Spectrum Guide to
MAURITIUS

STRUIK

Spectrum Guide to Mauritius

© 1997 Camerapix

Struik Publishers (Pty) Ltd
(A member of the Struik Group (Pty) Ltd)
Cornelis Struik House
80 McKenzie Street
Cape Town 8001
South Africa

ISBN 1-86825-810-6

This book was designed and produced by
Camerapix Publishers International
PO Box 45048
Nairobi, Kenya

Fax: (254-2) 217244
Tel: (254-2) 334398

Colour Separations: Universal Graphics
                          Pte Ltd, Singapore.
Printed and bound: Tien Wah Press, Singapore.

The **Spectrum Guides** series provides
comprehensive and detailed description
each country it covers, together with all th
essential data that tourists, business visitor
or potential investors are likely to require.

Spectrum Guides in print:
African Wildlife Safaris
Eritrea
Ethiopia
India
Jordan
Kenya
Madagascar
Maldives
Namibia
Nepal
Oman
Pakistan
Seychelles
South Africa
Sri Lanka
Tanzania
Uganda
United Arab Emirates
Zambia
Zimbabwe

Publisher and Chief Executive:
Mohamed Amin
Editorial Director: Brian Tetley
Picture Editor: Duncan Willetts
Text: Sue Heady
Editors: Barbara Lawrence Balletto and
Roger Barnard
Art Editor: Calvin McKenzie
Project Director: Rukhsana Haq
Graphic Designer: Lilly Macharia
Assistant Editors: Salim Amin and
Christine Pemberton
Production Editor: Karl Braunecker
Cartographer: Terry Brown
Typesetting: Rachel Musyimi
Picture Research: Abdul Rahman

Editorial Board

Spectrum Guide to Mauritius is the most recent addition to the popular series of high-quality and colourfully illustrated *Spectrum Guides* to exotic and exciting countries, cultures, flora, and fauna.

One of the world's most fascinating tourist destinations, the diminutive island nation attracts many people to its shores: visitors once bitten are forever smitten by this tropical paradise and return again and again. Yet until this book — the product of months of work by a dedicated team of writers and researchers in the *Spectrum Guides* editorial office and in the field in Mauritius — there were few, if any, comprehensive guides to its many attractions.

Most of the pictures are from the cameras of *Spectrum Guides* Publisher and Chief Executive **Mohamed Amin** his colleague, **Duncan Willetts**, who is equally renowned for his superb photography — both on land and under water, and photographer **David Lyons**. Mauritius, with its dramatic black cliffs, silver-sand beaches, rolling fields of sugar cane, marvellous mountains, and spectacular undersea sights, had long been a country they wished to capture on film, adding both inspiration and challenge to their outstanding photographic skills.

Project Director **Rukhsana Haq** organised the complex logistics and liason while **Sue Heady** laboured long and hard to produce a fascinating, in-depth, and readable guide book to this Indian Ocean country. An experienced writer and editor, she was born in Botswana and lived in Seychelles and Hong Kong before settling in England, where she now resides in between her frequent travels.

Refining the text and ensuring that *Spectrum Guides'* in-house style was maintained was the responsibility of American **Barbara Lawrence Balletto**, a writer and editor living in Kenya since 1986, and Roger Barnard, based in Britain.

Assistant Editor **Christine Pemberton** covered the length and breadth of Mauritius several times in checking and double checking facts and figures while Assistant Editor **Salim Amin** raised query after query.

Contributing his knowledge of birds of the Indian Ocean islands was British-born **Adrian Skerrett**, who now lives in Seychelles. A dedicated ornithologist, he is co-author of *A Birdwatcher's Guide to Seychelles, Beautiful Birds of Seychelles,* and *Spectrum Guide to Seychelles.* He is the Executive Officer of the Royal Society for Nature Conservation (RSNC).

Design and layout were in the hands of Kenyan **Lilly Macharia**, while another Kenyan, **Abdul Rahman**, oversaw photographic research. Kenyan **Rachel Musyimi** did the typesetting.

Above: Sun-lover soaks up the Mauritian rays.

TABLE OF CONTENTS

PART SIX: FACTS AT YOUR FINGER-TIPS

IN BRIEF

LISTINGS

MAPS

Half-title: Boat cuts a wake through the waters off Mauritius. Title: Jetski gives holiday maker the ride of a lifetime. Pages 8-9: Holiday resort of Ile aux Cerfs. Pages 10-11: Verdant landscape dominated at left by the balancing rock pinnacle of Pieter Both Mountain. Pages 12-13: Sheltered by a dreamy lagoon, the St Geran Sun Hotel, offers visitors a glimpse of paradise.

ETHIOPIA

SOMALIA

INDIAN OCEAN

KENYA

EQUATOR

Pemba

Zanzibar

Seychelles

Amirantes

Mafia

TANZANIA

Aldabra

Providence

Cerf

Agalega

Grand Comoro

Moheli

Anjouan

Mayotte

MOZAMBIQUE

*Mozambique
Channel*

Tromelin

**Cargados
Carajos**

MADAGASCAR

Rodrigues

MAURITIUS

Réunion

Mascarene Islands

TROPIC OF CAPRICORN

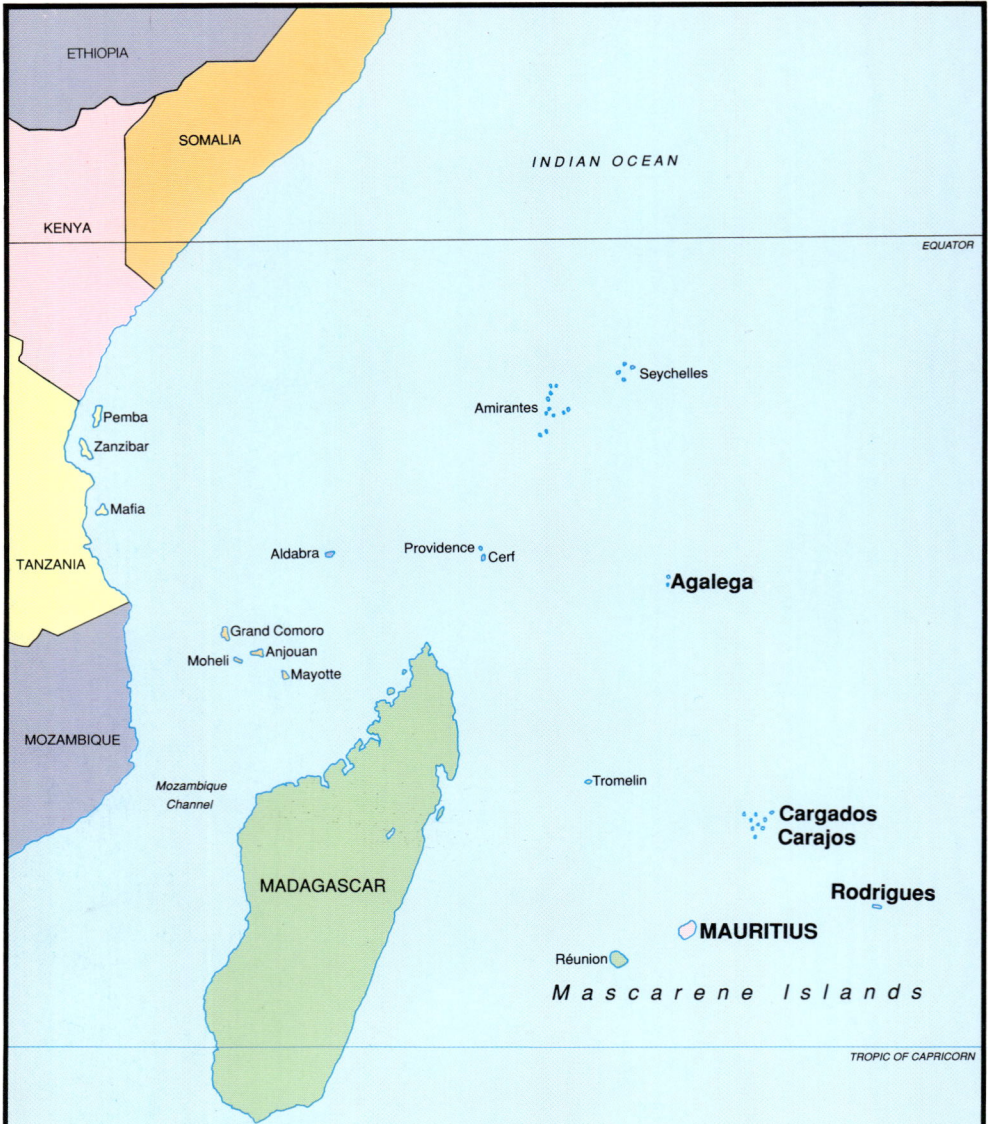

Mauritius & The Mascarenes

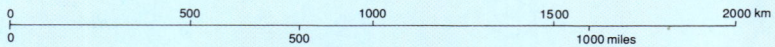

0		500		1000		1500		2000 km

0			500			1000 miles	

Mauritius

INDIAN OCEAN

SERPENT ISLAND

ROUND ISLAND N.R.

FLAT ISLAND

GABRIEL ISLAND

COIN DE MIRE ISLAND N.R.

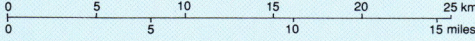

0   5   10   15   20   25 km
0   5   10   15 miles

Grand Gaube

Grand Baie

Goodlands

ÎLE D'AMBRE

Triolet

Piton

Rivière du Rempart

Pamplemousses

Terre Rouge

PORT LOUIS

La Nicolière Reservoir

Bon Acceuil

Centre de Flacq

PIETER BOTH
POUCE N.R.

BEAU BASSIN

Moka

St. Pierre

Trou d'Eau Douce

ÎLE DE L'EST

La Ferme Reservoir

ROSE HILL

Quartier Militaire

Bambous

CORPS DE GARDE N.R.

QUARTRE BORNES

Reservoir

Bel Air

Montagne Blanche

ÎLE AUX CERFS

Wolmar

PHOENIX

Piton du Milieu Reservoir

Sebastopol

Grande Rivière Sud-Est

VACOAS

Tamarin

FLOREAL

CUREPIPE

MT. LAGRAVE

Eau Bleue Reservoir

DOMAINE DU CHASSEUR N.R.

Tamarind Falls Reservoir

Mare aux Vacoas

Mare Longue Reservoir

Vieux Grand Port

ÎLE AUX BÉNITIERS

BLACK RIVER GORGES N.P.

PITON DE LA PETITE RIVIÈRE NOIRE

Rose Belle

New Grove

MAHÉBOURG

ÎLE AUX AIGRETTES

MORNE BRABANT

PITON DU FOUGÉ

MT COCOTTE

PITON SAVANNE

L'Escalier

ÎLOT FORNEAU

Chemin Grenier

Baie du Cap

Surinam

Rivière des Anguilles

Souillac

The Mauritius Experience

A common misconception is that Mauritius is simply a beautiful tropical island living off the legend of the dodo, as popularized in Lewis Carroll's *Alice in Wonderland*. In reality this Indian Ocean country has much more to offer than sun, sea, and sand, and the story of a sadly extinct bird species.

Those who arrive during the day will appreciate a bird's-eye view of the surrounding translucent waters, a breathtaking palette of green and blue that breaks lazily in a white haze onto silvery-sand beaches fringed by black volcanic rock. Passengers will also have a grandstand view of the interior, where majestic mountain tops dominate expanses of dense, verdant forest and seemingly endless sugar cane fields that — depending on the time of year — are sometimes yellow, sometimes green, and, at other times, surprisingly, pink.

Even at ground level, Mauritius continues to offer panoramic vistas on a scale hard to beat. Along the south coast, the seas dash in white anger against dramatic black cliff faces. Standing tranquil on the northern plain are colourful bougainvillaea in the foreground and sugar cane fields up to the Pieter Both peak in the distance.

Not that the island is without blemish. Many urban and rural buildings are generally unattractive. Concrete cubic monstrosities (with steel rods sticking out of the top floor in case the owner scrapes enough money together to add another floor) may make practical homes able to withstand strong cyclonic winds, but surely this objective could be achieved by more attractive means.

Thankfully, at least one Mauritian architect, Maurice Giraud — who has, among other projects, worked on Le Touessrok and Paradise Cove Hotels — and a local group calling themselves Friends of the Environment are doing all they can to make the island's modern architecture more appealing. Don't let this put you off, however, because the towns have redeeming architectural features.

For example, Port Louis, with its pre-20th century buildings around the Place d'Armes and the colonial houses lining its quiet back streets, has a charm of its own. Other old buildings are to be discovered elsewhere — in the highland area of Moka, for example. To be sure, the dodo still plays its part. Its relics are considered a highlight of the Natural History Museum in Port Louis.

It is enshrined for posterity worldwide by the saying 'dead as a dodo'; and the Mauritians have seized on its commercial potential by featuring dodos on such items as T-shirts, carved bookends, and children's books.

But that was one bird that was. There is much more on Mauritius to lure the ornithologist and rivet the bird-watcher. Extant are eleven species that are endemic. The most intriguing are the Mauritius kestrel — recently rescued from the jaws of extinction — and the pink pigeon and the echo parakeet, both still struggling to survive. In general, the country has fascinating flora and fauna — a veritable tourist paradise in which naturalists can have a field-day, especially since the Black River Gorges National Park makes most of these plants and animals easily accessible.

Mauritius also offers a wide range of sporting activities. There are perfect conditions for paragliding during certain summer months, several superb golf courses, numerous hiking trails, exciting horse treks in the mountains behind Port Louis, and a host of boar and deer to be hunted in season. Its mid-ocean position makes for excellent scuba-diving, surfing, a unique undersea walk, and some of the world's best game fishing. Another thing going for

---

Opposite: clockwise from top left: Young girl of Indian descent; Man radiates traditional Mauritius hospitality; Island beauty; Boy on Rodrigues.

Above: Oceangoing tugs at their berths, the 20th-century skyline of Port Louis rises up against a backdrop of green and beautiful mountains.

Mauritius as a holiday destination is its size — small, but big enough for each district to display its own individuality. The north is generally heavily given to tourism. The east and the south, being on the windward side, are characteristically wild. The leeward district of the west is quiet.

Though Port Louis and the surrounding highlands are urbanized, a trip to unspoilt Rodrigues is like travelling several decades back in time. In the evening, there is plenty of Western-style entertainment: restaurants offer a wide range of cuisine; shows (often with a local flavour) are performed almost every night in hotels, theatres, and nightclubs; live music and casinos are to be found throughout the island.

Ever since the Dutch made Europe's first recorded landing on Mauritius in 1598, the island has been a welcome landfall for far-from-home sailors, a haven of peace and repose, a blissful respite for those waiting to resume the rigour of a voyage.

And for those not enchanted on their first visit, make sure you come back. Mauritius will grow on you. The Nick Faldos and the Wilbur Smiths of the world, who have made numerous journeys to this Indian Ocean paradise, will testify to this.

Welcome.

Travel Brief and Social Advisory

Some do's and don'ts to make your visit more enjoyable.

Mauritius — everything under the sun

Because of its tropical island image, Mauritius has gained a reputation as one of the most paradisaical holiday destinations in the world. But it deserves more.

It should be better known to tourists for its diverse physical character, its fascinating flora and fauna and its wealth of opportunities for a wide range of visitors, be they sports enthusiasts, the back-to-nature types, or those simply keen to relax.

However, there is another wonderful element to Mauritius for the holidaymaker. It is the people. Their multi-cultural nature has become one of the island's best assets.

Immigrants from Europe, Africa, and Asia have brought with them their own distinctive traditions and these persist, making for an exciting and varied stay for visitors. They can, in a single day, eat gourmet French meals, visit a Hindu temple, watch a Creole sega show, and end up at L'Amicale, the casino in Port Louis where Chinese gambling games are still the order of the day.

The cultural diversity is emphasized by the many languages heard on the street, the multifarious modes of dress, the numerous Public holidays marking events of various religious groups, and a seemingly endless choice of wares from all over the globe to be found in the vibrant markets and shops.

Underneath these differences, however, the 'island culture' is reflected in the friendly, laid-back attitude of the people, and this is what unites them as Mauritians. It is this amicable attitude that ensures tourists enjoy their holiday, for visitors find hotel service convivial and often impeccable; they discover tour guides are informative, well-trained, and often fluent in several non-Mauritian languages; and they realize that the bystander in the street is happy to help with directions or a car breakdown.

Mauritians are proud of their country and want visitors to enjoy it, to experience the island at its best. This disposition is reflected by the Mauritius Tourist Promotion Authority (MPTA) and inbound tour operators who are all there to ensure that your visit is smooth and pleasurable. Enjoy!

Getting There

Air Mauritius, the national carrier, flies nonstop twice a week from London (Heathrow), four times a week from Paris (CDG), five times a week from Brussels, four times a week from Cape Town, twice a week from Manchester, once a week from Melbourne, twice a week from Vienna, once a week from Frankfurt, once a week direct from Munich, once a week from Zurich, once a week from Rome (Fiumicino), twice a week from Johannesburg, once a week from Perth and Melbourne, three times a week from Bombay, once a week from Singapore, and once a week from Hong Kong. It also flies once a week from Paris (Orly) via Frankfurt, once a week from Munich via Geneva, twice a week from Johannesburg via Durban, once a week from Johannesburg via Harare, once a week from Singapore via Kuala Lampur, twice a week from Nairobi via Antananarivo or Moroni and Antananarivo, twice a week from Antananarivo via Réunion, and seven times a day to and from Réunion.

Other airlines flying in and out of Mauritius include Air Austral, Air France, Air India, Air Madagascar, British Airways, Condor Airlines, Singapore Airlines, and South African Airways.

A permit is required from the Ministry of Agriculture and Natural Resources to import plants and plant material, including cuttings, flowers, bulbs, fresh fruits, vegetables, and seeds. All plant material is subject to examination and must be declared to Customs immediately on arrival. The law prohibits all imports of sugar cane and its products, soil, micro-organisms, and invertebrate animals. Facilities for examination and certification of plant materials are available at Réduit (Tel: 454-1091), and Sir Seewoosagur Ramgoolam (SSR) International Airport offices of the Plant Pathology Division of the Ministry of Agriculture, (Tel: 637-3194). All animals and animal material need an import permit from the same ministry, and a sanitary certificate of the country of origin. All animals must be declared to Customs immediately on arrival. Landing is allowed if certificates from the veterinary authorities of the exporting country are in conformity with the import permit. Dogs and cats undergo a six-month quarantine, birds and other animals up to two months. Additional information may be obtained from the Ministry's Division of Veterinary Services at Réduit (Tel: 454-1016).

Firearms and ammunition must be declared on arrival.

Getting Around

By road
Driving is on the left. Mauritius has a two-lane motorway (the M2) crossing the island from SSR International Airport in the south-east through Port Louis to Grand Baie in the north. There are also some excellent 'A' roads that run, for example, parallel to the west coast from Port Louis as far south as Black River. However, the 'B' roads are rough, as are roads on Rodrigues Island.

Once away from the beaten track, it is often difficult for visitors to distinguish between the 'B' roads and the private tracks meandering through the sugar estates. The lack of signposts simply makes things worse for those not in the know. Full-grown sugar cane creates its own problems. Drivers lose their sense of direction because all they can see is a 'tunnel' of sugar cane ahead.

As a rule, driving standards are low and accidents common. Drivers have the annoying habit of doing exactly the opposite of what European drivers would expect

them to do. For example, they pull out to overtake in front of an oncoming car, expecting the driver of the car on the other side of the road to slam on his brakes to avoid a collision.

Indicators are rarely used or, perhaps more correctly, never repaired. Many cars have no brake lights or headlights in working order. The most dangerous are the cars that drive at night with only one headlight on unlit country roads. It is all too easy to think that one-headlight cars are scooters and that there is space to overtake on your own side of the road, only to realize at the very last minute that the oncoming vehicle is, in fact, a one-headlight car.

Holiday drivers from the US and the European continent introduce another element. Because the British still ruled when cars were introduced to the island, cars must be driven on the left-hand side of the road. American and European holidaymakers often forget this, resulting in unfortunate accidents.

Pedestrians display kamikaze attitudes by walking side by side along the road, their backs to the traffic. Drunken pedestrians, who abound at the weekend, should be given a wide berth. Animals, particularly stray dogs, are other obstacles to avoid on the road.

Drunken driving does exist, particularly at the weekend, although the relatively recent introduction of breathalyzers may help to put an end to this problem.

In spite of the existence of speed traps, the upper speed limit (80kph on major roads) is often ignored, especially now that the booming economy has led to an invasion of fast cars.

Despite all this, if you drive gently and keep your eyes open, you are unlikely to experience any major problems. Wear your seat belt, as the law requires.

There are many car rental companies. Cars can be booked either in advance and picked up at SSR International Airport, where car company representatives are always on hand, or through hotels, inbound tour operators, and the car companies' own offices.

The standard of rental cars is generally high and international car companies such

Above: Four-wheel mobility gives tourists the freedom of the island.

as Avis, Europcar and Hertz operate in Mauritius. Rates vary according to the type of car hired — everything, from family saloons to mini-mokes, is on offer — and the duration of the rental. You can also hire a driver at an extra cost. Check with the individual car company for comprehensive and up-to-date information.

Mopeds and motorcycles can also be hired on the island — the majority of rental companies dealing in two-wheeled transport are to be found in Grand Baie and Pereybere. Bicycles can be hired from independent operators in these two areas and from a number of hotels. Given the somewhat frenetic road conditions, driving around Mauritius on a moped or a motorcycle is akin to writing your own hospital admittance slip, unless you are an experienced biker. Bicycles, however, are usually quite safe on short distances and are fun for visiting interesting sites close to where you are staying.

Exploring the whole island, however, is much easier and more comfortable by car. Those who don't wish to drive themselves can hire a chauffeur-driven BMW or rent a taxi for the day and hope that the driver does not mind doubling up as an informal guide. Taxis are usually metered, but day rates are always negotiable. The adventurous may decide to cross the island by bus.

Indeed, most parts of Mauritius can be visited using this method of transportation, which is extremely cheap.

By air
There is at least one daily return flight to Rodrigues from SSR International Airport. During the peak tourist season, there are two daily flights on most days. The ATR-42 turbo-prop plane journey takes an hour and a half. In 1996, a normal return flight costs Rs5,940 and an excursion return costs Rs2,800.

By boat
The one ferry operating out of Mauritius, the *Mauritius Pride,* has no fixed schedule but usually sails to Rodrigues and Réunion two or three times a month. There are three classes on the twenty-four-hour crossing to

Above: *Mauritius Pride*, the sole ferry, plies between Mauritius and the islands of Rodrigues and Reunion, usually two or three times a month.

Rodrigues: Class Excellence (twin-berth cabin) Rs 2,800 return (1,400 one way), Class Loisirs (seat only) Rs 1,800 return (Rs 900 one way), Economy Class Rs 1,300 return (Rs 650 one way). On the ten hour trips to Réunion there are two classes: For a cabin Rs 2,700 return (peak season), seat only Rs 1,900 return (peak season). Low season fares are Rs 300 cheaper. Children under 12 pay 50 per cent. One way is 60 per cent of the return fare. Bookings should be made well ahead of departure through the Mauritius Shipping Corporation on Tel: 242-5255. Island cruises — for example, to the islands of the northern coast — are offered by a number of charter operations (see the water sports section).

On foot

The mountains of Mauritius offer rugged and challenging walks. There are no venomous snakes, but stick to marked footpaths or, better still, take an experienced walker or guide. All walks can be completed by people of all ages and fitness levels, with good trainers or light walking shoes.

It is not advisable to drink from mountain streams. The water may look clear, but under the microscope it is likely to teem with parasites. Walkers should carry their own water (and food) as there are no snack bars.

The cooler months of May and June are ideal for walking, and it is also the time when the island's vegetation is at its best. Walkers should set off early in the morning ahead of the midday heat.

The people

The Mauritians are very friendly and helpful. Should you experience a flat tyre as you drive you will immediately attract five or six assistants. Always ask for permission before taking a person's picture. Having a camera poked in one's face by a complete stranger is not an action that many of us would appreciate. Although many are poor by Western standards, they do not appear to resent affluence, although they may try to take advantage of it now and again. Beach vendors, trying to obtain the highest price possible, expect tourists to haggle with them over prices. It is all part of the fun of selling. Be sure to buy only from vendors who display permits from the Ministry of Tourism.

Do not expect to get a great deal of help from the police. In Mauritius it often appears that officers of the law would rather be relaxing than working. Bribery and corruption are rife.

Safety
Muggings and violent crimes are unusual, but visitors should be on their guard as there have been some incidents in the tourist areas of the north. Women — alone or in pairs — are advised not to walk in the evening, but to drive or take a taxi.

Most crime is of a petty nature, such as urban pickpocketing. Do not leave valuables on the beach or in unlocked cars.

When they are not needed, money, passports, and airline tickets should be kept in your hotel's safe boxes.

Weather
Its proximity to the Tropic of Capricorn assures Mauritius a typically warm and humid sub-tropical climate.

There are two seasons: summer from November to April, when it is hot; and winter from May to October, when it is warm. Summer temperatures range from 24°C (75°F) at dawn to 30°C (86°F) at noon on the coast, while in winter you can expect about 18°C (64°F) at dawn to 24°C (75°F) at noon. The central highlands are usually five degrees cooler.

Cyclones occur between January and March, unleashing high winds, dark brooding clouds, and torrential rains. April to June and September to November are considered the best times to visit Mauritius.

Clothing
Light clothing made from natural fibres is useful all year round, particularly in the summer (November to April), when temperatures are higher. In winter (May to October), a few heavier items are essential as it can be chilly during the evening in coastal regions, and at all times of the day up in the highlands.

Mauritians, in contrast to many tropical islanders, generally dress smartly, so if you wish to feel in place in town and more expensive restaurants, you may want to take a few casually smart outfits. But it is not essential; it is understood that those on holiday prefer T-shirts, shorts, and flip-flops. Note that in some up-market hotels more formal evening dress may be required. For example, men may be asked to wear long trousers, other than jeans.

It is not advisable for women to sunbathe topless on public beaches.

Hats and caps are useful for all and essential for those who are bald or balding, as the sun, especially in summer, can be scorching. Sunglasses are vital against the harsh, glaring sun. Strong sunscreens (with a factor of fifteen or more for real protection) are recommended.

What to take
Almost all Western consumer goods are available in Mauritius. However, keep in mind that many cost more than they would back home.

Health
The only vaccination needed before a visit to Mauritius is yellow fever, and that only if you are arriving within ten days of leaving infected or endemic areas. The worst affliction visitors are likely to encounter is a mosquito bite. In rare cases, this could result in malaria, which is present in some rural areas — although not in Rodrigues.

Even on overcast days, never underestimate the strength of the sun. Even in the shade, one can suffer severe burns due to the reflection of the sun's rays off surfaces such as the sea and sand. Avoid lying out for several hours on your first day. Build up a tan slowly by spending short periods in the sun every day. Always wash fruit and vegetables carefully before eating them. It is better to drink mineral water than tap water to avoid stomach disorders.

Visitors who fall ill should seek treatment from a private doctor or clinic. Standards in public hospitals are not high. Clinic charges may be considered expensive,

Above: Although descendants of many races and many creeds, the people live in harmony, first and foremost as Mauritians.

Opposite: The intriguing mix of cultures and religions in Mauritius is colourfully reflected in much of the nation's architecture, such as this Hindu temple.

so it is advisable to take out travel health insurance before you leave home.

Photography

It is best to carry with you all the cameras, photographic equipment, and film that you need. A number of professional photographic shops on the island sell film but the stock may not be comprehensive.

One-hour processing is available for colour prints; the capital's professional photographic shops will also process slides (if given a few days). Photography is always best in the early morning or late afternoon.

Communications

Mauritius Telecom (MT) operates a fairly efficient and reasonably priced telephone system, but there is a shortage of telephone lines in some areas. For that reason, and because businessmen worldwide now like to be in constant contact, many people use Emtel, the local mobile telephone service.

Public phones are few and far between but can usually be found outside police

Top: Sugar cane, a dodo, and a deer adorn the Mauritius coat of arms.

Above: The colourful Mauritius flag, symbolic of the country's past struggles and present treasures.

stations and community centres. These take Rs5, Rs2, and R1 coins or MT cards, which can be bought from MT and shops displaying an MT card sign. For local telephone numbers dial 90 for Directory Enquiries.

International Direct Dialling services are available out of Mauritius and calls can be made either from public booths (using an MT card), from the MT offices around the island, or from hotel rooms, where a surcharge is usually imposed.

To make an overseas call, dial 00 plus the country code, the area code, and then the telephone number required.

The Mauritian postal service is efficient and post offices are found in most towns and villages. The main post office is located in a majestic old building on Port Louis's Quay Street (across the motorway from the main part of the capital), open between 0815 and 1115, and 1200 and 1600, Monday to Friday, and between 0800 and 1145 on Saturday. Postage depends on the size of the postcard — Rs10 for a large postcard and Rs4 for a small one for European destinations in 1995.

For postcards within the Indian Ocean rim — Réunion, Madagascar, Seychelles — the rates are Rs8 and Rs3 respectively.

When to go
The tourist season lasts throughout the year, but it peaks between the traditional European holiday month of August and the end of the Mauritian summer in April. European visitors sometimes find the winter months of May to August too cool for their liking, especially as they have left their own summer behind. However, the Mauritian winter provides excellent walking conditions. June to September is also when the island's hunting takes place.

Big game fishing enthusiasts should visit during the summer months (November to April).

Where to stay
There is a wide range of options from which to choose when it comes to accommodation. There are many small family-run hotels and, of course, a wide range of tourist-class and luxury hotels. The two main hotel chains are Sun International,

which operates the superb St Geran, Le Touessrok and Coco Beach on the east coast, and La Pirogue and the Sugar Beach on the west coast, and the Mauritian-owned Beachcomber Group, which operates six hotels of varying standards around the island, the flagship hotel being the Royal Palm on the north coast.

Other international hotel chains operating on the island include the Maritim, the Sofitel, and the Berjaya, all on the west coast, and Club Méditerranée in the north.

A full range of self-catering places, including serviced beach bungalows of a high standard, can be rented through companies such as Leisure Promotion.

There are also a large number of fairly cheap guesthouses or pensions, although the standard may not be as high as normally expected by international travellers.

National emblem

The national emblem, which is also used on the personal standard of the President of the Republic, incorporates sugar cane, a dodo, and a deer.

It was under British Governor Sir Henry Barkly — 1870 and 1873 — that the coat of arms was created. The first public unfurling of the flag with the first arms of the colony of Mauritius and therefore the first sight of what was later to become so familiar to the islanders took place on 25 May 1870 when the Duke of Edinburgh (1844-1900) landed from the warship HMS *Galatea* for a strenuous 10-day visit. He was the first member of the royal family to visit Mauritius.

Sugar cane has long been, and remains, the mainstay of the island's economy, while both the dodo and the deer are typically Mauritian.

The emblem's Latin motto is 'Stella Clavisque Maris Indici', meaning 'Star and Key of the Indian Ocean', indicating the important part the island played in colonial history. It could equally be true of its position today.

National flag

The national flag is made up of four horizontal bars of colour. From top to bottom, red represents the struggle for freedom and independence, blue represents the Indian Ocean, yellow represents the new light of independence shining over the island, and green represents Mauritius's lush landscape throughout the year.

National anthem

Motherland
Glory to thee
Motherland, O Motherland of mine
Sweet is thy beauty
Sweet is thy fragrance
Around thee we gather
As one people
As one nation
In peace, justice, and liberty
Beloved country may God bless thee
For ever and ever

National flower

This is the *Trochetia boutoniana* of the family *Sterculiaceae*, whose common name is *boucle d'oreille*. It is a multi-branched shrub or low tree with oval to elliptic leathery leaves, greyish on the upper surface and densely covered with short stellate whitish hairs underneath. The beautiful flowers are bell-shaped, 5 to 6 centimetres (2 to 2.5 inches) long. The five petals, veined with carmine on a whitish background, are edged with carmine. The five elongated calyxes are fused at the base and covered with whitish stellate hairs.

The genus *Trochetia* of the family *Sterculiaceae* is endemic to the Mascarenes. There are five species in Mauritius, of which one is thought to be extinct, and others in Réunion.

Above: Delicate beauty of Mauritius' national flower, Trochetia boutoniana *(boucle d'oreille)* a species endemic to the island.

Above: Detail of mosaic that adorns the church of Ste Croix in Port Louis.
Opposite: Fascinating murals adorn the exterior walls of the Temple of Shiva at Troilet.

Intricate Tapestry of History and Culture

By world standards, Mauritius is a fairly 'young' country. Although the first recorded sighting of Mauritius (and the other Mascarene islands) was made in AD 975 by an Arab named Hassan ibn Ali, he and his fellow explorers deemed it not worthy of settlement, because there were no inhabitants to convert to Islam and seemingly no commercial prospects.

At a later date, the Portuguese, too, dropped anchor off Mauritius, but also voted against putting down roots there, because the island offered no possibilities of trade, plunder, or winning Catholic converts. The Portuguese did, however, decide to drop off some pigs, goats, and cattle — which they hoped would reproduce, thereby supplying food for their return journeys — as well as monkeys and, unbeknown to them, rats, which, by eating the dodo's food and eggs, consigned the posthumously famous bird to extinction.

In the end it was the Dutch, in the early 17th century, who decided to set up a permanent base on Mauritius. Once settled, the Dutch decided to export the valuable ebony and ambergris found on and around the island. They also intended to grow crops, such as tobacco and sugar cane, and rear cattle to supply the Dutch ships that called at Mauritius. Slaves from Madagascar and convicts from Batavia (Indonesia) were brought in to help the Dutch.

The settlement unfortunately failed in 1658, but they tried again — more ambitiously — in 1664. Crops such as tobacco, sugar cane, indigo, and maize were cultivated on a commercial scale, while deer imported from Batavia flourished in the tropical forests. Forts were built, forests were cleared for timber, and domestic animals were raised for food.

But it still didn't work, for a number of reasons, including bad leadership. The Dutch withdrew in 1710, destroying buildings and stores they thought future settlers might use, but left behind their Malagasy slaves, sambhar deer, and — most importantly — sugar cane, which later would become the most important single product in the island's history. Meanwhile, the French, who had earlier laid claim to Réunion and Rodrigues, watched events carefully. In need of a good natural harbour in the Indian Ocean, they were keen to use Mauritius and, in 1715, claimed the island, renaming it Île de France.

It was seven years, however, before the French East India Company actually occupied the island, bringing with them various officials and settlers, more slaves from Madagascar, pirates and their women, and Swiss mercenaries recruited as the island's garrison. The cultural 'melting pot' that is now Mauritius was truly underway.

Like the Dutch before them, the French struggled to make things work, but stuck it out for another 14 years, when it became clear that the future of Île de France did not look good. There was no crop being grown commercially other than coffee (which was doing badly), and anarchy, disorder, and corruption were rampant. Enter Captain Bertrand François Mahé, Comte de La Bourdonnais, who took over as governor in 1735. The first 'national hero' of Mauritius, La Bourdonnais is credited with building the country's true foundations.

He started by moving all of the French Indian Ocean port facilities to Port Louis (from Port Bourbon). The population blossomed; so too did the facilities: a shipyard, a naval base, an armoury, warehouses, hospitals, houses, and a road system. Importantly, La Bourdonnais regulated food supplies by introducing manioc from Brazil, a crop suited to the tropical conditions of the island. He also ordered a garrison to patrol the forests for runaway slaves, and established much needed law and order on Île de France. His brother opened the first sugar factory.

La Bourdonnais's rule lasted until 1746, when France and Britain were heavily involved in the War of the Austrian Succession. Dupleix, commander of the French headquarters in Pondicherry, requested La

Bourdonnais to assist their efforts. La Bourdonnais thus led an expedition to India, defeated the British fleet, and blockaded the British headquarters in Madras, forcing it to surrender.

Although Dupleix wanted to plunder Madras and destroy it, La Bourdonnais felt that the British would pay a handsome ransom for it if it were left as it was, so he returned to Île de France.

Dupleix accused La Bourdonnais of accepting a bribe to preserve Madras, and La Bourdonnais was forced to return to France and was thrown into La Bastille. Although found innocent in 1751, he died two years later, at the age of 54.

Île de France remained under the French East India Company for another twenty years. In 1764, the French Ministry of Marine Affairs took over the administration of the island. Many of Port Louis's public buildings and fortifications were renovated and repaired, the harbour was restored, the shipyards were reorganized, and many new establishments — such as hospitals, a pharmacy, a bakery, a printing works, and a road construction department — came into existence. Most of this happened under the guiding light of Pierre Poivre, a former French East India Company agent.

Under Poivre's influence, trade flourished on the island, which began a period of great prosperity, helped along by the American War of Independence, during which the French supported the rebellious American colonists and an attack was launched on the British in India. Privateering became big business and the population of the island increased dramatically.

The French Revolution in 1789 changed everything. The new regime allowed a system of self-government to be set up in the colonies. In Île de France, a general assembly was elected, local district councils set up, and tribunals replaced courts of justice.

But the colonists' enthusiasm for the revolution was short-lived when, in 1794, France announced that slavery was to be abolished, which did not sit at all well with the Mauritians. From 1796, the island was in open rebellion and effectively an independent territory, where piracy reigned

supreme. In 1799, Napoleon Bonaparte took control of France and soon afterwards sent General Charles Decaen to 'reconquer' Île de France. The colonists accepted him as governor only on the condition that slavery be allowed to continue, which it did. The island prospered under Decaen's rule, but trouble was soon on the horizon.

In the early 19th century, Britain expanded its influence in the Indian Ocean and captured the Cape of Good Hope, which in effect isolated the Mascarene Islands from French help and began a British blockade of Île de France. Although the French successfully held off the British in an August 1810 battle, Decaen was caught by surprise in December of that year, and surrendered to British forces. The British vowed not to change the laws, customs, language, religion, or take control of any private property. The island's name reverted to Mauritius, and most settlers stayed on.

Shortly after the British takeover, 'sugar cane fever' swept Mauritius, encouraged by the British governor, Robert Farquhar. The island was transformed into a plantation colony, with sugar dealers and sugar planters forming a new class. The sugar industry, however, was threatened soon after its inception by an international campaign to free slaves. Opposition to abolition only faded away in 1835, when Britain agreed to pay two million pounds sterling in compensation to the slave owners.

The plantation owners then began to look to India for an alternative source of workers, who were brought to the island as indentured labourers. In the end, some 450,000 Indians came to Mauritius, bringing with them a number of problems: disease, crime, and food shortages among them.

Life on the island hit an all-time low in the last decade of the 19th century, when sugar and shipping declined drastically. For many years afterwards, sugar prices rose and fell, and the Mauritian economy with them. The British established naval and air bases in Mauritius during World War II, and the country organized its own local defence and sent many men to serve overseas. Once the war was over, local

Above: Early Mauritian Indian family. The Indians played a major role in the development of the country.

politics took front seat — particularly leading to the rise of the Labour Party, headed by Dr (later Sir) Seewoosagur Ramgoolam.

Eventually the party was in a strong enough position to push for self-government and independence, which it attained in 1967, with Dr Ramgoolam becoming Premier.

Emigration was encouraged in the 1960s (although less than 17,000 people left the island), and a series of plans was devised to boost the Mauritian economy. Foreign investment was encouraged through incentives, and tourism began to take root.

Tourism, along with the sugar industry and export manufacturing, continues to play an important role in the country's economy to this day. With its rolling sugar cane fields, beautiful mountains, silver-sand beaches, crystal-clear waters, and pristine areas of nature reserves, Mauritius continues to draw both naturalist and sun-lover alike to its shores.

Serene crater lakes are evidence of Mauritius's tumultuous volcanic past, and nature continues to change the face of the island, particularly in the south, where eroding waves have carved out dramatic cliffs, caves, and arches. Dense, luxuriant forest can be found to the east, where rainfall is most abundant, while the north features many beautiful beaches. It is to the highlands, however, in the centre, that most of the Mauritian population migrated, after a malaria epidemic around the turn of the century. This is where most of the sugar plantations spread out, as far as the eye can see; changing colour with the seasons.

Working the fields, running the businesses, and keeping the economy going are just more than a million Mauritians, who form a colourful kaleidoscope of customs and culture.

Although a melting pot of different races and religions, the people are, first and foremost, Mauritian — and proud of it, for reflected in the people's faces is the history of the country itself, formed from the machinations of many different nations but evolving into one that is uniquely Mauritian.

32

History: Corsairs and Colonists

Written in the ancient sediments of the Indian Ocean and its volcanic rocks, the story of what is now Mauritius actually began some eight million years ago, when the island is believed to have come into being. Only in the last 1,000 years, however, has man been aware of its existence because of its relative isolation from other land masses.

There is speculation that the forebears of the people who now inhabit Indonesia may have discovered the island on their way to colonize Madagascar 2,000 years ago, and that Phoenician sailors a thousand years before Christ may have chanced upon the island as they circumnavigated Africa, but there is no solid evidence.

Towards the end of the 10th century, Arabs from the Persian Gulf started to travel extensively to trade and spread Islam. They established several outposts on the east coast of Africa, which was already inhabited by the 'Zanj' people. The Arabs and the Zanj intermarried, creating a society called *Swahili* (literally meaning coastal) based on the Islamic culture.

One of the Arabs' most important contributions to this civilization was their boat-building skills. Their vessels could not venture very long distances without touching land, but, stopping off at either the Comoros or Madagascar, they could reach Mauritius and the other Mascarene islands.

The first recorded sighting of Mauritius was made in AD 975 by Hassan ibn Ali, who had set sail from Shiraz (in present-day Iran) at the head of seven ships and a band of Muslims. Most of his followers settled around what is now Mombasa and on the island of Pemba but one of the ships reached the Comoros (a name derived from the Arabic *komr*). From there, it continued on to Madagascar and then Mauritius.

In the course of their voyage of discovery, the Arabs must have either landed on, or at least sighted, all the Mascarene islands. They named them *Dina Mozare*, a corruption of *Diva mashriq*, or Eastern Isle (Mauritius); *Dina Arobi*, a corruption of *Diva harab,* or Desert Isle (Rodrigues); and *Dina Margabim*, a corruption of *Diva maghrebim* or Western Isle (Réunion). However, the Arabs do not appear to have settled on any of the islands, probably because they did not offer any immediate commercial prospects and there were no human inhabitants to convert to Islam.

The first European visitors to the Mascarenes were the Portuguese, great naval explorers who were spurred on by a religious crusading spirit and a strong desire to break the Arab monopoly on the profitable trade with the East. In 1498 Vasco da Gama discovered the route to India around the Cape of Good Hope and, on further trips to the East, the Portuguese chanced upon many of the Indian Ocean islands.

In 1507, Domingo Fernandez dropped anchor off Mauritius and named it Ilha do Cirne (Swan Island), perhaps after the flightless dodo which, with a little stretch of the imagination, did resemble a swan. However, it is more likely that, as was the custom, the island was named after the *Cirne*, the ship Fernandez captained.

Pero (also known as Pedro) Mascarenhas, a Portuguese pilot, is credited with the 1512 European discovery of Réunion, which he called Santa Apolonia, and it is after him that the Mascarenes are named. Much later, in 1528, Diego Rodriguez saw Rodrigues. Rodrigues has retained its Portuguese name, as have several neighbouring Indian Ocean islands, including Diego Garcia in the Chagos archipelago.

The Portuguese refrained from settling the islands because their main objectives of trade, plunder, and implanting the Catholic religion were not relevant to the uninhabited Mascarenes. The Portuguese also preferred to stay close to the bases they had established on the African and Indian coasts. However, they did at times use Ilha do Cirne as a supply stop and as a place to refit ships on their way to and from India and the East Indies.

Apart from introducing domestic

Above: Statue of Captain Bertrand François Mahé, Comte de La Bourdonnais, the first 'national hero' of Mauritius, who became governor in 1735. Above right: In the 1760s, trade flourished on the island, thanks to the astute guidance of Pierre Poivre, a former French East India Company agent.

animals such as pigs, goats, and cattle, which they hoped would multiply to supply food for return journeys, the Portuguese introduced monkeys and, inadvertently, rats, which destroyed the dodo's food and ate its eggs, consigning the bird to extinction.

In 1598, the first of the next wave of maritime supremos in the Indian Ocean, the Dutch, arrived in Ilha do Cirne, keen to develop trade links with the Orient to stop reliance on the Portuguese for Eastern goods. It was, however, by chance that Vice Admiral Wybrandt van Warwyck landed on the south-east coast of Ilha do Cirne.

His fleet, sailing from Amsterdam to the East Indies, took shelter there from a storm. Finding it uninhabited, Warwyck claimed it for the Netherlands and named the island Mauritius, after his *stadhouder* (head of state) Maurice (Maurits), Prince of Orange

and Count of Nassau. The annexation was quite a coup for the Netherlands, which was, at that time, rebelling against Spain, which also ruled over Portugal. The admiral and his fleet stayed just long enough to map the island. For the next 40 years the Dutch visited the island frequently as a convenient place on their way to and from the East Indies for refitting and replenishment. The first Dutch Governor of the East Indies, Pieter Both, on a journey home, was drowned off the island's west coast in 1615, and one of its most distinctive mountains is named after him. However, the Dutch did not try to settle, being more interested in trade than colonization.

In the early 17th century, the French and the English, together with the Portuguese and the Dutch, all traded with Asia — ships from the four countries called at Mauritius to pick up supplies. Rivalry was hotting up and, although all four were interested primarily in trade, a point came when they all wanted to establish and maintain bases to protect their Indian Ocean routes.

In May 1638, therefore, to forestall any settlement by the other three countries, Cornelius Simonsz Gooyer was sent to set up the first permanent Dutch base around the original landing place, now known as Vieux Grand Port, near Mahébourg. The Dutch named it Warwyck Bay. Gooyer, however, realizing the importance of the north-west, also sent a small detachment of troops to an area the Dutch called Noord-Wester Haven (north-western harbour).

Once settled, the Dutch realized the island had valuable ebony and ambergris (an odiferous substance found in the sea and in the intestines of sperm-whales, which is used in perfumery) that could be exploited and exported, along with the tobacco they set out to grow, to Europe. They also intended to grow crops and rear cattle to supply the Dutch ships that called at Mauritius. The settlers were instructed to prevent the English, French, and Portuguese from making any further use of the island. Over the next few years, slaves were imported from Madagascar and convicts were sent from Batavia (in modern Indonesia, where the Dutch had established a base in 1619) to help the settlers to fell the ebony forests and cultivate crops. So from the very first settlement the island's population was of mixed origin. Sugar cane, introduced (along with deer) from Batavia, was one of the crops grown.

Eventually, in 1658, the settlement failed, for two reasons. First, the Dutch felled too many ebony trees, creating a glut in Europe and drastically reducing the market price. Secondly, another Dutch settlement had been established in South Africa's Cape of Good Hope in 1652, which had taken over the most important function held by Mauritius: to supply Dutch ships sailing to and from the East Indies. In 1664, under the aegis of the Cape colony, the Dutch tried again to establish a base on Mauritius, perhaps thinking that two settlements would be better than one in the face of increasing rivalry from other European nations. This time the Dutch were more ambitious and attempted to cultivate, on a commercial scale, crops such as tobacco, sugar cane, indigo, and maize. Sambhar deer from Batavia thrived in the tropical forests and were hunted for food and pelts. Forts were built on the east coast for defence, forests were cleared for timber, and domestic animals were raised for food.

In 1710, the Dutch settlement failed for a second time. There was a lack of good leadership, lacking support from home; the number of settlers and slaves was never enough to establish a sound agricultural economy; the island was in some areas barren and rocky, in others thickly wooded; the Dutch were lazy; the absence of enough women made the settlers restless; and the Dutch Empire was based on trade and profit, so that Mauritius became more of a liability than an asset. In addition, because of cyclones, and escaped Malagasy slaves, who exacted their revenge for Dutch cruelties by destroying crops and slaughtering cattle, the island often failed to produce enough food for the settlers, let alone passing ships. Before the Dutch withdrew, in 1710, they destroyed all the buildings and stores. Yet, the Dutch contribution to the history of Mauritius is important. They left behind their Malagasy slaves, Sambhur deer, and sugar cane — set to become the most important single product in the island's later history.

The French, the last European nation to enter the Indian Ocean, staked their claim to Réunion and Rodrigues in 1638. Four years later, the French Eastern Company (the precursor to the French East India Company) set up its first trading post in Madagascar. In 1664, the French East India Company was founded, and a year later a settlement was established on Bourbon (as Réunion was then called), which became the main French outpost in the Indian Ocean.

Europe's settlement of the West Indies in the late 17th century drove the Caribbean pirates into the Indian Ocean, where, in Madagascar, they set up their own republic called Libertalia around 1685. However, from 1688, pirates also made use of Bourbon and, from 1697, visited Mauritius

Above: The *St Geran* tragedy inspired Bernardin de St Pierre's famous romantic novel, *Paul et Virginie*. Here, depicted in an old engraving in the museum in Port Louis, is the 'The Visit of Governor La Bourdonnais' in a scene from the novel.

to exploit timber to repair their ships. All ships plying Indian Ocean waters were preyed on; the British East India Company ships, in particular, suffered greatly. The rich booty captured from these heavily-laden merchant ships was taken to Libertalia to be sold to American traders, who encouraged piracy against the British.

Partly to control these pirates and partly because Bourbon's one disadvantage was lack of a good natural harbour, the French were keen to use Mauritius for themselves when the Dutch withdrew.

The year 1710 certainly marked the start of a new era for the Indian Ocean. The Mughal Empire, which had for long kept India unified, fell into decline. Local rulers started to exert their own authority and to declare war on one another. As a result, European merchants no longer felt safe in India and looked to trading bases elsewhere, which they owned and which they could fortify. French and English trading companies now wielded the greatest power

in India, the Portuguese having lost importance in the 17th century and the Dutch concentrating all their energies on the East Indian archipelago, now Indonesia. In 1715, Captain Guillaume Dufresne d'Arsel, sailed from the Red Sea port of Mocha to Mauritius and claimed the island for France, renaming it Île de France.

Seven years passed before the French East India Company actually occupied the island, in April 1722, with a motley crew of company officials and settlers from Bourbon; slaves from Madagascar, Mozambique, and West Africa; pirates and their women; and Swiss mercenaries recruited as the island's garrison. A larger party of settlers arrived from France a year later. It was at this time that Warwyck Bay became known as Port Bourbon and Noord-Wester Haven became Port Louis.

For 14 years, the French colony — which remained under Bourbon's control — suffered problems similar to those facing the Dutch. The island had few natural resources, it was ravaged by rats and by cyclones, the troops lacked discipline, and the settlers were uncertain where to establish their headquarters, although it was finally decided that Port Louis would be a good location as the prevailing winds made it easier for ships to set sail from there than from Port Bourbon.

In 1735, Île de France's population was no greater than 1,000 (including slaves), no crop was grown commercially other than coffee, which did badly, and anarchy, disorder, and corruption were rampant. Only with the arrival of Captain Bertrand Franç-ois Mahè, Comte de La Bourdonnais, who took over as governor of both Bourbon and Île de France in 1735, did Île de France's fortunes start to improve. A man with vision and ambition, Mahè was the first national hero of Mauritius and is credited with building its true foundations.

Realizing that a power struggle between France and Britain was beginning in the Indian Ocean and India, he immediately followed up on a decision made by his predecessor, Nicolas de Maupin, to transfer all port facilities from Port Bourbon to Port Louis. A well-equipped and well-protected port and naval base were constructed and a shipyard established.

The small settlement soon became a town, boosted by La Bourdonnais's decision to move the regional government seat from Bourbon to Île de France. Slowly, a civilized life evolved in Port Louis, attracting colonizers from Bourbon and France. In the first four years of La Bourdonnais's governorship, the population grew from under 1,000 to more than 3,000.

To suit the new headquarters and an expanding commercial centre, the thatched hovels were replaced by sturdy stone barracks and fortifications, an armoury and powder magazine, warehouses, a dry dock, hospitals, and houses, some of which survive to this day. Government House was built in Port Louis and an official residence for the governor, Mon Plaisir, was erected in Pamplemousses. Roads were opened throughout the island, facilitating internal communications.

More importantly, La Bourdonnais regulated food supplies, previously precarious because cyclones often destroyed crops, by introducing manioc from Brazil, a crop well suited to the tropical conditions of Île de France. Sugar farming also spread slowly — La Bourdonnais's brother opened the first sugar factory at Villebague in 1744. Other crops grown included maize, potatoes, rice (on a small scale), indigo, coffee, and cotton.

La Bourdonnais made another great contribution: law and order. Before his arrival, escaped slaves were always the bane of colonists. Their forays from their dense forest hideouts made life very difficult; but La Bourdonnais soon put paid to this by ordering a garrison to patrol the forests.

Keen to establish French dominance throughout the Indian Ocean, La Bourdonnais sent one of his officers, Captain Lazare Picault, to explore the islands north of Île de France. Picault landed on the largest of these islands and named it Mahé, in La Bourdonnais's honour. For a time, the islands were known as the 'Îles La Bourdonnais', but in 1756 they were renamed Séchelles (later corrupted to Seychelles) after the influential French family of Herault de Séchelles; but they remained a dependency of Île de France until 1814.

La Bourdonnais, however, failed in two objectives. First, he wanted to use the pirates to weaken Britain's position, but the French East India Company rejected this proposal. Secondly, he wanted to make Port Louis a free port. The company agreed to this proposal in 1742 but, in 1747, due to disappointing results, the free port status was withdrawn. Ironically, both proposals were to be revived later, with great success.

It was during Mahé de La Bourdonnais's administration that the island's most historic event occurred — the *St Geran* tragedy. In 1744, the ship known as the *St Geran* was wrecked during a storm off Île d'Ambre on the north-east coast and the event inspired Bernardin de St Pierre's famous romantic novel *Paul et Virginie*.

In 1746, with Britain and France heavily involved in the War of the Austrian Succession (1740-1748), Dupleix, the commander of the French headquarters in India's Pondicherry, sent an SOS to Île de France.

La Bourdonnais led an expedition of nine ships to India, defeated the British fleet, and blockaded the British headquarters in Madras, forcing it to surrender. Dupleix's aim was to plunder and destroy Madras, but La Bourdonnais argued that, left as it was, the British would pay a handsome ransom for it. As the two failed to agree, La Bourdonnais and his fleet returned to Île de France, leaving Madras untouched.

Dupleix accused La Bourdonnais of accepting a bribe to preserve Madras, and so La Bourdonnais was replaced as Governor.

On his return to France, he was thrown into the famous prison, La Bastille, and, although found innocent in 1751, he died a broken man two years later at the age of 54. Today a statue of La Bourdonnais stands in Port Louis facing the harbour, and the town of Mahébourg (founded in 1805) is named after him; so is the main Seychellois island of Mahé.

Île de France remained under the French East India Company for another twenty years after La Bourdonnais's departure. In that time, although a succession of four governors tried to encourage agriculture, little was accomplished because of the demands of the Seven Years' War (1756-63), which proved decisive in the struggle between Britain and France for control of India and the Indian Ocean.

Île de France played an important part in the war, being the nearest French naval base to the east coast of India. Île de France provided French forces with fresh supplies and helped repair damaged ships. In the end, the British won because their naval base in Bombay was a great deal closer to the action and because of the severe damage a cyclone caused to the French navy when it sought shelter on Île de France. The 1763 Peace of Paris allowed France to continue trading in India, but required that all French fortifications be destroyed.

During the last few years of the war, the Mauritians, with permission from island authorities, attacked ships flying the British flag, and thus protected their livelihood. Not exactly pirates, the Mauritians called themselves 'corsairs' because they did not attack ships of any nationality they thought carried worthwhile cargo, just those with British allegiance. While the corsair business thrived, the French East India Company suffered severely during the war and, under fierce criticism in France, where many objected to its trade monopoly, it sold Île de France — an island of 1,998 whites and 'free men' and 18,100 slaves — to the French king in 1764.

The French Ministry of Marine Affairs did not take over the administration of the island until July 1767, marking the start of a new era. On that day two senior royal officials landed in Port Louis: one was the new governor-general, who held supreme power as commander of the islands' naval and military forces, and the other the intendant, with financial and judicial responsibilities. The governor-general was Daniel Dumas and the intendant was Pierre Poivre, formerly a French East India Company agent, who was to make an outstanding contribution to Mauritian history between 1767 and 1772.

Poivre was a wise administrator who brought back prosperity and order to the island after the setbacks suffered by the French during the Seven Years' War.

It was mostly at Poivre's instigation that Port Louis's public buildings and fortifications, which were falling into ruin, were repaired; the harbour, which had silted up and was strewn with ships' wreckage, was restored; the shipyards, neglected since La Bourdonnais, were reorganized; and barracks, hospitals, a pharmacy, a bakery, a printing works, and a road construction department were established.

It was he who introduced spice plants from all over the world, particularly from South America, and offered tax incentives to plantation owners to grow them. Although this venture failed, it was under his guidance that the island began a period of great prosperity. Trade flourished from 1770, when the French East India Company's monopoly ended and the island's trading activities increased sharply. In 1769, a year before the liberalization of port activities, 78 ships visited Port Louis. By 1783, the annual figure had increased to 176. The growing prosperity was helped by the American War of Independence (1776-1783), during which the French

Government supported the rebellious American colonists and an attack was launched on the British in India. The British fleet was therefore engaged, and the people of Île de France took advantage of the situation to start raiding once more. Privateering became big business, with Île de France as the base for 29 privateer expeditions between 1779 and 1782; in 1781 alone there were 15. As the island's prosperity increased, so too did the population. By 1788, almost 43,000 people were living on Mauritius, more than double the number 20 years earlier.

Vicomte de Souillac, who was governor from 1779 to 1787, introduced an era of extravagance to the island. Port Louis became famous for its bright social life, with dancing parties everywhere, duelling, gambling, drinking, and hunting — much of it paid for by the privateers' booty that poured into Port Louis. Its markets became overstocked and from 1786 the American traders got even better deals on oriental goods than they would have done in Calcutta.

All that was soon to change. In 1789, the year of the French Revolution, Île de France replaced Pondicherry as the seat of government for all French possessions east of the Cape and, in January 1790, a ship arrived from France flying a new flag, the *Tricolore*. News of the revolution was, at first, welcomed by the islanders for it seemed to give them the opportunity to get rid of the authoritarian government of the Crown.

A feature of the new regime introduced by the revolutionary government into the colonies was a system of self-government. Thus, in Île de France, a general assembly (later called colonial assembly) was elected, local district councils were set up, and tribunals replaced courts of justice.

A National Guard replaced the island's militia; streets were renamed and revolutionary clubs opened. Church property was confiscated. White, red, and blue ribbons were worn. Even a guillotine was erected on the *Champ de Mars*, although it was only put to use when tested on an animal.

The colonists' enthusiasm for the revolution faded in 1794 when France announced that slavery was to be abolished. The Mauritians decided not to obey. Two years later, when two government officials arrived to persuade the Mauritians otherwise, the assembly expelled them. From 1796, Île de France was in open rebellion and, until the arrival of General Charles Decaen in 1803, was effectively an independent territory.

For many years, until the British took control of Île de France in 1810, piracy continued to be the islanders' main activity, spawning a new generation of privateers that included Jacques Hodoul and Robert Surcouf. The latter soon won the title of 'King of the Corsairs' for his bold defiance and daring acts. Fifty-one ships were employed in these operations and 119 vessels were taken between 1793 and 1802. The booty, seized mostly from British merchant ships from India, was sold to a large number of countries, including the United States and Denmark. Business with the United States flourished to such an extent that in 1794 Washington appointed a resident consul.

In 1799, Napoleon Bonaparte took control of France and, in 1803, sent Decaen to 'reconquer' Île de France. The colonists accepted him as governor on the condition that slavery continued. Decaen dismantled the machinery of revolutionary government, and all civil and military organizations were restored to their pre-1789 status.

Decaen was in the same league as La Bourdonnais and Poivre in administrative ability and innovation, but he was unpopular because of his dictatorial style. The changes that he made in Île de France — primarily in education and law — reflected Napoleon's activities in the metropolitan country.

Decaen founded primary schools and changed the name of Lycée Colonial — a central school opened a few years earlier — to Royal College. As in France, the college was expected to produce potential officers for the legion as well as to give students a

Overleaf: Ruins of an old sugar mill on an east coast plantation.

Above: The Naval and Historical Museum in Mahébourg holds many relics of the historic Battle of Grand Port.

sound general education. He also rechristened Port Louis, Port Napoleon, had it dredged again and built a second port, Mahébourg, on the south-east coast, close to Port Bourbon. It was later renamed Port Imperial, although it has since resumed its original name of Mahébourg. It was not built for commercial purposes, but only because Decaen realized the site's strategic importance. He was to be proved right in 1810, when the British attacked it.

Decaen adopted the Napoleonic code, adapting it to the island's special needs. The Code Decaen remains the basis of the Mauritian legal system to this day. Decaen also appointed district commissioners to replace the local district councils.

The years 1804-1805, when the island prospered and its social life thrived, coincided with the peak of trade between Mauritius and the Unted States. In 1807, when relations between France and the United States became strained, President Thomas Jefferson prohibited all American trading trips to Île de France. In the early

19th century, Britain — incensed by attacks on its Indian shipping routes by privateers based in Mauritius — decided to expand its influence in Africa and the Indian Ocean. In 1806, it captured the Cape of Good Hope, effectively isolating the Mascarene islands from French help, and so began a British blockade of Île de France that prevented ships from entering or leaving Port Napoleon.

In 1809, British forces occupied Rodrigues and prepared to attack the other two Mascarene islands. Bourbon, renamed Réunion during the revolutionary years, was taken in July 1810. A major battle was fought between the French and the British fleets off Vieux Grand Port on 24 August, 1810. After prolonged fighting, the French surprised even themselves by winning — it is the only French naval victory inscribed on the Arc de Triomphe in Paris.

It did not, however, delay the fall of Île de France for long. In December 1810, 70 vessels with at least 10,000 men on board left Rodrigues for Île de France. Making

Above: Painting of the Battle of Grand Port in the Naval and Historical Museum, with the British frigate *Magicienne* in the foreground.

use of a passage near Coin de Mire, they crossed the shallow waters to the north of the island and landed at Cap Malheureux. Decaen was taken by surprise, expecting their arrival closer to Port Napoleon. The British forces, commanded by General John Abercrombie, marched on the capital, meeting only token resistance. Decaen surrendered on 3 December because he had no chance of success against the British forces and because the settlers were indifferent to remaining French.

Generous capitulation terms allowed anyone not keen to stay under British administration to leave with all their possessions. The British also pledged to preserve the island's laws, customs, language, religion, and private property. The island's name reverted to Mauritius, and Port Louis was restored as the capital's name. Most settlers remained. The island was their home, but, perhaps, they also expected the colony to be restored to France.

Although Mauritius was to remain British for longer than it had been French,

it was the French occupation that really left its mark. French is still spoken and many place names remain French. The 1814 Treaty of Paris, reaffirmed by the 1815 Treaties of Vienna, gave Mauritius, along with Rodrigues and Seychelles, to Britain, thus closing them as French bases for further expeditions against British possessions. Réunion was returned to France because Britain considered it worthless as a naval base.

The first British governor, Robert Farquhar, had been installed in 1810 straight after the French capitulation, and he maintained absolute power. However, to veil this total authority, a council of government made up of the leading colonial officials — such as the chief justice, the chief secretary, the commanding officer of the garrison, and the controller of customs — was set up in 1825. There were to be no constitutional changes until 1885, but this did not mean that the Mauritian people did not have a say in matters. The chamber of agriculture, set up in 1853, was controlled

Above: Relics of Mauritius's past link with Britain, the initials 'VR' — for Victoria Regina — feature prominently in the Victorian ironwork gate at the Port Louis central market.

by the plantation owners and proved very powerful and effective as a pressure group.

Remarkably independent of London, Farquhar took advantage of the long time it took for dispatches to arrive to act as he thought. He won over the French settlers through scrupulous interpretation of the capitulation terms, even allowing them to continue the slave trade despite the 1807 law prohibiting it in the British Empire. However, in trying to help all elements of the population, he faced hostility from the plantation owners, who did not appreciate his efforts to improve the slave conditions.

Keen to develop the economy, Farquhar, after a particularly damaging fire in Port Louis in 1816, tried to establish the capital as a free port, hoping this would be an adequate compensation for stopping privateering. He also stimulated food production and road building, but he finally ran foul of the home government and was recalled in 1817. Three years later he returned, as Sir Robert, to govern until 1823.

A series of disasters, in addition to the Port Louis fire, occurred in the first two decades of British rule: outbreaks of smallpox, cholera, and rabies, and fierce cyclones, in 1818 and 1819 resulting in a large-scale destruction of houses and crops. Despite a recommendation from an 1822 Commission of Eastern Enquiry for Mauritius to be 'more Anglicized', there was no great influx of British settlers.

Charles Darwin noted some 20 years after the cession of the territory to the British, 'Although the island has been so many years under the British government, the general character of the place is quite French: Englishmen speak to their servants in French; indeed I should think that Calais or Boulogne was much more Anglified [than Port Louis].'

Following Farquhar's departure in 1823, and until 1849, Mauritius was subjected to a number of military governors, all of whom were universally disliked for their attempts to crush the opposition to the abolition of slavery and to Anglicize the island. Darwin, who arrived in Port Louis on the *Beagle* on 29 April 1836, for a 10-day stay, apparently liked Mauritius, wishing aloud, 'How pleasant it would be to pass one's life in such quiet abodes.'

At the beginning of the 19th century, encouraged by Farquhar, who realized that sugar cane was the only money-making crop able to withstand cyclones, a craze for cultivation of cane swept Mauritius. Plantation owners abandoned cotton, coffee, and indigo. Two factors were involved. First, Mauritius was no longer open to shipping from all countries because the navigation laws in force throughout the British Empire restricted trading in British ports to British or locally-owned ships. Secondly, the Cape of Good Hope, now also in British hands, was a flourishing port and thus a serious rival to the Indian Ocean island. Sugar, therefore, became the island's *raison d'être* for the next 150 years.

Another incentive to grow sugar came in 1825, when Britain decided to admit Mauritian sugar at the same rate of duty as that from the West Indies, with considerable implications for the future of the Mauritian economy. Within the year, production had increased from 10,869 tons to 21,244 tons. Within two or three years, sugar was undoubtedly the island's most important crop. The island, now transformed into a plantation colony, brought a new class into existence: sugar dealers and sugar planters. The latter, predominantly of European descent, established large sugar estates, and property became concentrated in fewer hands.

Shortly after it had been so successfully established, the sugar industry was threatened by an international campaign to free slaves, on whom the labour-intensive sugar industry depended. The plantation owners, whom the slaves outnumbered three to one, argued that not only were the slaves needed in the sugar cane fields, but that their release would create problems. Furthermore, the Britain-based Anti-Slavery Society campaigned for abolition without compensation to slave owners. The latter argued that slaves were a valuable form of property and that to abolish slavery without compensation would be robbery. A prominent member of the Anti-Slavery Society, John Jeremy, arrived in 1832 to press for emancipation, but it led to a general strike organized by the plantation owners, which brought life to a standstill. Jeremy was subsequently expelled. It was only when Britain agreed, in 1835, to pay two million pounds sterling in compensation that opposition to abolition faded away. Though 'freed', the slaves still had to go through a four-year period of apprentice-ship, in effect to work as forced labourers for the plantation owners for meagre wages. This period gave the owners time to find more labourers, at the end of which virtually all the slaves left the estates to live as smallholders on land too poor to have been claimed previously, or to work as unskilled labourers or fishermen.

The plantation owners looked to India for an alternative source of workers, who were brought over as indentured labourers to work for a pittance. A few arrived in 1830 and 1834, but the majority arrived between 1835 and 1909 (when Indian immigration was halted). Immigration reached its peak in 1858 and 1859, when demand for Mauritian sugar also surged. In all, around 450,000 Indian coolies were imported into Mauritius.

The profusion of immigrants brought numerous problems. Various diseases, such as cholera, were introduced; crime increased; and feeding the greatly swollen population became difficult. According to the 1851 census, Mauritius had a population of 180,823, and the number was to increase dramatically with the continued importation of indentured labour.

But not all immigrants were labourers. The Gujaratis, Indian Muslims, belonged to a more well-to-do social and economic class, as did the Cantonese from China. They were mainly in trade, and controlled the supply of basic commodities such as rice and cotton.

The sugar boom of the 1850s and 1860s and the need for greater imports to meet the demands of an ever-increasing population spurred shipping. But there were two other reasons: in 1851 the navigation laws barring foreign ships from entering Port Louis were repealed, and gold was discovered in Australia, causing large numbers of

Above: Devastating cyclone of April 1892 flattened most of Port Louis.

people to emigrate there. The latter resulted in Mauritius supplying European goods and locally produced sugar to the antipodean continent. Increases in shipping led to improvements, such as new dry docks, in the Port Louis harbour. In the 19th century there were some improvements in internal transport. Stimulated by the need to carry large quantities of processed sugar from factories to Port Louis for export, for example, railway lines were initiated. There were two lines: the Northern Line, completed in May 1864, ran from Port Louis to Flacq via Pamplemousses; and the Central Line, completed in October 1865, ran from Port Louis via Plaines Wilhems to Mahébourg. The lines were extended in the late 19th and early 20th centuries. But the economic boom was not to last.

A series of events in the second half of the 19th century did much to diminish Mauritian vitality, one being disease epidemics introduced by the indentured Indian labourers. Malaria alone killed 50,000 people between 1866 and 1868.

According to some historians, the opening of the Suez Canal in 1869 also contributed to the sapping of Mauritian wealth. Others say that it was, in fact, an advantage, because it brought the island closer to Europe — the sailing time was reduced to a month. Certainly, a regular shipping service (established in 1864) meant that Mauritius maintained very close ties with France and is one of the reasons why the island has enduring ties with its former metropolitan master. Mauritius, on the other hand, was no longer a strategically important outpost in the Indian Ocean and, perhaps most importantly, the Port Louis harbour failed to adapt fast enough to cater to the needs of steamships.

Economically, Mauritius started to feel the strain of relying on a monocultural crop, especially after 1863, when cane sugar was forced to compete with European beet sugar and cheaper cane sugar from Java and Cuba. From the 1860s to the beginning of the 20th century, the Mauritian sugar industry declined considerably.

Difficulties on the plantations compounded the problem. Fed up with living in utter misery, the indentured labourers became agitated. In 1871, a plantation owner, Adolphe de Plevitz, took up their cause, organizing a petition signed or marked by 9,000 Indians and presenting it to a sympathetic governor, Sir Arthur Gordon. The petitioners pressed for a royal commission to investigate the whole system of indentured labour in Mauritius. A commission was appointed in 1872 and its reports, published in 1875, recommended changes in the indentured labour regulations and its effective action to improve medical facilities on the sugar estates. In the last 20 years of the 19th century, more and more Indians moved away from the sugar estates for employment elsewhere or, having saved enough, bought their own subsistence-level smallholdings.

Constitutional changes also marked the last two decades of the century. In 1885, Governor John Pope Hennessy persuaded the Colonial Office to grant Mauritius its first elected legislative council.

The British administration introduced parliamentary elections and a limited franchise in 1886, as well as a Council of Government to which members had to be elected. Party politics followed the constitutional reforms of 1885, with the 'oligarchs' of the conservative Parti de l'Ordre dominant over the 'democrats' of Action Liberale until the early 1920s.

In the 1880s Joseph Conrad, who called at Port Louis as Captain Korzeniowiski, complained of long waits for ships' supplies and of high prices. Conrad — who painted a more detailed, and not altogether complimentary, portrait of contemporary Port Louis in his short story, *A Smile of Fortune* — resigned, rather than return to Mauritius. He described the ruling classes of that time as '. . . the old French families, descendants of the old colonies; all noble, all impoverished and living a narrow domestic life in dull, dignified decay. The men, as a rule, occupy inferior posts in Government offices or in business houses. The girls are almost always pretty ignorant of the world, kind and agreeable and generally bilingual; they prattle innocently in both French and English. The emptiness of their existence passes belief.' Life on

Mauritius seemed to hit an all-time low in the last decade of the 19th century. Sugar and, with it, shipping continued to decline, and there were a number of natural catastrophes and epidemics in 1891, 1893, and 1899. In 1892 a terrible cyclone hit Port Louis very hard, and in 1893 and 1896 fires destroyed large sections of the capital. These disasters led to the decline of Port Louis, as the population moved to the healthier climes of the highland areas, such as Rose Hill, Quatre Bornes, Vacoas, and Curepipe.

In general, then, at the start of the 20th century, Mauritius was economically depressed and over-populated. Yet Indians continued to arrive until they constituted the majority of the population. Recruitment of indentured labour ended in 1907, by which time the impact of Indian immigration had changed the course of the island's history.

At the same time, there was significant and continued emigration from Mauritius to South Africa and, by 1939, it was estimated that there were 16,000 Mauritian settlers in Durban alone. This did not solve the problem of over-population, but it did deprive Mauritius of some of its best men, since those who emigrated tended to be enterprising and to have capital.

The Indian majority came to wield great influence in all spheres; not only did their efficient workforce sustain the economy, they also proved vigorous in politics. After Mohandas Gandhi visited Mauritius in 1901, the Mahatma sent one of his representatives, Manilal Doctor (an Indian lawyer), to Port Louis in 1907 to stir the Indian community out of its apathy. His work appeared to produce results.

A 1909 British royal commission recommended that Indians be represented in the Council of Government and that the indenture system come to an end.

Mauritius was not directly involved in the First World War, but it was certainly affected by and suffered from it. A drastic reduction in shipping led to food shortages and subsequent price rises. However, the effects were not entirely negative. Mauritius benefitted when the price of sugar rose, as France and Britain, keen to stockpile food during the war, bought large quantities of colonial produce. This stock-piling kept sugar prices high for several years and brought a degree of prosperity to Mauritius not witnessed since the mid-19th century. At the same time, there was an increase in the number of Asian traders, who succeeded in securing an almost complete monopoly of the trade in food grains and cloth. After the war a campaign ensued for Mauritius to be returned to France, but the so-called 'retrocessionist' candidates were heavily defeated in the 1921 general election.

There was a short-lived post-war economic boom, especially between 1920 and 1923, when sugar exports hit another high. The boom then gave way to harsh conditions during the 1930s, when discontent was high and Mauritian politics stormy. Dr Maurice Curé, a member of the Council of Government, conducted a campaign for political reform and launched the Parti Travailliste (Labour Party), which worked tirelessly to increase political awareness and encouraged workers to fight for higher wages and improved conditions. The party played an important part in precipitating the disturbances which began on the sugar estates in July 1937, then moved to the Port Louis docks, and brought about the declaration of a state of emergency.

As a result, a commission of inquiry was set up, whose report of April 1938 was extremely critical of many aspects of the sugar industry. It recommended that a labour department be established and that the trade unions should gain recognition. But before anything could be done, global war broke out again.

While the First World War had had little effect on Mauritius, the same could not be said of the Second World War. The month-ly shipping service from France stopped. Japan's entry into the war and the fall of Singapore led to infrastructural development as the British established naval and air bases in Mauritius. Grand Port was used for warships, an airfield was built at Plaisance, a flying boat base was established at Tombeau Bay, and a large telecommunications station was built at Vacoas. Production of local crops was increased during World War II as rice supplies from India and Burma were cut off.

The island assumed a strategic importance when the Suez Canal was closed. Mauritius organized her own local defence and sent many men to serve overseas.

Once the war was over, the Mauritian people returned to their own problems. A 1947 commission suggested that the vote for Legislative Council elections be extended to all adults able to read and write simple sentences in any Mauritian language and to anyone who had served in the armed forces. This suggestion took effect the following year, the first constitutional change since 1885. In the 1948 election, there were 71,236 registered voters, representing two-fifths of the adult population. Significantly, a large number of workers, in comparison with just 11,426 in the 1936 election, took part.

The Labour Party, headed by Dr (later Sir) Seewoosagur Ramgoolam, won the majority of seats in the Legislative Council. The struggle to transfer power from the old oligarchy to the descendants of immigrants had begun. However, the Parti Mauricien, led by a Franco-Mauritian called Jules Koenig, remained the dominant party, supported by the nominated and official members of the council.

The 1953 election brought genuine democracy a step closer. The Labour Party increased its share of elected seats and demanded universal suffrage within 10 years, an increase in the number of elected members, and the establishment of a rule that ministers be responsible to the elected council. The Labour Party won all these demands. In the meantime, new irrigation reservoirs were constructed, roads were built to replace railways, and the harbour installation at Port Louis was modernized. Sugar continued to be the primary crop; as late as 1970 it represented 93 per cent of all Mauritian exports.

In 1958, universal suffrage — anyone over 21 who could write his or her name could vote — was introduced, enabling the Labour Party to consolidate its position at the expense of the more conservative opposition, now known as the Parti Mauricien Social Democrate (PMSD). Of the 40 elected seats, Labour took 24, the PMSD three, and the rest went to splinter parties

Above: The former Tyack home of Sookdeo Bissoondoyal is now a museum. Bissoondoyal, highly respected by the Indian community, formed the Independent Forward Block Party in 1957.

and independents. The Labour Party was now in a very strong position and able to press for more drastic changes: self-government and independence. The PMSD did not want independence because it represented two minority groups — Creoles (those of mixed race) and Francos — who feared dominance by the Indo-Mauritians. However, self-government was eventually reached in two stages. First, in 1962 Dr Ramgoolam became Chief Minister. A general election followed in 1966, in which the Labour Party won only 19 of 40 seats and was thus forced to form a coalition government. The second step took place in March 1964, when Dr Ramgoolam became Premier and the Executive Council became the Council of Ministers, responsible to the Legislative Assembly. It was a fragile coalition, however, and differences between the PMSD and the Labour Party persisted.

In 1965, Britain's Colonial Office declared that Mauritius would be granted independence as long as a general election showed that a clear majority of the population was in favour. Two years later, in the 'independence' election, 54.8 per cent voted for the 'Independence Party', an alliance of the Labour Party and two smaller parties, while the PMSD, which had campaigned for some form of association with Britain, gained 43 per cent of the vote.

The way was now clear for independence, and on 12 August 1967 Mauritius obtained self-government. The transition to full independence was not entirely trouble-free. It was a period marked by ethnic unrest, aggravated by a depressed economy and an increase in unemployment. Sadly, the racial troubles, largely between Creoles and Muslims, resulted in 100 deaths before British troops intervened to bring the bloodshed to an end.

Independence was finally gained on 12 March 1968. The coalition formed for the 1967 'independence' election disintegrated, and the Labour Party joined forces with the PMSD. As independence was already a reality, the major difference between the two parties had disappeared. Nonetheless, they had to compromise. For example, in pre-independence days, the Labour Party had called for the nationalization of the sugar industry to ensure an equitable distribution of wealth, but the alliance with the PMSD forced the Labour Party to drop the idea.

Meanwhile, a young Franco-Mauritian called Paul Berenger returned to Mauritius in 1968 after education in France to found a new opposition party, the Mouvement Militant Mauricien (MMM). His extreme left-wing policies appealed to young workers, in particular, and he quickly gained support.

In 1971, MMM members prompted a series of strikes. A state of emergency was declared and the MMM leaders were detained for a year.

Back in 1961, a survey entitled *The Economic and Social Structure of Mauritius*, which served as a guide to politicians and administrators, had pinpointed the following as major problems facing Mauritius: the economy's dependence on a single crop, sugar; the excessive population growth; and high unemployment. The solutions to these problems were thought to lie in diversification of the economy, a brake on the population growth, an increase in exports, and the creation of new jobs. Following independence, the government set about trying to produce these solutions.

A successful campaign by the Family Planning Association in the 1970s reduced the annual growth rate from three per cent in the 1960s to 1.7 per cent. The government encouraged emigration in the 1960s, although this policy led to less than 17,000 people leaving Mauritius.

Also, after independence, a series of national plans was devised by the Ministry of Economic Planning and Development. The First National Plan (1971-1975) was a great success. Jobs were created through the establishment of an Export Processing Zone (EPZ). Foreign investors were offered incentives and concessions to pour capital into EPZ enterprises, which provided jobs, helped to diversify the economy, and stimulated exports. By 1975, the EPZ, the most successful sector of which was textiles, had created nearly 10,000 new jobs.

Tourism was another major success story under the first national plan. In 1970, 25,000 tourists visited Mauritius. By 1974, the annual figure had grown to 73,000. Tourism earnings, in the meantime, had quadrupled, and the number of workers directly involved in the industry had trebled.

The second national plan (1976-1980) was not as successful as the first, perhaps a reflection of the state of the sugar industry, which suffered from falling prices after a 1974 peak. Even this minor hiccup stirred the plantation owners into action. The estates were further mechanized, waste products were put to greater use, and programmes were diversified. The sugar industry remains crucial to the economy.

A world economic depression caused sugar prices to slump and oil prices to rise, and the Mauritius rupee had to be devalued twice. The recession of the mid-1970s also had an impact on Mauritian politics. In the 1976 general election, blaming the recession on the government, the extreme MMM party won 40 per cent of the votes and 34 seats. The Labour Party won 28 seats and the PMSD just eight, but they were crucial seats; the PMSD now held the balance and decided to form a coalition with the Labour Party. After the general election, the Labour Party strongly felt that drastic changes were necessary as a remedy, but the old guard resisted this. A young, newly-elected member of the party, Harish Boodhoo, feeling dejected, decided to break away to form his own Parti Socialiste Mauricien (PSM).

In the 1982 general election, the PSM allied with the MMM to fight the Labour Party and the PMSD. The former coalition made a clean sweep of the seats. The Labour Party (led by Sir Seewoosagur) and the PMSD failed to return a single elected candidate. The only consolation for the Labour Party/PMSD coalition was their four 'best loser' seats. Anerood Jugnauth (later knighted), President of the MMM, became Prime Minister, with Boodhoo as Deputy Prime Minister and Berenger as Minister of Finance.

But the new government failed to deal with the social and economic problems facing the country. Within a year, the PSM–MMM coalition had disintegrated. Tension

Above: The first leader of independent Mauritius, the late Sir Seewoosagur Ramgoolam, and his wife.

between ministers came to a head, and Berenger and 10 other cabinet colleagues resigned. Arguing that the MMM's left-wing policies were not encouraging foreign investment and that Mauritius was in dire financial straits, in 1983 Sir Anerood broke from the MMM and formed a new party, the Militant Socialist Movement (MSM), which formed an alliance with Labour, the PMSD — under the flamboyant former mayor of Curepipe and Port Louis, the late Sir Gaetan Duval — and two other parties, and won the general election of August 1983. This gave the five-party coalition the mandate to implement less radical policies and to restore relations with more conservative foreign governments, including South Africa, upon which the Mauritian economy depended to a significant degree.

Prime Minister Jugnauth's new government took a number of steps to stimulate the economy. Company and personal tax ceilings were reduced from 65 to 35 per cent. Trade was liberalized and import duties were lowered from a maximum of 85 to 35 per cent. To encourage private sector in-

vestment, attractive incentives were offered to local and foreign entrepreneurs. At the same time, to improve the lot of the poor, subsidies on staple foods and social service benefits were raised. These steps significantly revived the economy and stabilized society considerably.

All seemed to be going well until 1986, when three Mauritian MPs were caught at Amsterdam's Schiphol Airport with heroin in their suitcases. A subsequent inquiry opened a can of worms, implicating other politicians in drug running. Deputy Prime Minister Boodhoo was expelled from office and later resigned his seat, his place being taken by Sir Gaetan Duval, who went on to compound his playboy image by admitting

Overleaf, clockwise from top left: Colourful dancers entertain the crowds at the island's National Day celebration; elegant Indian dancers take part in the festivities; members of the Mauritius armed forces march past the crowds; colourful National Day costumes highlight the country's many cultures.

51

he was bisexual. (These events were topped by the death at the age of 86 of the grand old man of Mauritian politics, Sir Seewoosagur Ram-goolam. Sir Gaetan died in May 1996.)

The scandals resulted in the next general election being brought forward by one year to 30 August 1987, which Sir Aneerood won decisively, thanks to an alliance with 39 of the 62 contested seats.

The MSM renewed its alliance with Berenger's MMM for the next general election, in September 1991, and achieved a landslide victory. Sir Aneerood Jugnauth remained Prime Minister, while Berenger became Foreign Minister. When Mauritius became a republic in 1992, Sir Veerasamy Ringadoo, previously the governor-general, was installed as the first president for three months before handing over to Sir Cassam Uteem, a former industry minister.

In this new stab at a coalition, however, Sir Aneerood and Berenger again failed to see eye to eye for very long and, in August 1993, the Foreign Minister was sacked. Shortly after that, the MMM split into two factions, one led by Berenger, the other by Dr Prem Nababsing, the latter remaining in alliance with Sir Aneerood's MSM.

In April 1994, the MMM faction led by Berenger joined Labour, now led by Ramgoolam's son, Dr Navin Ramgoolam, in a pact for the election in December 1995. Given the serious problems facing the ruling MSM/MMM Nababsing alliance — there was resentment at the Prime Minister's personality cult, and a senior member of the government was arrested in 1994 on a charge of murdering his wife — the Labour Party–MMM Berenger alliance romped home by a landslide 65 per cent.

Jugnauth tendered his resignation to President Cassam Uteem and Ramgoolam took over as Prime Minister. Ramgoolam, a Hindu like Jugnauth, and Berenger, a Creole, campaigned on a platform of sticking to the economic policies that had brought Mauritius prosperity rare in other African states. It was under Jugnauth, but with reforms set up by Berenger, that Mauritius became the success story of Africa in the 1980s, with Gross Domestic Product — GDP — growth of more than eight per cent a year.

Above: Cassam Uteem who became President of Mauritius in July 1992.

Above: Dr Navin Ramgoolam, son of the founding father of Mauritian nationhood, became Prime Minister in December 1995.

The Land: Beauty Forged by Fire

From the air the most dramatic physical features of Mauritius are craggy peaks, green sugar cane fields, and, in contrast, rich blue seas around the island. The mountains, which run roughly north-east to south-west, rise to over 800 metres (2,600 feet). But it is their profile, rather than their height, that is impressive; spindly and pointed peaks so steep and rocky that no vegetation of any kind grows there.

The lower slopes tend to be covered with forests and rough grassland, but it is the cane fields that dominate the plains, covering nearly 40 per cent of the total Mauritian land mass. Offshore, many different hues of blue colour the lagoon, which varies greatly in width depending on the reef's distance from the coast.

With the exception of the inner Seychelles islands, which are granitic, all of the world's islands are either coralline or volcanic. All three Mascarene islands — Mauritius, Rodrigues (a dependency of Mauritius), and Réunion — are volcanic. However, the Mascarenes are of different ages. Mauritius is the oldest, at eight million years, Réunion is about three million years old, and Rodrigues is just a baby at one-and-a-half million years old. Because of tectonic plate movement, volcanic activity still occurs in the Indian Ocean, but, above sea level, only in Réunion, where lava is spewed out regularly from the Piton de la Fournaise. Mauritius is entirely volcanic, except for marginal tracts of uplifted coral reef and beach material, and its physical relief has been created by lava flows. The first volcanic eruptions in the Indian Ocean's south-west are thought to have taken place about 13 million years ago, resulting in the undersea Mascarene Ridge, which runs from Seychelles in the north to Réunion in the south and forms the Mauritian base.

Five million years later, at the beginning of the Pleistocene era (the earlier part of the Quaternary period in which our ancestors first evolved), volcanic activity in two craters pushed land above sea level, forming an island that may have reached a height of more than 3,000 metres (19,800 feet). Subsequent explosions blew away the island's top to create a caldera. Weathering has reduced the caldera's walls to the present mountain ranges of Black River, Grand Port, and Moka. Secondary eruptions resulted in lava flows that only affected the island's south-west, creating, for example, the dramatic Baie du Cap cliff face. About four million years ago a new phase of eruptions opened up a chain of craters across the island from the south-west to the north-east, good examples of which are Trou aux Cerfs, Kanaka, and Mont Bar le Duc. Grand Bassin and Bassin Blanc are fine examples of crater lakes.

Other features dated to that period of volcanic activity include lava tunnels at, for example, Eau Coulée, which has a stream running through it; Petite Rivière, hung with stalactites, which twists underground for almost a kilometre; Trois Cavernes; La Caverne and Pont Bon Dieu; fumaroles at Eau Bouillie and Puits des Hollandais; and trachyte domes (made of rough, usually light-coloured, volcanic rock consisting mainly of potash felspar) at Mont Camisard and Piton du Milieu.

Around the same time a crater developed that produced, as lasting evidence of its existence, the islands of Coin de Mire, Flat, Round, and Île aux Serpents off the northern coast of Mauritius.

After another period of erosion, the last series of volcanic activity took place more than 100,000 years ago and its lava created the coastal plains. Perhaps as recently as 10,000 years ago, though, a succession of thin lava flows covered about 70 per cent of the present highlands.

Since then, submergence and emergence have occurred, so that in some places raised reefs and beaches are found as high as 20 metres (66 feet) above sea level.

Overleaf: Sunset over distant Round Island, seen from Serpent Island.

The most recent lava streams, which once ran down from the central crater, can still be seen, black and smooth, in the Roches Noire area in the north-east.

These lava flows fashioned undulating coastal plains, which are particularly wide in the north, east, and south-east. The largest plain is in the north and north-east, and covers about one-sixth of the total island, rising very gently to the highlands.

The island's present higher central plain, which rises to about 600 metres (1,970 feet), is all that is left of a vast crater. The mountain ranges surrounding the plain are all steeply inclined towards the interior, the broken remains of the crater walls. The Piton de la Petite Rivière Noire is the highest peak, at 828 metres (2,715 feet); Pieter Both is next at 820 metres (2,690 feet); then Le Pouce, the thumb-shaped mountain that looms behind Port Louis, at 812 metres (2,663 feet).

Smaller volcanic eruptions on the coast produced more crater wall formations, such as the towering Morne Brabant and, just offshore, Îlot Forneau in the south-west. A little further east along the south coast, at Baie du Cap, there is a better-defined formation, and the Vieux Grand Port bay has a large crater that can sometimes be seen under the sea from a boat.

Charles Darwin was impressed by the island's volcanic nature, writing in his diary in the 19th century, 'Captain Lloyd took us to the Rivière Noire . . . that I might examine some rocks of elevated coral. We passed through pleasant gardens, and fine fields of sugar cane growing amidst huge blocks of lava.' The mountain peaks, however, did not impress everybody. 'Quaint and picturesque groups of toy peaks' is how American writer Mark Twain once described the worn-down pinnacles.

The line of craters from north-east to south-west acts as a natural barrier to rain clouds blown by the prevailing winds from the east. Consequently, the greater part of the island's annual precipitation — up to five metres 16 feet a year — occurs on the eastern side of the mountain ranges, producing lush vegetation that's in contrast to the arid land on the western side of the ridge. Although experiencing a radial pattern of drainage, Mauritius is not an island of huge rivers. The Grand River South-East, the largest, is only 39.4 kilometres (24.5 miles) long. There are some 60 other small rivers, some of which are fast flowing, particularly in the rainy season; they have waterfalls and are used to generate power. However, most streams degenerate as they reach the coast and become rubbish-clogged trickles.

A 1949 geological survey by the University of Cape Town discovered no important mineral resources, but the deep weathering of the volcanic lavas has produced soils excellent for sugar cane.

The 330-kilometre (205-mile) coastline is almost entirely surrounded by coral reef, broken, for example, between Souillac and Le Bouchon on the southern coast, where the sea crashes against the black cliffs to create a rugged, wild coastline.

At Gris Gris in the south and Pointe aux Caves in the west, wave action has produced cliffs, caves, and arches. It has also brought sand ashore and created of beaches at many different points. At Le Morne and Albion, both on the west coast, sand spits have formed, and, at Riambel in the south, wind action has produced sand dunes. There are two excellent, natural harbours — Port Louis in the north-west and Mahébourg in the south-east.

Mauritius lies on a submarine shelf one to four kilometres (.5 to 2.5 miles) wide, except in the north where it covers an area of 24 by 20 kilometres (15 by 12 miles). The shelf then plunges steeply down to 3,600 metres (2.237 miles or 11,300 ft), the average Indian Ocean depth.

Marine plants and the larvae of sedentary marine animals were the first to colonize the island. Lichens encrusted the bare rocks and, as powdery soil formed, wind-, sea-, and bird-borne plants began to take root, many of them from Madagascar, the nearest major land mass, just 805 kilometres (500 miles) west of the Mascarenes. Eventually, the abundant rainfall and equable climate enabled the island to be covered by dense luxuriant forest of tall, slow-growing trees. The forest was divided into three areas: sea-level palm savannah; big trees such as ebony, *bois d'olive, bois du*

Above: Fitting together like pieces of an enormous jigsaw puzzle, sugar cane fields spread out across much of Mauritius.

natte, and *bois de fer*; and forests of tall straight woods like the *tambala coque*, the flying buttress, whose roots stand up well to cyclones. Today, 2,000 hectares (4,950 acres) of indigenous forest remain in Mauritius, mostly in the south-west and Machabee.

The original forest was inhabited by lizards, snakes, and other reptiles, which arrived by sea on the back of natural 'rafts' of twigs, branches, and creepers from nearby lands. One mammal (a large bat species) and a large number of birds were all brought by errant winds to their final destination.

The animal life settled and prospered. Over the years and across generations, new species evolved unique to the Mascarenes. There being no major predators (the lizards and the geckos feared only the owls and the small kestrels), many of these amazing creatures developed without natural defences. The tortoises grew huge and plodded along the path of life, while many of the birds had no need to fly. The most famous of the flightless birds is the dodo, which was fat and waddled along at no great speed; but there were also the aphanapteryx in Mauritius and the solitaire in Rodrigues.

With the arrival of nature's worst predator, man the extinction of these birds was inevitable. First seafarers, and then settlers, came with dogs, cats, pigs, goats, rats, monkeys — a dangerous predator, second only to man. Within a very short time, several unique species — including the dodo and the solitaire — had vanished.

In the waters around Mauritius and Rodrigues, sea turtles abounded, coming ashore to lay large numbers of eggs on sandy beaches. At Rodrigues, especially, thousands of sea cows (dugongs) were to be found in the lagoon. The waters teemed with fish of all types and sizes, as did the rivers, where early visitors also saw large eels. Much of this unique marine life dwindled significantly or completely disappeared. In the 1970s, naturalist Gerald Durrell wrote in his book *Golden Bats and*

Pink Pigeons, '. . . the indigenous flora and fauna of Mauritius can be said to be hanging on to its existence by its finger nails'. Durrell's Jersey Wildlife Preservation Trust has done much to rectify that situation in the last 20 years, helping to rescue the Mauritian kestrel from the brink of extinction (only four were left at one time).

Pear-shaped Mauritius occupies 1,865 square kilometres (720 square miles); its greatest length and breadth are roughly 62 and 48 kilometres (38.5 and 30 miles), respectively. The whole country, including its dependencies, covers only 2,045 square kilometres (790 square miles), but, because the islands sprawl so, the sea area is vast. Around Mauritius itself more than 15 islets lie in their own lagoons. North of the island, uninhabited except by wildlife, are five small islands: Serpent, Round, Flat, Gabriel, and Coin de Mire. Rodrigues lies 653 kilometres (406 miles) east of Mauritius, occupying 110 square kilometres (42 square miles); at its longest and widest it is 18 and eight kilometres (11 and five miles),

respectively. Rodrigues is like Mauritius in physical appearance, being little more than a mass of basaltic lava rising out of the sea. It is the only island in the Mauritius group with a large flat limestone outcrop — 810 hectares (2,000 acres) in size.

There are two prominent features — a central ridge that runs most of the length of Rodrigues, from which undulating slopes fall away into a very wide, shallow lagoon, and limestone caves at Caverne Patate à Butte L'Habe, a popular tourist attraction. Twice the size of the island, the 200-square-kilometre (77-square-mile) lagoon accommodates around 20 small islands. A host of white sandy beaches, well protected by the coral reef, surround Rodrigues, and there is only one natural harbour of any note, at Port Mathurin, the island's capital.

Originally Rodrigues was covered by luxuriant vegetation but, over the years, deforestation has resulted in soil erosion and islanders now toil constantly to eke out a living from the sparse, rugged slopes.

Further afield, Mauritian dependencies include the Cargados Carajos Archipelago, also known as the Saint Brandon Islands, 395 kilometres (245 miles) northeast, and the two Agalega Islands, 1,200 kilometres (745 miles) to the north, all coralline. Their physical appearance is, therefore, very different from that of Mauritius or Rodrigues. They are flat, with beaches of white coral sand.

Mauritius has also laid claim to the island of Tromelin, occupied by France, and would like to reclaim Six Islands, Peros Banhos, Solomon, and Diego Garcia in the Chagos Archipelago, which have, since 1965, been part of the British Indian Ocean Territory.

Mauritius in its entirety lies between 10° and 21° latitude and 57° and 58° longitude, just north of the Tropic of Capricorn. The nearest neighbour, only 220 kilometres (137 miles) away, is Réunion, which belongs to France. To the west lies Madagascar — 805 kilometres (500 miles) away — and the east coast of the African continent, some 1,800 kilometres (1,200 miles) distant. Western Australia is 5,854 kilometres (3,637 miles) to the east, and India 3,200 kilometres (1,988 miles) to the north.

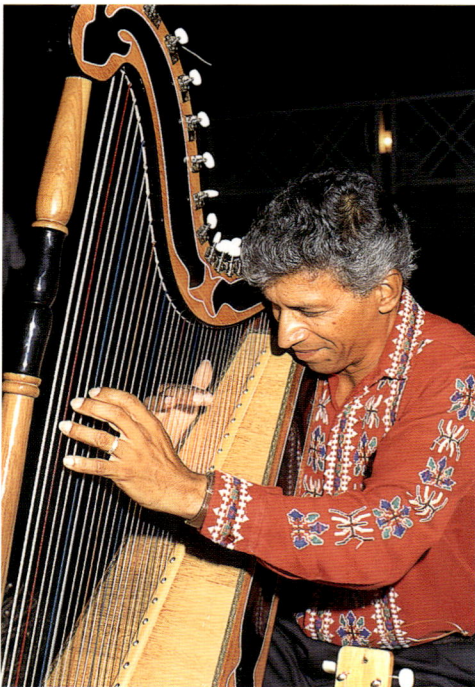

Above: Mauritian harpist plays a nostalgic air.

The People: Proud and Unique

Human settlement of Mauritius began in the 17th century, when the Dutch brought Malagasy slaves with them to work the land. Thus the population has been mixed from the word go. Later immigrants came from all over Europe (but particularly France), Africa, India, and China.

The constituent elements have, by and large, preserved separate communities and maintained their cultural origins and traditions. Different physical types exhibit various ethnic modes of dress, speak a variety of languages, and practise several religions.

However, it is impossible for Mauritians to consider themselves simply as French, Indian, African, Chinese, or whatever, for, whenever they return to the country of their forebears they soon realize that there has been such an evolution over the years that the tone and vocabulary of their language is often quite different. Distance and time have also changed them in other ways. From a religious viewpoint, Mauritians have, in most cases, developed their own typical rituals.

There is complete freedom of religion in Mauritius, and the variety of faiths is bewildering for such a small country. According to the 1983 census, 87 religious denominations and organizations existed in Mauritius, the main ones being Hinduism, Christianity, and Islam.

Christianity was the first to take root and over a quarter of a million subscribe to it, the majority being Roman Catholic.

Hinduism is practised by just over half the population, while about 16 per cent are devoted to Islam.

Most Sino-Mauritians are Roman Catholic, but China's ancient religions are observed by a portion of the population and some Chinese festivals are celebrated.

However, despite their mixed ancestry and religious backgrounds, most people regard themselves as Mauritians first, and their association with a particular ethnic or religious group takes second place.

A unifying factor is that the country is small and remote, and has one of the world's highest population densities. A good portion of the population lives in one of the country's five municipalities: Port Louis, Beau Bassin-Rose Hill, Quatre Bornes, Vacoas-Phoenix, and Curepipe. Each town features a main road, usually called Route Royale, on which most of the town's commercial activities are centred. Radiating from the Route Royale are any number of roads, most of which are shady residential thoroughfares. Others choose to live in or around a village, which generally boasts a cyclone shelter, structures little more than unfinished concrete blocks with steel rods poking out of the top (ready for the time when enough money is raised to build a second storey), various places of worship, and plenty of general stores. Some villages, such as Triolet, sprawl over a large area and are akin to small towns.

Indians

Today, the Indo-Mauritian community accounts for some 65 per cent of the island's population. In 1835, when slavery was abolished, Indians were quite few.

A century earlier, the Comte de La Bourdonnais encouraged Indian tradesmen and artisans to migrate to Mauritius. By the second half of the 18th century, they were involved in agriculture and were hired as domestic servants. Most were Tamils from southern India. By 1800, there were 6,000 Indians in Mauritius, representing roughly one-tenth of the population. The British brought more Indians to Mauritius in the early 19th century to build roads. However, most of the Indo-Mauritians are descendants of sugar workers who came as indentured labourers from India after 1830, to replace the freed slaves. These workers came from different parts of the vast subcontinent, but the majority were from the northern provinces of India and were Hindus.

By 1860, Indians already constituted around two-thirds of the population, a proportion that has been maintained ever since. In the 19th century, when some of

the sugar estates were sub-divided, those who could afford to bought small plots of land. More recently, since the 1950s when educational facilities became accessible to all, Indo-Mauritians have entered the civil service and various other professions.

They had different social, linguistic, and religious traditions, and it was only over time that they developed common traits and became known as Indo-Mauritians. Yet they preserve a sense of separate cultural identity through, for example, their unique religious festivals and, in the case of the Tamils — who still form the bulk of the labour force on the sugar estates — through their work.

The Tamils, the second most important Indo-Mauritian group, came in the 19th century. Tamil denotes the people, their country, their cultural tradition, and their language. As long ago as 1771 Pierre Poivre allowed them to build their first temple on the island. However, the first large temple did not open until the 1850s, in Terre Rouge. Tamil temples are always easily recognizable by their wide range of bright colours.

The Tamils of southern India are followers of Hinduism. But the Tamil religion practised in Mauritius has no counterpart in India.

The Mauritian Tamils are renowned for their seemingly masochistic form of the Hindu faith. They perform awe-inspiring rituals and observe such practices as fire-and-sword walking at certain times of the year. *Cavadee*, celebrated for Lord Muruga, is their most important, and most colourful, feast. Devotees carry a *cavadee* (literally a piece of polished wood) as a penance for wrongdoings, pierce their bodies with small silver needles and then carry their *cavadee* to the temple.

Hindu houses throughout Mauritius are easily recognizable by small shrines, festooned with red and white flags, erected in the garden to worship their god.

Weddings are of utmost importance and last for three days. It is not uncommon for a large marquée of bamboo or steel scaffolding and palm fronds or tarpaulin to be erected in a village or town for this purpose. The various stages of a wedding take

place in this marquée. Grand Bassin, in the south, is as sacred to the Mauritian Hindu, as the Ganges. Every February, the Maha Shivaratree festival is held at Grand Bassin. Devotees from all over the island come to spend the night by the lakeside in worship and then return to their homes in the morning with a little holy water from the lake to continue the ceremony in their local temples (the first of which was opened in 1867).

Other Hindu festivals include Diwali (festival of light), Raksha Bandhan (festival of the silken bond, now celebrated as Sisters' Day), and Ganga Snaan (which literally means bath in the holy Ganges).

The Muslims are the smallest group of Indo-Mauritians. Predominantly Gujarati, they came from west India — not as indentured labourers, but as free men engaged in trade. They formed a new 'middle class' on the island, and today are dominant in the rice and cloth businesses. The Mauritian Muslims are subdivided

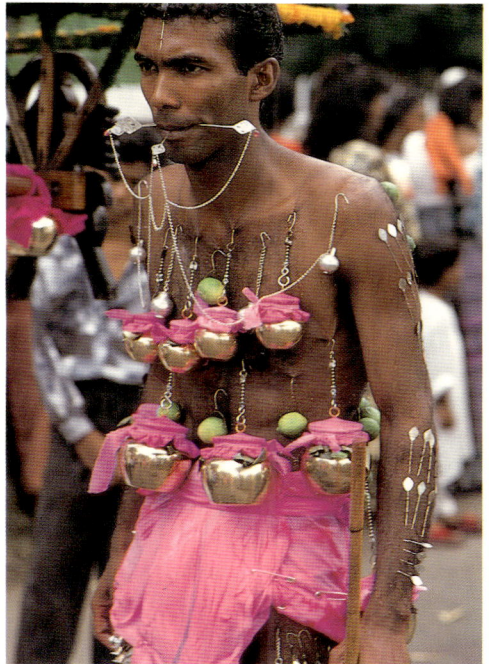

Above and opposite: *Cavadee* participants willingly pierce their bodies with small silver needles as part of the important and colourful Tamil religious festival.

Above: Proud of their individuality, yet working together as Mauritians, the country's youth attend a rally in Port Louis.

into Sunni, Shia, and Ahmadist sects. The Sunni, who constitute 95 per cent of the Muslim population, are further divided into Sunnee Hanafites, Meimons, and Sunnee Surtees. Meimons, who came from Gujarat, form an aristocracy and are often the textile and grain traders, playing perhaps the most important role among the Mauritian Muslims. They are responsible for the Jummah Mosque in Port Louis, on which the faith is focused.

The most important Muslim festival, Muharram (known in Mauritius as Yamsey oe Ghoon), commemorates the martyrdom of a grandson of the prophet. Other important festivals include Eid-Ul-Fitr, which marks the end of Ramadan, the culmination of a month of obligatory fasting and abstinence.

Creoles

The second largest group in Mauritius — representing about 30 per cent of the population — are the Creoles, the term usually referring to people of mixed African and European decent. In Mauritius, it is just as likely to refer to a mixture of any two or more of the country's four main groupings. Creoles hold jobs in all sectors of the economy, from the civil service through teaching and other professions, to managerial posts on the sugar estates. Those not so highly educated work as clerks, dockers, fishermen, and domestic help.

Chinese

The forefathers of the Sino-Mauritians were sailors, artisans, and small traders who arrived while Mauritius was under British administration, mostly from the south-eastern and north-eastern Chinese provinces. They were among the last immigrants to settle in Mauritius, with significant numbers arriving in the 1840s. By the 1920s, the Chinese had gained control of the retail trade, operating shops throughout the island. The Chinese are extremely hardworking — at school and in their chosen professions — and many of the younger generation, having attained a high level of education, are seeking employment outside the retail trade, in banks and businesses. As with Chinese immigrants all over the world, they tend to stick together to preserve their identity, although this has been difficult. As late as 1911, there were only 355 women out of 3,313 Chinese people. Moreover, the Chinese are prone to congregate in urban areas because many are traditionally retailers and shopkeepers. Indeed, Port Louis has its own 'Chinatown' or Chinese quarter. Many Sino-Mauritians originally subscribed to the Buddhist faith, and the first temple was opened in Port Louis in 1846. By the end of the 19th century, 92 per cent of the Sino-Mauritians followed Buddhism and other oriental religious beliefs, but others had converted to Christianity, as this was a prerequisite to marrying a Roman Catholic. By 1921, almost a third (2,000 of 6,745) of the Chinese had become Christians. By 1952, their number had overtaken that of those practising traditional Buddhism, a religion originating in India but introduced to Mauritius through China.

Europeans

Europeans are often referred to as the Franco-Mauritians, because the majority are descendants of French colonists and most still speak the pure French of their ancestors. Because many are descended from the early plantation owners, the Europeans dominate the sugar industry, but they also play an extremely important part in such other fields as commerce, trade, and tourism. An amazing thing about Mauritius is that, although it was a French colony for just 95 years and a British one for all of 158, France continues to wield more influence over Mauritius than Britain. This apparent incongruity results from the fact that the British offered the French generous capitulation terms when they conquered the island, pledging to preserve the existing laws, customs, language, religion, and private property. It also results from the French continuing efforts to maintain cultural hegemony in all French-speaking countries, including its former colonies. Many European, and also small numbers of Creoles, Indians and Chinese, are Roman

Catholics. Roman Catholicism was the first religion to be practised in Mauritius. In 1616 the first mass was celebrated by a Jesuit priest called Manoel d'Almeida, but it was not until 1722, when the French took possession of the island, that Roman Catholicism became the official religion. It remains the largest Christian group, but other Christian churches have established themselves. Anglicanism was introduced when the British captured the island in 1810.

In 1850, the Cathedral of St James in Port Louis was consecrated and, since 1854, Anglican bishops have presided over the well-being of the Anglican community. Other Christian groups active in Mauritius include the Presbyterians and the Baptists.

Language

While there are many languages, two are almost universally spoken and act as a unifying force. The first is Creole, a pidgin French that evolved in the early 18th century as a method of communication between slaves and their masters on the sugar estates. The language now has a very definite local flavour, being peppered with words or corruption of words from various languages and dialects. As Creole is associated with no particular ethnic group, it has become the lingua franca of all sections of the community and is certainly the most commonly used.

The second, English, is, like Creole, not associated with a particular ethnic group, but that is not the reason it is used across ethnic lines. The reason is that Mauritius was a British colony for over 150 years and the Asian immigrants realized that the way to achieve promotion in the civil service and to find a place in a British university was through the language of the colonial masters. But only from 1847 were court proceedings carried out in English and not until the 1940s did it become the medium of primary education. English remains the official language. The first settlers, the Dutch, left behind a legacy of Dutch place names, but did not have any other lasting effect on local linguistics. The French settlers introduced a language that still holds pride of place in Mauritian life. It is the

Above: Colourfully clad Mauritian dancer perfoms the erotic *sega* dance.

dominant language in the press, as well as of polite and formal conversation. Two factors explain the fairly high standard of French in Mauritius. First, there is the presence of the Alliance Française. Established in 1884, it is the oldest branch of that organization outside France. Secondly, a large number of higher education scholarships are provided by the French government.

The profusion of Indian immigrants, from the end of the 18th century, brought a number of new languages and dialects to the country. The initial wave of immigrants came mostly from southern India and, as a result, Tamil was the first Indian language spoken in Mauritius. Throughout the 19th century, Bhojpuri was the most widely spoken Indian language following the arrival of large numbers of indentured labourers from northern India. At the beginning of the 20th century, Hindi became an increasingly important language, but it is now used only in religious ceremonies and literary circles Bhojpuri, on the other hand, is still widely spoken. Telegu,

Marathi, Gujarati, Bengali, and Punjabi are also spoken. Muslim traders arriving in the 19th century brought Urdu to Mauritius. In the same century, Chinese immigrants introduced Hakka, Mandarin, and Cantonese.

In 1948, literacy in any local language became an electoral requirement. Since then, there has been a drive towards teaching all languages. In 1955, Asian-language classes were introduced in primary schools and, in 1974, in secondary schools.

By the 1980s, 22 languages were being spoken and the mother tongues of the islanders' forebears totalled 33.

Music, dance, and theatre

The *sega*, the closest thing the Mauritians have to a national dance, evolved many generations ago, much like the Creole language, as a means of communication. The Malagasy and African slaves brought to Mauritius by European masters initially had no common language and so, on the few occasions when they were allowed to gather, they expressed themselves and their feelings through song and dance.

Above: Representing a rainbow of cultures, students participate in a Port Louis youth rally.

Dancing the sega became not only a source of relief from the wretched daily lives of the slaves, but also an important means of social and cultural interaction. More precisely, the sega came to be an erotic dance played out between members of the opposite sex. There are no complicated moves in the sega. The feet are shuffled along the ground while the hips are gyrated.

The best place to see an authentic sega is the Chamarel/Black River area. The commercial versions of the sega performed in most hotels today are not a true representation of the traditional dance; although they are, nonetheless, colourful and entertaining. The music that accompanies these performances follows the traditional rhythms of the islands, even if, in many cases, the score is played by guitars instead of traditional instruments. The original instruments for a sega include the *ravanne*, the *bobre*, the *maravanne*, and the *tamtam*; the *ravanne* being probably the most important. It is a large tambourine made from a goat's skin (preferably that of a she-goat), which is traditionally heated over a fire before

play begins. The *ravanne* is then beaten by one of the musicians to produce the main rhythm and sets the pace for treading the measure.

The *bobre* is made from an arched piece of wood, to which is attached one or more dried gourds or pumpkins, a metal string, and a ring to vary the string's tension and thus tune the instrument. The *bobre* is, in other words, little more than a primitive type of guitar. The string is either played with a bamboo stick or plucked with the fingers in time to the *ravanne*'s beat.

The *maravanne*, a wooden box half filled with stones or dried beans, is shaken, creating an intricate beat. The *tamtam* is a big drum either carved out of a large tree trunk or made from a big wine cask.

Connoisseurs say there are variations between the Mauritian and the Rodriguan segas, the most obvious of which is that the Rodriguan version is closer to the original. However, there are subtler differences not so easy for the uninitiated to discern. For example, the rhythms are said to be similar but not identical, and only one couple

67

dance at a time in the Rodriguan sega, while all couples dance together to the Mauritian sega. One thing is for sure: the Rodriguan dances and music have been influenced by European modes to a far greater extent than the Mauritian. On Rodrigues, mazurkas and quadrilles are often danced to the strains of an accordion, steel triangles, coconut maracas, and, on occasion, a fiddle.

Definitely one of the best places in either Mauritius or Rodrigues to see traditional dancing is Ben Gontrand's house in Port Mathurin every Thursday evening. Each week a crowd congregates in the front room to be instructed in the intricacies of traditional dances. An accordion player, three triangle players, and a *maraca* player set the rhythm, soon accompanied by the sound of stamping feet on the wooden floor. The dances start slowly, but the beat soon quickens and, as the dancers work harder, excess layers of clothing are discarded. Onlookers are welcome, but restricted to the spacious verandah, which is a more than adequate viewing point.

Above: Elderly Triolet woman, witness to many changes in her years as a Mauritian.
Opposite: Young and old alike take part in their religion's festivities, such as this one at the Swastika Hindu temple at Forest Side in Curepipe.

A modern sega version that is popular among Mauritian youth is *seggae* — a cross between sega and West Indian reggae. Seggae from groups such as Ras Natty Baby and Natty Rebels, the best known, can be heard frequently on the local radio stations. The Natty Rebels often stage concerts — check for dates in the local newspapers — and cassette tape recordings of their music are widely available.

Mauritians often complain that too much attention is paid to the sega, for, with the multi-cultural composition of the country, several other forms of traditional dance are performed — but not as often.

Just as the Malagasy and African slaves turned to music and dance after their daily travails, so did the indentured Indian labourers. Classical Indian dances were accompanied by traditional percussion instruments such as the *dholok* (drum), *dholki* (large drum), *daf* (tambourine), *tavil* (drum from southern India), *tappu* (tambourine from southern India), and *tabla* (drums from northern India).

Today, the *dholok*, made from a hollowed tree trunk with a piece of goatskin attached to both ends, is played to the accompaniment of folk singers. *Dholok* and *jhaal* (copper cymbals of varying sizes) also play a central role in religious and cultural activities. The *tavil* and *tappu* are considered sacred instruments now played only during religious ceremonies. Traditional wind instruments, such as the *bansuri* (a north Indian flute) and the *nadaswaram*, are used in religious ceremonies as well as such social events as weddings.

Several hotels, including Paradise Cove, organize evenings of classical Indian dance, and at the Indian restaurant Indra, in Domaine les Pailles, traditional Indian *ghazal* music is performed on the last Saturday of every month. A few hotels, such as Sofitel Imperial Hotel at Wolmar, provide a venue for an evening of traditional Chinese performances.

The two theatres in the country, The Plaza in Rose Hill and the renovated Municipal Theatre of Port Louis, stage concerts and cultural shows. Check with local newspapers for details.

PART TWO:
PLACES AND TRAVEL

Above: Enticing view of the sea from the verandah of the Maritim Hotel in Balaclava.
Opposite: The majestic mountain of Le Pouce, as seen from Balaclava, dominates the skyline.

The North: Beautiful Bays and Beaches

The northern end of Mauritius is made up of the two districts of Pamplemousses and Rivière du Rempart.

The village of Pamplemousses, from which the district takes its name, was so called by the French because of the grapefruit-like trees that used to abound in the area. The French settled in Pamplemousses during the very first years of colonization in the 18th century, and it was home to several famous French figures, including the Comte de La Bourdonnais and Pierre Poivre. La Bourdonnais is credited with building the true foundations of Mauritius, while Poivre, another able administrator, led the island to great prosperity during the second half of the 18th century.

Under the French administration, Pamplemousses was divided into eight subdivisions. Today, there are 17 village council areas — Arsenal, Baie du Tombeau, Calebasses, Congomah, Crève Coeur, D'Épinay, Fond du Sac, Le Hochet, Long Mountain, Morcellement Saint André, Notre Dame, Pamplemousses, Plaine des Papayes, Pointe aux Piments, Terre Rouge, Triolet, and Villebague.

Rivière du Rempart is thought to have got its name from the very steep banks of the river (of the same name) that flows through the district. The district of Rivière du Rempart played a crucial part in the island's conquest by the British, for it was at Cap Malheureux, its most northern point, that the invading soldiers landed in November 1810. From there they proceeded to Port Louis, where the French were forced to capitulate.

Rivière du Rempart is now subdivided into 19 village council areas — Amaury, Amitié, Belle Vue Maurel, Cap Malheureux, Cottage, Esperance Trébuchet, Goodlands, Grand Gaube, Grand Baie, Mapou, Petit Raffray, Piton, Plaine des Roches, Poudre d'Or hamlet, Poudre d'Or village, Rivière du Rempart, Roches Noires, Roche Terre, and The Vale. A gently undulating plain covers much of the northern part of Mauritius, providing the ideal topography for sugar cane fields. As a result there are several sugar estates in the north, such as Beau Plan and Belle Vue in Pamplemousses, and Mon Loisir in Rivière du Rempart.

The northern plain is fringed by some beautiful beaches, most notably at Trou aux Biches, Mont Choisy, Grand Baie, and Péreybère. Given its image as a tropical island paradise, it is towards the beaches that most visitors to Mauritius gravitate, but the north also offers a chance to visit the Nicolière Mountains and the famous Royal Botanical Gardens at Pamplemousses, both inland.

For sports enthusiasts, there is plenty to do in this part of the island. For example, Trou aux Biches has a big game fishing centre and a nine-hole golf course. Watersports and scuba-diving centres are found in most large hotels, the unique experience of undersea walking takes place in Grand Baie, and there are opportunities to hire a yacht from a number of operators.

There is shopping galore for locally produced clothes and Mauritian artefacts in Grand Baie, and the model shipbuilding factory at Historic Marine can be visited in Goodlands.

A wide range of restaurants offer different cuisines in various hotels in the north, and in the villages of Trou aux Biches, Pointe aux Canoniers, Grand Baie, and Péreybère. Nightclubs and a jazz club are concentrated in Grand Baie and Péreybère, and Trou aux Biches has a casino.

Getting there

The main northern tourist centre of Grand Baie is 17 kilometres (10.5 miles) from Port Louis, 45 kilometres (28 miles) from SSR International Airport, 20.5 kilometres (13 miles) from Rivière du Rempart, 42.5 kilometres (26 miles) from Curepipe and 74 kilometres (46 miles) from Souillac. It is served by a good main road from Port Louis and a new motorway from Piton and Mapon.

North of Port Louis

SERPENT ISLAND

ROUND ISLAND N.R.

```
0        5         10        15 km
0     2      4       6       8    10 miles
```

FLAT ISLAND   GABRIEL ISLAND

INDIAN OCEAN

N

COIN DE MIRE ISLAND N.R.

Cap Malheureux

Marina Holiday Village
Anse la Raie

La Maison
Les Mascareynes Hotel
Paradise Cove Hotel

Grand Gaube

Péreybère
Hibiscus Village
Petit Paquet
St. François
Le Grand Gaube Hotel
Island View Club

Pointe Bernache

Colonial Coconut Hotel
Merville Hotel
Royal Palm Hotel
Le Canonniere Hotel

ÎLE D'AMBRE

Petit Raffray
Roche Terre

Pointe aux Canonniere
Le Mauricia Hotel
Club Mediterranée
Grand Baie

Goodlands

PLM Azure Hotel
Mon Choisy
Le Grand Bleu Hotel
Casuarina Village
Temple

St. Antoine

Poudre d'Or

Trou aux Biches Hotel

Etoile de Mer Hotel
Trou aux Biches
Fond du Sac

Anse du Bain
Pointe Lascars

Villas Pointe aux Biches
Colonial Hotel
La Sirene Hotel
Triolet

Pointe des Roches Noires

Au Soleil Couchant G.H.

Mapou

Piton
La Clémence
Roches Noire

Pointe Piments
Victoria Hotel
Balaclava

Rivière du Rempart

Maritim Hotel
Baie aux Tortues

Mon Loisir
Belle Vue Maurel

Moulin à Poudre
Botanical Gardens
Pamplemousses

Baie du Tombeau
Arsenal

Mon Goût
Petite Rosalie
Petite Julie
Amaury

Corotel Hotel

D'Epinay

Baie du Tombeau
Terre Rouge
Bay View Hotel

Villebague

R. du Rempart

R. François

Fort George
Sainte Croix

Congomah

R. Labourdonnais

La Nicolière Reservoir

NICOLIÈRE MOUNTAINS

Bon Acceuil

Les Mariannes

Centre de Flacq

Pont Bon Dieu

R. du Poste de Flacq

R. Coignard

PORT LOUIS

Above: Graceful curve of the Maritim Hotel beach with golf course in background.

When to go

Although pleasant at any time of the year, the best time to visit the north is April to June and September to November. You may wish to avoid the peak tourist season of December to early January (when holiday packages cost more), as well as the month of February, when it is hot, sticky, extremely rainy, and cyclones could occur.

Where to stay

In Balaclava, the Maritim Hotel; in Trou aux Biches, the Trou aux Biches Hotel; in Pointe aux Canonniere, Club Med, Le Canonniers Hotel; in Grand Baie, Le Mauricia, Merville Hotel, the Royal Palm; in Anse la Raie, the Paradise Cove Hotel, and in Grand Gaube, Le Grand Gaube. There are also plenty of middle-class and budget hotels, self-catering apartments, and bungalows in the north. See Listings.

Sightseeing

Start from Port Louis and travel **north** along the **motorway** leading out of the capital. An unmarked **left turn** at the **third**

roundabout onto the B29 leads to **Baie du Tombeau** (Tombeau Bay), which acquired its name from an ancient tomb containing the remains of George Weldon, an English governor of Bombay who drowned in the bay in 1697. His widow erected a massive monument in his honour (since vanished), which served as a marker warning sailors of the dangers of this stretch of coast.

The bay was certainly dangerous in those days. In 1615, four ships belonging to the Dutch East Indies Company were caught in a cyclone and headed for the safety of Port Louis. Just a few miles short of their destination, they were swept on to the reef at Baie du Tombeau. Three ships were wrecked and many lost their lives, including Admiral Pieter Both, who was on his way home to the Netherlands after a spell as the company's governor in the East Indies. In his memory, the Dutch referred to the bay as Pieter Both Baay. Now one of Mauritius' most celebrated landmarks, the cup-and-ball shaped mountain peak east south-east of Port Louis, is named after Both. During the early French settlement,

Above: Catamaran heels to the wind off Balaclava's Maritim Hotel with distinctive 811-metre (2,660-ft) Le Pouce in background.

the area was called Baie de la Maison Blanche (White House Bay) and Baie d'Orleans (Orleans Bay), but by the mid-18th century, the area had acquired its present name.

Today, Baie du Tombeau is little more than a dormitory village of Port Louis with some small industrial activities: a community centre, a private medical centre called Clinique du Nord, and Bay View hotel — boasting a Chinese restaurant with excellent views out to sea.

Further along the B29 road, which runs roughly parallel to the coast, the small, clean Corotel Hotel is on the left. Eventually the B29 reaches a T-junction at the A4, from where one turns **left** towards **Arsenal,** 1.3 kilometres (0.8 mile) further on.

Arsenal traces its name back to the 18th century when the governor, La Bourdonnais, built a house in the vicinity to weapons store all the island's ammunition. A **black cannon** on the village's central wall signifies its former importance as a munitions depot. Close by, the road bridges a small **lake** called **Bassin Merven,** named after a local who accidentally drove his car into it and drowned. There is little of interest in this quiet village except a **pottery** and the arsenal's **historic ruins** at **Ville Valio.** The only time the place seems to come alive is when a match involving the English football team Arsenal is being broadcast by the local television station; television sets are then surrounded by vocal supporters.

Just past Arsenal is **Moulin à Poudre** (Powder Mill). The mill was established by the French in the 18th century and remained in operation until 1810. The building later served as a state prison and now houses a skin disease infirmary. Nearby is the Sir Seewoosagur Ramgoolam National Hospital, which is not recommended — go to a private clinic if you need medical assistance. Just beyond the hospital, on the junction of the B18 and B11 roads, concealed in thick woodland, is a **monument** to Singhalese Prince Ehelepola, who was exiled to Mauritius by the British in 1825.

He died in Mauritius three years later. Opposite the black cannon on the wall in Arsenal is a **turning,** a continuation of the A4, about 500 metres (550 yards) along which there is a **signpost** to the Maritim Hotel and Balaclava, reached via the B41 road. The Maritim, set on 25 hectares (62 acres) of private land at **Baie aux Tortues** (Turtle Bay), played host to French president François Mitterrand when he attended the Francophone summit in Mauritius in 1993. The hotel is favoured by visiting businessmen because of its proximity to Port Louis.

Baie aux Tortues was given its name by sailors in the 17th century, probably because turtles used to crawl up the beach to lay their eggs. The underwater life in Baie aux Tortues is relatively untouched. In fact, it is thought to be the only Mauritian bay still 90 per cent comprised of live coral, and is therefore the site of Mauritius' first projected Marine National Park.

From Balaclava the road continues **north** towards **Pointe aux Piments** (Pimento Point, presumably named after the profusion of pimento bushes in the area), where the road meets the coastline, which it then follows closely.

Hotels include The Victoria, an addition to the Beachcomber Group and Villas Mon Plaisir. The remnants of the **Batterie des Grenadiers** are found at Pointe aux Piments, as is the Au Soleil Couchant guesthouse and a casual, 'sand under your feet' restaurant.

From Pointe aux Piments along the coast to **Trou aux Biches,** the open sea can be glimpsed through a forest of casuarina (or filao) trees. The waters off the beaches are not suitable for swimming, but marine life abounds in the many rock pools that have developed between the uneven fingers of black basalt stretching towards the coral reef. This coastline is excellent for watching the sunset as fishermen wade in the shallows for crab, octopus, or fish that may have been trapped in the rock pools at ebb tide. The B41 becomes the B38 road and all

along the coast towards Trou aux Biches are a number of weekend beach homes and hotels that include the Colonial Beach Hotel, Villas Pointe aux Biches, La Sirène, and Étoile de Mer. Trou aux Biches takes its name from the belief that at one time it was a watering hole for female deer. In the centre is L'Argonaute Coquillages et Artisanat, a shop that sells local handicrafts. Nearby is a run down **Aquarium,** which still provides a fascinating glimpse into the underwater world around Mauritius. More than 200 species of fish, invertebrates, live corals, and sponges are housed here in 36 tanks. One of the most popular tanks is inhabited by sharks, moray eels, and other deep water fish.

Just around the corner from the Aquarium is the Corsaire Club, from where big game fishing expeditions can be organized, and Le Pescatore, a restaurant famous for its seafood dishes and its romantic location right on the seafront.

The next **right turning,** the B36 road, also known as Shivala, leads to **Triolet.** Along it are two places of interest to watersports fanatics. Sun Sea & Snow Sports manufactures wetsuits in a variety of designs, colours, and thicknesses for clients around the world, but tourists can have wetsuits custom-made in two days for about a third of the price they would pay for an off-the-peg model back home. Sun Sea & Snow Sports is housed in what resembles a huge aeroplane hangar — set back from the road on the right. Just after the turning to Sun Sea & Snow Sports, the Island Style factory shop is on the left, the most popular boutique among windsurfing enthusiasts. It is on the outskirts of Triolet, the largest 'village' on Mauritius, which was named after Pierre Triolet, a building entrepreneur during French rule. Triolet sprawls over several kilometres and has a large population of Indo-Mauritians, many of whom are employed in the tourism and textile industries.

There is little of interest to tourists in

Opposite: Sailing is just one of the many watersport activities to be enjoyed off the north coast of Mauritius.

Above: Family enjoys the weekend on the public beach at Mont Choisy.
Opposite: Colourful tiger stands at the Shiva Shrine of the Temple of Maheswarnath at Triolet.

Triolet, apart from the beautiful **Mahe-swarnath temple.** The largest Hindu shrine in Mauritius, it can be seen soon after the Island Style shop. However, as it is a one-way system, those travelling by car must go past the **bus station** on the **left** and the Roman Catholic **Church of Notre Dame des Anges** on the **right,** before hitting the main road of Triolet, then **turn left** and **left again** to reach the **main entrance** to the temple. The Maheswarnath was completed in 1891 and renovated in 1989. Tourists may take photographs but should leave their shoes on the front steps.

Back in Trou aux Biches, a string of resort-type hotels await you, including the Beachcomber Group's Trou aux Biches Hotel, Casuarina Village, Le Grand Bleu, and PLM Azur, which stretch out along the coast. The Trou aux Biches Hotel, with an excellent beach, has the added attractions of a **casino** and a **nine-hole golf course.** The village of Trou aux Biches is also home to the Organization de Peche du Nord, which arranges **big game fishing** trips.

Trou aux Biches then becomes **Mont Choisy,** where a thick forest of casuarina trees skirts one of the most popular beaches on the island. Offshore, conditions are perfect for windsurfing, sailing, and water-skiing, while the long sandy beach is favoured by early-morning and late-afternoon walkers and joggers. Behind the beach and the casuarina trees is an old landing strip (now a football pitch) where two pilots — Hily and Surtel — made aviation history on 10 November, 1933, when they made the first flight from Mauritius to Réunion, a distance of some 220 kilometres (137 miles), in four hours.

At Mont Choisy the road meets a **T-junction,** opposite which is a **private road** marked 'Chemin Privé — Passage Interdit'. However, the public can drive along this private road edged with banyan trees and colourful tropical flowers if they wish to visit the **Mont Choisy Farm,** where grain-fed poultry, meat, and prawns are sold.

From the **T-junction** it is about a one-kilometre (half-mile) drive to **Pointe aux**

Above: Incredibly detailed model ships are produced in the workshops of Mauritian craftsmen.

Canonniers (Gunners' Point) via an avenue of flamboyant trees, which are particularly brilliant around December when the red flowers are in full bloom.

The Dutch called Pointe aux Canonniers both '*long hoeck*' (long point) and '*de vuyle hoeck*' (danger point) because so many ships were wrecked on the hidden reefs offshore. At first the French called the area Pointe Longue (long point), but when they started using the headland as a garrison they changed the name to Pointe aux Canonniers.

A **lighthouse,** opened in December 1855, was built on the site of the original French fortress, but it was closed down in 1932. It was needed to warn mariners of the dangers of the reef, which, between 1851 and 1883 alone, claimed 12 ships. Under British rule, the area was known as Gunner's Point, for it continued to serve as a military post, but it also became a quarantine area for boats arriving with cases of contagious diseases. Some shore battery **cannon** dating back to 1750 and the **ruins** of the lighthouse (which still stands by the remains

of the lighthouse keeper's quarters) can be seen in the tropical gardens of Le Canonnier Hotel. There are a couple of other hotels in Pointe aux Canonniers. Club Mediterranée (Club Med) is renowned for its excellent sporting facilities throughout the world, and the Mauritian resort is no exception. Many watersports are on offer, but a good number of land sports can also be pursued, including volleyball, football, golf, tennis, and darts. Sumptuous meals are provided and, in the evening, after dinner, club employees pool their resources to produce nightly cabarets and fashion shows. As at any Club Med, once you have paid for your holiday, everything — except souvenirs from the resort's boutique, excursions, and drinks outside of meals — is free.

The main building of another hotel in the vicinity, the 26-room Colonial Coconut, used to be a private house. It was built in the early 20th century of wood and 'ravenal' (the stem of the traveller's palm) walls, with a thatched roof. The walls are lined with colonial pictures of Mauritius

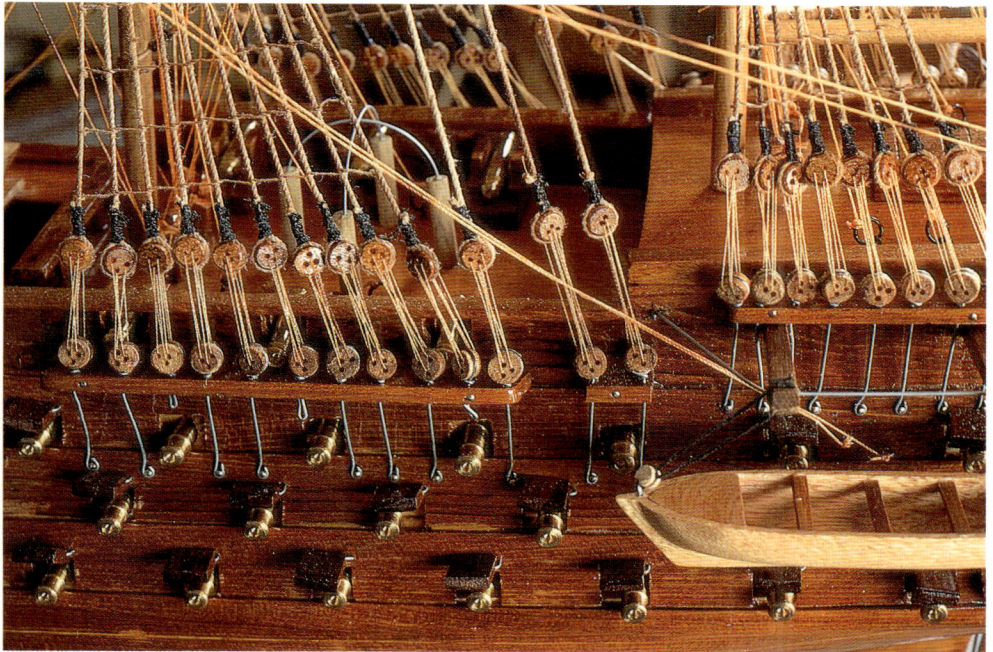

Above: Detail shows the painstaking work that goes into creating a model ship, each one a replica of a vessel that once sailed the seas.

and there is an impressive, if small, library of old books. The newer buildings accommodating the guest rooms have been constructed in traditional style and most offer views of Grand Baie.

A number of interesting **shops** are located on the main road that runs through Pointe aux Canonniers. Another branch of Island Style stocks surfing gear and beach accessories; Ceauneau House sells model ships, as does Galerie P Bauwens, although the latter has extended its range to include beautiful wooden furniture and clothing with a predominantly nautical theme; Galerie Hélène de Senneville offers a wide selection of Mauritian art and some brightly coloured handicrafts; and several shops, including Bonair Comptoir, sell locally produced clothes. At night, the same building that houses Galerie P Bauwens comes alive as a restaurant, Le Bateau Ivre, and as a nightclub at the weekend called Le Privé.

The Pointe aux Canonniers road continues **east** to Grand Baie, 2.8 kilometres (1.7 miles) away. At one point, just before Le Capitaine restaurant, the road borders the sea. Just offshore — if it's not out cruising — an **historic vessel,** the *Isla Mauritia*, is at anchor. Built in 1892, this ship will particularly appeal to sailing history buffs. It took Spanish boat builders two years to convert 90 tons of durable pine into the *Isla Mauritia*. Owned by three generations of the same family, she used to carry freight between Europe and Africa until 1959, when she sank in unusual circumstances. Salvaged and registered as a private ship, she was faithfully restored to her former glory in Scandinavia and now conforms to modern standards with regard to navigation and safety equipment. In 1988 she completed a six-month journey from Europe to Mauritius, where she plies the coastal waters carrying tourists on day trips. Her crew, dressed in naval rig, usually sail the boat to Baie aux Tortues, where they drop anchor, prepare a barbecue, and then allow passengers to explore the underwater world, ending the day

Above: The silver sands and turquoise waters of Trou aux Biches.

with an authentic *sega* (local dance) that involves audience participation. Just past Le Capitaine is another string of **shops,** including a host of clothes boutiques, such as Equateur, Fast Forward, and Chipie, which sell jeans, T-shirts, and jumpers; the Henry Koombs Gallery, where the art of one of the most popular Mauritian artists is displayed; Macumba, selling Indonesian and a few African handicrafts; and a well-stocked bookshop, Librairie Papyrus, selling postcards, books on Mauritius, and a wide selection of international newpapers and magazines.

Continuing along the **main road,** the Grand Baie **police station** is on the **left** and marks the start of the heart of **Grand Baie.** The Dutch called Grand Baie both Bogt Zonder Einde (Bay Without End) and Varekens Baay (Pigs' Bay), while the French called it Baye Profonde (Deep Bay) and, from the middle of the 18th century, Grand Baie.

Within the last 10 to 15 years Grand Baie has grown from a quiet little fishing village into a well-developed — some might say an overdeveloped — holiday resort. There is plenty of holiday accommodation, ranging from the luxurious Royal Palm to cheap pensions and self-catering bungalows.

During the day visitors amuse themselves by visiting the numerous souvenir shops and boutiques, such as Cotton Club, Habit, Floreal Knitwear, and Délire, that offer a variety of clothing; water-based activities such as scuba-diving, water-skiing, undersea walking, yacht charters — modern catamarans whisk guests out to the northern Îlot Gabriel and Flat Island on day trips — windsurfing, and kayaking. The pace of life is relatively slow and there is still something of a rustic charm to Grand Baie. It is still small enough to walk around, although during the summer heat it may be necessary, from time to time, to sit and enjoy a cooling drink on the way. Alternative modes of transport include bicycles, mopeds, motorcycles, and cars, all of which can be hired in Grand Baie. In addition, the area is well served by public transport. The **Grand Baie Yacht Club** is along the same road as the hotels

Above: Gleaming waters of a Mauritian beach resort provide opportunities for all water sports.
Overleaf: Sailing off into the sunset at Mon Choisy.

Le Mauricia Royal Palm, Merville Beach Hotel and the **conference centre** used for the 1993 Francophone Summit attended by, among others, France's President Mitterrand. The club offers reciprocal arrangements to yachtsmen from around the world.

Of the restaurants in Grand Baie, Palais de Chine is generally reckoned to offer the best Chinese foods, while Café de la Plage has a great setting on the seafront, Le Grillon is well-known for its seafood and Beatrice serves Italian food. Alchemy is a popular drinking spot. Special events are detailed in *Grand Baie News*, a free monthly publication found in many local shops and hotels.

A kilometre or so further along the northern coast, slowly but surely merging with Grand Baie, is **Péreybère,** named after Charles Péreybère, who owned a great deal of land here in the 19th century. Mainly because of its beach, which is excellent for swimming, Péreybère is very popular today, among both foreign visitors and Mauritians with weekend bungalows (known as *campements*). There are several casual restaurants in Péreybère, including the Café Péreybère, La Pizzeria, and a bar called Bounty. The two more up-market restaurants in Péreybère are Hibiscus, part of a hotel by the same name, which has a beautiful setting by the sea, and Épicure, serving European cuisine, to which the nightclub Secrets is attached.

On leaving Péreybère, the road passes close to **Paloma Beach,** where there are picturesque views across to the offshore islands of **Coin de Mire** and, beyond it, the islands of Flat, Gabriel, Serpent, and Round.

Coin de Mire is so called because it resembles the triangular piece of wood that used to be wedged beneath a cannon to give it the right elevation and trajectory.

Flat Island, which has a **lighthouse**, used to be a quarantine station (mainly for Indian immigrants) and, before the railway lines were opened, mules were bred there to transport the sugar from field to ship. At

Above: Translucent waters invite holidaymakers at Trou d'Eau Douce.

low tide, Flat Island is joined to the tiny island of **Gabriel** by a sand bank. Both are favourite haunts for day trippers who charter yachts from Grand Baie. **Round** and **Serpent islands** are misnamed. Mauritius's two endemic species of snake are found only on Round Island, which is not round, while Serpent Island has no snakes, and is round.

Round Island has been referred to as Mauritius's answer to the Galapagos Islands because, despite covering an area of only 150 hectares (370 acres), it is home to some tree, lizard, and snake species found nowhere else in the world — and has more endangered species per unit area than any other comparable spot on earth.

Round Island, which lies just over 22 kilometres (14 miles) off the main island, was made a nature reserve in 1984, managed jointly by the Government Conservation Unit, the Jersey Wildlife Preservation Trust, the World Wide Fund for Nature, and the Mauritian Wildlife Fund. It is of huge importance, because the endangered species found on the island once occurred on Mauritius, too, but they have become extinct there due to the introduction of rats, which eat plant fruit and seedlings and steal reptile eggs.

No rats have ever found their way to Round Island, although rabbits and goats were imported there in the 19th century and caused widespread vegetation destruction. The remaining population of these animals was removed in 1986, and the plants are beginning to regenerate. Plant life includes the last remnants of palm savannah, such as the famous bottle palm, the Round Island hurricane palm, a fan palm, and a vacoas. Another very rare plant endemic to Round Island and neighbouring Coin de Mire is *Lomatophyllum tormontorii*.

Round Island is famous for reptiles, most of which are restricted to the island. There are two species of endemic snake: the burrowing boa and the keel-scaled boa; three species of skink: the endemic Telfair's skink, Bouton's skink, and Bojer's skink; and three species of gecko: Guenther's gecko, ornate day gecko, and night gecko.

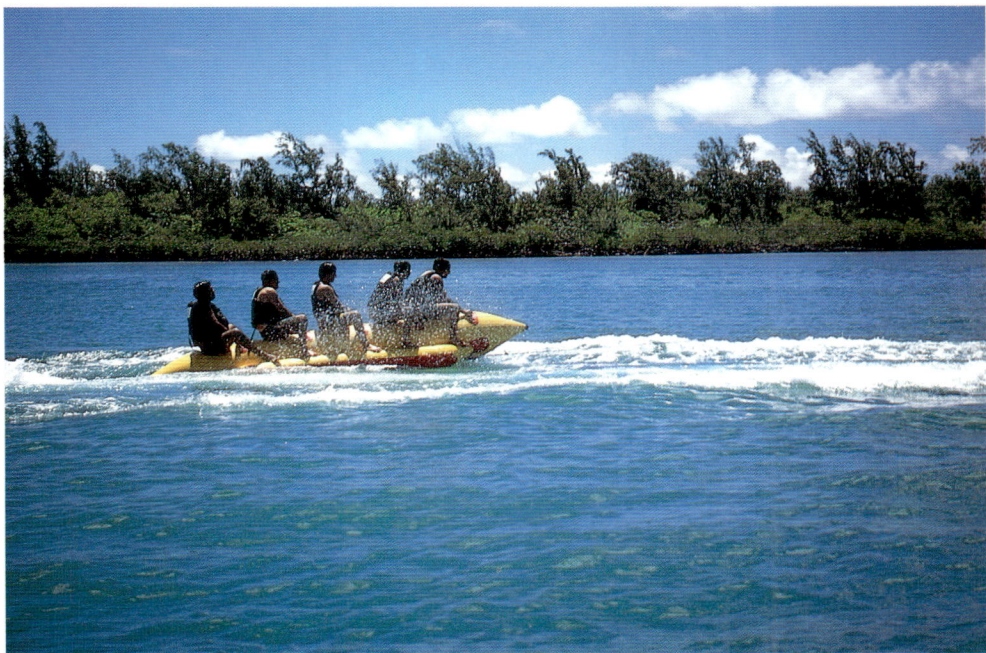

Above: Watersports are the *raison d'etre* for a Mauritian holiday.
Overleaf: Beauties of Mauritius — the richly varied shapes and colours of the andraeneum flower.

Round Island is also an important breeding ground for such fascinating seabirds as wedge-tailed shearwaters, white-tailed tropic birds, red-tailed tropic birds, and Trinidade petrels.

Visitors wishing to land on Round Island need a permit. Landing by boat is difficult due to strong currents, but special helicopter trips can be arranged.

Back on the northern coast, from Pérey-bère **east** until the church at **Cap Malhe-ureux** (Cape of Misfortune), all the sea views are occupied by grand houses hidden from the road by high stone walls. One of the old colonial style houses has been converted into an exclusive five-room hotel called La Maison.

Cap Malheureux lies about six kilometres (four miles) from Péreybère and is the most northerly point on Mauritius. It is thought to have acquired its name from the many shipwrecks that occurred offshore in the early years of colonization. It was at Cap Malheureux that the British landed when they conquered the island from the French in 1810. The small, simple Roman Catholic **church** of Notre Dame Auxiliatrice in Cap Malheureux is easily identified by its distinctive reddish-orange roof, from which one can admire the panoramic view. Coin de Mire, looking like a wedge of cheese, lies offshore, as do, in the far distance, Îlot Gabriel and Flat Island.

Further **east,** along the B13 at **Anse la Raie,** is the Paradise Cove Hotel, one of the Small Luxury Hotels of the World. With only 64 rooms, the hotel offers its guests a very personalized service and prides itself on always offering 'something more'. For example, the sporting activities available — in addition to the usual choices — include archery and kite flying.

From the Paradise Cove Hotel the B13 road zigzags its way through casuarina plantations and sugar cane fields, passing the hamlets of **Petit Paquet** and **St François,** until it reaches **Grand Gaube,** which takes its name from *gaube,* a Creole word meaning bay or inlet. It is predominantly a fishing village, but the

Above: Small, simple, but beautiful, the Roman Catholic church of Notre Dame Auxiliatrice in Cap Malheureux.

construction of two hotels — Le Grand Gaube and the Island View Club Hotel — means that it is frequented by tourists. Le Grand Gaube is the superior of the two hotels. From Grand Gaube, travel **south-westwards** to **Roche Terre** on the B14 road for four kilometres (2.5 miles), until you reach a **T-junction;** take a **left turn** on to the A5 in the direction of **Goodlands,** a town which acquired its name in the 19th century when a sugar estate flourished there. Another **sugar estate, St Antoine,** easily distinguished by the remains of its old factory chimneys and well-laid gardens at the entrance, still exists to the east of the town. Goodlands is now quite heavily industrialized and several textile factories are found there. So is **Historic Marine,** the largest Mauritian factory producing **model ships.** Established in 1982, Historic Marine claims to make the 'Rolls Royce' of model ships; in other words, the really top-quality models, and the prices reflect that claim.

Visitors are welcome to look around the workshops and the large room that dis-plays the factory's full range of products. From Goodlands, follow the B15 past St Antoine for three kilometres (two miles) to **Poudre d'Or.** Several claims have been made as to the origin of this name, which means gold dust. One is that a Polish explorer visiting Mauritius in the 18th century found gold dust there; another suggests that the sand on the beach is gold in colour; a third is that the name was inspired by the prosperous sugar plantations in the region.

Whatever the answer, Poudre d'Or has never prospered and today is no more than a fishing hamlet, from where it is possible to hire boats to **Île d'Ambre** and **Pointe Bernache,** uninhabited islands a 30-minute boat ride away, where the swimming and snorkelling are excellent.

In 1744, it was a storm off Île d'Ambre that led to the *St Geran* being wrecked on the reef. This event inspired Bernadin de St Pierre to write his famous romantic novel *Paul et Virginie.* The book is about a boy and a girl who grow up together and

Above: Once just an ordinary fishing village, Grand Gaube has now been transformed into a tourist haven. Overleaf: Mauritian fishermen haul in their bounty from the sea.

eventually fall deeply in love. Virginie goes to Paris to be educated and, on her return, her ship, the *St Geran*, is wrecked on the reef in sight of land. The adoring Paul is waiting for her, but Virginie refuses to be saved, because she is too shy to remove her cumbersome clothes. Instead, she drowns and her body is washed ashore. Paul dies soon after of a broken heart and their bodies are buried together.

From Poudre d'Or, continue for almost five kilometres (three miles) along the B15, past the **turning** to **Pointe des Lascars,** and then take the A6 to **Rivière du Rempart.** Pass straight through the town and, on the western outskirts, take a **right turn** towards an area called **La Clémence,** just after a striped pedestrian crossing, if you wish to visit Star Knitwear. The factory produces jersey-knit products for a large number of English high street stores and sells the excess in an on-site factory shop at very reasonable prices. From Rivière du Rempart, drive past the neat grounds of the **Mon Loisir sugar estate** and continue on to

Belle Vue Maurel. From there, follow the road to **Petite Julie** and then it is a 1.5-kilometre (one-mile) drive **south** to a **T-junction** on a corner. **Turn left** along the road **signposted Nicolière** and **Flacq,** which passes through a grand, shady avenue. Take a **right turn** sign-posted Nicolière, at the edge of **Villebague.**

Villebague is said to be the country's oldest **sugar estate,** with a château at Grand Rosalie, built by Governor Villebague (1756-1759). The château, not open to the public, is a copy of the headquarters of the French East India Company in Pondicherry, with 20th-century additions that include side turrets. The **remains** of the old **sugar factory** are listed as a **national monument.**

The road to **Nicolière** passes through a number of sugar plantations, the road creeping slowly uphill and then bordering the **reservoir** of La Nicolière (250 metres — 820 feet — above sea level), built in the 1920s to irrigate the northern plains. On the banks of the reservoir men are likely to be

fishing and women washing clothes. The road starts to twist dramatically uphill from this point through the rich green and thickly forested slopes of the **Nicolière Mountains.** Stunning panoramic views are afforded across the sugar plantations, liberally scattered with piles of black volcanic rock on what is appropriately called Plaine des Roches (plain of rocks).

On reaching a **T-junction**, take a **left turn** to visit the **Save the Cave project** at **Pont Bon Dieu.** The Wildlife Club of Mauritius has cleaned out a lava cave, traditionally used on the island for dumping rubbish, and created a local recreation site and point of interest.

Alternatively, from the **T-junction** take a **right turn** towards **St Pierre** and, two kilometres (1.3 miles) on, at a second **T-junction**, take another **right turn** to **Montagne**

Above: Memorial to the *St Geran*, which met its tragic end on the reef off Poudre d'Or.
Opposite: Never-ending sugar cane fields at Villebague, said to be the oldest sugar estate in Mauritius.

Longue. Pass the forestry nursery on the **right-hand** side of the road and, as you descend, there are excellent views of the northern plateau with Coin de Mire floating offshore in the far distance.

Along this road, in the settlements of **Les Mariannes** and **Congomah,** traditional village life continues almost untouched by modern development. On reaching a **T-junction** on the B20, **turn right** and then, within a kilometre (half a mile), **left,** along a tree-lined road towards **Petite Rosalie.**

Pass through **Mon Goût** before reaching **Pamplemousses,** where the white railings on the **right-hand** side of the road mark the edge of the **Royal Botanical Gardens. Turn right** where the road is signposted **Mapou** and the **entrance** to the gardens is on the right.

The Royal Botanical Gardens were renamed Sir Seewoosagur Ramgoolam Gardens in 1988 in honour of the late Prime Minister, but many still refer to them by their former name. The **fence** and **gates** are scrolled in wrought iron and gained a first prize in the International Exhibition at London's Crystal Palace in 1862. The gate was a gift from François Lienard, a Frenchman who lived in Mauritius. He was interested in natural history and created a museum in Port Louis that was destroyed by fire in 1816. There is an **obelisk** in the gardens commemorating him. Entrance is free. There are official guides (fee Rs50) but you may prefer to use the small comprehensive guidebook in English and French by A W Owadally, the Conservator of Forests, which is on sale just inside the gate.

The entire gardens occupy roughly 93 hectares (230 acres), of which a third is an experimental station. The gardens' origins go back to 1729, when a French colonist acquired about half the present site, then called Mon Plaisir. La Bourdonnais bought it in 1735 to create a **vegetable garden** (to the left of the present entrance) beside his own residence, named Mon Plaisir, to supply produce initially to his own household and, later, to the town and visiting ships.

When, in 1770, the gardens became the private property of Poivre, an able administrator as well as a keen horticulturist, Pamplemousses became famous. He

Above: Colonial gatehouse at the entrance to the impressive Sir Seewoosagur Ramgoolam Botanical Gardens in Pamplemousses.

introduced plants from all over the world as well as encouraging indigenous species to flourish. In 1810, the gardens reverted to government ownership.

The British neglected them until James Duncan was appointed their director in 1849. He stayed until 1864, introducing many trees, including the royal palms that add majestic splendour to the main avenue. Thousands of eucalyptus trees were planted after the malaria epidemic of 1866 so they could be transplanted to the island's swamps, which, it was hoped, they would dry out, reducing the mosquito-breeding grounds. Since 1913 the gardens have been under the control of the Ministry of Agriculture.

There are 500 plant species in the gardens today, of which 80 are palms and 25 indigenous to the Mascarene islands — among them stately palms, fruit and spice trees, ebony, mahogany, latania, and pandanus.

Highlights include the talipot palm, which waits 40 to 60 years to flower and then dies; and the huge 'Victoria amazonica' lilies from the Amazon in the water lily pond. The lily plants have circular leaves, with upturned edges, that may grow up to one metre (three feet) in diameter. The flowers, which do not last longer than 48 hours, change colour — cream with a heady fragrance one day and then pink the next.

Another pond contains the white-and-yellow flowers of the lotus lily, held in veneration by Hindus. The betel nut palm grows nearby. Its orange fruit contains the betel nut, which is sliced, mixed with lime paste, wrapped in a vine leaf, and chewed. It has a numbing effect, depresses the appetite, and stains the gums and lips an alarming red, but not permanently. The

Opposite: Ninety-three hectares (230 acres) of luxuriant flora await the visitor to the Botanical Gardens, which date back to 1729.
Overleaf: Giant Amazon lilies at the Botanical Gardens grow up to 1 metre (3 feet) in diameter.

Above: Ornate graves at the huge multi-faith cemetery in Terre Rouge. Opposite: Light and shadow play on lush foliage in the country's famous Botanical Gardens in Pamplemousses.

gardens' **Mon Plaisir building** looks impressive, but is not the original home of La Bourdonnais. It is an English-built office block, dating from around 1850. The first floor used to house a herbarium and a museum but is now used as an official reception room. There are offices downstairs. Mon Plaisir is a listed building, as is the **reproduction** of an early **sugar mill** nearby. Sir Seewoosagur was cremated outside the mansion, in front of which trees have been planted by visiting dignitaries.

There are several **animal pens** in the gardens. Among them is one dedicated to **giant tortoises,** brought from Aldabra in Seychelles in 1875 at the request of the Royal Society of Arts and Science, which feared they were on the brink of extinction. In Mauritius, the wholesale slaughter of tortoises began in the 18th century when sailors and colonists killed them for their meat. By the end of the 19th century they had become a protected species, thanks to a campaign led by famous British naturalist Charles Darwin. There is also a **deer park**

in the gardens accommodating **sambhar deer,** which were first introduced in 1639 from Batavia (now part of Indonesia). The several **monuments** there include a **slab of rock** that the sentimental believe marks the **graves** of **Paul and Virginie,** the fictitious lovers in Bernadin de St Pierre's book.

Opposite the **main gate** of the gardens is the basalt-built **Church of St François,** reputed to be the oldest Roman Catholic church in Mauritius. Built in the 1750s, certainly some of the country's oldest **graves** are found in the **cemetery,** including one belonging to Abbe Buonavita, Napoléon's almoner while he was in exile in St Helena, who settled in Mauritius after Napoléon's death in 1821.

From Pamplemousses, follow the A5 road **north** to a **roundabout**. Follow the **signs** for the M2 to Port Louis. *En route* to the capital, the motorway passes a huge **cemetery** where Mauritians of all religions are buried side by side. It is a 12-kilometre (seven-mile) drive back to Port Louis from Pamplemousses.

The East: Sugar Estates and Sandy Beaches

Eastern Mauritius is composed, in the main, of the two districts of Flacq and Grand Port.

The name Flacq can be traced back to the Dutch presence in Mauritius. Originally the area was called Groote Vlakte ('groote' meaning great and 'vlakte' meaning plain) because it is flat. It also came to be known as Boere Vlakte (Farmers' Plain) because of the rice and vegetables then grown in the fertile area. Vlakte was corrupted to 'Flacq' during the French administration.

The French separated Flacq into eight administrative units. It now has 22 village council areas: Bel Air Rivière, Sèche, Bon Accueil, Brisée Verdière, Camp de Masque, Camp Ithier, Centre de Flacq, Clémencia, Ecroignard, Grande Rivière Sud-Est, Lalmatie, Laventure, Mare La Chaux, Medine Camp de Masque, Olivia, Poste de Flacq, Quatre Cocos, Queen Victoria, Saint Julien d'Hotman, Saint Julien, Sebastopol, and Trou d'Eau Douce.

Grand Port takes its name from the long-established settlement of Vieux Grand Port. It is historically important, for the first Dutch colonizers settled in the area, as did the French at a later date. The Dutch called their first colony Warwyck Bay and, when the French acquired Mauritius in the early 18th century, they renamed the settlement Port Bourbon. In 1805, the French established Mahébourg across the bay and Port Bourbon was demoted to Vieux Grand Port (meaning Old Great Port).

Under French rule the Grand Port district was divided into eight administrative units. Today there are 24 village council areas: Bambous Virieux, Bananes, Beau Vallon, Bel Air (Sud), Bois des Amourettes, Cluny, Grand Sable, l'Escalier, Mahébourg, Mare Chicose, Mare d'Albert, Mare Tabac, Midlands, New Grove, Nouvelle France, Old Grand Port, Petit Bel Air, Plaine Magnien, Quatre Soeurs, Rivière des Creoles, Rose Belle, Saint-Hubert, Trois Boutiques, and Union Park.

Before the Dutch began felling trees, much of Flacq was covered by ebony for-

ests. The French continued the deforestation to build ships and houses. The district is now devoted primarily to agriculture, especially sugar cane. One of the island's largest sugar estates, Flacq United Estates Limited — FUEL — occupies large tracts of land.

From the village of Grande Rivière Sud Est south to Ferney, the coastal plain becomes a very narrow shelf between the sea and the Bambou mountains, which include Montagne Bambou at 626 metres (2,053 feet) and the aptly named Lion Mountain, 480 metres (1,574 feet). The coastal plain then widens once more to accommodate more sugar cane plantations, including those belonging to the Rose Belle Sugar Estate.

The eastern side of Mauritius is, in general, a lot wilder than the western, especially in the winter months of July and August, when strong south-easterly winds batter the coast. Parts of the east are a lot prettier than the north and west, because they are less developed.

There are some picturesque beaches around Roches Noires and a beautiful long sandy stretch at Belle Mare. Île aux Cerfs, close to Trou d'Eau Douce, is also well-known for sandy beaches, restaurants and watersports facilities. Inland, there are two scenic nature reserves — at Le Val and Anse Jonchée.

Sport lovers should visit Domaine du Chasseur at Anse Jonchée for hunting, or big game fishing. The east coast is fast developing a reputation for golf offering two courses — one nine-hole, the other 18-hole. Watersports and scuba-diving can be enjoyed at the big coastal hotels; there is a yacht charter operator at Trou d'Eau Douce.

The east coast is relatively quiet once the sun goes down. The hotels, including the 1996 Coco Beach, have their own after dinner shows and two — the St Geran and the Belle Mare Plage — have casinos, but there is little of interest to visitors in the villages themselves at night.

Pointe Lascars
ÎLOT DU MORT

Bras de Mer des Frégates

Piton

Rivière du Rempart

Pamplemousses

Pointe de Roche Noire

Coral Beach Bungalows

R. du Rempart

PLAINE DES ROCHES

Pointe Lafayette

La Nicolière Reservoir

Laventure

Pointe Radeau

Bras de Mer Belcourt

ÎLE MALNO

Poste de Flacq

St. Geran Sun Hotel
Sandy Bay Hotel
Coco Beach Hotel
Belle Mare Plage Hotel

Bon Acceuil

INDIAN OCEAN

Lalmatie

Centre de Flacq

Pointe des Puits

Belle Mare

△ MT. BAR LE DUC

Emeraude Beach Hotel

Vaitur Hotel

R. du Poste de Flacq

Le Palmar Hotel

Ambre Hotel

St. Julien D'Hotman

Ecroignard

Silver Beach Hotel

Residence Valmarin

Le Tropical Hotel

R. Colgnard

Trou d'Eau Douce

Quartier Militaire

Medine

Le Touessrok Sun Hotel

ÎLE DE L'EST

Bel Air

R. Seche

BLANCHE MOUNTAINS

Ernest Florent

Beau Rivage

ÎLE AUX CERFS

Piton du Milieu Reservoir

Montagne Blanche

Beau Champ

Pointe Grand Vacoas

R. du Boucan

Sebastopol

Deux Freres

Grande Rivière Sud-Est

Anse Cunat

Moonlight Bay
Protea Hotel

Quatre Soeurs

Pointe St. Lain

Grand Rivière Sud-Est

ÎLOT FLAMANTS

MT. BAMBOU △

Grand Sable

BAMBOUS MOUNTAINS

Pointe aux Roches

Petit Sable

△ MT. LAGRAVE

DOMAINE DU CHASSEUR N.R.

Pointe du Diable

French Batteries

Eau Bleue Reservoir

Hotel

Pointe Corail

Bananes

Le Val Nature Park

R. Champagne

LION MT. △

Pointe Bambou

Anse Jonchée

Providence

Ferney

Bois des Amourettes

Cluny

St. Hubert

R. Eau Bleue

ÎLE MARIANNE

R. des Creoles

Vieux Grand Port

Anse Colas

Astroea

Riche en Eau

Rivière des Creoles

Pointe Brocus

ÎLOT VACOAS

ÎLE AUX FOUQUETS

R. Bée Marique

Rose Belle

Deux Bras

Pointe de la Colonie

ÎLE DE LA PASSE

New Grove

Ville Noire

MAHÉBOURG

Monte Carlo Hotel
Croix du Sud Hotel

ÎLE AUX AIGRETTES

R. la Chaux

Croix du Sud Hotel

Tourist Rendezvous Hotel

La Chaux

Pointe d'Esny

AIRPORT

Plaine Magnien

Chante aux Vent Hotel

Mare Tabac

Shandrani Hotel

Blue Lagoon Hotel

Trois Boutiques

ÎLE DES DEUX COCOS

Pointe Vacoas

R. du Poste

Eastern Mauritius

0   2   4   6   8 km
0   1   2   3   4   5 miles

Above: Islamic mosque in Flacq.
Opposite: Grey stone Roman Catholic Church in Flacq.

Getting there

The base from which to explore eastern Mauritius, Rivière du Rempart, is 26 kilometres (16 miles) along the A6 road from Port Louis. Trou d'Eau Douce, one of the major tourist centres in the region, is 47 kilometres (29 miles) from Port Louis and 34 kilometres (21 miles) from Mahébourg. Mahébourg is eight kilometres (five miles) from SSR International Airport and 47 kilometres (29 miles) from Port Louis. All are served by a good network of roads.

When to go

The best months to visit the east of Mauritius in general are September to November, but scuba-divers should note that during July and August the sea off the east coast is usually too rough; dive centres have to transport divers to the north to explore the Mauritian waters.

Where to stay

At Pointe de Flacq, the St Geran Sun; at Belle Mare, the Belle Mare Plage Golf Hotel and Resort, Coco Beach Hotel; at Trou d'Eau Douce, Le Touessrok Sun; in Anse Jonche'e the Domaine du Chasseur. There are quite a few other hotels and resorts along the east coast of Mauritius. See Listings.

Sightseeing

The A6 from Port Louis leads to the town of **Rivière du Rempart,** a good starting point to take a tour of eastern Mauritius.

The Dutch settlers called Rivière du Rempart Rooi Rivier (Red River), but their French successors renamed it Rivière de la Terre Rouge (Red Soil River). The town eventually came to be known as Rivière du Rempart, probably because of the river's steep banks as it flows through the town's outskirts.

The modern Rivière du Rempart is a busy town that has gained prominence as an agricultural and industrial centre and as the constituency of the former Prime Minister, Sir Aneerood Jugnauth. The town specializes in producing a number of

Above: Colourful sari shop in Flacq.

aquatic plants, such as watercress and *brede songe*, which play an important part in Mauritian cuisine. The open-air market always offers a feast of colour and of fresh produce. Industrial activity is predominantly related to the textile industry.

From Rivière du Rempart, follow the B15 road around the coastal bulge known as **Roches Noires.** The road is lined with thick casuarina forests, through which are glimpsed wonderful shady vistas and snippets of translucent blue seas. Not surprisingly, this quiet, undeveloped part of the island is popular with Mauritians as a weekend retreat; consequently a number of bungalows hug the coast.

At the **southern** end of the Roches Noire bulge, one reaches a wild **beach** where a **monument** has been erected in memory of five soldiers of the Special Mobile Force (paramilitary police) who drowned at sea in July 1964 while on exercise.

From here to **Poste de Flacq** — some 2.5 kilometres (1.5 miles) away — the hilly road twists dangerously. To the **west** is **Plaine des Roches,** clearly taking its name

from the countless conical mounds of **black volcanic rock** protruding from the sugar cane fields. Poste de Flacq was originally called Haaven Voor de Sloep (Sleepy Harbour). This so easily applies to the settlement today, for modern Poste de Flacq is little more than a road junction with a few general stores. However, the outpost acquired prominence under the French when they established a military post there, hence its present name. It maintained its importance well into the 19th-century as the final destination on the northward railway line from Port Louis.

At the **crossroads** in the middle of Poste de Flacq, turn **east** to reach the **Kashinath Mandir,** or 'Floating Temple', a **Hindu temple** built on **Île aux Goyaviers** and linked to the mainland at low tide by a **causeway.**

From Poste de Flacq, take the **B23 road** and follow the **road signs** to **Centre de Flacq,** about five kilometres (three miles) away. The origin of this lively town's name is self-explanatory — it is in the middle of the district of Flacq. The importance of

Above: Mangroves and serene waters are shoreline features of Poste de Flacq.

Centre de Flacq has been raised by new industrial and commercial complexes.

Next to the **market** is the late 19th-century basalt **District Court House,** listed as a **national monument,** which is a copy of the Scottish ancestral home of Sir Arthur Hamilton Gordon, the British governor in the 1870s. The building also houses the Civil Status Office (equivalent to a registry office) where holidaymakers wishing to marry in Mauritius must obtain a licence.

Backtrack to Poste de Flacq and continue for 4 kilometres (2.5 miles) **south-eastwards** along the distinctly rural **B62 road,** which dips and curves with alarming frequency. Reaching a **T-junction,** take a **left turn north** to the St Geran Hotel; on the **right** is a 1996 space age beach resort, Coco Beach Hotel.

Many consider the St Geran the only place to stay in Mauritius, although the same could be said of Le Touessrok in Trou d'Eau Douce or the Royal Palm in Grand Baie. The St Geran is, without a doubt, special. It is often voted the best beach resort in the world and more than 50

per cent of its guests are repeat visitors. Top golfer Nick Faldo holidays there every year and novelist Frederick Forsyth is also a regular.

When it opened in 1975, the St Geran was the first Mauritian five-star hotel. Set on a palm-fringed beach, the highlights are its numerous restaurants, bars, sporting facilities — including the nine-hole Gary Player-designed golf course — and the casino.

A **right turn** at the **junction** of the **B62** and **B59** will lead to the 178-room Belle Mare Plage Hotel and Golf Club, a beach-fronted four-star resort offering a wide range of facilities. There are several restaurants, bars, a conference room, a well-equipped fitness centre, a casino, and an 18-hole championship golf course with an adjoining clubhouse housing another bar and restaurant.

Further **south,** the **B59** coastal road passes casuarina plantations through which the fine white sand of **Belle Mare beach** can be glimpsed. Very rarely crowded, since it is isolated from a major settlement

Above: The fabulous St Geran Hotel, often voted the best beach resort in the world.
Opposite: The Kashinath Mandir, or 'Floating Temple', a Hindu place of worship on Île aux Goyaviers.
Overleaf: The palm-fringed beach at the St Geran Hotel is just one of the resort's many attractions.

and lacks public transport, Belle Mare beach is among the island's best. The village is believed to take its name after Jean François de Belle Mare, captain of the Cambresis Regiment in Flacq in 1762. It used to be an important source of lime, which was used in sugar manufacture, cement production, and fertilizer for the surrounding agricultural land.

An abandoned **lime kiln** in the casuarina forest is now a viewing point, but only for inland scenes, because the casuarina trees have grown so tall they obscure much of the seascape.

Not far from the kiln, there is a **marble cenotaph** in memory of 150 passengers who died when a South African Airways plane crashed in the Indian Ocean in November 1987.

Throughout the length of the B59 coastal road, a number of hotels adorn the beaches of eastern Mauritius.

The Dutch set up Trou d'Eau Douce, naming the settlement Verscheluyl (Fresh-water Hole), after an underground spring in the bay. The French first called it Trou Frais but later changed its name to **Trou d'Eau Douce.** It is essentially a fishing village that, for some inexplicable reason, reflects the charm of a small Mediterranean port.

After passing through the village, the entrance to Le Touessrok Hotel and Île aux Cerfs (Stag Island) is on the **left.** Le Touessrok, sister hotel to the St Geran, is among the most romantic resorts on the globe, attracting some world-famous visitors since it opened, including Princess Stephanie of Monaco and the Duke and Duchess of York.

The reception area of the 200-room hotel is on the edge of a lagoon on the mainland, while the rooms are on a small, private island reached by a Venetian-style bridge. Several discreet beaches are tucked away between the rooms.

In addition, there are two islands nearby — **Île aux Cerfs** which is accessible to the

Above: Inviting reception area of Coco Beach Hotel which opened in March 1996.
Opposite: The often-calm waters of the east coast offer perfect conditions for water-ski enthusiasts.

public while **Îlot Mangénie,** a deserted island, is reserved for Le Touessrok's guests.

The hotel has several restaurants and bars, in addition to those offered on Île aux Cerfs and Îlot Mangénie, and a wide range of sporting activities, including use of the golf course at the St Geran. Le Touessrok operates a private water taxi service to Île aux Cerfs but another public water taxi leaves from the nearby town of **Beau Rivage** for the island. Île aux Cerfs is famous for its serene white sandy beaches, extensive range of watersports, and excellent restaurants. It is a favourite destination for tourists in search of pure idleness.

Turn **south** out of Le Touessrok's driveway onto the **B59 road** and follow it for about three kilometres (two miles) to a **T-junction,** where a **left turn** puts you onto the **B28,** in the direction of **Grand Rivière Sud-Est.** Pass through the hamlet of **Ernest Florent** and straight over the **Beau Champ Sugar Estate crossroads** to reach Grand Rivière Sud-Est, a quaint fishing village

where you can hire a boat to visit a **waterfall** upstream.

Grand Rivière Sud-Est is one of the oldest villages in Mauritius, having been established by the early Dutch settlers who initially referred to it as Groote Rivier (Great River) and then as Kattius Rivier (Kitten River). In the late 17th century the village was a centre for storage and loading of the huge number of ebony trees being felled by the Dutch for export to Europe. It was the French who changed the village's name in the 18th century to Grand Rivière Sud Est.

It continued to be important in later years as the last railway station on the Northern Line, but the station was closed in 1954. Now, the only significant activities are fishing and sand quarrying just offshore.

The **B28 road** continues **south** towards Mahébourg, crossing the mouth of Grand Rivière Sud-Est. The hilly coastal road then passes **sugar cane fields** prior to arriving at the hamlet of **Deux Frères.** There is some

113

Above: Silver sands and clear-blue waters at Le Touessrok Hotel, where water taxis ferry visitors to and from nearby Ile aux Cerfs.

disagreement as to how the hamlet came by its name. One theory suggests that it was named after two similar-looking local hills. Another idea put forward is that Deux Frères and the neighbouring Quatre Soeurs acquired their names when an estate belonging to the Cheron family was divided between two brothers (*deux frères*) and four sisters (*quatre soeurs*). Along this coastal route are stunning mountain landscapes and sugar cane fields, but no sandy beaches by the sea. Instead, the seascape is edged by muddy shingle, on which fishermen prepare bait for a day's work.

Three more hamlets — **Grand Sable, Pointe aux Roches,** and **Petit Sable** — are passed as the **B28 road** draws closer to Mahébourg, while **Île aux Oiseaux** and **Îlot Flamants** lie offshore.

The **ruins** of an 18th-century **French battery** built to guard an entrance through the reef are situated at **Pointe du Diable.** The walls, broken only by observation slits, are over two metres (6.5 feet) thick and the seaward facing cannons date back to the mid-18th century. From the battery there are excellent **views** of **Île aux Fouquets** with its **lighthouse** (a national monument) and a sprinkling of islands just inside the reef, including **Île de la Passe.** During the 1810 Battle of Grand Port, Britain captured Île de la Passe but it kept the French flag flying in order to trick French vessels into thinking it was safe. Pointe du Diable is so called because, according to oral tradition, a French vessel was once approaching the coast of Mauritius when its compass started going haywire. The engineer, bewildered, attributed it to some supernatural force and so the nearest land point was christened Pointe du Diable (Devil's Point).

Opposite top: Pleasure boat glides through the translucent waters near Le Touessrok.
Opposite: Colourful dancers entertain tourists with a sensual performance.
Overleaf: Paraglider takes to the skies — one of the unique activities to be enjoyed on a Mauritian holiday.

Above: Île aux Cerfs is famous for its extensive range of watersports.

Five kilometres (three miles) south is **Anse Jonchée,** a sweeping bay with calm water and panoramic views of Mahébourg and the mountains behind. Anse Jonchée is named after Jacques Thomas de Jonchée de la Goletterie, a captain of one of the French East India Company ships, who, in 1723, acquired land locally.

A large **sign** indicates the **entrance** to the **Domaine du Chasseur,** from which a rough track winds uphill through sugar cane and pineapple plantation to the estate's reception area.

The Domaine is a pioneer in the field of 'green tourism', offering a fascinating alternative to Mauritius's abundant sea and sand. In 1985, General Manager Alain O'Reilly, an Irish-Mauritian, acquired 1,000 hectares (2,470 acres) to start the Domaine

Opposite: Snorkellers about to explore the inner world of a Mauritian lagoon.
Overleaf: Tiny Hindu temple stands in solitude in sprawling sugar plantation in the Quartier Militaire region near St Julien.

from scratch, opening its doors to the public in 1988. Some of the last acres of private native forest are found within the reserve. The forest includes more than 40,000 ebony trees and other tropical flora, such as bergamot, eucalyptus, traveller's palm, and wild orchids. The Domaine is also full of exotic animals **(deer, monkeys, wild boar)** and rare endemic **birds,** including the **Mauritian kestrel,** a couple of which are fed daily by the staff.

Visitors can admire the forest and its inhabitants either along well laid-out trails or in Land Rovers on a bone-jerking safari along bumpy paths that lead to the summit. From the top of the estate, the panoramic coastal view takes in Grand Port, site of the famous sea battle between the French and the British in 1810.

More sporting visitors to the Domaine can hunt, by stalking or shooting the Javanese deer and wild boar that roam the estate freely. **Big game fishing** can also be arranged. The one restaurant serves only food produced on the estate. The menu includes a range of traditional Mauritian

Above: Restaurant at Domaine du Chasseur overlooks the chalets and the lush, exotic flora, giving the impression that one is 'dining in the treetops'.
Opposite: View towards Lion Mountain from the lookout at Domaine du Chasseur.

dishes, such as venison curry, roasted wild pig, fresh fish, and palm heart salad. The tables, cleverly terraced along the hillside, give the impression that one is dining in the treetops. There are chalets for short-stay rental. **South** from Anse Jonchée, past Providence, lies the hamlet of **Bois des Amourettes** (Wood of the Young Lovers). It either gained its name from the fact that the wood was frequented by French soldiers from the Mahébourg garrison and their lovers, or from a kind of wood known as bois d'amourette produced by a species of mimosa plant.

Bois des Amourettes was of strategic importance in World War II. The British constructed an oil terminal, which served a naval base, in Grand Port and also a jetty nearby for the discharge of crude oil. Today Bois des Amourettes, sandwiched between the aptly named Lion Mountain and the sea, is a good example of a typical east-coast fishing village. There are excellent **views** of Mahébourg as the coastal

road wends its way into **Vieux Grand Port,** the oldest settlement in Mauritius. This was where the Dutch landed when they claimed the island in 1598, naming it Warwyck Bay. The French later renamed the settlement Port Bourbon and considered making it the headquarters of the French East India Company until they conducted a feasibility study, which led them to choose Port Louis instead. Port Bourbon became Vieux Grand Port in the first decade of the 19th century when Mahébourg was built nearby.

Naturally, the **remains** of some of Mauritius's oldest **buildings** are to be found here. There is a **ruined tower** known as the **Tour des Hollandais,** even though it is believed to be the remains of a watch tower or mill from the French period, and some French-built **coastal fortifications** that are in various states of disrepair. Behind Vieux Grand Port, the crouching lion of **Lion Mountain,** rising to 480 metres (1,570 feet), guards the bay. **Ferney,** a short drive

from Vieux Grand Port, is one of the original Mauritian **sugar estates,** built by La Bourdonnais and a partner around 1740. The factory ceased operations in the 1980s, and its cane is now transported to Beau Champ for processing.

There is a very sharp **right turn** into the estate's entrance, though it is closed to the public. However, a magnificent **white colonial residence** and the estate's extensive **gardens** can be seen from the end of the driveway. A **monument** erected by the Société des Chasseurs de l'Île Maurice at the entrance commemorates the landing of the Dutch Governor Adriaan van der Stel aboard the *Capelle,* laden with sambhar deer from Java, on 8 November, 1639.

Another **monument** close by was erected in 1953 to commemorate the 1639 introduction of sugar to Mauritius by Governor Van der Stel.

As the **B28 road** continues **south,** it crosses **Rivière des Creoles,** where sari-swathed Indian women often wash bundles of clothes, and then spread the laundry out on the banks to dry.

Ville Noire (Black Town) is little more than an extension of Mahébourg (linked to it by the British-built Cavendish Bridge over the River La Chaux). The area is named after the African and Malagasy slaves who settled there.

Mahébourg was established very early in the 19th-century. The French governor, Charles Decaen, visited Port Bourbon, a little further along the coast, in 1804. Sensing its vulnerability, he abandoned it, instead building a new port at Pointe de la Colonie on the opposite side of the bay. Decaen named the new settlement Mahébourg in honour of Mahé de La Bourdonnais. But, for diplomatic reasons, he soon changed the name to Port Imperial.

Decaen did not build the new port for commercial reasons, but because he believed the site of far greater strategic importance should Île de France come under attack from foreign forces. Decaen was soon proved right.

When the British tried to take Port Imperial on 24 August, 1810, they were soundly beaten. Although the British initially captured Île de la Passe and lured the French fleet into the bay by keeping the French flag raised on the small offshore island, the French tacticians were one step ahead of the invading forces. They moved the buoys marking the passages through the reef and many British ships ran aground. This is the only French naval victory recorded on the Arc de Triomphe in Paris. But four months later, Île de France surrendered to the British, and Port Imperial once again became Mahébourg. The British linked it to Port Louis by rail and the town flourished, becoming the main settlement in the south. However, the malaria epidemic of 1866, which forced coastal dwellers to seek healthier surroundings in the highlands, and, in the 20th century, the closure of the railways resulted in Mahébourg's general decline. Today, it is of interest to visitors more for its history than for anything else.

Past the **Cavendish Bridge,** take a **left turn** and follow the **B87 road** through **La Chaux** to the hamlet of **Pointe Jerome,** from where there are excellent **views** of Mahébourg and, across the bay, Vieux Grand Port. The Croix du Sud Hotel at Pointe Jerome has a good beach and pleasant views.

Nine hundred metres (980 yards), from Croix du Sud lies **Île aux Aigrettes,** a 20-minute boat trip away. The island, some 20 hectares (49 acres) in area, was declared a **nature reserve** in 1965 and is now an internationally recognized conservation site. Many plant species on the island are found nowhere else in the world. They are the last remnants of the coastal vegetation that was once prevalent on Mauritius.

Île aux Aigrettes takes its name from a colony of egrets that inhabited the island until they disappeared in the 17th century. During the Second World War, Île aux Aigrettes was used as a military base and much of the native forest was cleared. Later,

Opposite above: Colonial-style building houses Mahebourg Museum. Opposite right: Trees have taken over the ruins of this Dutch-built monument at Vieux Grand Port. Opposite: Rusting remnant of imperial battles to colonise Mauritius outside Mahebourg Museum.

Above: Mahébourg cemetery with a majestic backdrop, Lion Mountain.

the island was privately leased for grazing goats. Acacia trees were planted as fodder and the acacia soon spread over large areas.

In 1985, the Mauritian Wildlife Fund established a plant rehabilitation and management project to restore the island's vegetation to its original condition.

The aims were to eliminate alien plants, such as acacia, from out-competing the native species; to propagate and replant native trees; to eradicate shrews, which eat the eggs and the young of endemic reptiles; to reintroduce endemic Mauritian bird and reptile species; and to create a showpiece of native Mauritian coastal habitat to be developed as a resource for education and public involvement in nature conservation.

Much progress has been made towards the aim of restoring the ecosystem as soon as possible to its original state of 350 years ago, before the advent of man. This land is now home to a pair of rare **Mauritian kestrels.** Eighteen Mauritian plant species found on Île aux Aigrettes are classified as endangered or very rare, including *bois de fer*, Île aux Aigrettes ebony, Île aux

Aigrettes orchid, *bois de boeuf*, and *bois de chandelle*.

The **B87** continues **south** from Croix du Sud through **Pointe d'Esny,** a popular place for weekend *campements* (as Mauritians call the seaside bungalows they use over the weekend), and then the road ends at the public **beach** of **Blue Bay.** Although a sign warns of the danger of swimming further than 50 metres (160 feet) out, calm waters separate the tiny **Île des Deux Cocos** from the mainland. Returning to Mahébourg, take the **main A10 road** out of town, in the direction of **Curepipe** to find the **Naval and Historical Museum.** The museum is housed in an 18th-century colonial building, which used to belong to the de Robillard family.

In the early 19th century, the commandant of the District of Grand Port, Jean de Robillard, lived there and, following the famous 1810 battle, turned his home into a hospital.

The commanders of the opposing fleets, a Rear Admiral Duperre and an Admiral Willoughby, were both wounded and are

Above: Seeking solitude in the shade, woman strolls along a tree-lined avenue near Mahébourg.

said to have convalesced in adjacent beds. In 1950, the government acquired the house and converted it into a museum. On the lower floor are a number of items (including the last biscuit ration) from the steamship *Trevessa*, which foundered 2,400 kilometres (1,490 miles) off the Freemantle coast in the 1920s. The crew abandoned ship in lifeboats, which reached Mauritius more than three weeks later. There are also old pictures of Mauritius, a painting of General Charles Decaen, pieces from the wreck of the *St Geran*, a section of the frigate *Magicienne* and some of its 12-lb guns.

The floor above has ancient maps and sea charts, old lithographs of Mauritius, La Bourdonnais's four-poster bed, and two wooden sedan-type chairs in which masters sat to be carried by their slaves. Outside, in the back garden, the governor's private **railway carriage,** despite its decayed state, gives an indication of Victorian extravagance, with its wooden louvred windows, plush chairs, and iron-trellised balcony. A **craft village,** opened in July 1993, is also located in the grounds. Eight wood-en huts, in traditional style, house people making and selling a wide range of goods made from leather, cloth, wood and other materials.

According to old folklore, in Mahébourg, one of the garrison's commanders in the 19th-century was a Waterloo veteran called J S Sedley, thought to have been a son of the Duke of Kent and, therefore, an elder half-brother to Queen Victoria. Given that he lived in Mahébourg for so long, one wonders whether any of his descendants remain there. If so, they would be distant kin of the British Royal Family.

From Mahébourg, follow the **A10 road** towards **Curepipe,** and the **Plaisance Airport** will be signposted to the **left.** Plaisance takes its name from a 19th-century estate owned by the de Bissy family. It was there, in 1875, that George Clark, an English school teacher, dug up the only set of dodo bones discovered so far. The first aeroplane to land at Plaisance was a military aircraft in November 1944, and regular flights started in February the following year. In 1955 there were just 161 landings,

Above: Fishing boats at low tide on the beach at Anse des Courants near Mahébourg.
Opposite: Fertile land surrounds the chateau at Riche en Eau, with Lion Mountain in the distance.

but in 1991 the annual tally had grown to 5,287. The Sir Seewoosagur Ramgoolam International Airport, as it is now known, had a new US$75-million passenger terminal in 1987 built to a design supplied by China; in recognition of this, the departure lounge has a ceramic depiction of the Great Wall of China. The terminal was designed to handle a million passengers a year by the end of the century. The duty-free shops sell a range of electrical goods, books, soft toys, and alcohol, and the departure lounge has a bar and a restaurant.

Continue along the **A10 road,** passing **under** the **motorway.** This route provides excellent elevated **views** of the **sugar fields.** In the village of **New Grove, turn right (north-east)** on the **Deux Bras Branch Road,** indicated by a small **green sign** by La Croisée Store. It is the **B7 road,** a hilly shady avenue that leads up to **Riche en Eau** via the hamlets of **Deux Bras** and **Astroea.** At Riche en Eau, the road reaches a plateau of sugar plantations with a dramatic backdrop of hills. A bumpy road

leads to **St Hubert,** passing a striking **colonial house** to the **right** and a quaint old **church.** Pass the Cent Gaulettes Police Station and follow the **signs** to **Le Val,** a **nature park** on the 3,000-hectare (7,410 acres) **Rose Belle Sugar Estate,** which is an example of the diversification projects now favoured by a number of sugar estates. In this particular case, freshwater prawns are specially bred in chemically treated water; anthuriums, grown for export, thrive in greenhouses; and huge plots of watercress and *brede songe* are produced for home consumption. There are also **deer** and **sheep** enclosures, a duck pond, and a **mini-aquarium** with eels and tropical fish. The drive up to the estate allows visitors to get well and truly off the beaten track, and offers some stunning vistas en route.

From Le Val, follow the **road** to a **T-junction,** where a **left turn** leads to **Cluny. Turn right** on the **B83 road** to get to the **motorway.** It is then a 25-kilometre (15.5 miles) drive to Port Louis.

The South: Rugged and Windswept

Most of southern Mauritius falls in the Savanne district, which takes its name from the large areas of savannah (tropical grasslands dotted with trees and shrubs) that flourished along the coastal plain in the 18th century.

At the beginning of the 19th century, under the French administration, the district was made up of two smaller divisions — Grande Savanne and Petite Savanne — but today is just one district with 12 village councils: Benares, Bois Cheri, Britannia, Camp Diable, Chamouny, Chemin Grenier, Grand Bois, Rivière des Anguilles, Rivière du Poste, Saint Aubin, Souillac, and Surinam.

The south is famous for its rugged scenery. From the sea, breathtaking black basalt cliffs contrast with a backdrop of rolling sugar cane fields, which gently rise to meet the undulating foothills of the Savan-

ne Mountains. Le Souffleur, a blowhole, and La Roche qui Pleure, an interestingly shaped basalt formation, are two particular features of this dramatic coastline.

There are some stunning beaches, such as Gris Gris, along the south coast, but many are unsafe for swimming. This is because the numerous rivers descending from the uplands have prevented the coral reef from gaining a foothold, thus depriving the area of gentle lagoons as found in the north and west of the island. One of these rivers, the Savanne, is well known for the pretty Rochester Falls, close to Souillac.

For the energetic, there are a number of sporting activities to be pursued on the south coast: interesting scuba-diving sites from the Shandrani Hotel, bracing cliff walks to be taken east of Souillac, and, for the more patient, birdwatching at Bassin Blanc. Those interested in 'doing' the sites should visit La Vanille Crocodile Park, close to Rivière des Anguilles. The most important settlement on the south coast is Souillac, where the Robert Edward Hart Museum, the Telfair Gardens, and Le Batelage restaurant (in the old port area) are to be found.

Getting there

The easiest point to start a tour of the south, Plaine Magnien, is about 44 kilometres (27 miles) from Port Louis, 8 kilometres (5 miles) from Mahébourg, and 24 kilometres (15 miles) from Souillac. It is close to the motorway and is served by a good network of roads.

When to go

The best months to visit the south of Mauritius are from April to June and September to November. Keep in mind that this part of the island is the breeziest, particularly when the trade winds blow during the Mauritian 'winter', from May to October.

Where to stay

There are at least four hotels of international standard on the south coast: the Shandrani Hotel at Blue Bay, one of the Beachcomber Hotels, the Berjaya Resort Hotel on a western headland near Ilot du Morne, Paradis Hotel and the Beachcomber Brabant. At Plaine Magnien, there is the very basic Tourist Rendexvous; and, near Pomponnette, the Pointe aux Roches Villas. See Listings.

Sightseeing

Head **south-east** on a **rough track** leading off the **A10 road** between Sir Seewoosagur Ramgoolam International Airport and Plaine Magnien village to get to Shandrani.

Situated on a private peninsula, overlooking picturesque **Blue Bay,** the 181-room Shandrani Hotel offers all the amenities of a top-class resort — restaurants, bars, evening entertainment, and a wide range of sports, including a nine-hole executive golf course and a scuba-diving centre, from where ancient wrecks just

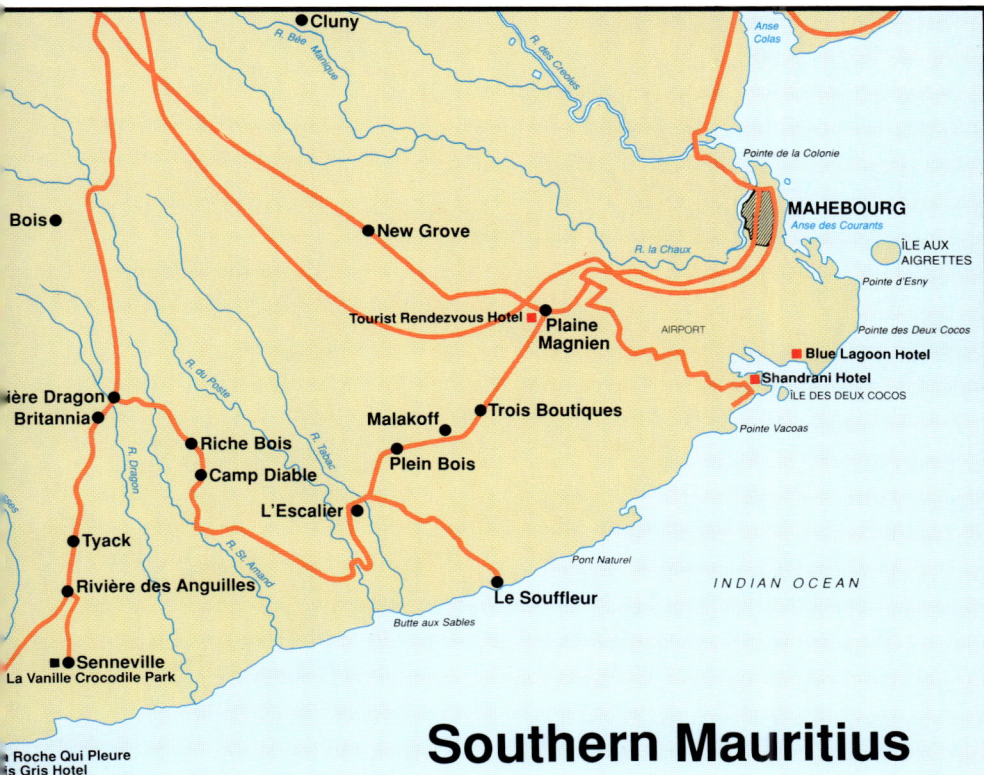

Southern Mauritius

© Camerapix

offshore are easily accessible. It is the hotel closest to the airport, just six kilometres (3.7 miles) away. **Plaine Magnien** is named after French colonist Marin Magnien, who started life as an employee of the French East India Company and rose to own the Plaine Magnien estate. From the Shell petrol station in the centre of Plaine Magnien, a **rough road,** the **B8,** leads to **l'Escalier,** passing through the hamlets of **Trois Boutiques, Malakoff,** and **Plein Bois.**

The village of l'Escalier takes its name from Baron Daniel l'Escalier, a French official who, in 1791, was appointed as civil commissioner of both Île de France and Bourbon (as Mauritius and Réunion, respectively, were then known).

Just before entering l'Escalier (which means stairs or steps), an **avenue** of bottle palms on the **left** borders the drive to the administrative offices of the **Savannah Sugar Estate,** which are surrounded by pristine plots of tropical flowers and offer stunning and extensive **views** of sugar cane fields below.

Immediately past l'Escalier Police Station, **turn left,** driving through the Savinia plantation, to reach **Le Souffleur** (The Whistler), a **blowhole** at the far end of a rocky promontory. Visitors used to be delighted by the ferocity of the water jet that shot skywards from the blowhole when the seas were rough, but now, after constant erosion, the jet is not as strong.

Nicholas Pike, the American consul in Mauritius in the 1870s, wrote of Le Souffleur: 'It rises nearly 40 feet above the sea, exposed to the full force of the waves and is perforated to its summit by a cavity that communicates with the ocean. When there is a heavy swell the waves rush in and fill up the vacuum with terrific fury. Wave on wave presses on, and there being no other outlet, the water is forced upwards, and forms a magnificent "jet d'eau" ascending to a height of 50 or 60 feet. The noise can be heard for two miles and when the Souffleur growls and roars, it is a sure indication of rough weather.'

Le Souffleur is still a popular and dramatic, if wet, picnic spot as angry seas crash down on the cliff face, sending sprays of salt water into the air. Permits to visit Le Souffleur, which are issued free, must be obtained from the estate office, near the police station. From l'Escalier, the **B8** continues **westward** across the **Du Poste** and **St Amand rivers**, which flow down from the Mare aux Vacoas region in the central highlands. There is a **junction** at **River St Amand,** where it is possible to follow the road **northwards** and, having passed through the hamlets of **Camp Diable** and **Riche Bois,** reach the **A9** at **Rivière Dragon. Turn left (south)** and almost immediately the road passes the immaculately maintained **Britannia Sugar Estate gardens.** This is one of the few sugar estates in Mauritius owned by a foreign company, the UK-based Lonrho Group.

From Britannia, it is a pleasant drive through avenued roads to **Tyack,** where the former home and now **Museum of Sookdeo Bissoondoyal** is to be found. Born in 1908, Bissoondoyal turned from school teaching to politics in 1948. Highly respected by the Indian community, he formed a political party called the Independent Forward Block in 1957 and, having been elected as a Member of the Legislative Assembly, retained that position until seven years before his death in 1977. The small Creole house in which he was born contains many of his personal belongings, including books. The museum is open to the public.

Tyack merges into the adjoining village of **Rivière des Anguilles** (River of the Eels), named after a river that flows just west of the village. The Dutch called it Palings Rivier, meaning Eel River. Rivière des Anguilles is an important commercial centre in the south. Particularly at the weekend, the market, filled with fruit and vegetable stalls, does a roaring trade.

From Rivière des Anguilles — it is a well-signposted two-kilometre (1.2-mile) drive south to **Senneville,** where **La Vanille Crocodile Park** is located. The park was opened in 1984 by Owen Griffiths, an Australian zoologist, and his Mauritian wife. They discovered that the area — a former vanilla-growing-region, hence the park's name — was ideal for farming **Nile crocodiles** for their skins. The first

Above: Distinctive red roofs of the 5-star Berjaya resort Hotels in the lee of 243-metre (797-ft) Le Morne Brabant on the south-west coast.

---

crocodiles — one male and four females — were imported from Madagascar and the park has been growing ever since.

The first crocodiles' babies were placed in heated indoor nurseries for about a year before they were released into ponds. Roughly a decade later, the park has crocodiles of all ages, all kept in secure enclosures with noticeboards giving details of the animals within. The park also exhibits a wide range of Mascarene animals and is now akin to a small zoo.

The park is well laid-out with a series of paths leading through tropical vegetation of exotic palms, freshwater streams, and indigenous flora, which systematically pass the pens holding crocodiles, **monkeys, deer, giant tortoises, tenrecs, rabbits, bats, wild pigs,** and a **giant Telfair skink** indigenous to Round Island. There is also an exhibition room containing specimens of Mascarene reptiles, such as the luminous green true chameleon and one of the largest species of lizard, the giant phelsuma from Madagascar. The park has a small

snack bar and a shop selling various products with a crocodile theme. Tourists might like to consider visiting the park at feeding time, usually between 1330 and 1400. From the park, backtrack to Rivière des Anguilles and follow the **A9 road south** towards **Souillac.** The A9 crosses the steep valley of Rivière des Anguilles, the boulder-strewn bed of which is covered in luxuriant tropical vegetation, such as traveller's palm.

Along the road lies the **Union** (also known as St Aubin) **Sugar Estate.** There are several impressive **colonial buildings** on the estate that can be seen from the main road. Pierre de St Aubin, a rich 18th-century plantation owner and businessman, held almost 400 hectares (988 acres) here and gave the estate his name.

There are sweeping **views** across sugar cane fields, spotted with isolated **Indian temples,** to the coast and the deep blue sea beyond.

Just as the A9 is about to enter Souillac, a **signpost** on the **right** indicates **Pepinière de Terracine,** a **plant nursery** that is

133

Above: Snack time: giant Aldabra tortoise at La Vanille Crocodile Park.

a diversification project of the Union Sugar Estate. Follow the road past the residential outskirts of Souillac, pass the Pepinière to the **left,** and then it is a bone-shaking journey through sugar cane fields to **Rochester Falls** on the Savanne River, which tumbles over upright columns of basalt rock from a height of 10 metres (33 feet). Young Mauritians will, if visitors are willing to pay, do daredevil dives from the top.

Back on the main **A9,** you soon reach the centre of **Souillac.** By the middle of the 18th century the French had named the estuary on which Souillac is situated Bras de Mer de la Savanne. When Vicomte de Souillac, Governor of Île de France between 1779 and 1787, encouraged the islanders to settle in the south, the town was named in his honour. Today it is the main town on the south coast.

A **left turn** into Monsson Street leads to Souillac's three main visitor attractions — Telfair Gardens, the Robert Edward Hart Museum, and Gris Gris.

It is worth stopping at **Telfair Gardens** for a picnic, a cool drink, or just a quiet break. The gardens are named after 19th-century plantation owner Charles Telfair, one of the few Britons to settle in Mauritius after the 1810 British conquest. In addition to owning the Bel Ombre sugar plantation, he was a keen naturalist and a founder of the Royal Society of Arts and Sciences in Mauritius. Huge Indian almond trees and banyans provide plenty of shade and there are a number of pavillion retreats.

For children there is a **play area** with swings and climbing frames. Neat lawns lead down to the water's edge, where the roar of the reef can be heard and very pretty vistas seen across the estuary. Do not be fooled by the inviting waters, however; it is dangerous to swim here.

On the far side of the estuary, **Souillac Cemetery** contains the **tombs** of many local figures, such as Robert Edward Hart and Baron d'Unienville, the 19th-century historian and first director of the Mauritius archives. Many tombs were destroyed by cyclone Carol in 1962, which is said to have strewn bones all over the cemetery.

Turn right outside the gardens to reach

134

Above: Prehistoric-looking Nile crocodile are raised at La Vanille Crocodile Park.

the **Robert Edward Hart Museum.** Born in 1891, Robert Edward Hart, a writer and poet, had his first work published in 1912 and left an important mark on Mauritian literature from the first half of the 20th century. In 1923 he succeeded his father as librarian of the Mauritius Institute, a position he held until his retirement in 1941.

As a place of peace and solitude in his retirement, Hart's friends clubbed together and offered him La Nef (The Nave), also called La Maison de Corail (The Coral House), in which the museum is now housed. The government bought the house in 1964 and, under the auspices of the Mauritius Institute, it first opened its doors to the public in November 1967.

The quaint bungalow — which, it has been noted, resembles the gingerbread house in the fairy tale *Hansel and Gretel* — contains numerous awards (some international), as well as some of Hart's poems, articles, books, and other personal belongings. The **views** from the front of the house are outstanding and no doubt inspired some of Hart's works. A little further along

the road from La Nef is **Gris Gris,** the southernmost point of Mauritius. There are several explanations as to how the area received its name. One is that Abbé de la Caille, who produced a map of Mauritius in 1753, had a passion for animals and, when his dog, Gris Gris, to whom he was devoted, died, he decided to name the promontory after him. Another is that its name comes from the veils of spray that are produced when waves break along this section of the coast. Yet another argues that Gris Gris is so named because black magic has been performed there and one of the local rocks looks like an old enchantress.

It is unsafe to swim at Gris Gris, but it is worth visiting for the **breathtaking scenery** and to feel the strength of the wind as it gusts inshore. The windswept coast here looks more like the Scottish highlands than a tropical island.

A **rough road** through cane fields follows an **easterly** path, beyond Gris Gris, to the **Foyer of Notre Dame de L'Unité,** a religious weekend retreat for Christians. Opposite the retreat, there are breaks in the

Above: The Union, or St Aubin, Sugar Estate, near Soullac, features several impressive colonial buildings.

vegetation that lead through to the clifftops; there are magnificent **coastal walks** to the east and back along towards Gris Gris. Quite close to the Foyer is a black basalt headland known as La Roche qui Pleure because, as the sea cascades around it, it seems to be weeping. The headland also bears a striking resemblance to Robert Edward Hart's profile.

Back in the centre of Souillac, **turn left** on reaching the **main road** and continue **westwards. Port Souillac** is on the **left.** Before Mauritius developed a comprehensive road and rail system, sugar was taken by overnight steamer from Souillac to Port Louis. Souillac's old port, redundant in the modern era, is now being converted into a visitor attraction.

In the shelter of the river estuary, Le Batelage, a restaurant serving a selection of Chinese, Creole and European dishes, is housed in a former sugar store building nearly 200 years old. Part of the port's quay is now the restaurant's terrace, which is well shaded from the tropical sun.

The restaurant is under private management, but the sugar store actually belongs to the Mauritian Government and was renovated with money provided by the French, on account of Souillac being twinned with a town of the same name in France. A section of the store not being used by the restaurant may eventually be turned into a museum dedicated to Charles Baudelaire, the 19th-century French poet who visited Mauritius on his travels. The National Coast Guard is housed next door to the sugar store.

Leaving Port Souillac, continue **west,** cross the **River Patates** on the back of an old **iron bridge** and, still on the **B9,** enter **Surinam,** which is thought to take its name from the Surinam cherry trees that used to grow in abundance in the area. Surinam is a large village with little, if any, interest to tourists.

However, just as the B9 enters Surinam, a **road** on the **left** has **signposts** to the **SSR Public Beach** and Villas Point aux Roches. From this beach to **Rivière des**

Above: Sparkling waters of a Mauritian estuary in Baie du Cap. The headland at right is M'maconde.

Galets in the west, there are almost five kilometres (three miles) of uninterrupted beach. **Riambel,** a hamlet on the coast, takes its name from the map produced by Abbé de la Caille in 1753. He named the area Ariambelo, a Malagasy word meaning sunny beach. Riambel, a shortened version of the original name, is reputed to have the island's best sand, which is used extensively in the local construction industry.

Riambel is a haven of peace and quiet. The hamlet's *campements* (bungalows) lie sheltered among a casuarina forest and enjoy enchanting views over the clear waters of the south coast.

There are several settlements along this stretch of road, such as **Pomponette** to the **west,** and **Pointe aux Roches,** where the small pension Villas Pointe aux Roches is found. The usually deserted beach in front of the pension is safe for swimming and, built on a rocky promontory, there is an **observation platform** from where there are incredible views of waves crashing ashore. In fact, the surf sends up so much spray that the views along the coast are hazy, and

visitors to the viewing platform are likely to be drenched. You pass a small **sugar estate,** Saint Felix, to enter **Galets,** a dusty hamlet at the mouth of the Rivière des Galets, named after the carpet of pebbles (*galets*) at the river mouth. The inhabitants are mainly fishermen and farmers.

At the **bus station** there are signs indicating a **right turn** for **Chemin Grenier** and **straight ahead,** along the B9, for **Baie du Cap.** To reach **Bassin Blanc,** a volcanic **crater lake,** follow the road to Chemin Grenier, passing through Chamouny and, if necessary, ask for directions because Bassin Blanc is not well signposted. Bassin Blanc can also be reached on the B89 road from Surinam via Mont Blanc.

Whichever route is taken for Bassin Blanc, it is sure to be ear-popping, for the road rises steeply, and bone-rattling, because these are bumpy roads with an inordinate number of hairpin bends. The scenery en route, however, makes it all worthwhile. The view of the rolling, sugar cane-clad foothills of the Savanne Mountains, backed by craggy mountain peaks

and fronted by the picturesque coastline, is awe-inspiring. Bassin Blanc, its banks covered with dense vegetation, is considered one of the best places on the island to spot endemic birds such as the **fody,** but visitors must be patient. Experts suggest spending about an hour by the lake to have a reasonable chance of spotting the local avifauna.

Back on the coast at Rivière des Galets, take the **B10** towards **Baie du Cap.** There is a small **iron bridge** over the Rivière des Galets and small **Hindu shrines** with red pennants are scattered among the casuarina trees to the seaside, while a stone-crushing quarry is to the land side.

Beau Champ is located on the coast of **Baie du Jacotet,** where, at low tide, it is possible to wade out to the isolated and uninhabited **Îlot Sancho,** a coral islet that may be small but has quite a history. It was the site of a violent British attack just prior to the French capitulation in 1810, and there is talk of treasure having been buried there.

There is some confusion as to how the bay and the river into it came to be named Jacotet. Some suggest it is because the trees on the banks of the river are often filled with frolicking *jacots* (Creole for monkeys); others say the two were named after a fisherman, Jean-Pierre André Jacotet, who lived nearby. Along this stretch of coast, huge rollers continually crash ashore, creating quite a picture.

The next hamlet, about five kilometres (three miles) to the **west,** is **Bel Ombre** (beautiful shadow), which takes its name from the **sugar estate** of the same name. The estate dates back to the second half of the 18th-century, but it really came to prominence in the following century when Charles Telfair (of Souillac's Telfair Gardens fame) acquired it. Telfair was something of an innovator and, on his initiative, Bel Ombre became the first estate to install an horizontal cane-crushing mill. He also transformed Bel Ombre into a 'model estate', ensuring that his slaves were well fed and properly housed.

The estate is unusual; much of the land under cultivation covers undulating terrain that lies at angles of up to 45°, causing cultivation, irrigation, and harvesting

difficulties. **West** of Bel Ombre, near the **cemetery** of **St Martin** (the next hamlet along the coast), a **cairn** marks the place where the survivors of the *Trevessa* landed in one of the ship's lifeboats in 1923. The *Trevessa* foundered 950 kilometres (590 miles) off Mauritius and the crew drifted in a lifeboat for 25 days before reaching land. Bits and pieces from the lifeboat, including a cigarette tin lid the survivors used to ration their daily water intake during their ordeal, are exhibited in the Naval and Historical Museum in Mahébourg.

Pass through the hamlet of **St Martin,** where typical island life goes on undisturbed, and the larger settlement of **Baie du Cap** is just a few kilometres further **west.** Baie du Cap is a small coastal village whose residents live on fishing and agriculture. A few general stores, a police station, a post office, a school, and a community centre — as well as a small beach — are found there.

To the **west, lava flows** have created dramatic cliff faces close to where Rivière du Cap flows into the long, large estuary of Baie du Cap. The raised **cement platform** crossing the estuary is known locally as 'the Irishman's Bridge'. It was at Baie du Cap that British navigator Matthew Flinders sought refuge in his unseaworthy ship of 1803 while returning from his second exploratory trip to Australia. His joy at having made it safely to land soon turned to frustration and anger when he found the French island at war with Britain and he was subsequently interned.

Rounding **Pointe Corail de La Prairie,** the mountain of **Le Morne** dominates the scenery. From **La Prairie Public Beach,** which, given its relative isolation, is usually quiet, Îlot Forneau can be seen offshore.

There is just one more hamlet, the laidback **l'Embrasure,** before the road reaches Le Morne and the start of the west coast.

Opposite: Local boy takes a daring dive off the rocks at Rochester Falls.
Overleaf: Although it's a rough drive to the Rochester Falls, the beautiful sights that greet the visitor makes it well worth the effort.

The West: Sunny and Serene

Much of western Mauritius falls within the Black River district. The area was known as Zwarte Rivier during the Dutch occupation. In the 18th century, the French translated the Dutch name directly into Rivière Noire, in turn translated by the British administration into Black River.

The area is thought to have taken its name from the Grande Rivière Noire, which flows through the region and is lined by black rocks.

Black River is sub-divided into 16 village council areas: Albion, Baie du Cap, Bambous, Bel Ombre, Cascavelle, Case Noyale, Chamarel, Flic en Flac, Grande Rivière Noire, Gros Cailloux, La Gaulette, Le Morne, Pailles, Petite Rivière, Richelieu, and Tamarin.

The western flanks of Mauritius enjoy far greater protection from the prevailing winds and rain than the east and, as a consequence, have a generally drier climate and a more arid landscape. For example, the Case Noyale area, particularly Petite Rivière Noire, resembles rural Rodrigues because of the slightly harsh landscape, which supports only corrugated iron shacks in the hamlet and a few goats that wander freely.

The protection provided by a string of mountains means calmer conditions off the west coast, leading to the formation of long, beautiful beaches, such as those at Le Morne and Flic en Flac. Being blessed with the best of both worlds, western Mauritius accommodates some of the few remaining tracts of luxuriant native vegetation, as in the Black River Gorges National Park.

In general, then, the western districts are characterized by extensive sugar cane fields, dominated by craggy peaks, such as Le Morne, the hills of the Black River Gorges National Park, and, further north along the west coast, Trois Mamelles.

For locals the most important settlement in the western districts is Bambous, but visitors will find Le Morne and the tourist centre of Flic en Flac of greater interest, although the latter has some way to go

before it can challenge Grand Baie in the north. There is much for sporting enthusiasts on the west coast — an 18-hole golf course at Le Morne, where there are also excellent calm conditions in the offshore lagoon for those wishing to learn a watersport, hiking and birdwatching in the Black River Gorges National Park, big game fishing from centres at Rivière Noire, seasonal surfing at Tamarin, and some great scuba-diving sites just off Flic en Flac.

Places of interest to visit include the Coloured Earths and waterfall at Chamarel; the Martello Tower in La Preneuse, the Casela Bird Park close to Flic en Flac, and the lighthouse at Pointe aux Caves, where the coastal scenery is very similar to the dramatic black basalt cliffs that dominate the south coast.

In the evening the international hotels provide an array of entertainment. Three of them — La Pirogue in Wolmar, the Berjaya Resort, and the Paradis-Brabant in Le Morne — have casinos. Flic en Flac has a number of restaurants for those willing to venture out of hotels.

Getting there
Le Morne, which marks the beginning of the west coast, is roughly 45 kilometres (30 miles) from Port Louis, 26 kilometres (16 miles) from Souillac, 50 kilometres (31 miles) from Plaine Magnien, and 58 kilometres (36 miles) from Mahébourg. It is off the main B9 coastal road.

When to go
The best months to visit the west coast of Mauritius are April to June and September to November. However, for those interested in hiking in the Black River Gorges, the cool months of May and June are considered more suitable. For big game fishing from Rivière Noire, the best season is November through April. Between June and August is the best time for surfing off Tamarin.

Where to stay

There are several top-class hotels along the west coast: in Le Morne, the Beachcomber's Paradis, and the Berjaya Resort Hotel in Wolmar, the Sun International and its twin, Sugar Beach Hotel, La Pirogue, and the Sofitel Imperial. See Listings.

Sightseeing

Le Morne is easily recognizable. It is a peninsula with a 243-metre-high (797-foot-high) table-topped mountain called Le Morne Brabant at its centre, and is the most westerly point on Mauritius.

Island folklore says that in the 18th and 19th centuries, runaway slaves used to hide among the precipitous clefts of the hillsides to evade capture and when slavery was abolished in 1835, officials were sent to Le Morne Brabant with the good news, but the runaway slaves refused to believe them and, rather than surrender, flung themselves from the mountaintop.

A **rough road** leads from the **B9** coastal road to the western side of Le Morne peninsula, where there are two hotel complexes. The more southerly of the two is the Berjaya Resort, a Malaysian-owned hotel opened in the middle of 1994. Like the other international-standard hotels on the island, it offers a range of facilities that includes restaurants, bars, evening entertainment, and a variety of watersports.

Just **north,** on the same road, is the hotel complex of Paradis, another Beachcomber Hotels property. The Paradis and the Brabant used to be run separately but now is a single entity.

The Paradis and the Berjaya stand right behind the secluded sandy beach that fringes the peninsula and are ideal for those — particularly beginners — wishing to indulge in watersports, because the lagoon is naturally calm, thanks to an unbroken reef. The Paradis has the added attraction of an 18-hole golf course. Both complexes have casinos in addition to evening entertainment.

Le Domino Seafood Restaurant is signposted on the rough road linking the hotels to the B9 coastal road. Set quite high on the slopes of Le Morne Brabant, it serves seafood lunches and Chinese specialities on

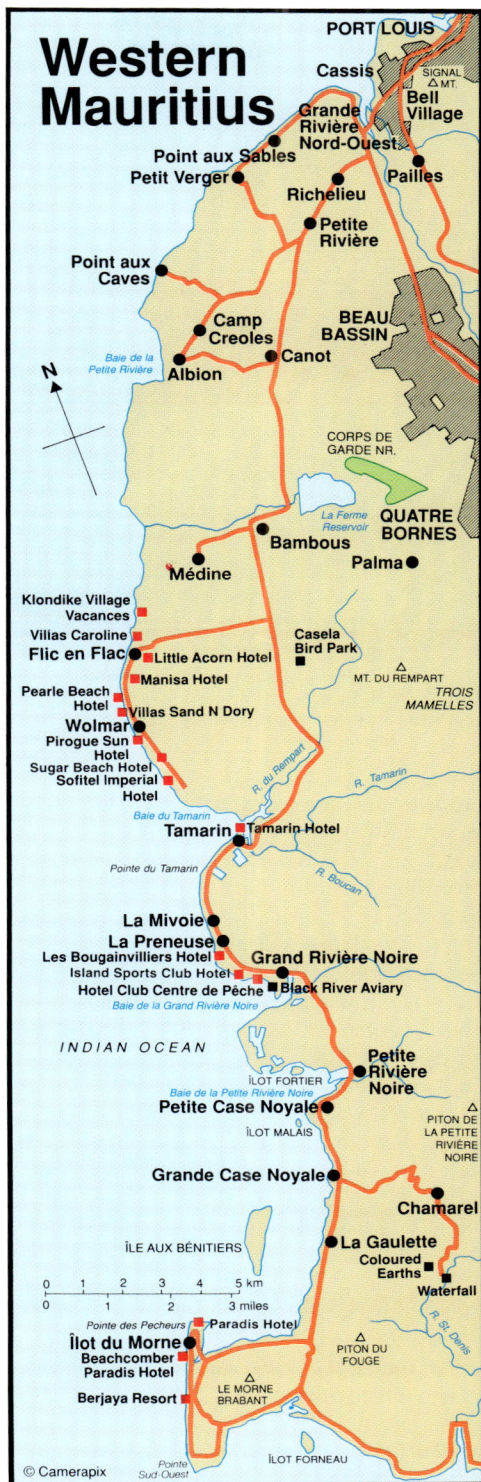

Western Mauritius

PORT LOUIS
Cassis
SIGNAL MT.
Bell Village
Grande Rivière Nord-Ouest
Pailles
Point aux Sables
Petit Verger
Richelieu
Petite Rivière
Point aux Caves
BEAU BASSIN
Camp Creoles
Canot
Baie de la Petite Rivière
Albion
CORPS DE GARDE NR.
La Ferme Reservoir
QUATRE BORNES
Bambous
Palma
Médine
Casela Bird Park
Klondike Village Vacances
Villas Caroline
Flic en Flac
Little Acorn Hotel
MT. DU REMPART
TROIS MAMELLES
Manisa Hotel
Pearle Beach Hotel
Villas Sand N Dory
Wolmar
Pirogue Sun Hotel
Sugar Beach Hotel
Sofitel Imperial Hotel
R. du Rempart
R. Tamarin
Baie du Tamarin
Tamarin
Tamarin Hotel
Pointe du Tamarin
R. Boucan
La Mivoie
La Preneuse
Les Bougainvilliers Hotel
Island Sports Club Hotel
Grand Rivière Noire
Hotel Club Centre de Pêche
Black River Aviary
Baie de la Grand Rivière Noire
INDIAN OCEAN
ÎLOT FORTIER
Baie de la Petite Rivière Noire
Petite Case Noyale
ÎLOT MALAIS
Petite Rivière Noire
PITON DE LA PETITE RIVIERE NOIRE
Grande Case Noyale
Chamarel
ÎLE AUX BÉNITIERS
La Gaulette
Coloured Earths
Waterfall
0 1 2 3 4 5 km
0 1 2 3 miles
Pointe des Pecheurs
Paradis Hotel
R. St Denis
Îlot du Morne
Beachcomber Paradis Hotel
PITON DU FOUGE
Berjaya Resort
LE MORNE BRABANT
© Camerapix
Pointe Sud-Ouest
ÎLOT FORNEAU

143

Above: Another beach resort on the northern headland of Pte des Pecheurs beneath 243-metre (797-ft) Le Morne Brabant in south-west Mauritius.

outdoor terraces with magnificent views along the west coast.

About six kilometres (3.7 miles) from Le Morne Peninsula is **La Gaulette,** an attractive village where the residents' gardens are full of tropical flowers and shrubs. A general store sells a few tourist essentials, such as suntan lotion and a small number of souvenirs. The village of **Grande Case Noyale,** six kilometres (3.7 miles) north of **La Gaulette,** is said to have been named after retired French soldier Pierre Marie Le Normand. He owned land and built a small *case* (Creole for house) on it to accommodate travellers who visited Mauritius. Noyale (using the first 'n' in the soldier's surname) would appear to be a corruption of the French word *royale,* meaning royal. Eventually, Le Normand was murdered by runaway slaves.

At the centre of Grande Case Noyale, **Mater Dolorosa,** a white **church** with a corrugated roof, was built in 1939 at the foot of a steep, winding **road** that leads through the thickly forested foothills of the Black River Mountains to Chamarel. En route, there are excellent **views** over the coast and Le Morne. Five kilometres (three miles) from Grande Case Noyale, the twisting road forks. The **left fork** leads to **Plaine Champagne** and the **right** to the tourist attraction of **Chamarel,** named after one Antoine de Chamarel, a former French army captain, who, in the 18th century, acquired land to farm vanilla, coffee, and pepper. Coffee is still grown locally today.

Chamarel has a church, a village hall, and the usual box-like houses found everywhere in Mauritius. It remains remarkably undeveloped despite the number of visitors who pass through to the **Coloured Earths** and the **Chamarel Waterfall.** In the 1960s,

Opposite: One of the island's last remnants of endemic forest cover at Black River Gorges National Park.
Overleaf: Spectacular vista in Black River Gorges National Park, looking toward Montagne de Rempart.

Above: Tourists explore the strange geological formations and copper and cobalt hues of Mauritius Coloured Earths.

the Coloured Earths were the first tourist attraction to be promoted in Mauritius. Today, samples are found all over the island packaged in tiny plastic tubes attached, for example, to key rings, which are sold in numerous boutiques and by beach vendors. The different-coloured sands can also be bought from the administration building at the entrance to the Coloured Earths site.

Visitors must pay a small entrance fee at the administration building if they wish to visit the Earths. Their rolling dunes, which are a combination of purple, red, blue, yellow, and rust, intrigue geologists. One possible explanation for this unusual feature is that the dunes are composed of mineral-rich volcanic ash, which has been eroded bare and coloured by oxidation.

As the land on which the Coloured Earths are found belongs to the **Bel Ombre Sugar Estate,** an example of the innovative horizontal mill introduced by Charles Telfair, a previous owner of Bel Ombre, stands in front of the administration building. The Chamarel Waterfall is close by. The 90-metre-high (295-foot-high) cascade is on the Rivière St Denis, which merges with the Rivière du Cap downstream, flowing out into the Baie du Cap on the south coast. From Chamarel, backtrack to Grande Case Noyale on the west coast and carry on along the **B9 northwards.** In the hamlet of **Petite Case Noyale,** opposite a quaint wooden **colonial building,** which houses a health centre, is the white entrance to a private **deer reserve** belonging to the Bel Ombre Sugar Estate. All the coffee grown around Chamarel is processed in a factory inside the reserve.

The next village, about one kilometre (half-a-mile) along the coast-hugging road, is **Petite Rivière Noire.** Most villagers are employed in the production of salt from sea water. The village **chapel** is a work of art crafted out of natural materials, including wood, straw, and aloe stalks.

Just outside the larger village of **Grande Rivière Noire,** about three kilometres (1.8 miles) to the north, there is a sharp **left-hand bend** where the **B9** becomes the

Above: Plush resort dominates the aquamarine waters of Blue Bay lagoon, south of Mahebourg.

A3, a far superior road. On this corner, **a rough track** off to the **right** leads to the **main entrance** of the newly designated **Black River Gorges (BRG) National Park.**

The park, which covers 3.5 per cent of the island, is the first of its kind in the country and was established in June 1994. Its 65.7 square kilometres (25 square miles) encompass the Black River Gorges and their environs, including the Brise Fer and Macchabée forests, Plaine Champagne, the Savanne Range, Bel Ombre forests, and much of the Black River Range.

The BRG National Park contains most of the remaining tracts of native forest — estimated at between 80 and 90 per cent — in Mauritius. Its primary purpose, therefore, is conservation, because the retention of the island's original vegetation is crucial for the survival of much of the endangered native fauna, such as the **pink pigeon, echo parakeet,** and **Mauritius fody.**

However, the park also offers recreation and education facilities. It is to be carefully zoned so that some areas offer open access to visitors, while other areas will only be reached along well-marked paths. The lower section of the park has been marked for recreation, the emphasis being on picnicking, camping, walking, biking, and having a good time.

The most important wildlife regions — at higher altitudes — will have restricted access, as many of the rare species are easily disturbed.

A **visitor centre** is to be constructed at the Black River entrance to the park. The government's National Parks and Conservation Service is training and certifying local people as guides who will come to a private agreement as to fees with visitors to the park. These guides will be contactable through the visitor centre.

Back on the **A3, Grand Rivière Noire** — more often than not called simply Rivière Noire or, in English, Black River — is very close. A **stone church** is on the **right** and a **National Community Health Development Centre** lies immediately to the **left.**

A **sign** to the **left** indicates the Hotel Club Centre de Pêche, where **big game fishing** trips can be arranged. The Black

River area is renowned for its big game fishing. The best times to fish are between November and April, when marlin, sailfish, wahoo, yellowfin-tuna, and various species of shark migrate to the warm waters around Mauritius and feed just beyond the reef, where the seabed falls abruptly to a depth of 600 metres (2,000 feet).

In the centre of the village are a number of general stores, and a **signpost** to the **left** points to the Black River Police Station. The **Black River Aviaries**, where much has been done to save threatened endemic birds from extinction, are near the police station. Entry is usually restricted to keen ornithologists and scientists.

Shortly after the centre of Rivière Noire, take a **left turn**, where there are **signs** to the **Martello Tower** and **La Preneuse**. Pass the old, quaint **Post Office building** and then travel along a narrow, shady **track** that leads past a **cemetery** and several attractive residential houses until the Martello Tower is reached.

The tower, along with three others, was built by British army engineers in the 1830s to control civil unrest and defend the island from foreign invasion. The British stole the Martello Tower design from Corsica at the end of the 18th century and then proceeded to build over 100 copies along Britain's south coast, and another hundred throughout their Empire, including those in Mauritius. Martello is a corruption of Mortella, the point on Corsica where the British first encountered this type of fortification. Martello Towers have very thick walls — varying between 2.5 and 4.5 metres (eight and 15 feet) — are circular, and are not very high. They all have a single external door high up and, when active, guns on the roof. Most, such as those in Mauritius, have four interior levels. The Martello Tower has been restored by the Friends of the Environment, a local body dedicated to improving the island's environment.

Behind the Tower is **La Prene-use Public Beach,** with stunning views along the west coast to Le Morne. La Preneuse, little more than a smart residential hamlet, was named after a French warship. In 1799 the ship was being chased by a British squadron and took refuge off the coast of Rivière Noire. The captain then ordered all the ammunition to be taken ashore and the area where the ammunition was landed became known as La Preneuse.

Continue north on the **track road**, which soon rejoins the main A3 road. **La Mivoie**, a picturesque hamlet that has effectively merged with La Preneuse, is home to the **Shellorama Shell Museum**.

Further **north**, about half-a-kilometre away, is **Tamarin**, which the Dutch named Molucque Reede (Oyster Bay). Only during the French administration did it become known as Bras de Mer du Tamarin, while the river that flowed into the bay was called Rivière du Tamarin after the tamarind trees there.

Access to the **public beach** is along a rough road close to the attractive Roman Catholic **church** of St Benoit. The Tamarin beach is relatively unspoilt, with beautiful **views** across the bay to the majestic peak of **Montagne du Rempart**. Along with Le Morne and a few other spots on the south coast, Tamarin is popular with surfers cruising the coast looking for the best waves to ride. Usually they find them in Tamarin, where waves of up to two metres (6.5 feet) occur between June and August. On the **opposite side** of the **main road** from the beach are **salt pans** where salt is extracted by a process of solar evaporation and then piled into huge rectangular pans.

Passing out of the **northern end** of Tamarin, the **A3** crosses the Rivière Boucan via the iron **Tamarin Bridge**, built in 1934.

The A3 continues through sugar cane fields to meet a **roundabout**, at which point the hills of **Trois Mamelles** provide a dramatic skyline. Take the A3 **northwards** towards Port Louis. From the roundabout, it is only a couple of kilometres (1.2 miles) until a **right turning** along a palm-lined **avenue** leads to **Casela Bird Park**. The park, established in 1979, stretches over

Opposite: The beautiful Chamarel Waterfall cascades into the gorge of the Rivierè St Denis, near the Coloured Earths.

Above: The 8-hectare (19-acre) Casela Bird Park contains more than 2,500 birds of more than 140 species. Opposite: Local men take a break under a banyan tree with its exotic cascade of aerial roots at Anse Noyale.

eight hectares (19 acres) and contains more than 2,500 birds of more than 140 species. There are birds from all the continents, but one great attraction is the **Mauritian pink pigeon**, one of the rarest birds in the world. Aside from birds, the park has **tigers**, fish ponds, **tortoises**, **monkeys**, and orchids. A small restaurant sells sandwiches, snacks, and drinks. It's worth stopping there just to admire the panoramic **view** of **Le Morne** and the rest of the west coast.

One kilometre (half-a-mile) further **north**, along the A3, a **road** to the **left** descends gently through sugar cane fields to **Flic en Flac**. This settlement owes its name to the Dutch, who called the area Friedland Flac after Friesland, a province of the Netherlands. A 1725 French map called the area Fri Lan Flac, later corrupted to Flic en Flac.

Mauritian poet Robert Edward Hart had a rather more imaginative idea for the origin of Flic en Flac, suggesting that it was an onomatopoeic phrase for the sound made when people trudged through the marshy land. Flic en Flac used to be a rather sleepy seaside village, but it is becoming more and more built-up and increasingly touristy, due to its closeness to Port Louis and the urbanized highlands. Now there is a wide range of places for visitors to stay and numerous restaurants at which to eat.

Unlike the tourist area of Grand Baie in the north, however, Flic en Flac has yet to develop an active nightlife. There is little of interest to see ashore — although Flic en Flac beach is spectacular for its whiteness and great length — but offshore a fascinating underwater world awaits discovery.

Pierre Szalay, president of the Mauritian Scuba Diving Association, operates a **dive centre** near the hotel called Villas Caroline, at the **northern** end of the beach.

Further **south** from Flic en Flac, along the coast, is the hamlet of **Wolmar**, with a couple of impressive hotels — La Pirogue and Sugar Beach (Sun International hotels) and the Sofitel Imperial Hotel.

Above: Slender automated lighthouse stands sentinel on the rocky headland of Pointe aux Caves.
Opposite: Sunset at Tamarin, where salt is extracted by a process of solar evaporation and then piled into huge rectangular pans.

From Wolmar, it is necessary to backtrack to the **A3**, as the road ends at the Sofitel Imperial. Back on the A3, **turn left** and continue towards Port Louis. The village of **Bambous** is less than three kilometres (1.8 miles) along the road. It was named after the extensive bamboo groves that used to cover the banks of the Rivière Belle Isle nearby. During the French occupation, Bambous was considered a desirable place to live. That was before the malaria epidemic of the second half of the 19th-century sent people rushing up to the healthier highlands. Today, Bambous is considered one of the most important villages in western Mauritius, because it includes the district court and a large state secondary school. The large basalt Roman Catholic **church** in the village is said to date back to 1841.

Carry on along the **A3**, **northwards**, and the hamlet of **Canot** lies along the road, just over four kilometres (2.5 miles). There, take a **left turn** and follow the **road** that twists through sugar cane fields in the direction

of **Albion**. Just before the village, **turn right** onto the **B78** towards **Camp Creoles**. Go through the Camp Creoles hamlet and take the first left for **Pointe aux Caves**, where there is a red-and-white striped **lighthouse** and stunning **vistas** along the west coast. The 30-metre (98-ft) high, lighthouse, built on a black craggy promontory in 1904, has 77 steps, and is the only fully automated lighthouse on the mainland. The lighthouse keeper, who lives in a bungalow nearby, will give a guided tour to visitors with a permit.

Tracks have to be retraced to the **B78 road**, where a **left turn** leads to **Petite Rivière**. From there it is possible to take either the **A3** directly into the industrial outskirts of Port Louis or the **B31** along the coast via Petit Verger and Pointe aux Sables to the capital.

Overleaf: Forested bowl of a volcanic crater and lake at Curepipe, circled by an observation road.

The Mauritian Highlands

Much of the highlands falls within Plaines Wilhems, the most densely populated district in Mauritius. It has four municipalities: Beau Bassin-Rose Hill, Quatre Bornes, Vacoas-Phoenix, and Curepipe.

How did Plaines Wilhems get its name? It is known that when the Dutch settled Mauritius, they stuck mainly to coastal areas, leaving the hilly interior mostly unexplored because it was covered by dense forest. Some believe it was named after a Dutch settler called Willem Willems, who had an estate on the inland plateau. Others think that the French named the area after Wilhem Leichnig, a German whom they found living on the plateau during their initial explorations into the interior. The French called it Plaines de Wilhems, later shortening the name to Plaines Wilhems.

Plaines Wilhems rose to prominence in the 19th century, when a cholera epidemic in the early 1860s, followed by a malaria outbreak between 1866 and 1868, led many inhabitants to flee Port Louis in search of healthier climes in the highlands — an exodus made possible by the opening of the Midland railway line in 1865. The latter meant that people could now commute daily between their homes in the highlands and their places of work in Port Louis. Between the 1860s and 1918, the population of Plaines Wilhems rose from about 30,000 to well over 70,000. All the necessities of civilized life — schools, social clubs, etc. — were soon established there.

The highlands remain popular residential areas, but an increasing number of Mauritians now prefer to live on or close to the coast to enjoy the benefits of the sea, sand, and sun, rather than endure the cold and damp of, say, Curepipe.

There are some beautiful colonial houses — but also some modern architectural disasters, it should be added — along the backstreets and shady avenues of the highland towns. Most can be viewed quite easily from the road. Those interested should visit the 19th-century municipality building and the early 20th-century Carnegie Library in Curepipe, as well as the 19th-century house called Eureka in Moka.

Other places of interest in this region include the SMF Regimental Museum in a solid stone building in Vacoas; the crater of Trou aux Cerfs, an excellent point from which to view the rest of Mauritius; the Botanical Gardens; the first model ship-building factory; an anthurium and andraeneum flower nursery in Curepipe; La Verrerie de Phoenix, the only glass-blowing factory on the island; and Domaine les Pailles, a reconstruction of Mauritian life in days gone by.

Not all of the highlights are found in built-up areas, however. They include the Black River Gorges National Park, where large tracts of native forest are protected by law and the scenery can be quite breathtaking; Grand Bassin, a crater lake sacred to the Mauritian Hindu community; and the Bois Chéri tea factory.

The Black River Gorges National Park also provides ample opportunities for keen walkers, as does the mountain of Le Pouce, which can be approached from Moka. In Vacoas, the 18-hole golf course belonging to the Gymkhana Club is open to visitors.

For those interested in shopping, the highlands are the place to head. Quatre Bornes is home to the Orchard Centre, a modern shopping facility packed with a wide range of stores, and the SPES handicraft shop. Floréal is the place for duty-free diamonds and knitwear. Curepipe is one of the best places on the island for browsing and has a wide range of shops, including a franchise of the French supermarket chain, Prisunic. Not to be outdone, Phoenix now has a franchise of the French supermarket chain, Continent.

In the evening, the highlands offer quite a range of activities. Highlights on a gastronomic tour include the five restaurants at Domaine les Pailles. After-dinner entertainment is provided by the Casino de Maurice in Curepipe and the Grand Casino at Domaine les Pailles, as well as by Sam's

The Mauritian Highlands

0 1 2 3 4 km
0 1 2 miles

INDIAN OCEAN

Robert Edward Hart Gardens

Sainte Croix

Cassis

Plaine Lauzun
Grand Rivière Nord-Ouest

SIGNAL MT.

PORT LOUIS

△ PIETER BOTH

Pailles
Domaine les Pailles

Coromandel

POUCE N.R. △ LE POUCE

MOKA MOUNTAINS

BEAU BASSIN

Eureka

Moka

St. Pierre

University

Mahatma Gandhi Institute

Le Réduit

La Ferme Reservoir

ROSE HILL

Belle Rose

Bambous

CORPS DE GARDE N.R.

Reservoir

Flic en Flac

QUATRE BORNES

CANDOS HILL

R. Terre Rouge

Palma

PHOENIX

MT. DU REMPART △

TROIS MAMELLES

VACOAS

Piton du Milieu Reservoir

R. du Rempart

R. Tamarin

Tamarin

FLOREAL

TROU AUX CERFS CRATER

Glen Park

R. Boucan

CABINET N.R.

Henrietta

Botanical Gardens

CUREPIPE

Tamarin Falls

PERRIER N.R.

Seizième Mille

PLAINES WILHEMS

Tamarind Falls Reservoir

Mare Longue Reservoir

Mare aux Vacoas

Nouvelle France

Grand Rivière Noire

PITON DE LA RIVIÈRE NOIRE △

BLACK RIVER GORGES

Le Pétrin

KANAKA CRATER ○

PLAINE CHAMPAGNE

Chamarel

Grand Bassin
LES MARES N.R.

BOIS SEC N.R.

Bois Chéri

La Flora

Coloured Earths

BLACK RIVER GORGES NATIONAL PARK

GOULY PERE N.R.

Grand Bois

R. dl Poste

Waterfall

R. St. Denis

△ MT. COCOTTE

R. Savanne

SAVANNE MOUNTAINS

Bassin Blanc ○

R. Paratis

Britannia

R. Diagon

R. des Galets

© Camerapix

and Moulin du Tango — the two night-clubs in Vacoas — and Palladium, on the motorway close to Réduit.

Getting there
The closest highland town to Port Louis, Beau Bassin, is less than 10 kilometres (6 miles) away from the capital, 11 kilometres (6.8 miles) from Curepipe, and about 33 kilometres (20.5 miles) from SSR International Airport near Mahébourg. A good motorway, the M2, runs through the highlands from Mahébourg to Port Louis.

When to go
The best months to visit the highlands are April to June and September to November, but take note that this region can be up to five degrees cooler than the coastal areas, so take an extra layer of clothing, especially during the winter months (May to October). The shops in Curepipe, Beau Bassin-Rose Hill, Quatre Bornes, and Vacoas-Phoenix open from 1000 to 1800 Monday to Wednesday, Friday, and Saturday, and from 1000 to 1330 on Thursday and Sunday.

Where to stay
In Quatre Bornes, the Gold Crest Hotel and El Monaco offer good quality accommodation and there are many smaller, basic hotels in the highlands, there are none of note. The closest hotels of international standard are on the west coast in Flic en Flac and Wolmar. See Listings.

Sightseeing
Heading **south-westwards** out of Port Louis through the suburban area of **Cassis** and **Plaine Lauzun**, the road reaches **Grand Rivière Nord-Ouest** (Great North-West River). The Dutch called this area De Waterplaats, meaning watering place, as many sailing ships put into shore at this point to take on fresh water from the river for their outward voyages. During the French administration the area was known as Baye St Louis after King Louis IX, and La Bourdonnais had an aqueduct built to convey water from the river to the capital. It acquired its present name in the mid-19th-century.

A **modern bridge** now crosses the Grand Rivière Nord-Ouest, but the **old iron bridge** can be seen clearly upstream. Dominating the neighbourhood is an imposing **derelict building** known as La Tour Koenig, which was built by the son of the first Koenig (now a well-known family name on the island) to settle in Mauritius. The son, a trained lawyer, was the first manager of the Mauritius Commercial Bank and had La Tour built in the style of a German castle to remind his father of his former homeland. La Tour is now a ruin, and although there have been several plans to renovate it, none has borne fruit.

There are several other **old buildings** of interest in Grand Rivière Nord-Ouest. One is a **stone corn mill** close to the old iron bridge — once used to grind locally produced wheat in colonial days. Another stone building called the **Borstal** was originally a hospital and has since been used for housing prisoners of war, as an asylum, and as an isolation centre. Close by is a building with Victoria Station carved under its eaves. Now a garage, it was a railway station when the railway lines were still in use.

Continue on the **main road south**, pass the industrial zone of **Coromandel**, and the first major settlement you reach is **Beau Bassin** (Beautiful Pond or Lake).

Some believe Beau Bassin takes its name from the pond now found in the courtyard of the town's Brown Sequard Hospital. Others think it was named after an experiment conducted in the Barkly Agricultural Experimental Station's 150-year-old artificial pond.

Originally Beau Bassin-Rose Hill was a predominantly rural area conceded on 30 April, 1759, by the French East India Company (at that time in charge of the island's administration) to Jean Baptiste Bourceret de St Jean. The two settlements developed, growing closer and closer together, and, eventually, in 1896, during British colonial control, Beau Bassin was twinned with Rose Hill for administrative

Opposite: Roaring waterfall tumbles into a gorge in the Balfour Gardens at Beau Bassin.

Above: Interior of the Church of Sacré Coeur, which has stood in the heart of Beau Bassin since the 1880s.

purposes. However, it was not until 1927 that the Town Hall of Beau Bassin-Rose Hill was built. Intentionally or not, Beau Bassin-Rose Hill is a combination of French and English, reflecting Mauritius's occupation by first the French and then the British. The municipality now has a population of about 95,000. Before the centre of Beau Bassin is reached, **turn left** at Tang Wai Supermarket on the corner of John Trotter Street, where there is a rusty, barely legible, **signpost** for **Balfour Gardens**.

Follow the road, passing big modern monstrosities that some call homes but which offer no warmth to the outside eye, and smaller, traditional Creole-style houses that give the impression of welcoming all, even strangers.

These residential streets, bordered by evergreens, are reminiscent of English villages, except that the Mauritian streets are far more orderly, being arranged on a grid system. Having followed John Trotter Street for some distance, **turn right** at Queen Alexander Street and then take the

first road on the **left** into A Hassenjee Street. The Balfour Gardens are straight ahead.

Balfour Gardens are named after Dr Andrew Balfour, an English sanitation expert who arrived in Mauritius in 1921. He considered the hygiene standards to be so low in Port Louis at the time that he recommended the building of a model housing estate for workers outside the centre of the capital. As a result, Bell Village — named after the then governor — was constructed in what are now the city's western suburbs.

The gardens are small and have quite recently been converted into a **children's playground**, with swings, climbing frames, and paths painted with miniature road signs, accompanied by tiny traffic lights. However, there is a **giant tortoise** enclosure and on the far side of the gardens there are **views** of the Moka mountain range to the north and a **waterfall**, which tumbles into an enormous gorge and then flows down into the Grande Rivière Nord-Ouest. At the head of the gorge stands a large white house, which, with its truncated ramparts, resembles a small castle. La Tour Blanche (the White Tower), as it was then called, was built in 1834 by John Augustus Lloyd, an English army captain. Captain Lloyd built stables alongside the house and kept the only elephant on the island. In 1836, Charles Darwin visited Mauritius aboard the *Beagle* and stayed at La Tour Blanche for a few days.

In 1946, La Tour Blanche became the home of Madame Dorothy Rouillard and her husband. The latter died in the late 1960s and, shortly before her own death in 1977, Madame Rouillard donated the house to the Catholic diocese of Port Louis. It was renamed Le Thabor, after Mount Thabor in Palestine where the Transfiguration of Jesus is believed to have taken place, and was converted into a monastery. In 1983, Le Thabor became a Maison de Formation du Diocese de Port Louis, a pastoral centre where children and adults are educated in the Christian way of life, and, in October 1989, welcomed Pope John Paul II on his official visit.

Le Thabor's setting is truly stunning. From the edge of the garden, which falls away suddenly and steeply into the gorge below, there are far-reaching views down the ravine to Port Louis in the far distance. The shady garden itself is a picture of tranquillity, filled as it is with twisted intendance trees, many of which are more than 100 years old.

From the 19th-century on, this area of the highlands attracted British settlers and diplomats seeking a place to live graciously, go horse riding, and garden to their hearts content. As a result it came to be known as the English Quarter.

From Le Thabor, return to the centre of Beau Bassin, via the one-way system. In the heart of the town stands the **Church of Sacré Coeur** (built in the 1880s) a small **market**, and an **old-style police station**.

Passing through the centre of Beau Bassin, the **main road** forks at a **roundabout**. Take the **right turn** and continue on up to **Rose Hill**, the centre of which is not much more than a couple of kilometres (1.2 miles) away.

Rose Hill is probably named after the colour produced by the sun's setting rays when they shed their light over the mountain of **Corps de Garde**, which overlooks Rose Hill, but it may also have taken its name from a 19th-century sugar estate called Mont Rose, which later became the Rose Hill Sugar Estate.

The Beau Bassin-Rose Hill **Town Hall** is on the **western** side of Route Royale, which is the **right side** of the road when approaching from Beau Bassin. Set well back from the main road, the extensive front lawn plays host to a **fountain** called La Fontaine des Arts, the work of two local artists, Neermab Hurry and Serge Constantin. The latter happens to be the art director of The Plaza Theatre in the Town Hall.

The **Plaza Theatre** opened in 1933 with a showing of a musical film, *Le Lieutenant Souriant* (The Smiling Lieutenant), starring Maurice Chevalier. It was never the intention that Town Hall's main auditorium should be called the Plaza Theatre, but in the 1930s, when it first opened, the municipality hired the auditorium out on certain days of the week to a cinematographic company that gave it the name of The Plaza, and the name has stuck ever since.

The Plaza, renovated in the early 1980s, is said to be the largest theatre in the Indian Ocean, seating at least 1,000 people. During the 1993 Francophone Summit it staged an official cultural evening which President Mitterrand of France attended.

The Plaza's productions include opera, pop concerts, and dance, and emphasize the island's cultural diversity as they are held in a number of languages, including English, French, Creole, and Indian. Check local newspapers for up-to-date listings of events.

There are several sections to the Town Hall aside from The Plaza. There is also the Max Moutia Theatre Museum, a library, and the Max Boullé Art Gallery.

The **Max Moutia Theatre Museum** is named after Max Moutia, a former inhabitant of Beau Bassin-Rose Hill, whose talent as a lyrical singer was greatly appreciated in Mauritius between 1938 and 1973 after he had already found acclaim in much of France. The small museum, attached to the very back of The Plaza, resembles the foyer

Above: Art deco façade of the Paris cinema in Rose Hill. Opposite: The Church of Sacré Coeur de Montmartre, with its towering spire, is situated across from the Town Hall in the centre of Rose Hill. Overleaf: The view from Pieter Both, the island's second-highest peak.

of an old theatre, with posters of past productions and photographs of members of the 1930s Mauritius Dramatic Club adorning the walls.

The **library** has a good Mauritian reference section and is situated next door to the Max Boullé Art Gallery. The latter does not have a permanent exhibition, but can be hired by local artists to display their work.

Next to the Town Hall, also set back from the road, is **Maison Carne**, a classic example of colonial architecture. Formerly a private home, it now houses offices that organize management training courses.

Turn left out of the Town Hall complex onto **Route Royale** and **left again** into Ambrose Street. Then **turn right** into Sir Edgar Laurent Street. Follow this narrow road to the **gates** on the **right** indicating **Craft-Aid**, a rehabilitation project that aims to provide creative and remunerative employment and training to the disabled. It was started in 1983 by Englishman Paul Draper, who has since moved on to set up a similar venture on Rodrigues. Among other things, the Craft-Aid workshop produces quality wooden furniture, pressed flower cards, bookmarks, and painted silk scarves.

Take the **road opposite** Craft-Aid to reach Hugnin Street. **Turn south** along Hugnin Street and continue along it until Sir Celicourt Antelme Street, where a **left turn** leads back to Route Royale and the centre of Rose Hill. There are two **churches** of interest in the heart of town — **Sacré Coeur de Montmartre**, opposite the Town Hall, and the older **Church of Notre Dame de Lourdes**, built in 1890, on the corner of Sir Celicourt Antelme Street and Route Royale.

Continue along Route Royale towards the **south** and **Quatre Bornes**. A hive of activity surrounds the town's roundabout on Route Royale. The **bus terminus**, from where it is possible to travel to most parts of the island, is located there, as is the

Above: An irresistible buy: brightly coloured andraeneum blossoms at the lively outdoor market in the centre of Quatre Bornes.

Post Office, formerly the railway station. Directly opposite is **Arab Town**, where neat stalls with pastel green corrugated roofs are manned by merchants displaying basketry, beachwear, and household games. A number of shopping centres and arcades have also sprung up in the vicinity, gaining Rose Hill a reputation as a shopper's paradise.

Other points of interest in Rose Hill include the **British Council**, with its library and a selection of fairly up-to-date British newspapers and magazines; the **market**, on the other side of Arab Town, where a wide range of meat, vegetables, fruit and flowers can be bought; and, close to the market, the **Dar-us-Salaam Mosque**, established in 1923.

From the Rose Hill **roundabout** follow Route Royale in a **south-easterly** direction towards the **M2 motorway** and Quatre Bornes. Go through **Belle Rose**, where the only decent **cinema** showing up-to-date Western movies, the ABC, is located and, just before the **motorway roundabout**, the

Roman Catholic **Church** of **St Jean** is on the **right**.

Follow the **signs** to Quatre Bornes (Four Boundary Stones), which takes its name from the fact that it has grown up where the boundaries of four sugar estates — Bassin, La Louise, Palma, and Beau Séjour — once converged.

Quatre Bornes, granted town status in 1895, is perfectly situated between **Candos Hill**, a small hillock to the south once used for military target practice, and the distinctive **Corps de Garde** to the west. Corps de Garde, during the French administration, is said to have served as a lookout post for runaway slaves. There are a number of **Hindu temples** on the lower slopes of the Corps de Garde that play an important part in the celebration of Cavadee, a solemn festival during which the entire Tamil community demonstrates its affection for and allegiance to the God Muruga. Devotees have their bodies pierced with *vels* (small silver needles) and carry a cavadee. While most walk barefoot to one of the temples,

Above: New shopping complex near the rapidly expanding town of Quatre Bornes.

some walk on wooden sandals studded with nails. Quatre Bornes itself is, in the main, uninspiring. It is largely residential, with a population approaching 70,000, and the central shops cater principally for the local people. However, the Orchard Centre, a new peach-coloured high-rise commercial block with several floors of **shops** that include home furnishing stores, clothes boutiques selling locally produced goods at reasonable prices, factory outlets, and electronic stores, as well as restaurants, has added to the town's attraction. A lively outdoor **market** is close to the Orchard Centre.

Travelling in a **westerly** direction, on the **opposite side** of the road from the Orchard Centre, is a **turning** into La Bourdonnais Street. The **SPES** (Société pour la Promotion des Enterprises Specialisés) **shop**, which is worth visiting for the wide range of locally produced artefacts on sale, is not far along the road. There are, for example, colourful ceramics, tropical mobiles, linen with a local theme, and lightshades made of unusual materials, such as the sugar cane stem, on offer. SPES was established in June 1967 by professionals and volunteers to help create jobs, to train people in skills such as weaving and ceramics that were previously non-existent in Mauritius, and to centralize handicraft activities on the island. It is an uphill battle, given the lack of a handicraft tradition in the still young and undeveloped Mauritian culture. It is far too easy to forget that the island has been inhabited for only 350 years or so and has yet to nurture a truly endemic identity.

The **B3**, or Route Vacoas, leads from Route St Jean in Quatre Bornes up to the municipality of **Vacoas-Phoenix**. The centre of Vacoas is just four kilometres (2.5 miles) from Quatre Bornes. On Abbé de la Caille's map of 1753, the town now known as Vacoas was marked as Mare aux Vaquas. However, on an 1807 map, its name had changed to Mare des Vacoas, and by the mid-19th-century was Mare aux Vacoas. It is evident from all these names that the town took its name from a profusion of local vacoa trees. Since 1968,

Above: Lush greenery surrounds the crater lake of Trou aux Cerfs, not far from Curepipe.

Vacoas has been linked with Phoenix, and the combined population of the two towns is in the region of 60,000.

The **B3**, once it reaches Vacoas, leads past Sam's and Moulin du Tango, two nightclubs in the same building that are popular with Mauritian residents. The **Eglise de Visitation à Vacoas** is on the **same side** of the road, a little further **south**. Just after the church, St Paul Avenue leads to the **east**. Continue along this road and the Vacoas-Phoenix **Municipality Building** is on the **right**.

The tree-lined roads (such as St Paul Avenue) and the cooler temperatures at this altitude have always attracted a steady stream of wealthy inhabitants to Vacoas.

This area is also home to the Special Mobile Force (SMF), a quasi-military police force established in 1960 when the British garrison left the island. The force undergoes rigorous training and is mainly employed in internal security and antiriot duties.

Just **north** of St Paul Avenue lies **Promenade Père Laval**, where the **SMF Regimental Museum** is housed in the former **Rum Warehouse Building**. The latter, a national monument, was originally constructed in the mid-1850s close to the central market in Port Louis. It was to have been a Presbyterian church, but the subsequent migration of people from Port Louis to the highlands put paid to this idea. In 1914, it became a rum warehouse for the Government's Customs and Excise Department. When it was decided to continue the motorway through Port Louis in the early 1980s, the rum warehouse was dismantled, its stones numbered and stored under the watchful eye of the SMF. Eventually, the SMF received the government's approval to rebuild the warehouse as a regimental museum.

It seemed more sensible, after all, to watch over the stones in some kind of solid form rather than just as a heap of rubble. Reassembling the rum warehouse was like trying to put together a 28,000-piece jigsaw, for that's how many stones the building has. Finally, on 8 July, 1993, the regimental museum was inaugurated by former Prime

Minister Jugnauth. The museum houses a wide and intriguing range of exhibits. As expected, there is a great deal of military memorabilia, including uniforms, guns, and regimental shields, but there are also Siamese twins joined at the pelvis, an amputated hand and a five-month-old aborted foetus preserved in glass containers, and a large Save-the-Whale *papier maché* display. The SMF Regimental Museum is situated just next to the 18-hole golf course of the Gymkhana Club. Established in the mid-19th century as a polo club for British army officers, it is now a private club with golfing facilities, tennis courts, a swimming pool, a snooker room, and a club house with a restaurant and a bar.

From St Paul Avenue take the Floréal Road **south** to reach **Floréal** itself, which comes under the jurisdiction of the municipality of Curepipe. The origins of the name Floréal are not clear, but it would appear to be linked to the luxuriant green vegetation in the area.

Floréal has been a coveted residential area since the early 20th century because it is not far from Port Louis and, due to its lofty location, has excellent views and cool temperatures, which make life more bearable during the hot Mauritian summers. Several embassies and diplomatic quarters are located in Floréal.

Floréal is also famous for the Floréal Knitwear factory, one of the largest producers of knitwear in the world, which has a shop where sweaters and T-shirts can be bought at very reasonable prices. Floréal Knitwear stores are also found elsewhere on the island. In addition, Floréal is home to the Adamas Duty-Free Shop, where diamonds can be bought.

On the way up from Floréal to Curepipe, there are **signs** to **Trou aux Cerfs**, a crater 200 metres (220 yards) in diameter, which is the result of volcanic activity that took place millions of years ago. Its banks are now covered with dense vegetation and its centre, once a watering hole for deer, is, to a large extent, choked with silt.

Perhaps more impressive than the inactive crater are the spectacular **views** from this elevated position. **Montagne du Rempart**, which Mark Twain described as a 'vest pocket Matterhorn', is to the **west,** flanked by the three peaks of **Trois Mamelles** that stand out, as Mauritians are wont to say, like three breasts. To the **northwest**, **Montagne St Pierre** is dwarfed by **Corps de Garde**, while in the foreground **Candos Hill** rises like a smooth molehill. To the **north** lies the sprawl of Curepipe and Phoenix and, in the far distance, Quatre Bornes, Rose Hill and Bassin. Just to the **east** of Rose Hill, the peaks of the thumb-like **Le Pouce** and the tiny ball that forms the head of Pieter Both are discernible among the jumble of **Moka mountains**.

Curepipe

From Trou aux Cerfs, roads wend their way down the hill, through the residential back-streets of **Curepipe** to the town centre.

There is more than one explanation as to how Curepipe came to be named. The first is that when the island was first inhabited, and there was no M2 motorway, it was a long trek across the island. The soldiers,

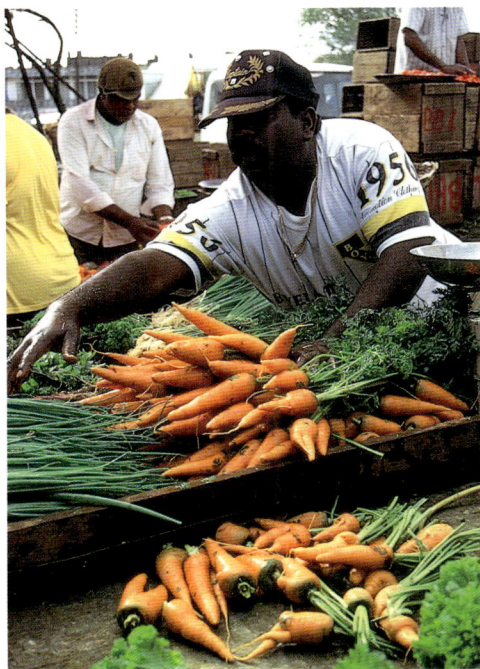

Above: Vegetable seller displays his wares at the Curepipe market.

Above: Curepipe's Town Hall, inaugurated in 1902, is a delightful Creole building with an impressive history and beautiful gardens. Opposite: Hindu faithful at Forest Side in Curepipe bedeck the Swastika Hindu temple with blossoms.

therefore, used to stop at this halfway point between the settlements in the south-east and the north-west to rest and to clean and refill their pipes. The second explanation holds that the town was named by a land-owner in the 18th century after his native village in south-western France.

In 1858, the population of Curepipe was just 200, but following the malaria epidemic of the 1860s, the settlement experienced rapid growth and now has a population of more than 60,000. Curepipe, at an altitude of 550 metres (1,804 feet), is the highest town in the highlands. The topography of the surrounding area and the height of the nearby mountains combine to produce a micro-climate that gives Curepipe the dubious honour of having the island's highest rainfall — over 3,000 millimetres (118 inches) a year. Mauritians refer to the two seasons in Curepipe as 'the rainy season and the season of rains'.

As a result, Curepipe often gives the impression of being a very grey town. In fact, Mark Twain described it as 'the nastiest spot on earth', but it has its highlights — if you are willing to dodge the raindrops. Curepipe's **Botanical Gardens**, set in the middle of one of the town's residential suburbs, are to the **south** of Trou aux Cerfs. The gardens, occupy just over two hectares (five acres), and are smaller than the Royal Botanical Gardens at Pamplemousses but are still spacious, charming, and beautifully laid-out. The gardens have a valuable collection of indigenous plants such as a *boucle d'oreilles* (literally meaning earring) tree, which takes years of tender care to nurture, and the only known example of the palm *Hyophorbe amaricaulis*, accidentally found when the area was cleared to make way for the gardens.

There are also elegant hurricane palms; the famous double coconut of the coco de mer from Seychelles; bottle palms; azaleas; Australian bottle brushes; a heart-shaped viah palm; a member of the arum family from Madagascar — which grows in an

attractive lake — and an enclosure that safeguards the rare *bois d'olive,* the *tambalacoque,* and the *bois de natte,* which are all protected species. There is only one written guide — *Le Jardin Botanique de Curepipe* by Guy Rouillard and Joseph Gueho. It is available from most good bookshops.

Curepipe's residential streets and houses are often unmarked. Efforts to introduce name and number plates have always failed. Secrecy seems to be the name of the game and, as if to emphasize this, houses are often concealed behind tall bamboo hedges. However, if you wish to see the **splendid old houses** you should travel along Pope Hennessy Street **eastwards** to meet Route Royale and on to the heart of Curepipe.

Turn south on to Route Royale at the Sik Yuen supermarket. **Royal College**, an austere grey building set in a large playground, is on the **right-hand** side of the road. The college was originally established in Port Louis, but following the 19th-century malaria epidemics and general migration to the highlands, it was transferred to Curepipe. The college moved into its present building, designed by French architect Paul le Judge de Segrais, in 1912, and only a few structural modifications have been made since. For example, the original wooden roof has been replaced by a concrete one.

A **war memorial** stands in front of the college, depicting a French soldier and a British infantryman standing united. Every year on 11 November there is a parade around the college in recognition of those who lost their lives in World War II. Behind the college are the Curepipe **Police Station** and the **District Court**, both old grey stone buildings. Opposite, on Sir Winston Churchill Street, stands the Continental Hotel.

Curepipe is famous for its shopping, although Port Louis and Grand Baie have as good a range of shops these days. The arcade underneath the old Continental Hotel, now closed, has an interesting array of **shops** and provides protection from the Curepipe rain. The arcade accommodates the antique shop Ville Valio, a good newsagent, as well as several clothes shops —

such as Cotton Club, the Spot, and Bonair — and a few shops selling tourist souvenirs. Rendezvous, a casual restaurant in the arcade, offers good Indian food.

Opposite Royal College, on Route Royale, are the Salafaa Arcades, a warren of **shops** that include pharmacies, clothes and shoe stores, snack bars, Chinese stores selling porcelain and silk, and a post office. Next to the Arcades is the Curepipe **market**, easily spotted thanks to the ugly chimney-like monstrosity that rises over it. Prisunic, in nearby Elizabeth Street, is a franchise operation of the French supermarket of that name and stocks wines, cheeses, and speciality foods freshly imported from France.

Evening entertainment in Curepipe is provided by the Casino de Maurice nearby.

On the road **south** of Prisunic is the **Town Hall**, Hotel de Ville (or Municipality Building, as it is variously called), a delightful Creole building with quite a history. Back in the late 19th century, a casino in Curepipe was bringing the city into disrepute, so the folk decided to establish a new venue for evening entertainment. At the same time Curepipe was given municipal status and it was deemed necessary to have a town hall befitting that status.

By coincidence, an imposing house, La Malmaison, was for sale in Moka, and the residents of Curepipe decided to purchase the house and transfer it to its present position. Unfortunately, La Malmaison was too big for the space provided, so the municipality acquired a local hotel and a convent and then destroyed both to make way for their new town hall. The cost of purchasing and moving La Malmaison was around Rs70,000 — considered a huge sum at the time. It was inaugurated on 23 December, 1902, by Sir Charles Bruce, the then governor.

In the Town Hall gardens there is a **monument** to the first French cartographer of Mauritius, Abbé de la Caille, whose 1753 map served as a model for all subsequent maps of the island. You can see copies of his work can be seen in the Naval and Historical Museum in Mahébourg. There is also a **bust** of the French poet Jean Paul Toulet and a **bronze statue** of Paul and Virginie, the ill-fated lovers of the St Geran

Above: French and British soldiers stand united on the war memorial that stands in front of Curepipe's Royal College. Overleaf: The natural lake of Mare aux Vacoas is the island's largest reservoir.

shipwreck, whom Bernadin St Pierre described in his famous novel. The **Carnegie Library**, next door to the Town Hall, is named after Andrew Carnegie, the wealthy Scottish-born American industrialist and philanthropist who set up a foundation that endowed public libraries throughout the world.

Mauritius came to benefit from the Carnegie Foundation thanks to American Captain Rossbain, who lived with his Mauritian wife in Curepipe at the beginning of the 20th-century. Having heard of the Carnegie Library in Seychelles, the American knew that the foundation was handing out money to establish libraries throughout the world. He wrote and asked the Carnegie Foundation if it would consider funding a library in Mauritius. After a great deal of correspondence, a donation was made and, in 1920, the library was finally opened. The Carnegie Library now has an extensive collection of books, many of them rare, on the Mascarene islands. It includes more than 2,000 books that used

to belong to Adrien d'Épinay, one of the island's first eminent politicians.

Facing Route Royale from the Town Hall and the Carnegie Library stands the awesome grey Roman Catholic **Church of Ste Thérèse**. Its construction was started by Abbé Comerford in 1868 to serve those who had fled the malaria epidemics on the coast, and it was consecrated on Christmas day 1872.

Model Shipbuilding

Follow Route Royale **south**, away from the town centre, pass the **model shipbuilding factory** of La Serenissima on the **right** and, a little later, take a **right** into the **B70** road known as Gustave Colin Street. Some way along the street, the **model shipbuilding factory** of Comajora is on the **right**. It is this establishment that started the model shipbuilding craze in the 1960s. In 1968, French Ambassador Touze recognized the talent of Jose Ramar, a local craftsman specializing in wooden products, and suggested that he produce replicas of old sea

vessels. Touze even helped the local craftsman by giving him the plans of old ships from his homeland. Ramar, therefore, started making replicas of several famous French vessels and quickly gained a reputation for his work — so much so that his models were soon being presented to such prominent visitors as Indira Gandhi, Prime Minister of India.

Further expansion to Jose Ramar's workshop led to the establishment in late 1970 of the Société d'Arts des Isles in Paris, which helped to distribute the boats, first in France and later throughout Europe. In order to increase the universal appeal of the model boats, the craftsman started sourcing ships' plans from various countries around the world, including Great Britain, the United States, Spain, and Holland. Before long, magnificent miniatures of the *Bounty*, the *Victory*, the *Endeavour*, the *Cutty Sark*, the *Golden Hind*, and even the *Titanic* were being produced.

Gradually, model shipbuilders sprang up all over the island and now over 100 factories of different sizes are producing boats of varying quality.

Another pioneer, further along the **B70**, Field Flora, on the **left side** of the road, was one of the first companies to start exporting the striking anthuriums and andraeneums found throughout Mauritius.

Back in 1967, when Maurice Bathfield started this line of work, he exported just 115 flowers a month to South Africa. In 1994, he was exporting an average of 50,000 flowers a month to Italy, France, and Ireland. At the peak of the flower season — i.e., the Mauritian summer — he was exporting up to 60,000 flowers monthly.

Anthuriums and andraeneums are not actually indigenous to the island — the prototypes were imported from Brazil just after the First World War and from Hawaii following World War II — so do not assume that they are the national flowers of Mauritius! The reason they are grown so widely for export is that they travel well, lasting up to five days in a box and more than two weeks once unpacked. It may only be slight, but there is a difference between anthuriums and andraeneums (an anthurium is smooth, an andraeneum has veins). There are different colours and various sizes available.

Visitors can see this for themselves at Field Flora, where Maurice Bathfield himself is likely to be on hand to explain the vicissitudes of the flower business. At the end of a visit it is possible to order flowers to be delivered direct to the airport and picked up prior to your departure.

From Field Flora, continue **westwards** for a couple of kilometres (1.2 miles) along the **B70** until a **T-junction**. There **turn left (south)** towards **Le Pétrin**. The road then passes through thickly wooded areas of pine, sugar cane, and scrubland to the natural lake of **Mare aux Vacoas**, the island's largest reservoir.

Mare aux Vacoas is surrounded by a high barbed wire fence, but at one point an open gate and steps lead up to the reservoir's edge. The lake is in the centre of such a high plain that Mauritius appears from this angle to have no mountains.

Continuing **south**, a **track road** leads to **Mare Longue Reservoir** to the **west**. The only way to travel this route is on foot or in a four-wheel-drive car. Further **south**, at the **junction** of Le Pétrin, there is a small **park building** and a placard showing a map of the five to 15 kilometres (three to nine miles) of walk to **Tamarin Falls** and **Macchabée** in the **Black River Gorges National Park**, both of which are accessible from this point. Le Pétrin will eventually become the main access point to the Black River Gorges National Park from the highlands and it is hoped that wardens will be stationed there to provide information, maps, and brochures.

In late 1994, the **road** that led **south** from Le Pétrin was blocked by landslides that occurred during the terrible cyclone that hit Mauritius earlier that year. However, it is now possible to travel its full length, down through beautiful tracts of virgin forest to Chamarel.

Opposite: Young anglers try their luck near the Tamarin Falls.

Above: A number of temples and shrines dot the shores of Grand Bassin, an important place of Hindu pilgrimage.
Opposite: The shrine of Lord Krishna and Radha Rani in a lakeshore Hindu temple at Grand Bassin.

Sacred lake

The road that leads **east** from Le Pétrin passes, after two kilometres (1.2 miles), **Grand Bassin** (Ganga Talao as it is known to the Hindu community), a **lake** occupying the crater of an extinct volcano.

When indentured labourers started to arrive from India in the 1830s, what they missed most was the Ganges (Ganga), the sacred river of the Hindus, which, they believe, embodies purity and divinity. As it was impossible for the labourers to return to India to visit the Ganges, they brought the Ganges to Mauritius.

In 1897, Shri Jhummon Giri Gosagne, a Hindu priest in Mauritius, envisioned the waters of Grand Bassin coming from the Ganges. News of this dream spread quickly among the island's Hindu community, and the following year, during the festival of Maha Shivaratri, some pilgrims decided to trek to Grand Bassin to collect the lake's water to be offered to Lord Shiva.

Since then, an increasing number of Hin-

dus have made the pilgrimage to Grand Bassin every year during Maha Shivaratri. Over time, a number of **Hindu temples** and **shrines** have been built on the banks of Grand Bassin and, in 1972, some water from the sacred Ganges was poured into the lake. Since then, Grand Bassin has been known as Ganga Talao (the Lake of the Ganges).

The annual pilgrimage to Grand Bassin has become a very important feature in the religious calendar of the Mauritian Hindu community, and it is estimated that some 250,000 people join in every year.

Bois Chéri tea factory

From Grand Bassin, the twisting **B88** follows an **easterly** course through **tea plantations**, where women can be seen picking prized top leaves. An avenue of rich red cannas to the right indicates the entrance to the **Bois Chéri tea factory**.

Tours of the factory are willingly conducted. The tour includes the drying

Above: The Mahatma Gandhi Institute, established to promote Indian culture in Mauritius, lies just off the motorway en route to Moka.

rooms, the grade selection process (ten different grades of tea are produced), and the room where the leaves are packed into tea bags. The factory produces two types of tea — natural and vanilla — and exports to South Africa, France, and the United Kingdom.

From Bois Chéri, continue **eastwards**, pass through **Grand Bois** and, in under two kilometres (1.2 miles), you will reach the **A9**. Turning **north**, follow the road for five kilometres (three miles) until it meets the **A10,** and continue to head **north**. The A10 was the main road linking Mahébourg to Cure-pipe before the motorway was built. At **Seizème Mill**, **turn east** to join the **M2 motorway**, where the **signs** for Port Louis should be followed.

The motorway goes through **Phoenix**, which is twinned with Vacoas and is said to have been named after a 19th-century sugar estate and factory. It is now an important industrial town.

To the **east** of the Phoenix **roundabout** is Mauritius Breweries, which produces soft drinks and two international award-winning beers — Phoenix and Stella — as well as Guinness, under licence. Next door to the breweries is La Verrerie de Phoenix (The Phoenix Glassworks) — opened in February 1991 by Mauritius Breweries, Phoenix Camp Minerals, and the Centre d'Embouteillage Saint-Georges — which recycles the waste glass the companies produce.

La Verrerie is the only **glass-blowing factory** in Mauritius and has just three young blowers, trained by Belgian specialists, who produce up to 300 pieces a day; some blown, some moulded. The glassware produced comes in a wide range of colours — the green pieces are made from Sprite bottles, the brown ones from Phoenix beer bottles, and the clear pieces from Coca-Cola bottles. Powders are added to the clear glass to produce colours such as blue. Visitors to La Verrerie are very welcome. There is no entry fee, the blowers can be seen in action, and there is an adjoining showroom where a full range of glassware in different colours is on sale. The **road** leading to the **west** of the Phoenix **roundabout** takes you to the Mauritius Underwater Group (commonly called MUGS) headquarters. A large anchor has been laid to rest close to the clubhouse, which is no more than a large wooden hut.

MUGS
MUGS was founded in the early 1960s, when growing interest led local scuba-divers to believe that some sort of discipline and a set of standards should be imposed on the sport. As a result, MUGS is now affiliated to the British Sub Aqua Club (BSAC). MUGS really services Mauritian residents keen to scuba-dive — visitors to the island are likely to find the hotel dive centres and the independent operators on the coast more suited to their needs.

The MUGS premises are shared by the Mauritian Marine Conservation Society, which holds regular meetings and slide shows there. The society was set up to highlight awareness of damage to coral reefs. It aims to educate by slide shows and lectures, carry out marine surveys, and, in due course, establish marine parks — the first of which has been earmarked for Baie aux Tortues, in front of the Maritim Hotel on the west coast.

Next door to the MUGS clubhouse is the Phoenix Factory Shop, where locally produced clothes can be bought at discounted prices. Opposite the MUGS premises is a new Continent supermarket.

From the Phoenix **roundabout** continue **north**, following the **signs** to Port Louis. On the **opposite side** of the **motorway**, a mock Italian mansion-style building is a popular nightspot called Palladium.

At the next **roundabout**, just over two kilometres (1.2 miles) away, take the **first turning** towards **Le Réduit**, and the University of Mauritius campus is straight ahead. Set among a mix of modern and colonial university buildings are divisions of the Ministry of Agriculture and La Clinique Mauricienne, one of the top private medical clinics on the island. There is also a nice little **post office** housed in an old stone building.

To the west of the university is **Le Château de Réduit**, the official residence of the President, the gates to which are guarded by policemen.

Le Château — or Le Réduit (the Refuge), as it is now commonly known — was constructed in 1748 for French Governor Barthelemy David as a country residence and safe place for the families of French East India Company employees in the event of an invasion, although there are rumours that it was also built as a hiding place for one of his mistresses.

The original wooden château was subsequently damaged by cyclones and it is now made almost entirely of stone. When the railway lines opened in the 1860s, the governor had his own coach (now in the garden of the Naval and Historical Museum in Mahébourg), and a special stop was made at Le Réduit to allow the governor to board and alight.

The gardens of the château used to be open daily to the public, but these days they are only open on special occasions. Return to the Réduit **roundabout** on the

Above: Statue of the much-revered Mahatma Gandhi marks the entrance to the Mahatma Gandhi Institute near Moka.

motorway and follow the signs to Moka, which derives its name either from an important coffee trading town of the same name on the Red Sea or from a particular variety of coffee that used to grow in the area.

Off the motorway, en route to Moka, the road passes the Mahatma Gandhi Institute, established to promote Indian culture in Mauritius. Take the only left turning in Moka, and a signpost to the right indicates the way up to the mountain of Le Pouce. It is not difficult to walk up Le Pouce, especially if approached from the east. From Le Pouce, looking over the Pailles Valley, the views of Port Louis and its harbour are breathtaking.

Alternatively, if you carry straight on along the road, a private road on the left leads to Eureka, La Maison Creole, built in 1856 by an Englishman who sold it to Eugene Leclezio, the first Mauritian judge of the Supreme Court. A few years later it was put up for auction and his son, Henri Leclezio, speaker of the Legislative Council, put in a bid, crying 'Eureka' when his bid was accepted. Hence its name.

The younger Leclezio devoted his life to restoring Eureka into a home, which was to

Top: The Moka District Court House, a fine example of the colonial architecture still found in Mauritius. Above: Sign of the countryside — oxcart warning near Moka.

Top: The beautiful Eureka, or La Maison Creole, built in 1856, is now a museum and a stunning example of colonial architecture.

Above: Model of the now-extinct dodo at Eureka.

become the birthplace of his descendants. It remained a private home until 1986, when the Leclezio heirs turned the house into a museum and opened it to the public.

Eureka

Eureka is well worth a visit. With the Moka mountains rising steeply behind it and the front gardens tumbling down into a ravine, the house itself — constructed entirely of wood — is a stunning example of colonial architecture and has an amazing 109 doors. Inside, the high-ceilinged rooms contain fine examples of antique furniture that reflect the home's glorious past, as do the many photographs and paintings of days gone by.

From Eureka, take a **left turn** away from Moka and follow the **road** down to the **M2 motorway,** where a **right turn** leads back to Port Louis.

After five or six kilometres (three or four miles), as the road starts to descend into Port Louis, **Pailles,** which takes its name from a special grass that used to grow in this area and was used as fodder (*pailles*) to livestock in the Port Louis district, lies to the **east** of the motorway.

Domaine les Pailles

Follow the **signs** to **Domaine les Pailles,** a re-creation of Mauritius as it was in days of old. The Domaine includes a traditional **sugar cane mill** and an adjoining **distillery,** a **spice garden,** an **historic train** (in miniature), exquisitely fashioned replicas of 18th-century **horse-drawn carriages,** swimming pool, and a 'crazy golf' course. Visitors can also hop into Land Rovers to explore the nearby mountains where **deer, monkeys, white-tailed tropic birds,** and the rare **Mauritian kestrel** may be seen.

Les Écuries

Nearby are **Les Écuries** (The Stables), a well-equipped **equestrian centre** run by Remi Barrot, a former French national rider and a graduate of Saumur. Visitors to the centre can trek for a matter of hours or (once a month) overnight in the hills encircling Port Louis and participate in dressage and show-jumping lessons. An instructor is also on hand to teach those interested in learning to drive horse-drawn carriages. East of Les Écuries, a new **racetrack** to challenge the Champs de Mars in Port Louis is in the early stages of development.

Also in Domaine les Pailles are five restaurants, two housed in exact reproductions of colonial architecture, which offer a range of French, Indian, Chinese, Creole, and Italian cuisines. For evening entertainment, a jazz band plays in the French restaurant every Wednesday, Friday, and Saturday. The Indian restaurant has traditional ghazal music on the last Saturday of the month, and the Italian pizzeria plays host to a modern pop and rock band on Saturdays. The Grand Casino du Domaine is located in the same building as the Chinese restaurant. From Pailles, return to the **M2 motorway** and the suburbs of the capital are almost immediately north.

Above: A popular equestrian centre on Mauritius, Les Écuries, at Domaine les Pailles.

Opposite top: Fine lines of the casino at Domaine les Pailles.

Opposite: Spectacular views abound from Domaine les Pailles.

The Islands: A World of Their Own

Rodrigues

Rodrigues is the small, quiet, and often forgotten younger sister of Mauritius. There, insular island life continues at such an unhurried pace, so undisturbed by modern distractions, that Rodrigues is often compared to the Mauritius of several decades ago.

There is reason to believe that Arab explorers were the first to set eyes on the island now called Rodrigues. On the world map drawn up by cartographer Cantino in 1502, Rodrigues is marked as Dina Arobi, probably a corruption of the Arabic *diva harab* (desert isle).

The first European to espy the island was Portuguese adventurer Diego Rodriguez, after whom it is named, in 1528 — nearly 30 years after the Portuguese discovery of Mauritius. It was another 10 years before Rodrigues made its first appearance on Portuguese maps. However, the Dutch are believed to have been the first to go ashore in September 1601. The reasons why Rodrigues remained untouched by man for so long include its small size, its mid-oceanic isolation and the formidable reef that surrounds it, making access by sailing ship extremely hazardous.

The French took formal possession of Bourbon (now Réunion) and Rodrigues in 1638, just as the Dutch were establishing their first settlement on Mauritius, but they did not immediately colonize the island.

The first settlement on Rodrigues resulted from an unusual series of events. In 1685, the Edict of Nantes, which 87 years earlier had granted religious freedom to Protestants in France, was revoked and resulted in many Huguenots (French Protestants) fleeing their homeland in fear of Roman Catholic persecution.

In 1689, a plan was developed whereby 10 Frenchmen, led by François Leguat,

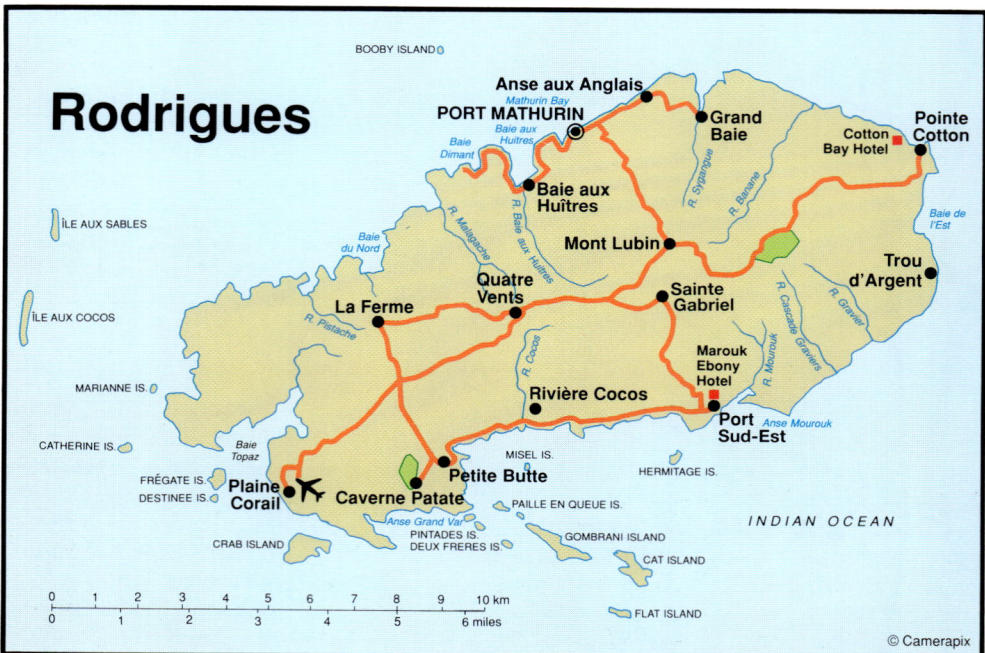

Rodrigues

would found a Huguenot utopia on Bourbon. Once settled, they were to be joined, within two years, by more Huguenot refugees.

The ship bearing the 10 men finally set sail in 1691, but bad weather prevented it from reaching either Bourbon or Mauritius and instead it went on to Rodrigues. The men waited two years for more Huguenot refugees to arrive, but none ever did. At first, the 10 were happy with their lot. Thanks to copious supplies of food already on the island — fish, crayfish, oysters, turtles, birds, wild fruit, and vegetables — they did not go hungry. Neither did they go thirsty: fresh water from the island's streams and a crude wine they made from coconut milk provided sufficient drinks.

However, after two years, the Huguenots began to long for some female company, so they built a boat of sorts and successfully sailed to Mauritius. There they were initially welcomed by the Dutch, but then the latter became suspicious of the refugees and imprisoned them. After some time the French were sent to the East Indies, from where they finally made their way back to Europe.

Leguat wrote a vivid account of this adventure, entitled *Voyage et Aventures de François Leguat & de ses Compagnons en Deux Îles Désertés des Indes Orientales,* which was published in book form in 1708.

In 1725, Desforges-Boucher, Governor of Bourbon, read Leguat's book and was inspired to send an official French colonization party to Rodrigues in Louis XV's name. The settlement, whose inhabitants were ordered to catch tortoises as food for the settlers on Île de France (as Mauritius was then called) and for visiting French ships, failed and it was not until 1750 that a permanent French colony was established on Rod-rigues.

The French settlement, numbering hardly more than 100 residents, including slaves, lasted until 1809 when the British seized the island and used it as a base from which to launch attacks on Île de France. The latter was successfully annexed the following year and, in the 1814 Treaty of Paris, Britain officially took possession of the renamed Mauritius and Rodrigues islands.

Rodrigues, however, was neglected by the British governors, whose attention was focused on Mauritius. It was not until 1882 that a governor even deigned to set foot on the island.

After 1810, Rodrigues was administered by the most senior settler on the island. His workload was not demanding. The population, just under 200 in 1838, led a simple life dedicated to producing salted fish and rearing pigs and poultry for consumption in Mauritius.

By the end of the 19th century, even though the population of Rodrigues had grown to more than three thousand, its links with Mauritius were still tenuous. In fact, Rodrigues received so little support from the main island that it was, on occasion, threatened with famine.

Rodrigues continued to be administered as a dependency of Mauritius until independence in 1968. It is now represented by two members in the Legislative Assembly. The Mauritian government has a Ministry of Rodrigues that appoints an Island Secretary to look after the 35,000 Rodriguans.

As a result of the island's settlement pattern, and in stark contrast to the Indian dominance of Mauritius, Rodrigues's population is mainly of European and African stock, the latter being descendants of slaves brought over by the early French settlers. Several languages are spoken, but Creole, French, and English dominate. Roughly 95 per cent are Roman Catholic.

Of volcanic origin, Rodrigues is the youngest of the three Mascarene islands, being only one and a half million years old. It is also the smallest, being just 108 square kilometres (42 square miles) in size, 16.5 kilometres (10.2 miles) long, and 7.5 kilometres (4.6 miles) wide.

Rodrigues is the most easterly of the three Mascarene islands, and the most isolated. The nearest land mass is Mauritius, 653 kilometres (405 miles) to the west. To the east, the western coast of Australia is several thousand kilometres away.

The geography is quite similar to that of Mauritius but the island boasts a unique system of limestone caves. The island is dominated by a central ridge about 10 kilometres (6.2 miles) long that tapers off in the

west into a coral plain, but there is nothing that can be called a mountain. Mont Limon, at 396 metres (1,300 feet), is the highest point on the island.

Despite the relatively low altitude, there is a dearth of flat terrain because a series of deep ravines stem from the central ridge to both the north and the south. These ravines open up into valleys that range in width from 200 metres (650 feet) at Anse Mourouk to 400 metres (1,300 feet) at Rivière Coco. In order to provide adequate land for building development, a number of extensive reclamation projects have been initiated along the northern coastline close to the capital of Port Mathurin.

Its coast is not particularly rugged, but there are only a few good sandy beaches and just one fine harbour, at Port Mathurin. The island is protected by an all-embracing coral reef that has a few narrow openings, just two of which can be navigated, and then only at some risk.

Originally, Rodrigues was thickly forested, but an extensive programme of felling trees for timber in the period immediately after 1750 and, more recently, over-grazing, have wiped out the original plant community. Secondary growth is limited.

At least eight endemic plant species have become extinct and only 38 species or subspecies of endemic flowering plants survive. Of these, 21 are endangered, seven vulnerable (likely to become endangered), and eight rare. About 64 hectares (158 acres) of Rodrigues are now protected in two nature reserves, where very rare plants such as the *café marron* (only four plants are known to exist — two in Rodrigues, two in London's Kew Gardens) and *bois pasner* are to be found.

There have been attempts at reafforestation and a great number of acacia trees have been planted. However, far from preventing soil erosion, these trees, given the rather melodic name of *picon loulou* by the islanders, grow fast and create extensive shade because of the wide span of their branches, which results in nothing being able to grow around them. Soil erosion is, therefore, aggravated. Most of the island's rugged landscape is now barren, but it displays warm hues that are predominantly yellow and brown.

Offshore, Rodrigues is surrounded by a huge lagoon of about 200 square kilometres (77 square miles), stunning not only because of its size, which is roughly twice that of the island itself, but also because of the many colours — yellows, greens, blues, and black — reflected in its waters. More than a dozen islets dot the lagoon, of which two, Île aux Cocos and Île aux Sables, are nature reserves, being important breeding grounds for four tern species.

The island has some interesting natural fauna, such as birds, lizards, snakes, and other reptiles, but there used to be many more. Rodrigues was once home to 16 endemic species of reptiles, birds, and bats. Now, just 300 years after the island was first colonized by man, only three remain — the Rodrigues fruit bat, the Rodrigues fody, and the Rodrigues brush warbler. All three have been close to extinction as a result of destruction of their habitat. Today, while their numbers are either steady or show an upward trend due to the better protection of their habitats, they are still endangered.

Thousands of giant tortoises used to inhabit the island. Alfred North-Coombes wrote: 'Giant tortoises take 30 to 40 years to reach maturity and may live for as long as two to three hundred years. It was only the isolated position of these islands, the absence of man and natural enemies, which favoured this development to an almost fabulous extent. Indeed, Leguat says that they were so numerous at Rodrigues "that sometimes you see two or three thousand of them in a flock; so that you may go above a hundred paces on their backs . . . without setting foot on the ground".' It is estimated that, from 1750, not less than 10,000 giant tortoises a year were hunted as a precious source of food for the inhabitants and ships' crews. Eventually, they became extinct around 1800.

A flightless bird, the solitaire, which evolved on Rodrigues, also became extinct

Opposite: Some fine, sandy streches of beach can be found on Rodrigues, which is protected by an all-embracing coral reef.

Above: Rodriguan fishermen display their catch.

around 1770 because of both ruthless hunting and its natural habitat being systematically destroyed. Turtles and dugongs used to abound in the seas off Rodrigues, large numbers of the former appearing on the beaches to lay their eggs, but no longer.

From this beautiful, but somewhat desolate landscape, the Rodriguans manage to eke out a basic living from subsistence — and some commercial — farming and fishing, as well as a fledgling tourism industry.

Getting there

Rodrigues, 653 kilometres (405 miles) east of Mauritius, can be reached by air and by sea. A return daily flight from SSR International Airport in Mauritius conveys passengers to Rodrigues. During the peak tourist season, this service is increased — on most days of the week — to two flights a day. The journey, in an ATR 42 turboprop plane, takes an hour and a half.

The *Mauritius Pride* ferry sails from Port Louis to Rodrigues two or three times a month, but on no fixed schedule. Regulars advise those contemplating the ferry journey to fly to Rodrigues and go back by ferry to Mauritius as the trip to Rodrigues is against the prevailing winds and much rougher. For fares for the three classes on offer and departure dates, contact the Mauritius Shipping Corporation in Port Louis.

Getting around

There are various ways of getting around Rodrigues. The easiest is to join an organized tour or to hire a four-wheel-drive car with or without a driver–guide, as there is only a limited bus service, which starts at 0545 and ends at 1730.

Rodrigues is also an ideal place to put on walking boots, pack a picnic in a rucksack, and spend several hours hiking on hilltops. En route, walkers will be captivated by the scenery, charmed by the friendliness of the local people, and, because of the island's small size, need never worry about getting lost.

When to go

Rodriguan summers (October to April) are hot and wet. Winters (May to September)

Above: Rodrigues is well known for its basketry, produced on the roadside by a number of artisans.
Overleaf: Although a tiny town, the Rodrigues capital, Port Mathurin, is the heart and soul of the isle.

are warm and dry. Scuba-divers should note that the one diving centre is closed during July and August.

Where to stay
There are only three hotels of note on Rodrigues. The more up-market Cotton Bay Hotel is on the east coast at Pointe Cotton, the smaller Marouk Ebony Hotel is on the south coast at Paté Reynieux and Beau Soleil Hotel is in Port Mathurin. In addition, several guesthouses operate in and around Port Mathurin. See Listings.

Sightseeing
The easiest place to start a tour of Rodrigues is the capital, **Port Mathurin.** Located on the northern coast, it is a tiny town recognized as the heart and soul of the isle. The official residence of the island secretary, the island's administrative offices, and the sea port are all located there.

It is worth spending some time wandering around Port Mathurin to admire the **island secretary's house** and the few other colonial homes remaining, and to visit a number of **shops** selling local handicrafts.

Since 1989, Rodrigues has had its own Craft-Aid, managed by Paul Draper, the Englishman who founded the original workshop of the same name in Rose Hill, Mauritius. The Craft-Aid shop is in Jenner Street, while the production centre, which employs some 20 people, is located in Victoria Street. However, a new centre at Camp du Roi on the outskirts of Port Mathurin opened some time in 1994. The Craft-Aid employees produce leaf collages, coconut jewellery, potpourri, wooden furniture, and parts for model ship factories, most of which can be found on sale in the shop.

The Port Mathurin **market** is worth a visit, particularly very early on Saturday morning, when it is at its most colourful. It is important to get to the capital relatively early on any day of the week, because the town closes down around 1500 and is fast asleep no later than about 1800, except on Friday night, when it is likely to be quiet

by 2100. About two kilometres (1.2 miles) to the **east** of Port Mathurin is **Anse aux Anglais,** once considered a desirable place to live, and **Grand Baie,** where there is a well-sheltered beach. While driving to Grand Baie, watch out for the cattle that wander across the roads and marvel at the sure-footed goats that cling to rocky outcrops high up on the hillside.

A couple of kilometres to the **west** of the capital is **Baie aux Hûitres** (Oyster Bay), where the local fishing community lives and substantial stretches of land have been reclaimed but have yet to be developed.

Further along the coast road, at **Baie Diamant,** there are extensive mangrove swamps.

From Port Mathurin it is a steep, twisting three to four kilometre (1.8 to 2.4 mile) drive up a **narrow road** to **Mont Lubin,** the second largest settlement after the capital, and probably the most visited town purely because it is in the island's centre and acts as an intersection from where roads run north to Port Mathurin, east to Pointe Cotton, south to Port Sud-Est, and west to the airport at Plaine Corail.

Take the road **east** and just outside Mont Lubin lies **Mont Limon,** the highest point on the island. It is worth the short but steep scramble up from the road to the top, from where it is possible to enjoy a 360-degree panorama of Rodri-gues and its surrounding lagoon.

Continue along the road to '**Atelier des Frères Leopold**' in **Palissades,** where any number of workers can be seen producing the basketry for which Rodrigues is well known. A wide range of goods such as hats, mats, bags, and panniers, is produced from local vetiver, aloe, and vacoas plants.

Proceeding towards **Pointe Cotton,** the road twists and turns, rises and falls, passing general stores but no villages of any great size. Rather than living collectively, the people tend to live at a distance from one another, surrounded by the plots of land on which they subsist. This pattern of settlement is most evident just after sunset, when numerous lights appear widely scattered over the landscape.

This particular habit has led to problems as far as the installation of utilities is con-cerned, but gradually more and more dwellings are being introduced to the modern world. For example, in 1972 only 0.6 per cent of the island's households had electricity, compared with 70 per cent in 1990, though this has led to a proliferation of unattractive overhead power lines that criss-cross Rodrigues and link the remote homesteads to the electricity supply.

Some of the island's electricity (less than 10 per cent) is produced by **wind turbines,** which stand close to the road at Trèfles. From this landmark it is all downhill to Pointe Cotton, where the Cotton Bay Hotel is located. This 48-room hotel offers a high standard of accommodation over-looking a sandy beach, and serves up some of the best Rodriguan cuisine. The Cotton Bay offers all the facilities expected of a good hotel, including a wide range of sporting activities, such as scuba-diving, tennis, volleyball, kayaking, and mountain biking.

Rodrigues is said to offer some of the best diving sites in Mauritius because of the island's isolation and the fact that the lagoon has not been subjected to fishing on a large commercial scale. Traditionally, fishing activities are limited to small wooden boats, propelled by poles. In addition, lagoon fishing is controlled so that nets are only used for six months a year, giving the fish time to reproduce. As a result, the outer reef, in particular, is totally unspoilt and teems with underwater life.

According to Neill Ions, the diving instructor at **La Licorne,** the only **diving centre** on the island, diving falls into two broad categories: inside the lagoon and outside. He describes dives inside as 'typically deep ravines gouged into the reef by centuries of tidal erosion, characterized by strong currents and visibility rarely more than 15 metres (50 feet). They are not all suitable for beginners, but they form the main fish feeding grounds and the rewards that go to those willing to brave the elements amount to a visual extravaganza. Vertical, coral-lined cliff wall overhangs, deep chasms weird rock formations and

Opposite: Squid hangs to dry on Rodrigues, many of whose residents make their living from the sea.

complex cave systems can be found.' The coral reef of the outer lagoon is pristine. T V Bulpin writes in his book *Islands in a Forgotten Sea*, 'In these jewellery boxes of the sea there is a fantastic variety of strange and colourful creatures. In fact, there can be few places on earth inhabited more densely than the dreamlike jungles of these coral reefs.'

From Pointe Cotton, **Trou d'Argent,** considered by many as the most beautiful spot on Rodrigues, can be reached by various transport methods. It is possible to make the whole journey on foot (the return trip taking three hours), to take a mountain bike as far as the hamlet of St François and then walk (a two-hour trip), or to take a boat as far as St François and then walk (another two-hour trip). At Trou d'Argent, expect to be inspired by dramatic cliff faces, a sea-coloured spectrum of greens and blues flecked with white, and the fresh sea breeze.

To reach the south coast from Pointe Cotton, it is necessary to drive back up to Mont Lubin and then down the **road** to **Port Sud-Est.** En route from Mont Lubin, stop at the small village of **Saint Gabriel,** the heart of the Roman Catholic Church.

Work started on the **church,** or 'cathedral' as it is sometimes called, in 1934 and, due to a few hiccups along the way and to its ambitious dimensions, it was finished only in 1941. Specially trained donkeys and hundreds of volunteers carried the sand, cement, lime, timber, blocks of coral for the walls and corrugated iron for the roof to their present resting place, 300 metres (984 feet) above sea level. The church stands 50 metres (164 feet) long by 19 metres (62 feet) wide and is 15 metres (49 feet) high, with twin towers 16 metres (52 feet) high. There is seating for 1,750 worshippers and standing room for another 250.

On Sundays, it is impossible, immediately before or after the service, to drive down to Saint Gabriel because the road is full of worshippers walking to and from the church. However, it is well worth a visit on the Sabbath, if only to watch the multitude of young men lined up to admire the pretty young girls closely guarded by their mothers. As the Rodriguan society is very conservative, this is usually the only chance that the boys and girls get to see one another away from home. From Saint Gabriel, the five-kilometre (three-mile) **road** down to Port Sud-Est has panoramic **vistas** of the southern coast and the many islets in the extensive offshore lagoon, while *paille-en-queue* **(white-tailed tropic birds),** with their distinctive long white tails, fly around the inland valleys. The views are breathtaking.

Once in Port Sud-Est, a small fishing village, the main attraction is the scores of women who, wearing large rubber boots and carrying a pronged harpoon, wade through the lagoon at low tide hunting octopus.

To the east of Port Sud-Est is **Paté Reynieux,** where the Marouk Ebony Hotel is situated. With only 30 rooms, this hotel is smaller than the Cotton Bay and offers a more limited number of amenities, but it does have a swimming pool and, among other facilities, provides for mountain biking and watersports, such as windsurfing and kayaking.

To the **west** of Port Sud-Est, the **road** hugs the coast, passing through tiny fishing hamlets where small wooden boats are pulled up onto land once the day's work is done. Outside the houses, octopuses are hung up to dry. The octopus, a speciality in Rodrigues, is collected all year round for export to Mauritius. In 1991, around 600 tons of this delicacy were dispatched to the main island.

Many of the houses are built with white blocks made of coral fashioned from quarries in Petite Butte. Huge slabs of coral are extracted from the quarry face and then sawn into blocks, currently sold at Rs10 each.

From Petite Butte the **road** heads inland in a **northerly** direction. Watch out for a **rough track** to the **left** (west) side of the road from Petite Butte, which leads to **Caverne Patate.**

The cave is entered through a hole in the middle of a field and the 20- to 30-minute walk along the cave reveals some amazing stalactite and stalagmite formations, many of which have been given names by the locals. Look closely, for example, and there

Above: Visitors stroll along the white beach of Île aux Cos, a small island off of Rodrigues.

is Winston Churchill (without his cigar), the leaning Tower of Pisa, an elephant, and a puppy. The cave is open to visitors twice a day, at 1000 and at 1300. Permits have to be obtained from the island's administrative offices in Port Mathurin. Visitors should ensure they carry a powerful electric torch with them.

From Caverne Patate follow the **road,** via either **La Ferme** or **Quatre Vents,** to **Mont Lubin,** about 13 kilometres (eight miles) from the cave. From Mont Lubin, the way is **signposted** back to Port Mathurin.

One excursion must be made from Port Mathurin. **Île aux Cocos,** a **nature reserve** and **bird sanctuary,** is a slow, enjoyable 90-minute ride as the local sailors skilfully guide the boat through the shallow waters of the lagoon that surround Rodrigues. En route, the crew trail lines behind the boat hoping to catch fish for lunch. Just in case they fail to get a bite, a feast of fresh lobster, fish, and chicken is brought from Rodrigues and barbecued on the beach once the boat has arrived at Île aux Cocos.

Then there is time for an hour-long walk around the sandy perimeter of the island. It is possible to see the remains of the **coconut plantation,** after which the island is named, and to admire the picturesque barren slopes of Rodrigues from afar, all the while being dive-bombed by any number of terns and numerous other seabirds.

Before catching the boat back to Port Mathurin, make time for a quick dip in the crystal-clear waters surrounding Île aux Cocos.

Evening entertainment is limited on Rodrigues, for most inhabitants tend to rise before daybreak and retire early. However, there are four restaurants in Port Mathurin (Le Solitaire, Le Capitaine, Le Paille-en-Queue, and Le Lagon Bleu); one in Mont Lubin (Phoenix D'Or); and one in Mangues (John Resto Pub), where it might be worth trying to get a meal fairly soon after sunset.

The two hotels, the Cotton Bay Hotel and the Marouk Ebony Hotel, probably make greater efforts to offer typically Rodriguan dishes than do the restaurants. They also make greater use of the wide range of fresh seafood on offer. The few evening events of interest to visitors include the traditional dance nights every Thursday organized at the old-style Creole home of Ben Gontran in Port Mathurin. A band — an accordionist usually accompanied by triangle and maracas players — sets the pace, while instructed by Ben, pairs of dancers two-step their way around the floor. The music and the sound of dancing feet on the wooden floor boards create quite a cacophony. The dances, such as mazurkas and quadrilles, include the sega and some influenced by European numbers. The dancing starts at about 1930 and lasts for an hour. Tourists are welcome to watch or join in the action. Friday is the one night of the week when Port Mathurin really comes alive. The place to be is Le Solitaire, where the weekly sega show is followed by a disco. There is also a night-club at Baie aux Huitres called Vibrason.

Cargados Carajos Archipelago (St Brandon)

From the middle of the 16th century, this archipelago appeared on Portuguese maps as Sao Brandao. The origin of this name is unknown. The Portuguese also called the islands Cargados Carajos. The Portuguese *coroa dos garajaos* translates into English as the reef of the garajaos, a particular type of seabird. The islands did indeed teem with sea-birds and, in the 19th century, guano was the islands' main export. Since the 1830s, however, the rich fishing grounds offshore have been of greater importance.

Getting there

The Cargados Carajos, 370 kilometres (230 miles) north-east of Mauritius, is not tourism-oriented. A visitor's permit is needed from the Outer Island Development Corporation, and this is not usually granted to women. The corporation will also assist with travel and accommodation requirements, which are likely to revolve around a private yacht charter, although, on very rare occasions, passengers can board the fishing boats around the islands.

When to go

As a non-tourism island, no particular season is recommended, although the 'winter' months of May to September are warm and dry.

Where to stay

There is no tourist accommodation.

Sightseeing

The Cargados Carajos is an archipelago of 22 coral atolls (usually referred to as St Brandon, the main island's name). Due to their coral formation, the scenery is very different from that of volcanic Mauritius.

The islands are flat, have white sand beaches and, as there is very little soil, the vegetation consists mainly of scrub, casuarina trees, and coconut palms. A number of islands are so low that the high tide sometimes swallows them.

The three main islands are Cocos in the south, Albatross in the north, and, in between, Raphael. The last, sometimes known as Establishment Island, is the administrative centre, inhabited by men employed by a Mauritian company to fish the offshore waters. There is also a meteorological station. No women are allowed on the island. There are excellent scuba-diving sites off the archipelago.

Agalega

Agalega's name is derived from the fact that the discoverer, Juan de Nova, came from Spain's north-western province of Galicia: A'galega means Galician.

When the British acquired Mauritius in 1810 at the end of the Napoleonic Wars, Agalega was occupied by a French privateer who had been granted a licence by the last French governor, General Decaen, to set up a coconut plantation worked by Malagasy slaves. Because of the importance of coconut oil to the Mauritian economy, the concession holder was also allowed to pursue non-agricultural work.

Mauritian and Seychellois companies exploited Agalega from the 1930s to 1975, when the Mauritian Government took

Above: Many inhabitants of Agalega make their living on the coconut plantations, which provide the main source of copra to Mauritius.

control. Seven years later, the Outer Island Development Corporation was formed, and it now runs Agalega and all the other Mauritian islands, except Mauritius itself and Rodrigues.

Getting there
Agalega, 1,200 kilometres (745 miles) north of Mauritius, has no tourism potential. A visitor's permit is needed from the Outer Island Development Corporation, who will assist with travel and accommodation arrangements, mainly a private yacht charter, or — on rare occasions — a fishing trip.

When to go
No particular season is recommended, but the 'winter' months of May to September are warm and dry.

Where to stay
There is no tourist accommodation.

Sightseeing
The two coral islands — **North** and **South** — lie only 560 kilometres (348 miles) south of Seychelles. The islands are separated by a 2.5-kilometre (1.5-mile) sand bank that can be crossed at low tide; but, taken as one, Agalega is roughly 24 kilometres (15 miles) long, and never more than 3.5 kilometres (two miles) wide.

The tallest points are 15-metre-high (50-foot-high) sand dunes; there is next to no soil on the island. The only vegetation is scrub and coconut trees.

The 400 or so inhabitants live in either of two settlements, **La Fourche** and **Vingt Cinq,** on North Island, and divide their time between work on the **coconut plantations,** which are the main source of copra to Mauritius, and fishing.

There is a **meteorological station** at **Port Sainte Rita** on South Island.

PART THREE: THE CAPITAL

Above: Port Louis street vendor displays his colourful wares.

Opposite: The towering Pieter Both peak, with sprawling Port Louis in the background.

Port Louis: A Mix of Old and New

Although the Dutch landed on the south-east coast when they first visited Mauritius in 1598, subsequent exploration revealed that the north-west coast offered equally safe anchorage on the leeward side. The latter point was of great importance in the days of sailing ships, for it made putting out to sea so much easier.

The Dutch called their landing point on the north-west Melukesereede (Turtle Bay) because of the large number of turtles and tortoises ('as fat as pigs', according to the diary of Matelief de Jonge) found there.

However, disaster struck when Pieter Both, the first governor of the Dutch East Indies, was on a trip back to the Netherlands. His ship put in just south of Melukesereede at the inlet now known as Baie du Tombeau in February 1615. A storm blew up, the ship was wrecked, and Both was drowned.

This catastrophe made the Dutch wary of anchoring on the north-west coast and so when they came to establish a permanent settlement in 1638, Warwyck Bay, their original south-east coast landing point, was chosen as the preferred site.

However, the first Dutch governor, Cornelius Simonsz Gooyer, realized that enemy vessels planning an attack on the island were likely to make use of the sheltered north-west and so he established a small garrison there. On early Dutch maps, the present site of Port Louis is marked as Noord-Wester Haven (North-Western Haven).

The French settlers arriving in 1722, under the command of Monsieur Denyon, renamed the two Dutch harbours: Warwyck Bay became Port Bourbon and Noord-Wester Haven became Port Louis. It is possible that Port Louis was named either in honour of Louis XV (still a child at the time) or after Port Louis in Brittany, from which many French sailors, who had set sail for India via Mauritius, came. Or perhaps it was a combination of the two.

It was Denyon's successor, Nicolas de Maupin, who decided that Port Louis offered far greater possibilities as a harbour than Port Bourbon, and he moved the French East India Company seat to the north-western settlement. However, it was De Maupin's successor, the Comte de La Bourdonnais, who really developed the potential of Port Louis after his arrival in 1735. La Bourdonnais found Port Louis 'in exactly the same state as nature had first formed it'. The site was not particularly promising as it was divided by a swampy gully. Furthermore, much of the land was covered in dense vegetation.

Only one area had been cleared, the present Place d'Armes, and around it were crowded some 60 or so French East India Company huts. La Bourdonnais soon built a well-equipped and well-protected port and naval base. He then set about demolishing the old huts and replacing them with stone buildings. It was under La Bourdonnais that a degree of civilized life finally evolved in Port Louis.

The Seven Years' War (1756-1763) established the importance of Port Louis as a base from which to attack the British in India. It also led to Port Louis becoming a haven for privateers. In other words, Mauritius-based vessels were given permission to prey on ships flying the British flag. In 1767, when the French crown took control of Île de France (as Mauritius was then known) from the French East India Company, two administrators — Daniel Dumas and Pierre Poivre — arrived. The latter soon realized that Port Louis needed to be improved and, before his departure in 1772, delapidated buildings were repaired and the silted harbour dredged. In addition, trees were planted, footpaths constructed, and roads paved. Vicomte de Souillac, who governed Île de France from

Overleaf: Battered through the years by cyclones and hurricanes, the capital of Mauritius, Port Louis, survives and continues is dynamic growth as it sprawls along the coast and reaches ever deeper inland.

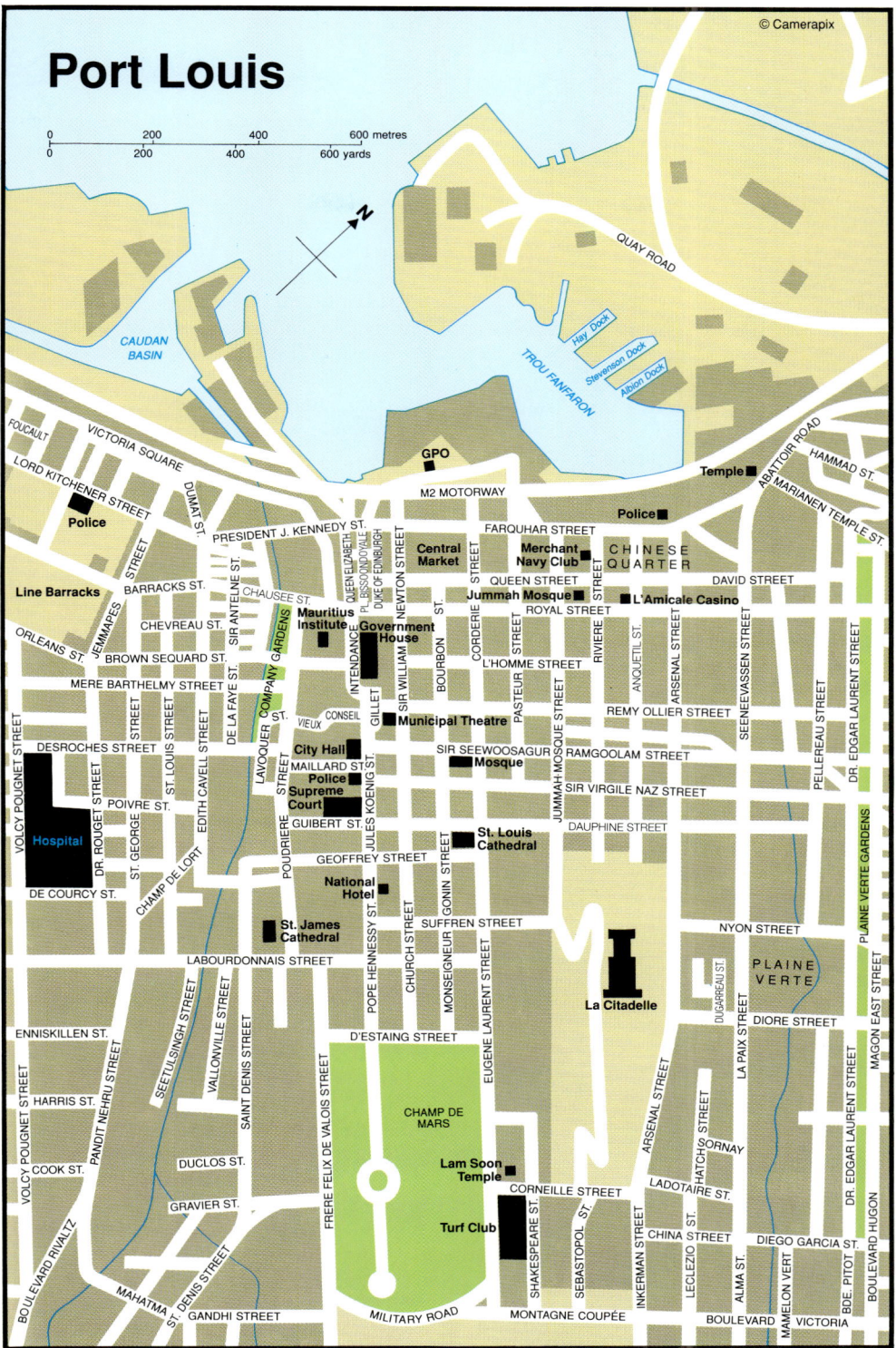

Port Louis

© Camerapix

0 | 200 | 400 | 600 metres
0 | 200 | 400 | 600 yards

N

CAUDAN BASIN

QUAY ROAD

TROU FANFARON

Hay Dock
Stevenson Dock
Albion Dock

GPO

Temple

M2 MOTORWAY

Police

HAMMAD ST.
ABATTOIR ROAD
MARIANEN TEMPLE ST.

FOUCAULT
VICTORIA SQUARE
LORD KITCHENER STREET
Police
DUMAT ST.
PRESIDENT J. KENNEDY ST.
FARQUHAR STREET

STREET
BARRACKS ST.
Line Barracks
JEMMAPES
CHAUSSEE ST.
Central Market
Merchant Navy Club
CHINESE QUARTER
DAVID STREET

CHEVREAU ST.
SIR ANTELNE ST.
QUEEN ELIZABETH
PL BISSONDOYALE
DUKE OF EDINBURGH
NEWTON STREET
CORDERIE STREET
Jummah Mosque
QUEEN STREET
L'Amicale Casino

ORLEANS ST.
BROWN SEQUARD ST.
Mauritius Institute
INTENDANCE
Government House
BOURBON
ROYAL STREET
RIVIERE
ANQUETIL ST.
ARSENAL STREET
SEENEEVASSEN STREET
PELLEREAU STREET
DR. EDGAR LAURENT STREET

MERE BARTHELMY STREET
DE LA FAYE ST.
COMPANY GARDENS
LAVOQUER STREET
VIEUX CONSEIL
SIR WILLIAM
GILLET
L'HOMME STREET
PASTEUR
REMY OLLIER STREET

DESROCHES STREET
DR. ROUGET STREET
ST. LOUIS STREET
EDITH CAVELL STREET
Municipal Theatre
SIR SEEWOOSAGUR
Mosque
JUMMAH MOSQUE STREET
RAMGOOLAM STREET
SIR VIRGILE NAZ STREET

POIVRE ST.
City Hall
MAILLARD ST.
Police
Supreme Court
JULES KOENIG ST.
DAUPHINE STREET

Hospital
ST. GEORGE
CHAMP DE LORT
POUDRIERE STREET
GUIBERT STS.
GEOFFREY STREET
St. Louis Cathedral

DE COURCY ST.
National Hotel
POPE HENNESSY ST.
GONIN ST.
NYON STREET

St. James Cathedral
LABOURDONNAIS STREET
SUFFREN STREET
CHURCH STREET
MONSEIGNEUR
EUGENE LAURENT STREET
La Citadelle
DUGARREAU ST.
PLAINE VERTE
MAGON EAST STREET
PLAINE VERTE GARDENS

ENNISKILLEN ST.
SEETULSINGH STREET
VALLONVILLE STREET
D'ESTAING STREET
ARSENAL STREET
LA PAIX STREET
DIORE STREET
DR. EDGAR LAURENT STREET

HARRIS ST.
PANDIT NEHRU STREET
SAINT DENIS STREET
CHAMP DE MARS
HATCH STREET
SORNAY
BOULEVARD HUGON

VOLCY POUGNET STREET
COOK ST.
DUCLOS ST.
Lam Soon Temple
CORNEILLE STREET
LADOTAIRE ST.
CHINA STREET
DIEGO GARCIA ST.

BOULEVARD RIVALTZ
GRAVIER ST.
Turf Club
SHAKESPEARE ST.
SEBASTOPOL ST.
INKERMAN STREET
LECLEZIO ST.
ALMA ST.
MAMELON VERT
BDE. PITOT

MAHATMA
ST. DENIS STREET
GANDHI STREET
MILITARY ROAD
MONTAGNE COUPÉE
BOULEVARD VICTORIA

Above: Port Louis' 19th-century fortress, La Citadelle, now restored, stages pop concerts.
Opposite: Port Louis, with its bustling port, is surrounded by a backdrop of green-cloaked hills.

1779 to 1787, oversaw many changes in Port Louis, including the construction of La Chaussée — a causeway that crossed the swampy gully and united the two parts of Port Louis. Today, La Chaussée is one of the city's main streets.

Port Louis had been made a free port in 1770, causing prosperity to reach new levels. This boom continued throughout the War of American Independence (1778-1783), when privateering once again flourished.

However, it was during the French Revolution that Port Louis really became a 'nest of corsairs'. Between 1793 and 1802, 119 foreign vessels with booty valued at around UK£ 2,500,000 were seized and brought to Port Louis.

General Charles Decaen arrived in 1803 to take control of Île de France and decided to fortify Port Louis, which he renamed Port Napoleon. However, his fortifications did not stop the British from conquering the island in 1810, when Port Napoleon once again became Port Louis. Sir Robert

Farquhar, the first British governor, rebuilt some streets and restored its churches.

Auguste Billiard, a French traveller, wrote a detailed account of Port Louis when he stayed there in 1817, noting that Port Louis was already an Eastern city, and he was right. Of the 25,000 inhabitants, only 3,000 were Europeans. The city was split into three main divisions: one for Europeans, one for coloured people and freed slaves, and one for Indians. There was also a small Chinese enclave. He noted that many led a luxurious lifestyle, there being a 'season', from June to October, when balls, festivities, plays, and race meetings took place.

Beginning in 1825, the many buildings of Port Louis that had been destroyed by the huge 1816 fire were rebuilt, and the market moved to its present position. In 1832, a general strike was organized to protest the arrival of John Jeremy, a prominent member of the British Anti-Slavery Society, which fought to abolish slavery in all British colonies. As a result, the following year

Above: The capital's busy port: export manufacturing plays a key role in the Mauritian economy.

Governor William Nicolay ordered Fort Adelaide (now also known as La Citadelle) to be built on a small hill in Port Louis as a measure to help control any future uprisings. The Commercial Bank, established in 1838, was not the first bank in Mauritius — a number had existed since 1812 — but it is the only one of the early banks that still survives and plays its part in the financial life of Port Louis.

Port Louis's municipal charter, published in December 1849, came into force on the first day of the following year. Municipal elections were held in February 1850 and the first mayor, Louis Lechelle, took office on 4 March.

Mauritius boomed in the 1850s and 1860s, thanks to great fortunes made from the sugar industry. Naturally, as the capital of the island, Port Louis benefited from this as shipping movements increased. The quays were extended, dry docks built to repair ships, and banks and commercial activity prospered. Between 1851 and 1861, the town's population increased from 49,909 to 74,128. Between 1866 and 1868

a mysterious disease, later identified as malaria, swept Port Louis, killing as many as 200 people a day, and many of the town's inhabitants fled to the highlands of Plaines Wilhems, which were, by then, easily accessible by train. As if that was not enough, four cyclones hit Port Louis shortly after the epidemic, the last one destroying 59 shops, 411 big houses, 477 smaller houses, and 1,319 huts. As a result, Port Louis went into decline as a middle and upper-class residential area, and its population fell from around 75,000 prior to the epidemic to 50,000 in 1918. The decline was compounded in the early 20th-century by its failure to make adequate port provision for steamers.

Today, like the phoenix rising from the ashes, Port Louis is again booming, reflecting Mauritius's rapid economic development, and it now has a population of over 130,000. Growth is not without problems, however. One of the most serious, an unlikely one on a tropical island, is congestion. Motor vehicles began to replace animal-drawn carriages after the First

Above: Port Louis is a city of contrasts, with modern skyscapers mixing with colonial mansions and traditional wooden houses.

World War, and their ever-increasing numbers now look set to choke the capital.

Port Louis is a city of contrasts; a mix of old and new. While modern skyscrapers dominate the centre, quiet backstreets are still filled with colonial mansions and traditional wooden houses with shady courtyards, providing pleasant respite from the city's hustle and bustle and the summer's scorching heat.

The island's one motorway runs through the capital — and it is not uncommon to see Indians pushing huge carts of fresh produce towards markets along it while brand new Mercedes and BMWs flash past. On the streets, hawkers, their cardboard boxes stuffed with goods, stand outside brand-new shopping arcades reminiscent of English suburbs.

At night Port Louis is very quiet. The capital's liveliest area is probably the Chinese Quarter, where entertainment is provided by the casino L'Amicale, and where the clientele play *quatre quatre* (fantan) endlessly. However, the renovated

Municipal Theatre may enliven the city in the evening.

Getting there

Port Louis is 17 kilometres (10.5 miles) from the main tourist centre at Grand Baie and 45 kilometres (28 miles) from SSR International Airport. A good motorway, the M2, runs from the airport to Port Louis.

When to go

The best months to visit Mauritius in general are April to June and September to November. However, during this period and the ensuing summer months until March, it is better to avoid the oppressive midday heat in Port Louis. Visit the city early in the morning or late in the afternoon. Note that Port Louis shops usually open between 0930 and 1700 from Monday to Friday, and between 0900 and 1200 on Saturday. Those interested in attending a race meeting should visit Mauritius in the winter months between May and October, the horse-racing season.

211

Above: A panoramic view of the nation's capital from La Citadelle, also known as Fort Adelaide.

Where to stay

There are a variety of good hotels including the 109-room La Bourdonnais on the waterfront which opened at the end of 1996 and hotel Le St Georges. The nearest beach hotel is the Maritim Hotel in Balaclava, a 12-kilometre (7.4 miles) drive away.

Sightseeing

An easy starting point for a tour of Port Louis is the majestic **General Post Office** (GPO) on the waterfront on the **western** side of the motorway. The GPO building, construction of which is believed to have started shortly after the British took possession of the island in 1810 but which was not completed before 1868, is a national monument.

When Sir William Gomm was appointed governor in 1842, he set about improving both internal and international postal communications. However, it was not until a postal ordinance came into effect at the beginning of February 1847 that the way was paved for the introduction of postage stamps and a network of inland post offices. On 21 September, 1847, Mauritius made history by becoming the first British colony to issue its own postage stamps. In 1875, there were 33 post offices in Mauritius and by 1964 there were many more as the closure of the railway lines resulted in some of the stations being converted into post offices.

To the **right** of the GPO there are several interesting **19th-century buildings,** most of them former warehouses. One, once a granary used for storing rice, is now the GPO's parcels building. There is also a **Philately Museum** in this complex with interesting displays of Mauritian and collector's stamps — with particular emphasis on stamps from the Indian Ocean region.

Directly opposite the GPO, across the motorway, is the fresh-meat section of the **Central Market** which is unmistakable by its smell. To the **south** of the market there are a number of **19th-century warehouses** where the Banque Nationale de Paris Intercontinentale, tourist **shops,** such as Argonaute and trendy clothes **shops,** like Équateur, Habit, and Pardon are located. The

Above: Storm clouds drift over the mountains behind Port Louis' waterfront.

heart of the city is **Place Sookdeo Bissoon-doyal,** commonly known by its old name, **Place d'Armes.** At the end of the Place, near the sea, is a **statue** of Comte de La Bourdonnais, the island's most famous colonial administrator. Just inland, there is an **inscription** and a Fleur de Lys commemorating the 250th anniversary of the founding of Port Louis in 1735.

Three **busts** of modern Mauritian politicians — Doctor Maurice Curé (founder of the Labour Party), Renganden Seeneevasen, and Emmanuel Anquetil — also stand there.

Parallel to the tree-lined Place d'Armes are the twin avenues named after Queen Elizabeth II and the Duke of Edinburgh. These avenues are flanked by some of the **oldest buildings** in Port Louis, as well as one of the newest — the monolithic headquarters of the State Bank of Mauritius on Queen Elizabeth Avenue.

Close to the State Bank are two beautiful examples of colonial architecture that have, fortunately, been preserved. One, tucked just behind and to the side of the State Bank, is the **IBL building** — IBL being a major Mauritian conglomerate — which is to the east of the other, the 19th-century **Mercantile Bank Building,** which now houses the Hong Kong Bank. Originally built as a private residence in about 1840, it has been a bank since the latter part of the 19th century. Mercantile Bank acquired The Bank of Mauritius in 1916. In 1959, Hong Kong Bank bought Mercantile. The name was changed in 1989. On the opposite side of the Place d'Armes, on Duke of Edinburgh Avenue, are the offices of British Airways and Singapore Airlines, as well as Carri Poule, one of the best Indian restaurants on the island. Along the central Place d'Armes is a taxi rank. At the head of the Place d'Armes is **Government House,** originally no more than a wooden hut covered with palm leaves.

Under Governor Nicolas de Maupin, in charge of the island between 1729 and 1735, a one-storey stone building called La Loge was built.

In 1738, La Bourdonnais added a second stone storey, two galleries on the front

wings facing the Place d'Armes, and two one-storey wings at the back. It was at this time that the building, the oldest one still intact in Mauritius, was renamed Hotel du Gouvernement or Government House. It remained the governor's residence until 1748, when Le Château de Réduit was built. All subsequent governors preferred the lower temperatures and substantial gardens at Réduit to the heat and humidity of Port Louis. Government House was subsequently repaired and extended, most notably under the first British governor, Sir Robert Farquhar, who oversaw the addition of a wing at the back as well as a large reception room in the left wing (later used by the Legislative Council). In 1883, the first telephone line connected Government House to Le Château de Réduit. Government House is still the seat of government, but parliamentary issues are debated in the modern Legislative Assembly Chamber just behind it.

In the **courtyard** of Government House is a **statue** of Queen Victoria. Originally erected in Victoria Square (now the southern bus terminus), the statue was moved to its present position after Queen Victoria's death in 1901.

Behind the memorial to Queen Victoria is a **statue** of Sir William Stevenson, governor from 1857 until his death in 1863. Arriving just a year after a serious outbreak of cholera, Stevenson insisted on reforming the island's quarantine system and enforcing its health laws. He also did a great deal of work for the island's youth, establishing an orphanage for 200 Indian children, reforming the education system, and increasing the number of government schools.

The **wrought iron gates** in front of Government House remain closed except on official occasions, such as the formal opening of the Legislative Assembly.

Facing Government House are two **statues** — one of Sir John Pope Hennessy, the British governor from 1883 to 1889, and the other of Sir William Newton (1842-1915), a British-trained barrister born in Port Louis. Both statues were originally unveiled on the Municipal Theatre site, but were moved to their present position early in the 20th-century.

Hennessy was responsible, in 1883, for installing a telephone system in Port Louis and, in 1885, electric lighting in the civilian hospital. He was popular among the people because he believed in giving the locals more responsibility. However, this policy lost him the support of his own officials and he was subjected to a commission of inquiry, which suspended him from duty. It was Newton, a member of the Council of Government, who, in 1886, was sent to London to defend Hennessy, which he did successfully. Hennessy was reinstated and spent the last year of his administration encouraging agriculture, particularly tea production.

Nearby, on the corner of La Chaussée and Intendance Street, stand the **Treasury Buildings,** which date back to the 1880s. Built of stone with an overhanging first floor verandah of wood, they house government offices.

Next door to the Treasury Buildings, on La Chaussée, is the **Mauritius Institute,** whose origins can be traced back to the 1880s. The institute is a department of the Ministry of Arts and Culture, which promotes arts and culture. To this end, the institute operates the **Natural History Museum** and the **Public Library** (both in the Mauritius Institute building), the Naval and Historical Museum in Mahébourg, the Sir Seewoosagur Ramgoolam Memorial Centre for Culture in the Plaine Verte area of Port Louis, the Sookdeo Bissoondoyal Museum in Tyack, and the Robert Edward Hart Museum in Souillac.

The Natural History Museum is located on the ground floor of the cream-coloured Mauritius Institute building. The museum's origins go back more than 150 years to 1842, when the Museum Desjardins was opened to the general public by the Natural History Society of Mauritius. The museum was transferred to the Mauritius Institute building in 1885. Museum Desjardins housed specimens of marine species and

Opposite: Elegant facade of Port Louis' State Bank building.

Above and opposite: Relic of a colonial past, Queen Victoria still stands guard outside Government House in Port Louis.

birds, which form the nucleus of today's Natural History Museum. In one room there are stuffed specimens of endemic birds — including the star attraction of a skeletal dodo — and of introduced birds and mammals, the huge skull of a sperm whale, and a whale suspended from the ceiling. There is also a skeleton, which, although not complete, is the only one that exists of the now extinct Mauritius red rail (aphanapteryx), a contemporary of the dodo. In another room there are all sorts of stuffed fish — including some very strange looking specimens — shells, starfish, corals, crabs, turtles, tortoises, butterflies, insects, and charts claiming to explain the meteorology of Mauritius.

The Public Library is located on the second floor of the Mauritius Institute building. Both a lending and a reference library, it houses more than 50,000 books and reference works, as well as a substantial number of magazines and periodicals. A special UNESCO section is attached to the reference library. Opposite the Mauritius Insti-

tute building, on La Chaussée, is a duty-free shop. Next to the Mauritius Institute building are the **Company Gardens,** where the French East India Company had its original headquarters. The area also saw service as a market and fairground before being developed as a cool haven in the heart of a hot city. Under La Bourdonnais, the area around La Chaussée was not much more than a marshy gully where people were buried in the worst possible conditions. When Port Louis suffered three terrible cyclones betweeen 1771 and 1773, followed by an outbreak of smallpox, pigs ransacked graves and rooted out corpses, littering the streets with rotting flesh. Only then did Governor Chevalier Desroches, ignoring church accusations of irreverence to the dead, transfer the cemetery to Cassis, in the western suburbs.

Two **lion statues** mark the **entrance** to the gardens, which are popular with Port Louis workers looking for a quiet, cool place to eat their lunch. A small **kiosk** in the gardens sells local handicrafts, and

Above: The Treasury Building, which dates back to the 1880s, is built of stone with an overhanging first floor verandah of wood.

there are several **statues** dedicated to interesting people.

Remy Ollier, whose statue is near the entrance, was a teacher in the 19th century who turned to journalism to help make ends meet. He took up the coloured population's cause and published his thoughts in the newspaper *La Sentinelle de Maurice*, which first appeared in 1843. Two years later, Ollier unfortunately met an untimely death. There is also a **statue** of Adrien d'Épinay (1794-1839), who was one of the island's first politicians of importance. Trained as a lawyer, he established the first independent newspaper, *Le Cerneen*.

When John Jeremy, a prominent member of the Anti-Slavery Society, arrived in Mauritius in 1832, it was d'Épinay who organized a general strike that brought life to a standstill, resulting in Jeremy's expulsion. D'Épinay's son, Prosper, a well-known sculptor, created this statue of his father.

Leoville l'Homme's **statue** is at the far end of the gardens. A librarian, teacher, poet, and journalist, he founded and edited

several newspapers. All along La Chaussée are **shops** selling a wide range of electrical goods — on hire purchase, if necessary — and a good professional photographic laboratory called Scott Photo Products. At the end of La Chaussée is **Line Barracks,** a fine, strong, and impressive example of early French colonial architecture. In 1736, La Bourdonnais ordered the barracks to be built for 6,000 men in an attempt to bring discipline to the soldiers who had, until that time, been billeted privately. However, much of the work was carried out in the 1760s, when Antoine-Marie Desforges-Boucher was governor.

The barracks remained under army control until 1922, when they were handed over to the government. Since then, they have housed the police headquarters and the passport and immigration office.

Turn **south-east** along Saint George Street and on the corner with Brown Sequard Street stands the **Church of the Immaculate Conception.** Originally, it was little more than a small wooden house

Above: Upper balcony view of the ornate stage and dome of the recently renovated Port Louis Municipal Theatre.

where meetings were held by a missionary, the Reverend Jacques Lebrun, sent to Mauritius in 1814 to introduce Catholicism to the black population, but it is now an impressive stone edifice built in the Gothic style.

From Saint Georges Street, **turn left** into narrow Brown Sequard Street, where there are a couple of stunning shuttered, white **colonial buildings.**

Continue along the street until the **Company Gardens** in Manilal Doctor Square are reached. Here are found several more **statues,** including one of Manilal Doctor, who arrived in Mauritius from India in 1907, at Mahatma Gandhi's prompting, to stir up the Indian community into playing a more active part in local politics and thus improve their lot. It would appear that his work bore fruit, for a 1909 British royal commission recommended that Indians be represented in the Council of Government and that the indenture system end. Manilal Doctor also established the first Indian newspaper, *The Hindustani*, in March 1909.

A **statue** of Charles Edouard Brown Sequard also stands in the Company Gardens. Born in Mauritius, he went to France to study medicine, making some fundamental discoveries in human physiology.

On returning to Mauritius in 1854, he was able to apply his knowledge to the struggle against the cholera epidemic. For his outstanding work, he received numerous local and international awards.

Another **monument** in the gardens is dedicated to the memory of Soeur Marie Barthelemy, who also worked with 19th-century cholera victims, while yet another commemorates the abolition of slavery in Mauritius.

On the corner of Poudrière and Malle-fille streets is **Galérie d'Art de Port Louis,** where local art is exhibited. Continue along Poudrière Street, in a **south-easterly** direction, as far as a 'No Entry' sign just beside the yellow Central Electricity Board building. Walk around the **barrier** and up the cobbled Rue du Vieux Conseil.

At the top of the incline a whitewashed

Above: The Mauritius Institute building, which houses the country's Natural History Museum — with its star attraction of a skeletal dodo — on its ground floor.

colonial building, called La Maison du Poéte, is used now and again for literary and artistic exhibitions.

Just along the street is the Musée de la Photographie (Photography Museum), housed in a beautiful old warehouse that used to belong to the Municipality of Port Louis. The museum, opened in July 1993, has a delightful collection of old newspapers, photographs, photographic equipment, and postcards, as well as a slide projector carrying old transparencies of Mauritius that depict, for example, the Place d'Armes in times gone by and mugshots of the first Indian immigrants. The Rue du Vieux Conseil also accommodates a branch of the Galerie Hélène de Senneville and Le Café du Vieux Conseil, an oasis of tranquillity in the heart of Port Louis serving light, informal lunches. The café is in the courtyard of 18th-century buildings erected on the orders of Intendant Poivre.

At the far end of the Rue du Vieux Conseil, on the corner of Gillet Square and Remy Ollier Street, is the 19th-century Municipal Theatre of Port Louis, reopened in late 1994 after extensive renovation. Designed by French architect Pierre Poujade, the theatre's foundation stone was laid by the first British governor, Sir Robert Farquhar. Opened on 12 June, 1822, it has contributed greatly to the city's cultural life. It originally seated 850 people, in classical style, with boxes for all the important members of government and society. Before its renovation, visiting French troupes performed plays and opera, and it is now becoming a centre of cultural activity once again. Turn south along Jules Koenig Street. City Hall, whose opening coincided with the city status being granted to Port Louis by Queen Elizabeth on 25 August, 1966, is on the right. Outside the building is a spiral staircase with a clock perched on top of it.

The monument was constructed to symbolize the days when watch-towers were erected over Port Louis to warn of fire outbreaks. Opposite City Hall is the Emmanuel Anquetil building, which

220

Above: Giant green turtle specimen on display at the Natural History Museum in Port Louis.

houses government offices. Further along Jules Koenig Street, on the same side as City Hall, are the 18th-century **Supreme Court buildings,** which surround a shady **courtyard.**

Opposite them is a large open-air car park, at the far end of which is **St Louis Cathedral,** the third church to stand there. The first, under the French, was a wooden structure called the Parochial Church of St Louis. Cyclones reduced it to a crumbling ruin early in the 19th century, but it was reconstructed under Governor Farquhar in 1813. A report in 1925 showed the walls to be in such a state of disrepair that the whole church was demolished and rebuilt. The present church was consecrated in 1932.

The lion-headed **fountain** outside the cathedral dates back to 1786, when it was erected on the order of Vicomte de Souillac. Water was funnelled down from the mountain of Le Pouce and disgorged from the mouths of the four bronze lion heads, providing a large section of the people of Port Louis with fresh water. Just next to the

cathedral is the **Episcopal Palace,** a fine example of a 19th-century mansion with colonnades, high ceilings, and wide verandahs. If you continue along Jules Koenig Street, it becomes Pope Hennessy Street. In the latter, the offices of the Mauritius Export Development and Investment Authority (MEDIA) are in the British American Insurance (BAI) building on the **left,** opposite the disintegrating remains of the Luna Park cinema. MEDIA is an important port of call for those wishing to do business in Mauritius. It is the island's focal point for investment and export promotion activities and provides support facilities to potential investors and industrialists. Next door to the BAI building is the National Hotel, one of the oldest on the island, which now only functions as a restaurant.

Turn in a **south-westerly** direction along La Bourdonnais Street and take the **first right** to reach the **Anglican Cathedral of St James.** It has a very simple wooden interior with an intricate **stained glass window** behind the altar. The cathedral used to be a gunpowder store and, as a result, the nave

Top: From leather handbags to shark jaws, souvenirs galore can be found in this Port Louis shop.
Above: Hindu deities, multi-coloured bangles, brass — Port Louis shops sell everything under the sun.
Opposite above: Palm-lined mall in downtown Port Louis.
Opposite: Customers browse in a market area jewellery store.

Above: Neatly drawn geometrical shapes of Mauritian sugar fields.
Opposite: Artistically arranged onions at the Port Louis market.

walls are about three metres (10 feet) thick. It was hastily turned into a church in 1812 when the island fell into British hands and a Protestant place of worship was required, but it was not completed before its consecration in 1950.

The cathedral's **bell** originated from La Villebague, a sugar cane plantation belonging to French Governor Magon, but Sir Robert Farquhar had it transferred to Port Louis to be installed in the belfry. On the opposite side of La Bourdonnais Street is a **narrow road** called Frère Felix de Valois, at the **north-western** end of which **traditional houses** hide behind high walls, shaded by tropical trees growing in their courtyards. The **south-eastern** section of Frère Felix de Valois Street borders the **Champ de Mars,** at present the island's only **racecourse.** The Champ de Mars takes its name from the large piece of ground located between the Military School and the River Seine in Paris, formerly used for military parades. Mars was the god of war in the Roman pantheon. Cradled by the rolling foothills

of the Moka mountain range, the Champ de Mars was also a training ground for soldiers during the period of French administration. It was also the island's main meeting place, and people used to stroll in its formal gardens at weekends when bands played.

In 1812, Colonel Edward Draper converted it into a racetrack. Draper was an English army officer whose passion for racing led to the foundation of the **Mauritius Turf Club,** the oldest track in the southern hemisphere and reputedly the second oldest in the world. The racing season lasts from May to November, the Mauritian winter months. All of the meetings, save one, are held on Saturday afternoon and each features seven races. Horse-racing is highly popular among the Mauritians, and the crowd, which usually averages 20,000, is always out to ensure a fun climax to the working week; it is a relaxed and colourful spectacle. The Champ de Mars is also the venue for the annual Independence Day celebrations on 12 March. There are two

Above: Thousands of punters cheer on their favourites at port Louis racecourse, the oldest in the southern hemisphere, founded in 1812.

Opposite: Colourful Indian temple in Port Louis is one of many religious sites to be found in the capital.

national monuments in the grounds of the Champ de Mars. One is an obelisk known as the **Malartic Tomb,** erected in memory of French Governor Anne Joseph Hippolyte de Malartic, who took control of the island in 1792 and tried his best to spare the country from total disorder following the 1789 revolution in France. The obelisk fell down during the fierce cyclone of 1892, but was re-erected the following year. The second is a **statue** of King Edward VII, and is the work of Mauritian sculptor Prosper d'Épinay, who, it is said, was a friend of the British king. Edward died in 1910 and the statue was erected two years later.

On the far side of the racecourse, on the corner of Dr Eugene Laurent and Corneille streets, is the predominantly red **Lam Soon Temple,** which, with its ornate carvings and smouldering offerings of incense, is a fairly typical example of a Chinese temple.

Continue up Corneille Street to reach **La Citadelle** (also known as **Fort Adelaide**), from where there is a panoramic **view** of the entire town. The fort was built between 1834 and 1840, following the problems associated with the attempted abolition of slavery, as a lookout post from which to monitor any further threats to civil order in the town. The fort is named after Queen Adelaide, wife of King William IV, the British monarch who reigned between 1830 and 1837.

For many years La Citadelle was abandoned and fell into ruin, but it has been renovated in recent times and is now used as a venue for pop concerts. From La Citadelle, travel down Jummah Mosque Street until Sir Seewoosagur Ramgoolam Street (better known by its old name of Desforges Street) is reached and **turn north-eastwards** towards Plaine Verte. Hidden behind a high brick wall is an **old wooden house** with a shady courtyard now known as the **Sir Seewoosagur Ramgoolam Centre for Culture.**

Visitors to the island cannot fail to notice the importance of Sir Seewoosagur

Above: Tombs and memorials to those who shaped the Mauritius of today in a Port Louis cemetery.

Ramgoolam to Mauritius. His name, or sometimes just the initials SSR, decorates buildings, streets, and complexes, all over the country. SSR International Airport is an example.

Sir Seewoosagur has been called the architect of Mauritian independence and the father of the nation, and is highly revered. Born into a poor family on the Beau Champ Sugar Estate in 1900, Sir Seewoosagur worked hard to pass through school with flying colours. In 1920 he went to England to study medicine. On his return, he moved into a house on Desforges Street and set up a medical practice.

Dr Ramgoolam soon became interested in politics and, in 1940, Governor Bede Clifford nominated him to the Legislative Council. Dr Ramgoolam later became a municipal councillor and, in 1958, was proclaimed Mayor of Port Louis. Four years later, as Mauritius moved closer to self-government, Dr Ramgoolam was made chief minister and, in 1964, Premier. The following year he was knighted by the Queen and in 1967 Mauritius attained independence. From 1983 until his death in 1985, Sir Seewoosagur was the governor-general. The Sir Seewoosagur Ramgoolam Centre for Culture was opened in September 1987 in his former home — he lived there between 1936 and 1983. The house, a national monument, is also the birthplace of Dr Maurice Curé, one of the founders of the Labour Party.

Several rooms are open to the public, including a consultation room where all Sir Seewoosagur's medical equipment, medical books, prescription forms, and a doctor's certificate are to be found. Other rooms contain photographs of official functions

Opposite (clockwise from top left): Bust of Doctor Maurice Curé stands in the Place Sookdeo Bissoondoyal, also known as the Place d'Armes; Statue of Sir John Pope Hennessy, the British governor of Mauritius from 1883 to 1889, faces Government House; Bust of Raoul River in the Company Gardens; Memorial to Sir William Newton, a British-trained barrister born in Port Louis stands next to that of Hennessy's.

Dr MAURICE CURE
3rd September 1886
1st March 1977
This plaque was unveiled
by
His Excellency
SIR VEERASAMY RINGADOO,
G.C.M.G
Governor-General
on 1st March 1989
in the presence of
THE RT. HON. ANEROOD JUGNAUTH
P.C.Q.C
Prime Minister
and
HON. ARMOOGRUM PARSURAMAN
Minister of Education,
Arts and Culture

SIR JOHN POPE HENNESSY K.C.M.G.
GOVERNOR OF MAURITIUS
1883-1889

WILLIAM NEWTON

Above: Ornate shrine of Twanntai, god of problems and of health, inside the Nam Sun Chinese Pagoda on Corneille Street in Port Louis.
Opposite: Ornately carved door marks the entrance to the Jummah Mosque in the country's capital city.

and his personal belongings. From the SSR Centre for Culture it is a short **north-west-wards** walk to the **Chinese Quarter.** This is a colourful part of the city with a myriad of **shops** selling specialist foods and traditional medicines, which advertise their trade in Chinese characters and in French. There are some good Chinese restaurants there, which are particularly fun to visit during Chinese festivals, when special foods are prepared and the atmosphere is electric with fireworks.

L'Amicale, a casino where Chinese gambling games are played, is on the corner of Royal and Anquetil Streets, the entrance being on the latter. It is an integral part of the city's small Chinatown and is one of the the few sources of evening entertainment in Port Louis.

The **Jummah Mosque,** a little further along Royal Street towards the city centre, is the focal point for the Muslim population. Built in the mid-19th century, it is the largest mosque in Mauritius and is a place

of meditation rather than a tourist attraction. Non-Muslims are not allowed beyond the courtyard. During Eid-Ul-Fitr, an important Muslim festival celebrating the end of Ramadan — the fasting month — hundreds of devotees converge on the mosque.

Towards the waterfront, the **Merchant Navy Club,** on Joseph Rivière Street, welcomes all visitors to the island, in particular seamen. The club, which is housed in a building dating back to the 1850s, used to offer accommodation to travellers when hotels were few and far between, but now it offers little more than a cool, wooden-floored bar serving drinks and simple snacks. There are table tennis, snooker, and pool facilities in the bar area.

From the Merchant Navy Club it is a short walk along Queen Street to the colourful **Central Market,** which is at its bustling best on Saturday morning. The tin-roofed, cobble-paved market, completed in 1844, is divided by Farquhar Street into two sections. On entering the market, note

231

Above: Old Chinese temple on the slopes of Signal Mountain near Port Louis.

the **wrought iron gates,** decorated with flowers and other artistic touches that also carry the initials VR in memory of Victoria Regina (Queen Victoria). The section on Queen Street has two sides. The one where fruit and vegetables are sold is particularly colourful between December and February, when a wide range of tropical fruits — including lychees, mangoes, and pineapples — are on sale. The most popular stall has tisanes to cure every problem imaginable, including dandruff, gout, eczema, and hernia. The other section sells tourist **souvenirs,** such as spices used in Indian cooking, basketry, jewellery, and clothing. Be prepared to bargain hard. Just across Farquhar Street is the second half of the market, which is dedicated to fish and meat, and easy to find because of the smell. In the outskirts of Port Louis, there are several sites of interest that are best visited by car.

To reach **Signal Mountain,** which is located to the **south-west** of the capital and has stunning views of Port Louis, the harbour, and the west coast, travel along La Bourdonnais Street from the **traffic lights** on Pope Hennessy Street. Cross a river and, on the corner with Mère Augustine Place, stands a modern high-rise building called C&R Court. On the 10th floor is an American-style steakhouse, where it is possible to enjoy a good view of Port Louis as well as a meal. Continue along La Bourdonnais Street until the road ends. A guard mans the gate at the beginning of the **track** up to Signal Mountain. To proceed further a permit must be obtained during office hours from the Ministry of Local Government, on Saint Georges Street. The gates up to Signal Mountain are closed at 1800. From the Signal Mountain **gatehouse,** continue **westwards.** A **monument** to Marie Reine de la Paix is on the **left.** Erected just after World War II, this monument is a place of pilgrimage. In 1989, when Pope John Paul visited Mauritius, he celebrated mass there attended by thousands of Mauritians.

Follow the road to its natural end and you reach the suburb of **Bell Village,** an area developed in the early 1920s, when

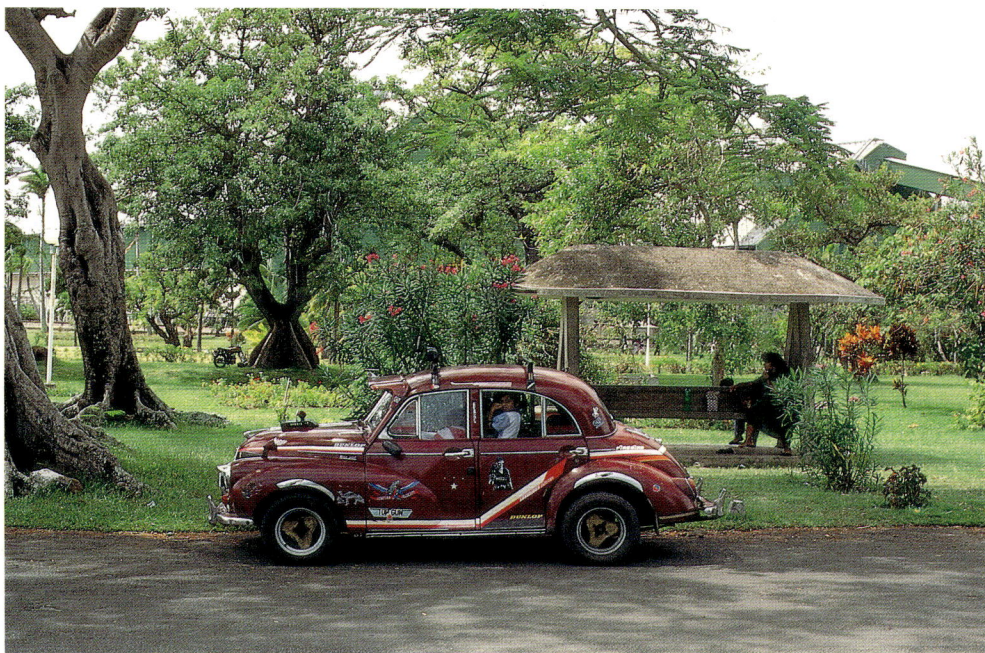

Above: Customized Morris Minor at the beautiful Robert Edward Hart Gardens in Cassis.

sanitary conditions were dreadful and Dr Andrew Balfour suggested that a model housing estate for workers be constructed outside the capital to improve their lot. Sir Hesketh Bell, Governor of Mauritius between 1916 and 1924, agreed and ordered Bell Village to be built. Bell Village is now an important cultural centre. Both the long-established Alliance Française, which actively promotes the French language and culture, and the African Cultural Centre, which houses a library and documentation unit, are on Victor Hugo Street.

Nearby is the Chinese Cultural Centre, housed in a typical modern Chinese monolith with just a touch of traditional decor. It was established in the mid-1980s to offer Chinese language and cultural lessons. The suburb next to Bell Village is called **Plaine Lauzun,** after Lauzun, commander of a French cavalry unit, who used the site for training. Modern Plaine Lauzun is an industrial zone that is home, among others, to International Distillers, makers of the locally made and ubiquitous Green Island rum. North of Plaine Lauzun is the suburb

of **Cassis,** thought to have taken its name from the acacia plants that grew in abundance locally, but it is also possible that it was named after a small French town close to Marseilles called Cassis. The French Cassis is well-known for its wines and creeks, and a proverb goes: 'Whosoever has seen Paris and not Cassis has seen nothing.' The same probably cannot be said of the Mauritian Cassis, but there are a few points of interest in the suburb.

The **Saint Sacrament Church** of Cassis is a fine piece of Gothic architecture. The building of the church was financed by a wealthy physician, Doctor Thomy d'Arifat, who died before the church was completed in 1879. Although its original purpose was to serve the wealthy inhabitants of Port Louis, it became known as the Cathedral of the Poor following the malaria outbreak and subsequent exodus of rich people to the highlands. From the church, turn into Ménagerie Street and follow the road around, turning **right** just in front of the solid wall of the **Muslim cemetery.**

Pass the **Al Noor Mosque** and take a

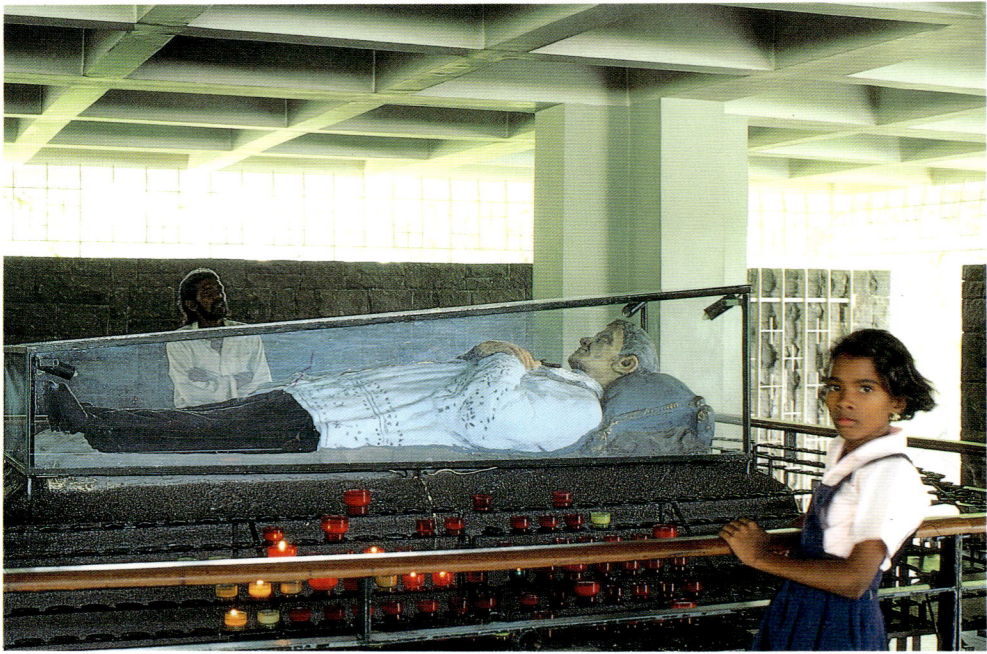

Above: Effigy of Père Laval, a 19th-century missionary, at the Sainte Croix church.

left turn into Reserves Street, and the **Robert Edward Hart Gardens** are at the end of the road, on the **left.**

The gardens contain two **national monuments** — a **bust** of Lenin (the Russian revolutionary) inaugurated by Sir Seewoosagur in 1972, and a **monument** commemorating the French landing and possession of the island by Dufresne d'Arsel in 1715. The palm-filled **gardens** are a pleasant place for a stroll, although it is just as easy to drive around them, and there is a children's play area. From the gardens, Cassis Street leads to the **motorway,** from where the city centre is easily accessible.

On the other side of the capital, in the north-eastern suburbs, is an area called **Sainte Croix,** where **Père Laval's shrine** is located. To reach it, take the motorway **northwards** until a **roundabout** indicates Sainte Croix to the **right.** Take this exit, follow the road to a **T-junction,** turn right and then take the first turning on the **left.** Sainte Croix is straight ahead.

Père Laval, a 19th-century missionary who dedicated his life to improving the lives of the poor and the sick, died in 1864. His body is buried at in the cemetery of the Sainte Croix church, sometimes referred to as the Lourdes of the Indian Ocean because sick pilgrims visit the shrine in the hope of a miracle cure. Every year, in early September, an overnight pilgrimage takes place, which, in 1993 alone, attracted 200,000 people. Just beside the church is a small museum devoted to Père Laval.

Opposite: Outlying suburb of Port Louis dominated by magnificent Le Pouce Mountain in the background.

PART FOUR: SPECIAL FEATURES

Above: Brilliant red mantle is an easily distinguishable characteristic of the male Mauritius fody.
Opposite: Richly coloured national flower of Mauritius, Trochetia boutoniana.

Birdlife: Past Domain of the Dodo

It is almost impossible to consider the birds of Mauritius without reflecting on the sad tale of the dodo, doomed to extinction almost as soon as the first Europeans landed on the island. Moreover, the dodo is not the only weird and wonderful land bird to have been lost forever from Mauritius's original unique avifauna. However, before mourning the dead it is fitting to praise the living, for Mauritius remains a Mecca for bird-watchers in search of special island forms found nowhere else on earth.

Back in the 1970s, it seemed as if the dodo's fate would continue to be repeated over and over again. The **Mauritius kestrel** was down to a population of just four known birds and probably ranked as the rarest bird in the world at that time. Also on the way out, it seemed, were the pink pigeon and the echo parakeet. Without desperate action to reverse the fortune of these and other endemic Mauritian birds, future visitors would have been able only to reflect on what a wonderful place it must once have been.

Fortunately, due to local and international endeavours, it still is a wonderful place. Gerald Durrell and the Jersey Wildlife Preservation Trust were leading players, together with the Mauritian Wildlife Fund and others. Their 'man on the spot' in Mauritius was Carl Jones, now a legendary figure in ornithological circles, having achieved what many believed to be impossible.

Captive breeding, habitat management, blood, sweat, and tears all played a part in the story. Mauritius kestrels reared in captivity have been reintroduced into the wild. Nest boxes have been erected and, though sometimes hijacked by Indian mynahs, a combination of efforts has slowly brought about an increase in the number of birds. Reintroduced into three mountain areas, there are now over 300 wild Mauritius kestrels, which include about 60 breeding pairs. This is a phenomenal success story, beyond perhaps the wildest hopes of all, except such visionaries as Carl Jones and Gerald Durrell. Another 'hopeless case' was the **echo parakeet** and, indeed, it is not yet close to being taken off the danger list. But there are some signs of hope. The bird declined as the native forest of Mauritius contracted. It reached the stage where attempts by echo parakeets to breed appeared to have been virtually abandoned. There are some signs that the trend has been reversed, with a slight increase in numbers in recent years.

More spectacular has been the **pink pigeon** programme, with the hundredth captive bred pigeon released in late 1994. The wild population is now well in excess of this figure — a dramatic success considering that in 1986 the total population may have been as small as 20.

Other rarities include the beautiful **Mauritius paradise flycatcher**, whose population also suffered a steady decline throughout most of the human history on Mauritius. It now survives in the patchy remnants of such indigenous forests as Bassin Blanc.

Then there is the **Mauritius cuckoo-shrike**, perhaps a fraction less common than the flycatcher. Indeed, some writers considered it doomed early in the 20th century. It has defied their dire predictions but remains very rare, with probably fewer than 200 surviving pairs. Unfortunately, although they feed mainly on insects, they are also partial to pink pigeon eggs when these are available, a not particularly helpful habit for those who wish to save both species from extinction.

The **Mauritius fody** is rarer still, with a population of perhaps 90 pairs. Some blame their decline on competition with the Madagascar fody. However, the Mauritius fody is mainly insectivorous, while the

Opposite: The Mauritius kestrel, once thought to be doomed to extinction, has made a remarkable comeback, thanks to some dedicated conservationists.

Madagascar bird is principally a seed eater and, while there is some overlap, the true reasons for the decline of the Mauritius fody may be more to do with habitat destruction and rat predation. Not all the unique birds of Mauritius are so rare. The **Mauritius grey white-eye** is common in hotel grounds, gardens, and, indeed, all over the island. This is the only species to have adapted well to man's arrival. The noisy social bird moves through the vegetation in groups of up to 20, feeding on insects and sometimes nectar. Throughout the native forest there are more grey white-eyes than all other native species combined.

Strangely enough, by contrast, another very closely related bird, the **Mauritius olive white-eye,** has suffered a huge fall in numbers, with probably less than 150 pairs surviving, though the number is difficult to assess accurately as the birds range over a large area, often remaining silent and inconspicuous within the undergrowth of the south-western forests of Mauritius.

Far less silent, but also found in the native forests, is the **Mauritius black bulbul**. Once it was a popular game bird and had this practice continued it would probably now be extinct. Fortunately, today the Mauritians recognize the value of their special birds and, though numbers remain low, there is hope that the bulbul's most critical days are now over.

Apart from the direct consequences of human exploitation, habitat clearances, and introduced rats, cats, and monkeys, Mauritius's unique avifauna has also had to face competition from a whole host of introduced birds, such as the world's most successful bird colonist, the **house sparrow**, and the noisy, ubiquitous **Indian mynah**. **Red-whiskered bulbul** are also common, the legend of their origin being that a single pair that escaped from a cage during a 1892 cyclone gave rise to the entire population now common all over Mauritius.

The **ring-necked parakeet** is fairly common, especially where maize or other grains are abundant. Indeed, this introduced bird — another late 19th-century escape artist — is a pest on agricultural land. **Barred ground doves** — deliberately introduced during the French era — are fairly common, too. These tame, endearing birds feed on the ground, often meandering around the chairs and tables of restaurants and hotels searching for scraps. Sometimes they are seen feeding with **spotted dove**, also introduced during the French period. Before all these man-made changes occurred, seabirds were undoubtedly far more common, but today it is still possible to enjoy many tropical specialities. The **brown noddy, blue-faced booby,** and **sooty tern** breed on Serpent Island. **Red-tailed tropicbirds** and **wedge-tailed shearwaters** breed on Round Island, while on the mainland of Mauritius, **white-tailed tropicbirds** are a fairly common sight.

But to get back to the world's most famous extinct species, though the last **dodo** died more than 400 years ago, the legend lives on. This was just one of the 11 species on Mauritius eliminated in historical times (compared with nine species on the list of survivors), but it is by far the most widely known. It was the Dutch settlers who first named it, giving it the title *Valghvogel*, which means 'disgusting bird'. The later name dodo was also Dutch meaning a sluggard. The European navigators of that era were interested in birds solely as a resource, and the dodo was not a favourite on the menu. As one Dutch captain wrote in 1602, 'even a long boiling would scarcely make them tender'. As other birds were plentiful, he noted, his men became disgusted with dodo meat. Dodos were easy to catch, and many were killed for killing's sake. However, the *coup de grâce* was given by introduced animals, which preyed on the adults, chicks, and eggs.

So strange was the dodo's appearance that it took some time before its nearest relative was identified. Some thought it to be some kind of ostrich, others a kind of vulture, and others still an albatross. The last dodo was long dead when, in the middle of the 19th century, Professor Reinhardt of Denmark surprised the scientific world by claiming the dodo was a giant flightless pigeon. It took some time for this insight to be universally accepted.

Today it is believed that, millions of years ago, a race of pigeons arrived in

Mauritius, probably from neighbouring Madagascar. They found an island with no mammal predators, an avian paradise, with nothing to challenge the dominance of birds. In such a haven, flight became unnecessary. The dodo's fate was sealed, for, when man and his entourage of animals arrived, the means of retreat was gone. The last dodo was seen on Mauritius around 1672.

All that remains today is a skull, a right foot, and some scientific plates of the left eye at the Oxford University Museum. But, as Joseph Connolly noted in *The Sunday Times* in 1995, 'The dodo may be dead, but it sure as blazes won't lie down.'

Even more important, the loss to the world of such a natural treasure emphasizes the importance of conservation programmes such as those to save the Mauritius kestrel, the pink pigeon, and the echo parakeet. Come what may, we have to make sure they never become as 'dead as a dodo'.

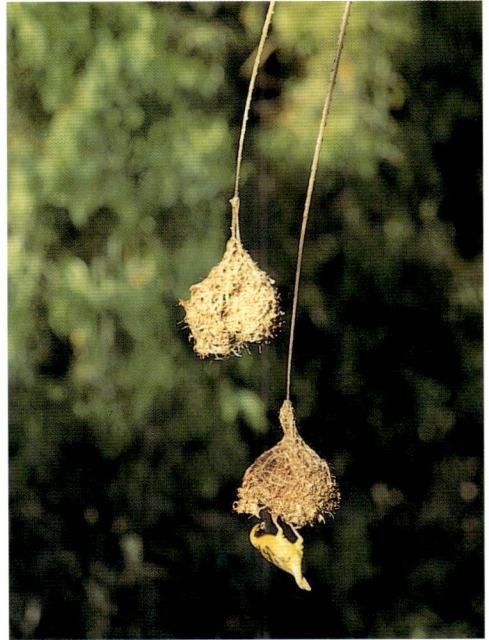

Top: Blush-pink beauty of the Mauritian pink pigeon.
Above: Village weaver birds building their woven nests in the forests of the Moka Mountains.

Marine Life: Waters Teeming with Wonders

Mauritius controls millions of square kilometres of the Indian Ocean. It has the right to exploit these waters, to fish and otherwise harvest the ocean, and to extract minerals and salt for its benefit. At the same time, it has a duty to care for the waters that it controls, to prevent pollution, to monitor fish stocks, to prevent overfishing, and to regulate fisheries and catching methods.

To conserve the marine life in its waters, underwater fishing with spearguns is forbidden, the size of fishing net meshes is controlled, and casiers and seines are forbidden at certain times of the year.

The Mauritian authorities have always banned dynamite fishing, because it causes permanent damage to the underwater world, especially the corals. They also ban indiscriminate collection of live corals, which, once taken out of water, break easily, lose their beautiful colours, and smell badly once the polyps have died. Only dead corals and shells that are washed up on the beach may be taken home.

To help restock the devastated lagoon, old barges have been sunk to create fish refuges.

Fish life

The types of fish found in Mauritian waters vary tremendously.

Sharks and other predators are mostly found in deep waters, but are sometimes spotted just outside the reef and within the lagoon itself, especially near reef passes, such as at Blue Bay and Mahébourg. Seven types of shark have been identified. The most common is the *requin chasseur*, but the *requin lezard* (**milk shark**), *requin renard* (**thresher shark**), *requin marteau* (**hammerhead shark**), *requin bleu* (**blue shark**), **mako**, and *l'endormi* (**lazy shark**) are not uncommon.

There are three types of rays and skates, the *diable de mer* or *mante* (**devil ray**) —

the largest of all living rays — the *raie chauve-souris* (**spotted eagle ray** or **duck-bill ray**), and the *trembleur* (**electric ray**). Such small fish as **sardines, herrings**, and **pilchards**, found in large shoals offshore, are of great economic importance as exports, as well as providing a major source of food for the islanders.

Four types of eel are found. The **Plotosidae** include **catfish** and **barber eels**; the **Echelidae** are elongated eels with pointed tails; the **Congridae** are large eels, while the **Muraenidae** are dangerous predators usually hiding in holes and suddenly emerging to catch their prey. Of the latter, there are over 20 species.

Serranidae are of interest to gourmets, for the group includes *vieilles, merons, garoupas,* and *serrans,* which are all, especially the *vieille ananas* and *vieille rouge,* popular fish for eating. Other fish generally found in large shoals and important as food are *sarde* (**red snapper**), *bourgeois* (**red emperor**) and *sacrechien.* The latter is particularly prized.

Capitaine, **silver bream, red mullet,** and **carangue** are also found in the lagoon in large shoals and make for excellent eating, especially the capitaine.

Larger game fish found in Mauritian waters include **Spanish mackerel**, which is valuable as both food and, between September and December when it is found in large shoals outside the reef, as a game fish; **yellowfin tuna**, which is fished extensively and, quite possibly, overfished as it is exploited by the Mauritian tuna fishing and canning industry, which sells it both frozen and in cans; **bonito,** an important food fish often canned and sold as tuna; and **wahoo,** much sought after by big game fishermen.

The greats of big game fishing, such as marlin and sailfish, are often found in Mauritian waters. **Black marlin** are common and are caught regularly by big game fishermen using long lines. The largest **blue marlin** caught in Mauritian waters weighed more than 700 kilos (1,540 lbs).

Above: Beautiful but harmful: the spines of the lionfish can inflict painful and serious wounds.

Sailfish, so called because they have a huge dorsal fin resembling a sail, are also popular game among deep sea fishermen. Naturally, as Mauritius is surrounded by a reef, there are hundreds of thousands of colourful reef fish in the lagoon. They include **butterfly, coral, clown, damsel, rainbow, parrot,** and **angel fish.**

There are also a number of unwelcome fish in the lagoon, like *laffes* and **scorpion**. The *laffe laboue*, commonly known as a **stone fish**, is like a chameleon and takes on the appearance of the stones and corals, among which it lies on the sea bed. It remains there motionless to await its prey and then inflicts a poisonous sting that can be very painful and fatal. It should not be touched, but if it does strike, the affected part of the body should be put in very hot water (as the venom is thermolabile, i.e., decomposes in heat) until medical help is obtained. The *laffe corail* or **scorpion** also has a very effective camouflage, poisonous spines, and should not be touched. The *laffe volant* or **common lionfish** is reddish-brown with white and orange stripes — it swims slowly and majestically, like a large bird flying. Its flowing spines can inflict painful and serious wounds, so it should not be touched.

There are five families of small, solitary, strange-looking fish in Mauritian waters that protect themselves from predators through a particular piece of body armour. The **puffer fish**, which inflates its body with air or water until it becomes spherical and the skin spines become erect, is a fairly common example.

Freshwater fish

There are several forms of freshwater fish in Mauritius. There are three indigenous species of freshwater eel.

The largest, the **mottled fin eel**, can grow up to two metres (6.5 feet) long. It has a pale yellow belly, mottled sides, and a dark green-brown back, so that it blends well with pebbly river beds. The **plain long-finned eel** can grow up to 1.2 metres (four feet), has a pinkish belly and a rich dark brown back. The smallest, the **short-finned eel**, grows to 70 centimetres (29

Top: Indian longfin bannerfish, colourful denizen of the coral reefs.

Above: The poisonous scorpion fish camouflages itself well in soft coral.

Above: Beauty where you least expect it: detail of the upper side of a sea cucumber, or sea slug.

inches) and is olive in colour. There are also three types of indigenous freshwater fish. The **freshwater carp** weighs up to 1.5 kilos (3.3 lbs); the chitte is similar to the carp but is more cylindrical; and the **river goby**, known locally as *cabot*, is a small fish that sticks to rocks by means of a ventral concave membrane. All are good to eat.

There are three introduced freshwater river fish. The **gourami** was brought over from the East Indies prior to the 19th century. The **goldfish**, called *dame cere* locally, is similar to the carp, but was imported from the East Indies, and is brownish. The **tilapia**, introduced as recently as 1950, can weigh up to a kilo (2.2 lbs).

Crustaceans

There are several types of indigenous freshwater prawns of gastronomic value.

The **river prawn**, or *camaron*, lives in well-oxygenated waters where it hides under large stones. Camaron in red sauce,

served with heart of palm, is a traditional Mauritian dish. The **colocasia prawn** or *chevrette de songe* is four to five centimetres (1.5 to two inches) long and is found in the sluggish sections of streams and rivers. The *betangue*, about the same size as the colocasia prawn, hides under pebbles in shallow rivers with a fairly strong current. Small prawns, collectively called *petites chevrettes*, are usually one to three centimetres (half to one inch) long and inhabit the shady rivers areas, close to the bank.

The only introduced freshwater crustacean is the *rosenberghi*, which is successfully farmed in ponds. It can grow up to 12 centimetres (4.7 inches) long.

Mauritian sea waters also play host to a large number of prawns. The ones mentioned here are of gastronomic importance. The **bambous prawn**, or **tiger prawn**, is found off the west coast, where it can weigh up to 40 grams (1.4 oz). The *Penaeus caniculatus*, which reaches six centimetres (2.3 inches) in length, is found in lagoons all around the island, but is most frequently fished just off Morne Brabant and

Above: Mauritius has several types of shore crabs, many of which camouflage well with the sand.

Riambel. In addition, Mauritian waters are home to a number of freshwater and sea water varieties of crab. The most often eaten are the **thalamites** or *carrelet batard*, the *crabe malgache,* the **reef crab,** and the *carrelet* **crab**.

The carrelet is the most highly prized in gastronomic circles, probably because it can grow up to 25 centimetres (9.8 inches) wide and has large pincers filled with succulent flesh. It favours brackish water and is, therefore, found in river estuaries and mangrove swamps.

The blue and red *carcassaille* is one of the most visually attractive crabs in Mauritius. They are found all along the rocky coastline.

In addition, Mauritius has a number of shore crabs, including five types of small **ocypod crabs,** locally called *cambresis* and found on the white sandy beaches. The most common is the **ghost crab**, so called because it camouflages well with the surrounding sand. Along muddy shorelines, four crab species, known as **calling crabs** or *ucas*, are likely to be found, all with bright colour markings. Beyond the beach, two land crabs, known to the locals as *tourlourous*, are renowned for the large burrows they dig.

Five types of lobster exist there. Only two — the **blue lobster**, or *homard canal*, and the **reef lobster**, or *langouste* — are caught frequently and appear regularly on restaurant menus. The blue lobster is the larger.

There are also at least 1,000 different species of shell, including **conches, cowries,** and **cones**, in Mauritian waters, but the Fisheries Act of 1980 made live shell collecting illegal, so remember that shells should be admired, but not touched. Specimens of the many local shells can be seen at the Natural History Museum in Port Louis.

Opposite: Lyretail coralfish, golden gems of the Mauritius' coral gardens.

Wildlife of Mauritius

Land mammals

The only endemic mammals when the Dutch first landed on the island in 1598 were several bat species.

The four types of **fruit bat** then on the island are thought to have made their way to Mauritius from the East Indies some time prior to the 17th century. *Pteropus niger* survives to this day in the Black River Gorges area. Colonies can be seen at dusk flying to feed in eucalyptus and sisal trees.

Pteropus subniger, the smaller of the two bats, disappeared from Mauritius around 1864, hunted to extinction by the settlers, who had no difficulty catching them as they took refuge in hollow tree trunks during the day.

A smaller bat in the same family, *Pteropus rodricensis*, is endemic to Rodrigues. Due to its small population, it is legally protected. *Pteropus mascarensis,* once confined to Round Island, is now extinct.

There are two insectivorous bats, the **Mauritius tomb bat** and the **free-tailed bat**. They are thought to be rather recent additions to the bat population. Both species shelter in caves during the day and can sometimes be seen around street lamps catching insects at night.

The **black rat**, also called **tree rat** because it likes to climb trees, is thought to have swum ashore from ships wrecked on Mauritius's protective reef prior to the 17th century. The first sighting of a black rat was in 1606, by which time it had probably already started destroying the island's endemic populations of snakes, lizards, Telfair's skink, and Gunther's phelsuma. Today, the black rat lives in forests, where it continues to destroy birds' eggs and nestlings, but is, on rare occasions, seen in towns.

The **long-tailed macaque** (*jacot* or *singe* to the locals) is believed to have been introduced from the East Indies by Dutch settlers. Considered nothing but a pest, the macaque feeds extensively on seeds, resulting in the rarity of a number of tree species and, like the black rat, tends to ransack birds' nests for eggs and nestlings.

Pigs were introduced by the Dutch in 1606. A report written by Lamothius, the then governor, noted that, by 1690, a feral pig population was flourishing in the woods. As early as 1709, hunting parties were organized to cull the huge herds of pigs. Wild pigs (known as *cochon marron*) are still to be found, but not in such large numbers.

Deer were introduced in 1639 by Dutchman Adrian van der Stel. Fifty years later, Lamothius, reported that the deer 'were present in abundance'. They remain so to this day. Deer (*cerf* to the Mauritians) are also now reared in feed-lots and the flesh exported or consumed locally.

In 1709, Captain de la Merveille found a number of **wild cats** while hunting around Baie du Tombeau and wrote that they had been introduced 'to destroy the rats that plagued the country'. Wild cats — *chat sauvage* — although rare, still roam the island today. Dogs were released into the wild during the early colonial days, but once deer hunting grounds were established, they were tracked down and destroyed.

The **brown rat**, also called the **Norway rat** and **common rat**, or simply *le rat*, is thought to have arrived around 1735. Unlike the climbing black rat, the brown rat burrows and is a good swimmer, and it has been accused of causing the disappearance of nesting seabirds from the small islands off Mahébourg.

The **house mouse** is thought to have arrived in Mauritius in the first half of the 18th century. Today *la souris*, as it is known locally, is found in forests as well as towns.

The first recorded sighting of the **black-naped hare** was in 1753, when Abbé de la Caille mentioned its presence on his visit to map out the island. Believed to have been introduced from India, black-naped hares (*lièvres* to the locals) are still common in Mauritius, and hare hunting is a popular

Above: Javan Rusa deer, introduced to Mauritius in 1639, graze peacefully in a nature reserve.

sport among the people. The **shrew** — known as *le rat musquet* — is thought to have been introduced from India in the middle of the 18th century. It feeds on insects and, in turn, is food for young Mauritius kestrels.

The **tenrec**, or **hedgehog**, is a brown insectivorous mammal native to Madagascar that was introduced to Mauritius in the late 18th century. The tenrec, which is called *tendrac* or *tangue*, hibernates in June, re-emerging in September for summer.

The **mongoose** was first introduced in the mid-19th century, but was soon eradicated by the settlers who realized that it was destroying some of their domestic animals, such as chickens.

A plague epidemic in 1899 prompted the British authorities to bring a number of male mongooses from India to control the rat populaton, which carried the vector of the disease. Unfortunately, and somewhat predictably, there were some females among the mongooses, and their numbers soon multiplied. As a result, the mongoose is now a permanent denizen.

Sea mammals

In the 17th century, there was only one endemic sea mammal in Mauritius, the **dugong**, common particularly in the lagoon surrounding Rodrigues. Notes written at the time describe the dugongs as follows:

'They measure 15 to 16 feet in length and weigh from 800 to 900 or even 1,000 pounds, yielding a delicious meat, one of the best that can be found on land or sea'. Rodrigues supplied Mauritius with salted dugong and, by the early 19th century, dugongs had become extinct in this part of the world.

In July 1991, the Mauritian Wildlife Fund, the Government of Mauritius, and the Whale and Dolphin Conservation Society began a joint project to survey the species and numbers of **whales, dolphins**, and **turtles** in Mauritian waters.

At least eight whale and dolphin species were recorded, and the National Parks and Conservation Service lists 10 whales —

Above: Fruit bat at La Vanille Crocodile Park — one of two types of bat still extant in Mauritius.

minke, sei, Bryde's, fin, short-finned pilot, southern bottlenose, humpback, Blainville's beaked, killer, and sperm — and four dolphins — **Risso's, spotted, spinner,** and **bottlenose.**

Reptiles

Reptiles followed the birds and the bats in the animal colonization of Mauritius. The birds and the bats had been carried to the island by winds, but the first reptiles — tortoises and lizards — arrived from other lands on rafts of branches and creepers. Gradually, over thousands, if not millions, of years, these animals evolved into species unique to Mauritius. Some have survived, many have not.

When the Dutch first settled Mauritius in 1638, the island teemed with two types of **giant Mauritius tortoise**, both considered endemic. These reptiles fed on the fruit of an endemic latan tree (*Latania lodigesii*). The fruit ripened and fell to the ground between June and September and

the tortoises would then gorge themselves, thus building up a thick layer of white fat 'as tasty as any European butter', wrote François Leguat, one of the first settlers on Rodrigues, who later spent time in Mauritius. The egg-laying season followed the feeding season. The female tortoises laid their eggs in soft soil or sand — one reason for their extinction, for the wild pigs introduced to Mauritius early in the 17th century dug up the eggs and ate them. The other reason for the extinction of the Mauritian giant tortoise is that they were considered a precious source of meat and were taken aboard ships on long voyages as a food supply. By 1696, Leguat had noted that the tortoises were rare, and by 1753, when the cartographer Abbé de la Caille walked across the island, he noted that he did not see any.

In the first half of the 18th century, Rodrigues had a very large population of these two types of tortoise, both endemic. However, from 1750, it is thought that at least 10,000 giant tortoises a year were hunted, the vast majority being shipped to

Above: An adult female Round Island keel-scaled boa, one of two snakes endemic to Mauritius.

Mauritius for food. The last giant tortoises on Rodrigues are believed to have disappeared in a 1795 fire. A number of **Aldabran tortoises** are kept in pens in the Royal Botanical Gardens at Pamplemousses, Balfour Gardens in Beau Bassin, and the Maritim Hotel in Balaclava.

The **radiated Malagasy tortoise** has been kept as a domestic pet for the last 200 years and a number can be seen in the Casela Bird Park on the west coast. The **green turtle** and the **hawksbill turtle** were seen frequently at certain times of the year during the Dutch settlement.

Herbert Hugo, governor of Mauritius (1673-77), wrote a journal in which he described how the turtles came ashore during September and October to lay eggs. As soon as they had returned to the sea, wild pigs would emerge from the forest to dig up the nesting holes and devour the newly laid eggs. Now, the green turtle is sometimes seen in open waters around Mauritius, but only at certain times of the year, and the hawksbill turtle is very rarely seen at all. They are more commonly seen off

the shores of Agalega. The **loggerhead turtle** and the **leatherback turtle**, both vagrants, are very rarely sighted in Mauritian waters. The **soft-shelled turtle** was introduced from China in the 1920s. It inhabits lakes, rivers, and other freshwater areas, but is rarely seen.

Both the **Round Island burrowing boa** and the **Round Island keel-scaled boa** are endemic to Mauritius. These snakes used to be found on Mauritius itself, but now may be seen only on Round Island, off the northern coast of Mauritius, and, even then, very rarely. The Round Island boa has burrowing habits like certain sand-burrowing boas of North Africa and has the conical head of a burrower. Measuring roughly 95 centimetres (37 inches) long when fully grown, it has a brown back and a pinkish belly marbled with black and olive green. Another burrowing snake, the **Mauritius burrowing snake**, is now extinct. The Round Island keel-scaled boa is larger than the burrowing boa, reaching up to 150 centimetres (59 inches) long in adulthood, and has a flatter head. The young are

251

Above: African bullfrog, *Bufo regularis*, makes an impressive display.

orange, but the adults assume a green shade, presumably for camouflage, as they are arboreal.

The **adult wolf snake**, introduced accidentally from India, is brown with yellow markings and can reach a length of up to 90 centimetres (35 inches). It inhabits hot and dry places, and is sometimes an unwelcome visitor in houses, although it is inoffensive. The **blind snake** probably arrived also by accident with goods imported from India in the late 1860s. It is small, black, and likes to live in humid places under stones. Both the blind and the wolf snakes are common. The **sea snake**, which lives in open waters, is very rarely seen.

The **agama lizard** was introduced from Réunion in 1900 and is now common in forest areas. The **giant skink, Telfair's skink, Bojer's skink,** and **Bouton's (snake-eyed) skink** were all probably carried to Mauritius on tree branches that were torn away from the banks of Malagasy or African rivers following floods or a bad storm. At one time, the skinks inhabited Mauritius itself, but predators, in the form of intro-

duced rats and mongooses, soon resulted in the extinction of the giant skink. Today the other three species, all endemic, are classified as rare and are found in their largest numbers on Round Island, off the northern coast of Mauritius. Telfair's skink, named after the 19th-century plantation owner and keen naturalist Charles Telfair, is now confined to Round Island. It can grow up to 40 centimetres (16 inches) long and is thought to have come originally from Australia. Bojer's skink is found on Round Island, neighbouring Île aux Serpents, and Île aux Fouquets off the southeast coast. Bouton's skink, which also hails from Australasia, lives on Round Island, Île de la Passe off the south-east coast, and on the mainland at Cap Malheureux, on the northern coast.

The **outdoor lizard**, a native of Madagascar, is pale olive green and lives under the bark of trees. It is rarely sighted.

The **house (stump-eyed) gecko, common house gecko, rough-skinned house gecko, tree gecko,** and **mourning gecko** are all introduced species thought to have

Above: Guenther's gecko, found only on Round Island, is more primitive than the other four species of Mauritian gecko.

drifted to Mauritius on trees branches, etc., from Madagascar or India. These geckos, generally pale pink, brown, or grey, are common (apart from the mourning gecko, which only lives on Rodrigues and is rare) and live indoors.

The **night gecko** is a small species believed to have arrived only recently on Round Island, Île aux Serpents, and Coin de Mire — the islands off the northern coast of Mauritius. There it has established a sub-species, the **lesser night gecko**. Both are strictly nocturnal and are brown.

The **common day gecko, Rodrigues day gecko, forest day gecko** and **ornate day gecko**, all endemic, are considered the real gems of the Mauritian reptile world because of their beautiful colouring. Their tails are an azure, while their bodies are bright green with red spots. It is only the different red back markings that set the four apart; you really have to be an expert to distinguish them. Unlike many gecko species that are nocturnal, these four have adapted to diurnal life, their skin colouring

serving as useful camouflage among forest vegetation. Unfortunately, *Phelsuma edward-newtonii* is now extinct, though there are specimens in museums. **Guenther's gecko** is more primitive than the other four species still in existence here today. It is brownish and active at dusk.

Endemic to Mauritius, it is now confined to Round Island. The **giant gecko**, similar to Guenther's gecko, once lived on Rodrigues but is now extinct.

The **Nile crocodile** is an introduced species bred at Le Vanille Crocodile Park for its skin.

Amphibians

There are only two amphibian species on Mauritius, both introduced and both found in and around lakes, rivers, and other freshwater formations and in forested areas. The **common toad**, introduced in 1922 to control a sugar cane pest, is known to the Mauritian people as *crapo*. The **Malagasy frog** was introduced from Madagascar in 1792. The locals call it simply *grenouille*.

Insects and arachnids

Several ant types inhabit Mauritius. The **black ant** is usually found trespassing in sugar bowls. The **red ant** will sting if its short grassy ground nest is trodden on. The **white ant,** or **termite**, is known locally as *caria*; it builds nests in the trunks of dead or dying trees and sometimes in wooden houses. **Cockroaches** are common, as are a number of **bee** and **wasp** species. The most dangerous of these are the **black carpenterbee** and the **yellow wasp**; both inflict nasty stings if antagonized.

Many butterflies flutter around, and the most common are listed here. The *Papilio demodocus*, originally from Madagascar, has brown wings peppered with golden flecks, the lower sections of which are imprinted with a blue and red eye spot. It lays its eggs on the leaves of the lime tree.

The *Papilio manlius*, which is endemic, has predominantly black wings marked with patches of bright turquoise. It also lays its eggs on the leaves of the lime tree.

The *Junonia rhadama* sports purplish blue and grey wings, and is named after a famous Malagasy king, while the *Amauris phaedon* has predominantly brown wings speckled with cream, the lower sections having a cream band.

The *Cathopsilla thaurana* displays wings that are totally yellow, but with a stronger yellow shade close to the body and a paler yellow out to the wing tips.

The most interesting of the Mauritian arachnids is the **grey spider**, with legs of bright orange. It is often to be spotted in the middle of a web spun — more often than not — between electric wires. Its yellow silk was used by ladies during the French period to knit a pair of gloves that was presented to Josephine de Beauharnais on her marriage to Napoléon in 1796.

Large **centipedes** and **scorpions** with offensive bites are found on Rodrigues.

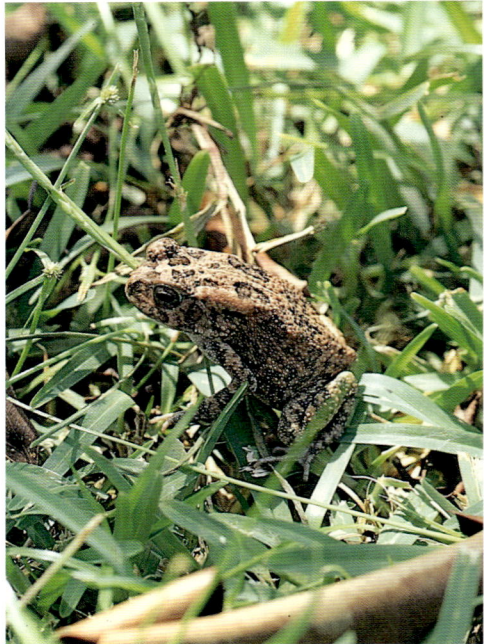

Above: Malagasy frog, introduced to Mauritius from Madagascar in 1792, is one of only two amphibians on the island.

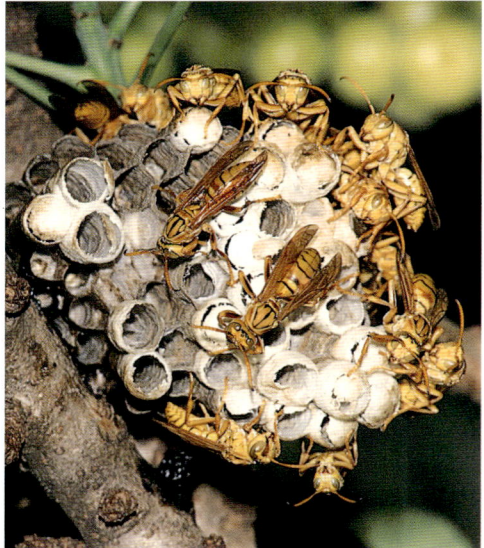

Above: Vicious when disturbed, Mauritian yellow wasps, also known as hunting wasps, swarm around their nest.

Flora: Exotic and Luxuriant

Very little remains of the native Mauritian forest. What does exist is to be found in the south-west and is now protected within the boundaries of the Black River Gorges National Park. The ruggedness of the terrain, mostly superficial lava flows, and the hilly topography have allowed this part of the virgin forest to remain intact.

Following the end of volcanic activity, marine plants were the first form of vegetation to appear. Later, as powdery soil started to materialize from the lava flows, seeds and plants are thought to have been brought by winds, sea, and birds and then began to establish themselves. Many originated in Madagascar, the nearest major land mass, just 805 kilometres (500 miles) to the west.

By the time the Dutch arrived, at the end of the 16th century, Mauritius was covered with luxuriant vegetation thanks to abundant rainfall and an equable climate. In 1638, an English sea captain, Peter Mundy, wrote of Mauritius: 'We came about the north side of the said Island, all towards the Sea Shore as fine a country as a man can Desire to beeholde, although wooddy.'

The tropical vegetation could be divided into three categories — sea-level palm savannah; huge trees, such as ebony, *bois d'olive*, *bois du natte*, and *bois de fer* in the middle ranges; and forests of tall straight trees, such as the *tambalacoque* in the upper reaches.

Nature was not to remain undisturbed for long after the Dutch advent. The settlers headed straight for the ebony forests, a wood much in favour in Europe during the 17th century, and proceeded to fell trees indiscriminately. By 1650, so much ebony had been exported to Europe that the market was glutted, and the price dropped dramatically.

In later years, much of the virgin forest was felled to make way for roads, the widespread planting of sugar cane, and urban development, and to provide wood for the domestic construction industry. By 1880, less than four per cent of Mauritius's native forest remained. Today, it is estimated that less than one per cent of the island's original pristine vegetation survives.

However, man has not been the only enemy of the original forest. Native plants suffer competition from two introduced and fast-growing species, **Chinese guava** (*Psidium cattleyanum*), which actually originated from Brazil, and **privet** (*Ligustrum robustum*) from Sri Lanka. These prolific species shade out the native tree seedlings and starve them of space and nutrients. As one local naturalist has put it, 'As a rule of thumb, once you've worked out what the guava plant and privet look like, everything else is native.'

Introduced animals have also caused problems for the flora. Monkeys eat the fruits of native plants, pigs uproot seedlings when they have germinated, and deer browse on them.

Many indigenous trees and plants have been destroyed over the years, but Mauritius still has some 900 flowering plant species native to the island and about a third of these are unique. Thirteen of these are among the rarest plants in the world, and well over 100 species are critically endangered.

One of the rarest plants in the world, a member of the coffee family called *café marron*, is endemic to Rodrigues. It was thought to be extinct until a single bush was discovered in 1980. Another bush has since been found, and cuttings sent to Kew Gardens in London have taken root, but still there are only four plants in the world.

Another plant has been rediscovered. A specimen of the endemic Mauritian species *bois chèvre* was recorded in the 1950s, but no further specimen was recorded until November 1990, when one was found surviving on an inaccessible cliff face. In February 1991, three more were located on the summit of a remote mountain. This species is now being propagated in the Government Nurseries in Curepipe.

It is at Macchabée and Brise Fer, in the

Above: Delicate pastel beauty of a Mauritian iris.

Black River Gorges National Park, that many endemic trees can still be found. The canopies of the ancient giant trees, such as the *natte*, *makak*, *tambalacoque*, *bois d'olive*, and *colophane*, intermingle at heights of up to 20 metres (65 feet), while their buttress roots intertwine at ground level, ensuring a firm hold against the strong winds that develop during cyclones.

A charming story is told about the *tambalacoque*. Various botanical gardens and the government nurseries in Mauritius have tried to germinate the *tambalacoque* seed, but without success. As the *tambalacoque* was common when the dodo was still alive, the story relates how the dodo used to eat the tree's fruit and, as it digested the flesh, its gastric juices worked on the hard seed. By the time the dodo expelled the seed from its body, it was soft enough to germinate. Now, without the dodo to assist, the *tambalacoque* is close to extinction. An intriguing tale, but untrue.

Thanks to the 'International Plant Programme' launched in 1984 by the World Wide Fund for Nature, it is hoped that the country's remaining endemic species will be saved from extinction. In conjunction with the Forestry Service and the Royal Society of Arts and Sciences, the Mauritian Wildlife Fund has established six forest vegetation plots, ranging in size from one to 10 hectares (2.5 to 25 acres), which are fenced to keep out deer and feral pigs.

Conservation workers remove the introduced vegetation to allow the native species to regenerate. They also plant seedlings of rare Mauritian species, which are propagated in the Government Nurseries in Curepipe.

In the older established plots, the difference between the vegetation in the fenced area and that in the surrounding forest is dramatic. The unmanaged forest is dominated by guava and privet, while the fenced plots have a great variety of plant species. The vegetation in the plots is less dense and has a more complex vertical structure, with four or five vegetation strata. The greater amount of light reaching the forest floor encourages a ground cover of native ferns, and the lack of competitive

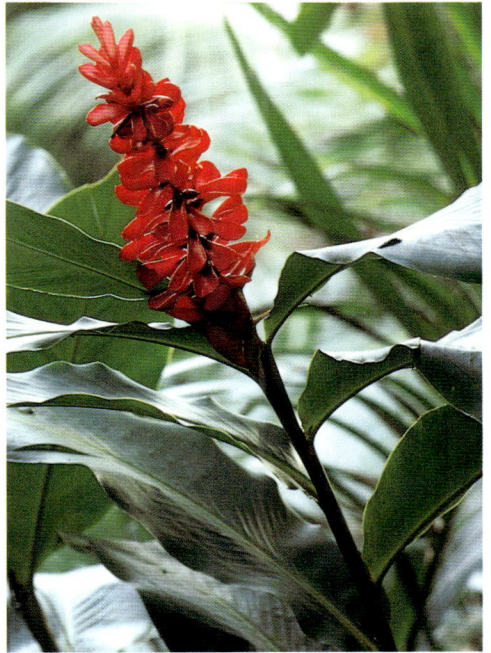

Top: *Hibiscus rosasinensis*.

Above: *Ipomea*, known as Morning Glory.

Top: *Hedychium flavuum*.

Above: *Alpina purpurata*, known as Red Ginger.

Above: Betel nuts ripen in the Mauritian sunshine.

weed species allows endemic tree seeds to germinate and sprout. The older plots are now showing significant signs of native tree regeneration. More common types of flora all around Mauritius include **screw-pines**, known locally as *vacoas*, which are most often found in marshy areas. They are easily recognized by their exposed roots which appear to prop up the tree. The **blue latan** is similar to the vacoas, but its bark has a slight blue tinge, hence its name.

The most common of the introduced trees is the **casuarina**, known locally as a *filao*. It resembles a pine and is found in large numbers growing close to beaches throughout Mauritius. It was introduced from Malaysia in the 18th century.

The east and south-east coasts support **mangrove** swamps. The mangrove is the only tree species to live in salt water.

Another easily recognizable tree is the **banyan**, an import from India which grows roots that hang down from its branches.

Given its tropical vegetation, a number of **palm** species, including the spectacular **traveller's palm**, are found in Mauritius.

One of the most distinctive trees, and one of the most attractive when it flowers in summer, is the **flamboyant**. Between November and January, this tree is ablaze with red flowers. Aside from the ubiquitously cultivated **anthuriums** and **andraeneums,** colourful **poinsettias, hibiscus, orchids,** and **bougainvillea** are among the flowering plants found on the island.

The national flower is the endemic *trochetia*, which is rarely seen, as it grows mainly in such inaccessible places as the south face of Le Morne Brabant. It is a delicate rose pink, bell-shaped blossom that hangs down from a nobbled stem crowned with leaves. The Black River Gorges National Park is the best place to visit the Mauritian native forest, but for those not interested in hiking, or without the time to visit the park, try the Royal Botanical Gardens in Pamplemousses or the Botanical Gardens in Curepipe.

The Sweet Success of Sugar

If the Dutch left Mauritius a great legacy, it was sugar cane. The crop plays a crucial part in the physical and economic fabric of Mauritius. The sugar fields make an immediate visual impact on the visitor and are responsible for changing the character of the island's landscape throughout the year.

When the cane reaches a certain height, the road user can see nothing but what is directly in front of him, but when the cane is harvested, sweeping vistas across the land and sea suddenly reveal themselves. Meanwhile, on the economic front, sugar cane has been at the heart of the island's prosperity for many years.

Along with a number of other plant species, it was introduced from Java by Dutch Governor Adrian van der Stel in 1639, and a plaque commemorating this fact has been erected on the Ferney Sugar Estate close to Vieux Grand Port. At first, the expressed sugar cane juice was used to distil only arrack, a crude form of liquor, but in 1696 the first sugar was produced.

Initially cane cultivation spread slowly under French rule. Only when La Bourdonnais introduced the first sugar factory in 1743, was sugar produced on a significant scale.

By 1755, enough sugar was being produced to meet the needs of Île de France, the neighbouring island of Bourbon, and the sailing ships that called at Île de France.

Cultivation increased significantly in the second half of the 18th century, especially during the War of American Independence (1776-1783). Much of this was due to the demand for arrack, which was popular among the French soldiers and sailors who visited the island. By 1786, there were 10 sugar factories on the island.

The first governor following the British conquest in 1810 was Sir Robert Farquhar. He realized the economic potential of sugar, given that the island was in the cyclone belt where less sturdy crops were unlikely to survive, and encouraged landowners to plant more cane.

After 1815, Mauritius experienced remarkable growth in its sugar cane culture. Thanks to the new impetus, 106 mills were in operation in 1820 and, by 1825, sugar production had reached 10,800 tons (more than three times the output in 1801).

The introduction of the first horizontal roller mill by Charles Telfair at the Bel Ombre factory in 1819 and the use of a steam-driven mill for the first time in Mauritius at the Belle Mare factory in 1822 certainly helped to increase production. Previously, mills had relied entirely on slaves and oxen to turn the rollers to crush the cane (a replica of this ancient method can be seen at Domaine les Pailles, on the outskirts of Port Louis). By 1853, all the animal-driven mills had been replaced by mechanized mills.

The British decision in 1825 to admit Mauritian sugar at the same duty as sugar from the West Indies led to the further expansion of sugar-growing on the Indian Ocean island. The decision was to dictate the economic pattern for years to come.

In just one year, between 1825 and 1826, sugar production increased from 10,869 tons to 21,244 tons. Within two or three years, it had become the most important crop.

But, just as the island's sugar industry was beginning to flourish further, the anti-slavery movement came into prominence and threatened to bring the industry to a halt. Opposition to abolition was only overcome when Britain agreed to pay compensation to the slave owners. In 1835 the slaves were emancipated and the plantation owners received UK£ 2 million, to be invested in the sugar industry to help boost production. There followed a boom that was to last for 10 years.

An alternative source of labour was found — indentured labourers from India.

Overleaf: Chateau de Ville Bague stands in immaculate gardens, surrounded by the deep green of its surrounding sugar plantation.

A few Indians had started to arrive in Mauritius from 1829, but large numbers were not brought into the country until after the abolition of slavery.

By the 1840s, Mauritius was the chief sugar producer in the British Empire, and by 1854 exports exceeded 100,000 tons a year. In the meantime, other crops, such as coffee and indigo, had largely been abandoned due to the greater profits sugar offered. Sugar yields peaked in Mauritius in 1865, when 165,000 tons were produced. One reason for this apex was the increase in demand for sugar from Europe. In 1820, the average per capita consumption of sugar in Britain was 7.6 kilos (17 lbs). By 1860, it had risen to 15.8 kilos (35 lbs).

Another reason for greater production was technological advancement. For example, the introduction of the American vacuum pan process resulted in greater efficiency in the extraction of juice, an increased yield from the cane, and a more reliable, and refined, sugar quality.

The disadvantage of the technological progression, however, was that the heavy capital cost of new machinery inevitably meant that it was no longer possible for each estate to have a mill for processing its own cane. The number of sugar factories in Mauritius fell from 222 in 1853 to 104 in 1892 — and to just 60 in 1908. At the same time, the number of estates was increasing and their average size diminishing.

There were other problems. A malaria outbreak in 1866 resulted in coastal estates being abandoned. Competition also multiplied, as countries like Indonesia and Cuba were able to produce sugar more cheaply, and European farmers, often with government subsidies, produced more and more sugar from beet.

So, despite the fact that Britain's consumption grew significantly, Mauritius no longer benefited from this comsumption upsurge.

During the last 30 years of the 19th century, the Mauritian sugar industry was more or less stagnant and production levelled out at around 130,000 tons annually.

To compound its problems, the wholesale London price, which had remained fairly steady up to the early 1880s, fell by almost 50 per cent between 1883 and 1887. The sugar boom was over for the time being.

These setbacks led the plantation owners to improve their cultivation techniques and manufacturing processes. New cane varieties were introduced, as were chemical fertilizers and chemical control in the sugar factories. An agricultural research laboratory, the Station Agronomique, was established in 1893. Its work was taken over 20 years later by the government's newly created Department of Agriculture.

This period of technical progress led to a number of other institutions being created, all of which contributed to advances in the industry. In 1919 the plantation owners united to form a sugar syndicate. At first it included only 70 per cent of the producers, but that percentage increased gradually over the years and since 1956 it has controlled the whole of Mauritius's sugar production.

From 1919, the industry enjoyed prosperity for a time. In 1920, Mauritius sold about 225,000 tons and, for the next three years, enjoyed a small boom. It was not to last long. As the price went up, so too did other costs, including overheads.

In the world depression of the 1930s, the Mauritian sugar industry hit a rough patch. Sugar prices fell, and to make matters worse, a serious cyclone struck Mauritius in 1931, destroying a significant proportion of the crop.

The bad years brought to a head growing rumblings of dissatisfaction with the political and economic state of affairs. In 1937, the Labour Party, which stressed workers' economic, social, and political grievances at its meetings, played an important part in stirring up strikes on the sugar estates. Plantation owners, for the first time, found their power seriously threatened. A commission of inquiry was critical of many aspects of the industry. Little changed as far as the life of the workers was concerned, but the plantation owners continued their quest to improve the

Opposite: Harvesting sugar cane on a Mauritian plantation.

Above: Mauritius is ideal for sugar cane cultivation, which needs plenty of sun and water.

industry by setting up the independent Mauritius Sugar Industry Research Institute in 1953.

The institute maintains divisions relating to plant breeding, botany and irrigation, pathology, entomology, soils and plant nutrition, cane and food crop agronomy, biometry, and sugar technology.

The sugar industry enjoyed another boom in the early 1970s that peaked in 1973, when a record 718,464 tons was produced. The following year, sugar and molasses represented nearly 90 per cent of the total domestic product. Once again, the upturn did not last long. While prices fell, wages rose substantially.

Perhaps some good has resulted from these negative developments. The high wages have forced the industry, with government approval, to resort to greater mechanization and to make maximum use of all parts of the crop by developing a wide range of by-products. Sugar dominance has decreased and the industry is playing an important part in the struggle to diversify the island's agricultural sector

so that Mauritius is not dependent on a single crop. Tea is the country's next most important agricultural crop after sugar, while others of importance include tobacco and fibre.

A wide range of vegetables is cultivated. Many of them are inter-cropped between rows of sugar cane in an effort to increase the proportion of food produced and thereby reduce the need to import large quantities of food, which has led in the past to an unfavourable balance of trade. This policy has met with considerable success: total foodcrop production increased from 39,000 tons in 1975 to more than 56,000 tons in 1991.

The trouble is that few crops are able to withstand the cyclones as strongly as sugar, and few seem to flourish as well in the difficult agricultural conditions of the island's rock-strewn landscape.

Cane fields still cover around 84,000 hectares (207,480 acres), which accounts for at least 40 per cent of the island's surface and over 90 per cent of the cultivated land, producing annually over six million tons of cane and around 650,000 tons of sugar — 590,000 tons of which is exported to the European Union. Approximately 55 per cent of the land under cane is owned by the 18 large estates, which also have their own sugar factories. The rest belongs to some 35,000 smallholders.

Today, sugar and molasses exports are not as important as they once were, but they still represent about 30 per cent of total exports. The share of sugar in the Gross Domestic Product is 10 per cent. The industry provides direct employment to more than 40,000 people (over 14 per cent of the working population).

Mauritius produces a large range of sugars, including demerara, golden granulated, golden caster, light and dark muscovado, and light and dark bakery.

The three important by-products are molasses, bagasse, and filter scums.

Most of the molasses is exported, but a small proportion remains in Mauritius and is used to produce rum, power alcohol, denatured spirit, redistilled alcohol, vinegar, drugs, and perfume. Cane spirit is manufactured from redistilled alcohol and local distilleries now produce a range of liquors, including gin and brandy, under licence from foreign firms.

Bagasse is mainly used to raise the steam necessary for the operation of the sugar factories. In some factories, part of the excess bagasse is burnt to generate electricity for the national grid. Bagasse-generated electricity represents 15 per cent of the overall electricity available on the grid. Bagasse is also used as a fertilizer by the anthurium and andraeneum plantations.

Filter scums contain a small amount of phosphoric acid and are applied to the fields at planting time as a fertilizer.

Sugar cane cultivation

Sugar cane, a tropical plant requiring strong sunlight and abundant water, is a giant grass that regenerates once it has been cut. In general, fresh cane is planted every eight years. Before planting, tractors are used to prepare the land. When new land is cultivated, rocks are removed and drainage ditches excavated with the help of bulldozers. Furrows are usually spaced at intervals of 1.6 metres (5.2 feet). Planting is carried out with short sections of cane called 'setts', about 40 centimetres (15.7 inches) long, which are laid in the furrow.

Each sett has several 'eyes' from which the plant and its root will grow. Planting is usually done manually, although mechanical planting is gradually being introduced. The planting season extends from the beginning of the year to September. Where rainfall is insufficient, irrigation is employed to nurture the cane.

To grow strong, healthy cane, the application of fertilizers is essential. Weeds are dealt with through the use of chemicals, whereas cane pests are culturally, biologically, or chemically controlled. Artificial ripeners are sprayed from helicopters in some areas to increase the sucrose content at the beginning of the harvest.

The cane is ready for cutting between 11 and 18 months after planting. Trashing is generally carried out immediately before the harvest to obtain cleaner canes and to facilitate harvesting.

Where the trash canopy is very thick, the fields are burnt prior to being harvested. Harvesting is usually carried out from June to November.

Cane cutting is mostly done by hand, but loading onto containers is about 50 per cent mechanized. Mechanical harvesters are gradually being introduced, but, at present, mechanically harvested cane represents only about three per cent of total production. Cane is then loaded onto trucks and taken to a factory.

Visits to sugar estates can be arranged either through local tour operators or through the public relations office of each individual estate. The estates are quite willing to take small groups or families on a tour of their sugar factories.

Sporting Mauritius

Mauritius offers visitors numerous sporting activities. Of the wealth of watersports, two of the most popular — big game fishing and scuba-diving — are detailed elsewhere. There are also many land-based sports.

Watersports

Undersea walking

For a really special experience — unless you've been to the Bahamas, the only other place in the world which operates this service — walk under water during your stay in Mauritius.

Sea walkers must don a large helmet for their underwater experience. A sophisticated system of compressors, air reservoirs, and valves on a boat moored at the site supply the helmet with constant fresh air.

Undersea walking is a particularly good way for children and non-swimmers to view marine life, but it is a fun activity for all, as underwater guides point out the numerous species of coral, hand out pieces of bread on which hundreds of fish flock to feed, and take photos to ensure this unique experience is not forgotten.

Undersea walking is available only at Grand Baie. The boat with the compressors and other essential equipment is permanently moored at the nearby Pointe aux Cannoniers, an area where walkers are assured of clear, calm seas and plenty of fish all year round.

For more information, contact Undersea Walk on Tel: 263-7820 or 423-8822.

Water-skiing, windsurfing and boating

Most hotels have their own boathouse offering a wide range of watersports: water-skiing, windsurfing, use of pedalos, canoes, and trips on glass-bottom boats. In the majority of cases, these activities are free to hotel guests.

Yachting

Hop on board a catamaran and sail the coastal waters to gain a totally different perspective of Mauritius. A fleet of catamarans particularly suited to the shallow lagoon waters can be used to explore the unspoilt and otherwise inaccessible inlets along the coast, as well as Îlot Gabriel and Île Plate.

Catamarans of varying sizes can be hired for day trips, sunset cruises, overnight breaks and weekend retreats. Lunch — usually freshly caught fish barbecued at the back of the boat — is served on board during day trips. Some yachts can arrange the hire of snorkelling, scuba-diving, water-skiing, fishing and wind-surfing equipment. For something completely different, you can charter the *Isla Mauritia*, a tall 19th-century ship from Yacht Charters.

For more information, contact:
- Yacht Charters, Royal Road, Grand Baie Tel: 263-8395, Fax: 263-7814
- Croisieres Australes, Gustave Colin Street, Forestside Tel: 675-1453, Fax: 675-6425
- Croisiere Oceane, Trou d'Eau Douce Tel: 419-2767
- Aquarius, Royal Road, Grand Baie Tel: 423-5566
- Croisieres Turquoises, Riche en Eau Tel: 631-9835, Fax: 631-9379

Landsports

Golfing

Mauritius is fast becoming a favourite holiday destination for keen golfers because it now has three 18-hole courses.

The Belle Mare Plage Golf Course is the most recent addition, having opened in January 1994. A par-73 course designed by South African professional Hugh Baiocchi, the Belle Mare is a demanding course with no margin for error. Every hole is flanked by hazards that include water, thick undergrowth, trees, and volcanic boulders. Given its location on the east coast, strong offshore winds mean that an even greater

Above: Zebra fish swarm around young girl as she experiences the wonders of an undersea walk in a Mauritian lagoon. Weighed down by the head visor through which oxygen is pumped, sea-bed walkers can enjoy the wonders of the inner universe just beneath the surface.

Right: Youngster smiles in delight as he takes his first steps underwater in a world of jewelled fish. Mauritius is one of only a few places in the world where undersea walking is organized.

Above: Verdant palm-fringed golf courses such as this lure golfers to Mauritius year after year.
Opposite: Carol Chan San, international mountain bike star of Mauritius, pauses during training in the highlands.

emphasis is placed on accuracy. The Paradis Golf Course in the south-west at Le Morne is the most picturesque of the three 18-hole courses. On one side of this par-72 course, designed by South African David Dulton, is the open sea; on the other is the majestic mountain of Le Morne. One advantage with both these courses is that they are located close to hotels, so golfers staying there can walk out to the first tee and, if they lack the stamina to play 18 holes straight off, can play nine holes in the morning and the second nine in the afternoon.

The third 18-hole golf course forms part of the private Gymkhana Club in Vacoas, which allows visitors to play for a green fee. The course is not, however, as challenging as those at the Belle Mare or Le Morne.

The St Geran, Trou aux Biches and the Shadrani hotels have nine-hole courses. The Gary Player-designed St Geran course has always been popular with tourists. In addition, the Maritim hotel has a short 'executive course' — all the holes are designed as par-3s. All the golf courses will supply clubs, and there are professionals on hand to provide tuition. For more information, contact the hotels or the Gymkhana Club directly.

Hiking

Dramatic mountain scenery, exotic vegetation, and varied fauna make Mauritius an interesting destination for keen walkers.

The Black River Gorges National Park (in the south-west) is popular among walkers because of its waterfalls and large tracts of native forest on which the island's endangered native fauna, such as the rare Mauritian kestrel, pink pigeon, and echo parakeet, depend for survival.

The park, first of its kind in Mauritius, was established in June 1994 and has 51 kilometres (32 miles) of footpath covering most of the island's wild walks. Eventually, the park will set up an information centre with licensed guides to assist visitors. Even now, walkers can hire the services of an experienced guide, such as King How, who is familiar with a wide range of walks lasting between three hours and three days (if visitors wish to camp as well). All of these walks are fairly easy and can be completed by all calibres of walker. While walking, King How provides a steady stream of information on the ecology, plants, birds, and geology. King How speaks French, English, and Creole, and charged between Rs150 and Rs200 a person a day in 1996.

Three of the walks recommended by King How are detailed below.

• **Le Pétrin–Macchabée Forest– Manava Gorges–Trois Bras** (15 kilometres — nine miles). En route, walkers may see Mauritius echo parakeets, white-tailed tropic birds, Mauritius fruit bats, Indian ring-necked parakeets, Mauritius cuck-oo shrikes, Mauritius kestrels, wild deer, wild pigs, tenrecs, and monkeys. Between January and May, edible Chinese guavas are also found on the walk.

• **Le Pétrin–Macchabée Forest– Mare Longue Forest–Brise-Fer Forest– Tamarind Falls Reservoir** (15 kilometres — nine miles). The pink pigeon and Mauritius echo parakeet may be seen en route, and King How will point out two sample plots of indigenous and endemic plants. The Brise-Fer peak can be incorporated into the walk, but adds an extra hour to the time taken.

• **Plaine Champagne–Black River Peak–Chamarel Church** (eight kilometres — five miles). The highlight is lunch on Black River Peak, the highest point on the island. On the way to and from the peak, white-tailed tropic birds, Mauritius fruit bats, Indian ring-necked parakeets, Mauritius cuckoo shrikes, wild deer, wild pigs, tenrecs, and monkeys may be seen. Between January and May, edible Chinese guavas can be picked along the path.

Intrepid walkers wishing to explore the numerous mountain and coastal hikes on their own should get hold of a copy of either Alexander Ward's *Climbing and Mountain Walking in Mauritius* or Robert Marsh's *Mountains of Mauritius, A Climber's Guide*. Ward's book, the first on the subject, aroused popular interest in mountain excursions in general, but Marsh's is far more comprehensive. Unfortunately, both books are out of print and hard to come by, but they might be found in some public libraries.

A few tips from Marsh's book include visiting the Ministry of Housing for comprehensive maps and wearing decent footwear, such as trainers or ordinary walking boots (alpine boots are not needed).

The best thing about climbing Le Pouce, Marsh writes, is the view to the west over Port Louis, the harbour, and encircling hills, and the panoramas to the east over sugar cane fields. Pieter Both, Marsh admits, may look difficult to climb because it is such a slender peak, but it is actually as simple as climbing a ladder, as the Special Mobile Force has set solid iron rungs into the rock. However, by 1996 these rungs had already began to corrode and visitors should check with the authorities before attempting this climb.

Lion Mountain on the east coast is not that high, writes Marsh, but it is impressive, solid, and occupies a position of strategic importance overlooking Vieux Grand Port. It would, no doubt, have been an ideal place from which to watch the famous 1810 battle between the French settlers and the British invaders. Today, Lion Mountain provides an excellent view of Mahébourg, the offshore lagoon islets, and the wooded Bambous slopes and Creole Mountain ranges.

The best walking months are cool May and June when the island's vegetation is also at its most colourful, but as long as walkers begin early enough to avoid the midday summer heat, walks can be made all year round.

For more information, contact King How on Tel: 242-4052.

Horse riding

Les Écuries (The Stables) at Domaine les Pailles, just south of Port Louis, is the main equestrian centre. Opened in August 1991, Les Écuries were planned and are managed by Remi Barrot, a former French national rider in three-day events who graduated from France's National Riding School.

Les Écuries houses 45 horses, six of which are the only trekking steeds in Mauritius, and they are ideal for both beginners and advanced riders. Treks take place in the morning and last for a couple of hours. The hourly cost is Rs500 (as of mid-1996), which includes insurance and riding equipment (hat and boots). Les Écuries advises all riders to wear long trousers and to book at least 24 hours in advance.

Once a month, usually to coincide with the full moon, Les Écuries also organizes an overnight trek. Riders trek for an hour and a half and then are supplied with a barbecue supper, after which there's time for a sing-song to the accompaniment of harmonica and guitar.

The night is spent in lodges with basic bathroom facilities, with the ride back to base in the morning. Non-riders who wish to accompany their families can be taken up to the lodges by a Land Rover. The cost (including insurance, lodging, meals, and equipment rental) was Rs1,000 a person in mid-1995. Dressage and show jumping lessons can be arranged on request at Rs500 an hour.

Les Écuries also has eight unruffled Welsh ponies for children between the ages five and 10. If the children can already ride, Les Écuries will take them out trekking; otherwise beginners take lessons in the ring. In mid-1996, the cost for children was Rs150 an hour for trekking or in the ring. For more information on all activities, including lessons on driving horse-drawn carriages, you should contact Remi Barrot at Les Écuries on Tel: 208-1998.

The following hotels also organize horse riding for their guests: Ambre, Belle Mare Plage, Le Paradis, Le Pearle Beach, Le Touessrok, Le Tropical, Les Orchidees, Maritim, Sandy Bay, and Silver Beach.

Hunting

June to September is the traditional hunting season, when wealthy landowners — for example, in Plaine Champagne and Case Noyale in the south-west of the island — invite friends to hunt the many Javanese deer they keep on their estates.

There is only one private estate in Mauritius, the Domaine du Chasseur in the south-east, where visitors can hunt all year round for a fee.

Hunters either stalk their prey or shoot from miradors (raised observation posts where the hunters sit and wait for beaters to drive the deer into fire range). Hunting helps the estates to cull the animals; 400 deer must be killed every year to keep the numbers manageable.

All essential hunting equipment is provided by the Domaine, which will also arrange for any trophy (the head of a shot deer) to be stuffed, mounted, and freighted back home. Prices vary according to the type of deer shot.

For more information, you should contact the Domaine du Chasseur at Anse Jonchée on Tel: 6345 097.

Paragliding

Those who relish flying high with kestrels may wish to paraglide over the Domaine du Chasseur, where several rare Mauritian kestrels are known to reside.

In August 1992, the French Paragliding champion asked Alan O'Reilly, Director-General of Domaine du Chasseur, the nature reserve in the south-east, to allow him to paraglide from the estate's mountain tops. He found five excellent spots from which to lift off and the sport has become so popular in such a short time that the island had its own annual international event in November 1993 when 47 of the world's top paragliders descended on Mauritius to compete.

Tourists wishing to paraglide were provided with all the necessary equipment and driven in four-wheel-drive vehicles to one of the various take-off points high on the hillside. Each participant had a radio with its own frequency, so he could call the Domaine once he had landed and needed to be picked up. The best paragliding

Above: Hunting is allowed on private estates in Mauritius, such as Domaine du Chasseur, and helps cull the animals: some 400 deer must be killed every year to keep the numbers manageable.

months are between September and April, when there is little wind and the well-heated earth produces thermal currents, giving paragliders the chance to soar in the skies for longer. However, in the second half of 1996, para-gliding had come to a temporary halt and enthusiasts should ask if facilities are available. Call the Domaine du Chasseur at Anse Jonchée on Tel: 6345 097.

Overleaf: Water-skier leaps the wake carved by his speed boat.

A Diver's Paradise

The popularity of scuba-diving is increasing rapidly among visitors to Mauritius due to improved diving facilities and greater international exposure to the fascinating undersea world waiting to be explored.

In 1993, 30,000 tourists (Almost one in 10) went scuba-diving at one of the 24 fully equipped diving centres. A decade earlier, there were only 12. Not surprisingly, the majority of the centres are on the coast and 90 per cent are based in hotels.

The Mauritian Scuba Diving Association (MSDA) regulates and promotes the local industry, ensuring that all the dive centres are run by qualified and experienced dive masters.

All the dive masters, who have been trained according to international standards, such as PADI, NAUI, and BSAC, are recognized by CMAS, the World Underwater Federation. All the diving centres are now to be run by instructors with a minimum of two stars.

The MSDA is fully active in the international scuba-diving arena and likes to be up-to-date on developments. In 1992, Mauritius played host to the first diving medicine congress in 12 years, and in September 1995 it is due to hold an international CMAS meeting.

The island also boasts a very active local diving club, the Mauritius Underwater Group — MUGS — which caters for locals and long-term residents.

According to Mauritian regulations, visitors must always dive with an instructor to keep an eye on the depths attained and the time spent underwater. A boat must always escort divers, and there will be extra oxygen supplies and a first-aid kit either on the accompanying boat or back at the home diving centre.

Should divers run into problems, three doctors trained in underwater medicine are available to treat such cases. There is also a decompression chamber at Vacoas in the centre of Mauritius, a maximum of an hour's drive from any coastal point.

According to local law, divers must be subjected to a medical check-up before they are allowed in the decompression chamber, which is open 24 hours a day. Diving centres supply all the necessary equipment, such as regulators, pressure gauges, and inflators (also known as buoyancy control devices, BCDs), but divers are welcome to bring their own. Diving charges are usually the same whether a diver uses his or her own equipment or the centre's.

Most centres organize two dives a day, although some arrange three in the peak tourist season. Some also organize night dives. A great advantage of diving in Mauritius is that it is possible, from most centres, to make two dives a day because so little time is wasted on travel — dive masters frequent dive spots no more than an hour away by boat — and so enthusiasts can dive in the morning, return to their hotel at lunchtime for a little siesta and dive again in the afternoon. Most centres are closed on Sunday.

Fifty per cent of the diving centres run scuba-diving courses that can be completed during a one-or two-week holiday — the PADI and NAUI centres offer open-water courses and the BSAC centres offer first-grade courses. Mauritius provides some excellent conditions for learning to dive because the surrounding lagoon is fairly shallow and it is possible to start diving lessons in the sea rather than a swimming pool. After qualification, most diving in Mauritius itself is done just outside the reef at depths from three metres (10 feet) to 30 (100 feet) or more metres.

Scuba-diving is possible all year round, except when there are cyclones (which normally occur in January and February). However, diving centres located on the east coast usually take divers overland to other

Opposite: Diver's torch illuminates a spectacular but dangerous lionfish, common to the Indian Ocean waters off Mauritius.

Above: Group of blackspotted sweetlips shelter in a coral overhang.

parts of the island, such as the north, in July and August, and dive from there, as the sea is often too rough in the east during these winter months. The MSDA only allows people aged 16 or above to dive, and they must have a doctor's certificate. Scuba-diving enthusiasts can buy custom-made wetsuits from Sun Sea Snow Sports in Trou aux Biches (Tel: 261-5174) at about a third of the cost in Europe.

Once in the water, visitors can expect to discover a captivating world where both small tropical reef fish and larger predators inhabit a seascape — predominantly volcanic, but colonized by corals — as rich and diverse as any terrestrial scenery. There are, for example, large sandbanks, rocky outcrops, volcanic and coralline reefs, and steep reef slopes to be explored.

Pierre Szalay, the 1994 President of the MSDA, has been diving around Mauritius for more than 10 years. 'I have worked almost everywhere in the world,' he says, 'and I still consider Mauritius the most exciting place to dive. This is not the place for gigantic scenery — if one is looking for vast, breathtaking views, it is better to dive in the Red Sea — but here [Mauritius] everything is delicate. The sites are small and you can see almost everything you can dream of.'

Divers in Mauritius must learn to appreciate the diverse landscape and to observe closely the minute detail of its marine life. For example, there is a greater variety of corals and more species of fish than are found in the Red Sea. Another advantage Mauritius has over the Red Sea is that it is far away from any major sea route and is not, therefore, subjected to the same level of pollution.

Due to the cyclones that Mauritius frequently experiences, the reefs are made of very strong corals, while the more fragile corals are found at greater depths. In all, very many different species of coral are to be found in Mauritian waters, and there is a wide variety of shells, including some endemic ones, like the Barthelemy cone.

The Mauritian waters are home to a great number of small reef fish, but coastal spots with big fish are limited. Lobster and

Above: One of the many wonders of underwater Mauritius: a feathery white fan worm.

crayfish are common. Many small reef fish are unique to Mauritius or the Mascarenes. There is, for example, a small black coffer fish with white spots that's very common in Mauritian waters, but is found nowhere else in the world. Only three people in Mauritius are allowed to collect tropical sea fish, and they find new fish and new species every year. For example, in 1991 they found 12 new species.

One collector, Daniel Pelicer, is something of a legend in Mauritius. He made a documentary about his work in 1991 entitled *Daniel and his Fish*, which won a number of international awards.

The fish collected are sold to aquariums around the world. The amount collected is very small — Daniel, for example, collects in one month what a single *garoupa* eats in one day — but the up-to-date information they generate is greatly appreciated by scientists and the diving centres.

The local scuba-diving community's motto is 'Look, but do not touch'. Since 1971, all scuba-divers and snorkellers have been forbidden to take corals and shells from the ocean or to use spear guns to catch fish.

The Coast Guard, which enforces these laws, has grown stronger ever since the late 1980s when, instead of just having big boats that could cruise the main shipping channels, it was equipped with small rubber dinghies that allow them to enter the reef and check activities in the lagoon.

Dynamite fishing was practised before 1980 — not because it was legal, but because dynamite was easily available as it was being used in the road construction industry. The only reason the locals have stopped dynamite fishing is because the type of explosives used in the last decade on land is not effective under water.

About 15 years ago, the Mauritius Marine Conservation Society (MMCS) — in part to counter the destruction by dynamite fishing but also to provide some alternative dive sites — started sinking old boats to create artificial reefs. Mauritius was the first country in the world to initiate such a programme and the MMCS has since been recognized by UNESCO for its work, which

Above: School of humpbacked snapper skim above the surface of a coral reef.

it has fine-tuned to an art following detailed studies on local marine ecology. So far, about 10 boats have been sunk in water 20 to 40 metres (65 to 130 feet) deep. Only recently has the establishment of a marine national park come close to fruition. At the end of 1994, it was hoped that the first would be inaugurated in Baie aux Tortues, Balaclava, on the west coast.

Now there are hopes to establish another protected area in Blue Bay.

A few of the best dive spots in Mauritius are listed below according to region.

Northern dive spots

The northern offshore offers a platform reef rich in fauna and flora. There are plenty of local dive spots for those with little experience, but some spots close to Coin de Mire are not for the novice because they are exposed to the ocean swell.

Aquarium

There the water reaches a maximum depth of 20 metres (65 feet), so it is possible to spend considerable lengths of time underwater. It is one of the most frequently visited dive sites in Mauritius, with an exceptional range of fish and corals; hence its name. Moray eels inhabit crevices and hump-backed scorpion fish are often seen.

Whale Rock

There are several spots, varying in depth from 18 to 45 metres (60 to 150 feet), which feature large black slabs of volcanic rock, plus black coral, huge gorgonians, and canyons; the top section has lots of small reef fish, such as angel fish and *garoupa*.

At greater depths, there are larger fish, including sweetlips, parrot and moon fish, barracuda and bottom snappers, and, if lucky, divers may see crayfish and dog-tooth tuna. Between 20 and 36 metres (65 and 120 feet) down, the landscape is impressive and green moray eels may be encountered.

Above: Diving in Mauritian waters reveals a myriad of beautiful fish and spectacular coral formations. Overleaf: Scuba-diving is possible all year round in Mauritius, and half of the diving centres in the country run courses that can be completed during a one-or two-week holiday.

Les Charpentiers (Coin de Mire)

Around 20 to 25 metres (65 to 80 feet) on a wall in front of the island of Coin de Mire, which drops down to a hundred metres (328 feet) or more; four sites can be visited, some as a drift dive; for experienced divers; lots of oyster clams, feather-duster worms, parrot fish, wahoo, dogtooth tuna, barracuda, and shoals of large kingfish are to be seen as well as dorado and whitetip sharks.

Stella Maru

A maximum depth of 30 metres (100 feet); a recent wreck, one of the 10 boats sunk by the MMCS to create artifical reefs — it is an old Taiwanese trawler, lying on its starboard side; a good alternative dive; plenty of tropical reef fish, such as boxfish and triggerfish on the natural, nearby reef, and scorpion and lionfish around the wreck.

Flat Island

Up to 50 metres (165 feet) deep; an all-day trip made only during the summer months when the seas are calm; a drift dive in the Valley of the Sharks, a rocky area with little coral growth, where whitetip and grey reef shark congregate.

Eastern dive spots

The east coast has some of the most beautiful dive sites in Mauritius, but they are often difficult to reach because this is the windward side of the island and so the sea can be rough. Due to this sea movement, the marine life is rich and diverse.

St Geran

Less than 10 metres (33 feet); an ancient wreck — the same one that features in Bernadin St Pierre's novel *Paul et Virginie*; some 'pieces of eight' can be found among the lumps of coral, and the ship's anchor and cannon are visible; a visit to the St Geran means a long boat trip.

St Geran Passe

Less than 20 metres (65 feet); a drift dive through a pass in the reef; the gentle current carries divers past huge parrotfish, coral walls, and a mass of brilliantly coloured tropical fish.

Roche Zozo

A maximum depth of 40 metres (130 feet); beautiful landscape with rich coral life.

Canyon Lobster

Less than 30 metres (100 feet), averaging 20 metres (65 feet); a dive through a pass in the reef with crayfish and lots of big fish, including tuna and, at certain times of the year, whitetip sharks.

Southern dive spots

There are not as many dive sites in the south as in other parts of the island, but there is still variety — shallow dives and some fantastic deep dives.

Bill's Murenes

Less than 30 metres (100 feet); a family of large, tame moray eels.

HMS Sirius

Up to 25 metres (80 feet); an ancient wreck. Although there are thought to be around 300 authentic wrecks, there is little left of most of them because the ships were made of wood and have disintegrated under water over time, but parts of *Sirius*, the only one known to lie in the lagoon, remain intact, protected by the fine silt continuously discharged by nearby rivers. A British warship, *Sirius* sank on 25 August, 1810, when she was set alight by the French. Once the fire reached the gunpowder store, *Sirius* met her death with a big bang. As a result, the wreck is scattered. Parts of the ship's remains, which provide shelter for trumpet, scorpion and butterfly fish, wrasse, and crayfish, have been invaded by white whip-like coral.

Western dive spots

Dive spots off the west coast are among the most popular because they are on the leeward side of the island, where conditions are calm and visibility rarely falls below 30 metres (100 feet).

Another advantage of the west coast dive spots is the great wealth and the variety of the underwater scenery — there are shallow water platforms of less than 20 metres (65 feet) to be explored, as well as steep slopes where the sea floor descends very quickly to more than 30 metres (100 feet).

Top left: Sabre squirrelfish.
Left: Indian Ocean giant clam.

The Cathedral

A maximum depth of 30 metres (100 feet); a very famous dive spot in Mauritius; fantastic landscape; essentially a wall dive to 30 metres (100 feet), where there is a three-metre-wide (10-foot wide) entrance to a large cave. The cathedral is about 15 metres (50 feet) wide with a three-metre-high (10-foot-high) arched roof; at the far end of the cave is a chimney or shaft about two metres (6.5 feet) wide that ascends vertically to the reef; marine life of interest includes large oyster clams, lobsters, soldierfish, squirrelfish, kingfish and lionfish, as well as fire and black coral.

The Aquarium

A shallow dive of not more than 15 metres (50 feet); small cliff faces, gullies and crevices; plenty of squirrel, soldier, angel, and butterfly fish, as well as *garoupa*, tame moray eels, and plenty of anemones; corals include the thick black wire and the colourful soft varieties.

Shark Point (also known as Rempart l'Herbe)

Between 40 and 60 metres (130 and 200 feet); normally made as a drift dive along a steep slope; hard and soft corals, also lots of big fish, including shoals of kingfish, barracuda, wahoo, tuna, and — throughout the year — reef sharks, while, on occasion, hammerhead sharks and large rays have been spotted.

St Gabriel, Kai Sei 113, and Tug II

Between 20 and 35 metres (65 and 115 feet); three ships scuttled to create artificial reefs as part of the MMCS programme; Tug II is highly recommended for those interested in shells.

Rodrigues dive spots

Dive spots in Rodrigues fall into two broad categories — inside and outside the reef.

Aquarium

A depth of only six metres (20 feet); inside the reef; this dive spot takes its name from the fact that it is always teeming with many different varieties of brightly coloured reef fish so tame that they can be fed by hand; a favourite with beginners.

Aquarium Passe

Twelve metres (40 feet) deep; Aquarium Passe is a narrow passage between one and five metres (three and 16 feet) wide that leads from the Aquarium through the reef to an area of cathedral-like archways; not for beginners because a strong current runs out to sea against which divers must fight with the help of a fixed rope on their return to the Aquarium.

Francois Passe

Twenty to 30 metres (65 to 100 feet); inside the reef; a fantastic canyon in which divers drift with the current for almost half-a-kilometre; huge shoals of king and unicorn fish, tuna, and barracuda are to be seen, and, fairly frequently, turtles.

Deux Maisons

Thirteen to 28 metres (40 to 90 feet); outside the reef; a good dive for all levels of diver; coral encrusted mountains and valleys.

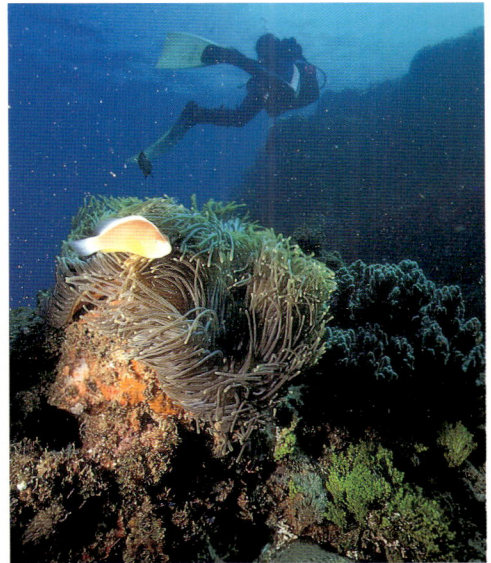

Above: Diver zooms in to explore skunk anemonefish living in symbiosis with its host sea anemone in a Mauritian coral garden.

A Day at the Races

Mauritius has a little-known attraction which is increasingly popular on this tropical hideaway — horse racing. Given its idyllic island image, Mauritius seems an unlikely setting for such a sport. All the more surprising, then, is the fact that the Mauritius Turf Club and its track, the Champ de Mars (also known as the Hippodrome), are the oldest of their kind in the southern hemisphere and reputedly the second oldest in the world.

Founded in 1812 by an English army officer, Colonel Edward Draper, the club and course maintain an international flavour typical of all aspects of Mauritian life, thanks to the island's chequered past. After the British conquest in 1810, Draper wasted no time in setting up the 'Sport of Kings'.

The site retained its French name, which roughly translates into English as 'military ground', giving some indication of the site's original use.

Draper oversaw the building of the oval 1,300-metre (1,420-yard) track and supervised the first meets, at which horses belonging to the English garrison and ridden by young army officers were raced. The French settlers soon showed an interest and entered their own horses. By the late 1830s, many French residents had become deeply involved in running the club, among them Adrien d'Épinay, one of the island's leading politicians and painters of the day, who acted as a steward. Under his and others' patronage, horse racing soon became firmly established.

These days, the Mauritius Turf Club is not the domain just of descendants of French and British settlers. The island's Chinese population plays a large part in horse and stable ownership, and some of the most successful trainers have been of Indian origin.

There are Mauritian jockeys — the vast majority of them amateurs — but each training stable also employs a professional, most of whom are South African, although a few come from England and Australia. In an attempt to reduce the reliance on foreign professionals, the Mauritius Turf Club launched a recruitment and training programme in the mid-1980s. It is a sign of the interest in horse racing on the island that over 1,000 applications were received from youngsters who dreamt only of racing thoroughbreds on the Champ de Mars.

The horses, too, are imported, as there is no thoroughbred culture in Mauritius. Two attempts at breeding produced only moderate success and none of the local horses could match the foreign thoroughbreds. Once again, most of the imported stock comes from South Africa, because European horses tend to arrive in poor condition and then need a long time to acclimatize. Over a hundred horses are imported annually from South Africa.

The 23-meet racing season takes place in 'winter', between May and November. All meetings, bar one, are held on Saturday afternoon. The exception is on a Sunday, when the longest race, and one of the four main races of the season — the Maiden Cup — is run. Each meeting features seven races, run over distances varying between 1,325 metres (1,448 yards) and 2,400 metres (2,624 yards). The oval, right-handed grass track, on which the straight is a short 225 metres (246 yards), can safely accommodate 11 runners.

Race days are naturally a fun climax to the end of the working week for the local people. But for tourists, whether avid racegoers or not, a day at the races should not be missed. The Champ de Mars is located on the outskirts of Port Louis and race days definitely add a touch of colour to the somewhat drab capital.

Islanders from all walks of life stream in from distant towns and villages to try their luck or simply enjoy the spectacle. It is not unknown for workers suddenly to discover a sick relative or a previously unobserved religious festival so they can attend race meetings.

While the crowd, which usually averages over 20,000, mills around the track, their senses are continuously entertained

Above: Horses spring from their stalls at the start of one of the main events.
Overleaf: Race nears its finish at the Port Louis racetrack cradled by the foothills of the Moka Mountains.

by piped theme tunes from popular soaps, the smell of fried food, the sound of bookies shouting the odds as they jostle for business, and the sight of punters as they study the form and share tips.

Hawkers and bookmakers do a roaring trade as full employment and a booming economy mean that people have extra cash to spend on leisure activities. Punters, exhausted from cheering for their trusted mounts, quaff drinks and sample snacks while placing bets of anything between 10 and tens of thousands of rupees on the next race.

Until recently, the bookmakers monopolized the betting and only allowed racegoers to place their bet on a win, but for the last few years computerized, on-line betting has been in operation. This tote system allows various betting combinations to be made, including the 'Pick Six', one of the most popular bets, which turned into a national fixation in early 1993, when the pool reached a record 20 million rupees.

Betting is certainly big business there, and 18 million rupees has been known to be staked at a single meet. Having made their bets, the spectators take up position close to the track. The majority stay in the arena, set inside the track, where there is no entry fee.

Aside from the track, there is plenty of activity to keep any less than ardent racing fan interested. In the clubhouse, the paddock, and the private boxes, a touch of age old elegance remains. Well-dressed officials keep a watchful eye on the weigh-ins, horse parades in the paddock, and the presentation of prizes. And the setting itself is stunning. A backdrop of gaunt copper-toned mountains acts as a natural amphitheatre to the drama played out in the vast plain of the Champ de Mars below.

Big Game Fishing

The seas surrounding Mauritius offer some of the world's finest big game fishing grounds. This is not just another wild claim; it is backed by solid facts.

Mauritius held the all-tackle world record for Pacific blue marlin (a 500-kilo — 1,100-lb — specimen) for 16 years until the record was broken in 1982. Giant-sized blue marlins have been boated with regularity in recent years, with at least 20 weighing in at over 450 kilos (990 lbs) and the biggest, caught in 1985, reaching the 630-kilo (1,386-lb) mark. Around 150 marlins (blue and black) are weighed in each year in Mauritius, but many more are lost as, on average, only one in five marlins hooked is boated. The tourist brochures go so far as to boast that Mauritius is one of the few places where giant-sized blue marlin of up to 450 kilos (990 lbs) can be hooked within five minutes of boarding a boat.

The reason for these excellent fishing records is that the sea falls away to 600 metres (2,000 feet) just a kilometre and a half (one mile) from the island's coast. It is in deep waters such as these that the big predators, such as black marlin, blue marlin, sailfish, wahoo, yellowfin tuna, bonito, and shark are normally found.

Particularly good fishing grounds are found just off the west coast from Rivière Noire, where the submarine foot of Le Morne Brabant reaches out into the sea, creating a maelstrom of tidal currents that attract bait fish, which, in turn, bring out the giant marlin and tuna.

Large catches require excellent paraphernalia to land them, and Mauritian boats are well-equipped with ship-to-shore radio and trolling equipment for both live bait and plastic lures, considered as standard. All the charter fishing boats use heavy-duty Penn International or Shimano reels, while lighter rods are available for bait when fishing for smaller skipjack tuna. Some boats also have electronic equipment to help pinpoint the elusive areas, which yield the big fish. Great boats and their equipment are of no use, however, unless they are skippered by experienced hands, and big game fishers will find Mauritian boats captained by locals who know the waters well, including tide movements, currents, spawning seasons, and the best baits.

Not all the fish hooked are landed. As a general rule, big game fishers now only keep what they and the crew want to take home to eat. At an increasing number of big game fishing centres, the excess fish weighing over 90 kilos (198 lbs) that are hooked, are simply tagged and then released back into the sea — once their length and size have been recorded.

The idea is to combine sport with conservation. Fishing enthusiasts still have the opportunity to land 'the big one', but the fish are saved from death and returned to open water once their details, which provide useful information for marine research institutes around the world, have been noted. However, the final decision on whether a fish is landed or not remains with the angler.

The two main deep sea fishing centres are in Rivière Noire and Trou aux Biches, both of which are on the west coast. In Rivière Noire, there is the Hotel Club Centre de Pêche, while the Beachcomber Fishing Club at Le Morne and the big game fishing centres at the Sofitel Imperial and La Pirogue in Wolmar are not far away. At Trou aux Biches, the Corsaire Club is near the well-known restaurant, Le Pescatore, where fishing enthusiasts can have their prize catch cooked. Fishing expeditions can be arranged through most hotels and inbound tour operators, such as White Sand Tours.

Given the early start to most fishing expeditions, those fishing enthusiasts staying on the east coast may like to consider incorporating a helicopter trip from their hotel to one of the west coast's big game fishing centres. It could mean as much as an extra hour in bed.

Although it is possible to go big game

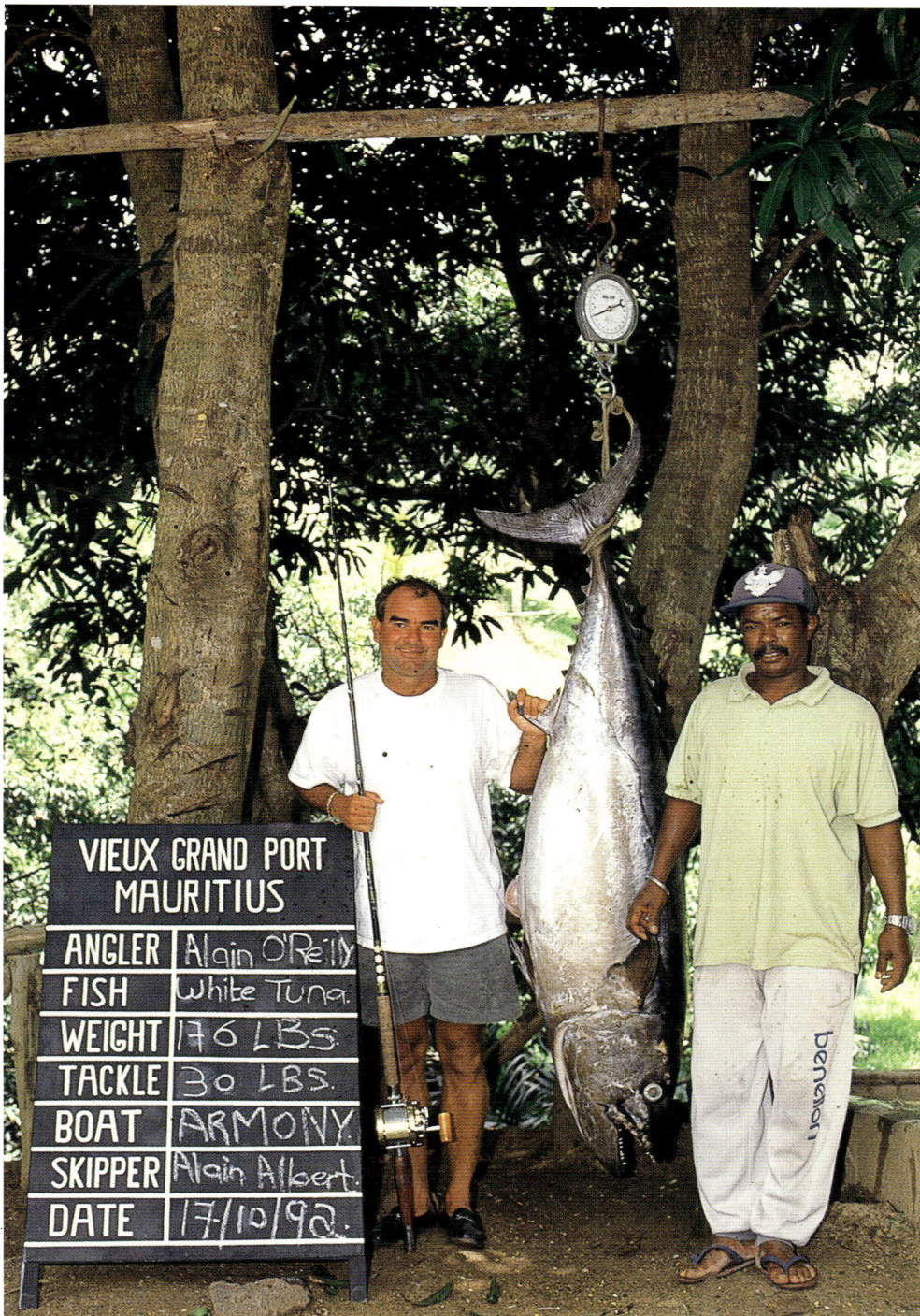

VIEUX GRAND PORT
MAURITIUS

ANGLER	Alain O'Reilly
FISH	White Tuna.
WEIGHT	176 LBS.
TACKLE	30 LBS.
BOAT	ARMONY
SKIPPER	Alain Albert.
DATE	17/10/92.

Above: Game fishing enthusiast weighs in a giant of the deep at a Mauritian big-game fishing venue.

fishing all year round, the best season is from November to April. Those keen to participate in competitions should note that there is a week-long Green Island International Marlin Competition every year, usually in February. Teams of four vie to land the greatest weight in fish and points are awarded on a per-pound basis.

The big game fish caught in Mauritian waters include the **blue marlin**, one of the most powerful fish in the Indian Ocean and one that creates challenges for anglers all over the world; the **black marlin**, another powerful fish that usually exhausts anglers with its runs and jumps (generally larger than the blue marlin); and the **striped marlin**, an acrobatic fish that spends as much time in the air as in the water when it is on the end of an angler's line. It does not grow to the same size as the blue and the black and is not common in Mauritian waters, but some are recorded every year.

Sailfish, which fly in the air when hooked in an aerial display of fury, normally weigh in at about 50 kilos, (110 lbs), so anglers should use a lighter tackle to get the best from the fight.

Yellowfin tuna, found in Mauritian waters in their largest numbers during March and April, usually weigh in between 65 five and 90 kilos (143 and 198 lbs), while **skip-jack tuna** (bonito), huge shoals which drive the bait fish to the surface where sea birds feast in large numbers, and captains watch for the flocks of sea birds to indicate where they should troll their lures.

Prolific runs of **wahoo** start in September; boats fishing have returned with as many as 24 in an afternoon. It is said to be the fastest running fish in the Indian Ocean.

Barracuda are also caught, but are not very common.

Big game fishers can expect to come across **blue, hammerhead, mako, tiger, black fin, white fin,** and, very occasionally, **great white sharks. Dorado** are plentiful and can be caught at any time of the year.

For those who have never been big game fishing, but are tempted to give it a try, here is a personal account that may just persuade you. Ernest Hemingway wrote about big game fishing with such passion that it is hard for anyone not to be fired by his enthusiasm. He once summed up the excitement he felt about fish, writing that 'they are strange and wild things of unbelievable speed and power and a beauty, in the water and leaping, that is indescribable, which you would never see if you did not fish for them, and to which you are suddenly harnessed so that you feel their speed, their force and their savage power as intimately as if you were riding a bucking horse'.

Potential fishers, armed with a sense of adventure and anticipation, must be prepared to rise early — at six or earlier — to enjoy a full day's fishing.

Once out on the water, the fresh sea breeze of the awakening day, accompanied by the hum of the engines and the reassuring rush of water as the boat cuts through the ocean waves, is exhilarating.

It is not long before the crew move into action aboard the boat and the game begins. The process of trolling — dragging bait through the water behind the boat to attract the game fish — starts. Several factors affect big game fishing, including the boat speed, the lure (plastic bait), the water temperature, seasons, and tides.

Outriggers (long poles on either side of the boat) increase the chances of a fish striking because they enable more lines, with different baits, to be trolled. But whether a big fish bites or not eventually comes down to luck, although it does help to have an expert on board.

As a result, deep-sea fishing often requires the simple wait-and-see strategy. For keen fishers this is where the thrill enters into the game. The sighting of a possible bite, the first assault on the bait, and the sounding of the alarm on the rod as a fish is hooked and the line runs off the reel at an alarming pace, are all reasons for the adrenaline to start pumping.

So fishermen settle in for a long wait, mesmerized by the rise and fall of the boat's wake. Multi-coloured lures dip and dive in the deep blue-green water, chased by white horses. False alarms there are in plenty; lines tangle, seaweed is caught, and choppy seas slacken lines. Then, the first bite strikes. The line starts to run off the reel, slowly at first, and then with a screech as the rod bends and the huge weight of the hooked fish pulls the line through the depth of the water. All hell breaks loose.

Stations are manned amid cries of 'Yo fish' and 'Stop the boat'. The serious fisher rushes to the chair, straps on a shoulder harness, braces his feet against the transom, and rams the rod into a holder, while the crew take in the extra lures to avoid entanglement and all others run to their cameras.

The game begins and tension mounts. The angler in the chair has to be careful that the fish is well and truly hooked, otherwise he may lose it there and then.

Aficionados will explain that it is not knowing what will land on their line — a half-kilo (one lb) bonito or a 50-kilo (110-lb) marlin — that keeps them riding out to sea time and again to fish.

Certain fish, however, are more attractive simply because they are such a challenge to catch with a rod and reel. Instead of submitting calmly to their fate when hooked, these fish put up such a fight that very often they get away from all but the expert angler. It is for this reason that deep sea fishing has come to be known as 'big game' fishing.

This time there is a sailfish on the line. Considered one of the most beautiful ocean fish by many, it is also one of the most playful. Leaping high out of the water, the hooked sailfish spreads its sail (a large dorsal fin) until it is stiffly erect in an agile display of aerobatics.

This sport is certainly not for the faint-hearted. Reeling in fish is hard work. For the next 20 minutes or so the fisherman's back strains as he pumps and reels his rod, which bows to a perilous degree out to sea. Eventually, the sailfish pulses its final death throes and the game comes to a successful conclusion with the landing of the first fish of the day. Once on board, it is obvious why these fish are considered beautiful, so rich are the blues and purples of its sail.

Catching fish is, without doubt, exhausting — it can take more than an hour to reel in a large fish, by which time the arms and back are aching and the hands are likely to be blistered, especially if it is a marlin, which is immensely powerful and, when hooked, explodes from the sea at more than 40 kilometres (25 miles) an hour. It is an awesome sight, and a thrilling challenge for the person at the end of the rod.

For some beginners, one trip is enough to satisfy the curiosity, but for others, big game fishing becomes an addiction, and many more holidays will be spent out at sea. For all, though, fanatics or not, a day out on the big blue sea can be a thrilling experience.

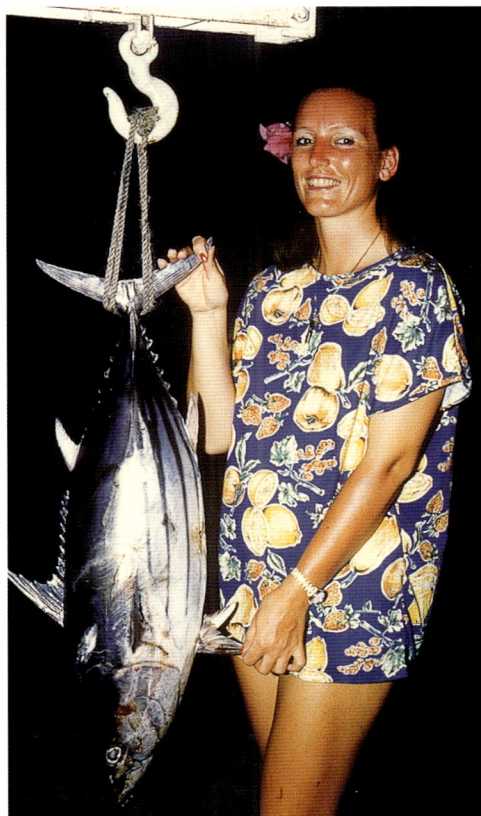

Above: Fighting fish of Indian Ocean which took one bite too many.

Mauritian Art and Crafts

Like many Mauritian avifauna, the most famous Mauritian artists — Chazal and Herve Masson — are dead. And, like the dodo, Chazal appears to be better known than any living artist.

His originals, mostly naïve depictions of flowers, birds, and fish, are much sought after and command high prices when compared with the works of other Mauritian artists. One of the largest collections is at the Paradis Hotel in Le Morne, where Chazal gathered much of the inspiration for his work. In addition to his originals, prints and objects — such as ashtrays adorned with examples of his trademark naïve style — can be seen all over Mauritius.

The style of Herve Masson, who died in 1990, 10 years after Chazal, is quite different. Masson was not a typical island artist producing naïve paintings, like Chazal. Rather, he produced figurative oils that gained recognition in the United States and France, where he exhibited.

Today the most prominent contemporary Mauritian artist is probably Henry Koombes', the only one to have his own gallery. Located on Route Royale in Grand Baie, the gallery displays a wide range of his work, including paintings, prints, lithographs, etchings, and sculptures. Koombe's style is very distinctive, verging on the comic, and appeals particularly to the younger generation.

Most of the other popular artists exhibit their work in one of the three galleries belonging to Hélène de Senneville, who opened her first showroom in Grand Baie in 1987 and has been working with, and encouraging, local artists ever since.

Ms de Senneville feels that there was a need for a gallery some years before she opened one, as there was already a demand for indigenous island art. 'At that time, perhaps the young people were directing their energies into creating T-shirts and clothes, much more basic things.'

Another likely reason for the lack of art in those days was the shortage of materials in Mauritius, and the high taxes on the supplies that were found locally. Now it is much easier and cheaper to obtain the essential materials.

But, according to Ms de Senneville, one of the characteristics common to several of the local artists' work is the small sizes of their pictures, harking back to the days when paper was so precious that they used to divide a sheet into several smaller pieces.

The one criticism she levels at some local painters is: '. . . if it works well, they won't work at their art. They won't work at it and say it doesn't matter if it's no good, it's not for sale, I'll consider it as a part of my work, something for my personal progression. No, they will paint because it's a good sale.'

What sells in Mauritius is figurative art, which coincides with the conservative tastes of the public, who like to buy paintings of subjects with which they are familiar, such as a particular mountain or a favourite beach, and with the choice of tourists who purchase paintings that will remind them of what they have seen once they return home.

There are other reasons why Mauritian art is conservative.

The country has no art school, so while a few have been lucky enough to train overseas, most local artists are self-taught.

Perhaps, more importantly, believes Ms de Senneville, 'We don't have museums. In Europe, young people sit in museums, copying, learning, and drawing until everything is stuck in their mind, and then they can do their own interpretation. Here, their museum is nature and the people, so that's why all the art in Mauritius is very figurative because they paint what they see.'

As a result, the galleries exhibit what Ms de Senneville describes as the 'blood' of Mauritius. 'The blood of Mauritius is nature, the coconut tree, the sea, the pirogue (a type of boat), the mango, the Indian woman, all that is the theatre of Mauritius, scenes of island life,' she explains. The

Above: One of the most popular Mauritian artists today is Danielle Hitié, who produces typical Mauritian scenes in water-colours.

most popular medium of Mauritian art is undoubtedly water-colour, but local artists are turning more and more to acrylics.

There is, however, a wide range of mediums on display in the galleries, which means that there are prices to suit every pocket. Hélène de Senneville's galleries display the works of both Chazal and Herve Masson, although never in any great numbers. Pictures produced by contemporary artists are more plentiful.

Today's popular artists include Danielle Hitié, who produces typical island scenes — such as Creole houses and Mauritian labourers — in water-colours, both as originals and as seriagraphs. Hitié is one of the few Mauritian artists who make a living from art — the others have to have a second job to survive — and recently exhibited in Switzerland.

Serge Constantin, who takes his inspiration largely from Matisse and likes to sketch, is, nonetheless, willing to try various mediums and has produced lithographs, engravings, and oils. Herve de Cotter reproduces scenes from everyday Mauritian life in a very naïve style in a number of media, including acrylic, gouache, and pastel.

Vaco Baissac does very simple drawings that he then colours in, using a variety of bright shades, resulting in a painting that rather resembles a stained glass window.

Bernard Debergh paints high quality oils, employing a very classical, figurative style and, according to Ms de Senneville, 'captures the sea like no one else'.

Aside from art, the galleries stock a number of local handicrafts, such as wall hangings made from steel and wooden book ends. Ms de Senneville started producing such items following a visit to Indonesia in the mid-1980s.

'I went to Bali,' she says, 'and saw all these brightly coloured wooden things and thought that Mauritius should be producing the same kind of things, so I started a workshop here.

Before that, all the handicrafts here were brown, such as model ships and dodos

Above: Life in Mauritius is colourfully portrayed in Dominique Masabot's painting, 'Isle Maurice'.

made from wood. For me, that's not Mauritius. Mauritius is about colour, life, it's joyful.' Since Ms de Senneville set up her production unit, her idea has been copied many times over and there are now a great number of colourful products on sale throughout the island. They are among the most noticeable local handicrafts, alongside model ships.

It is impossible to visit Mauritius without coming across the model ships for which the island is well known. And, not surprisingly, the boats come high on the list of items tourists buy as souvenirs.

The model shipbuilding industry has come a long way since 1968 when French Ambassador Touze recognized the talent of Jose Ramar, a local craftsman specializing in wooden products, and suggested that Ramar produce replicas of old sea vessels.

Further expansion at Ramar's workshop led to the establishment in late 1970 of the Société Art des Isles in Paris, which helped to distribute the boats first in France and, later, throughout Europe. To increase their universal appeal, the craftsman started sourcing ships' plans from various countries, including England, America, Spain, and Holland, and before long magnificent miniatures of the *Bounty*, the *Victory*, the *Endeavour*, the *Cutty Sark*, the *Golden Hind*, and even the *Titanic* were being produced.

Gradually, model shipbuilders sprang up all over the island, and now there are over a hundred factories of varying sizes producing boats of varying quality. The largest, with some 150 employees, is Historic Marine (in the northern town of Goodlands), which was established in 1982 and prides itself on producing the 'Rolls Royces' of model ships.

Plans from naval museums around the world ensure faithful reproduction of ancient vessels, some of which — special orders for large boats — take as long as 18 months to complete, while the smaller models take about a month to make.

The reason the boats take so long is that everything is done by hand. Burmese teak and South African mahogany are used to build the main frames, which are assembled using adhesive rather than nails. One employee works on one boat, so that even-

tually he becomes a specialist producer of that particular model. Only the finishing touches of copper and bronze fittings, cloth sails, and rigging are done by another worker. In 1988, Historic Marine expanded its production to include marine furniture, such as writing desks, jewellery boxes, and chests — also made from teak and mahogany. In addition, the factory makes lacquer boxes and lacquered half hulls of boats, which are mounted for hanging on walls.

Tourists are welcome to visit Historic Marine to see the ship models being made and to wander around the large showroom displaying a full range of products.

Historic Marine, Zone Industriel de St Antoine, Goodlands, Tel: 283-9304. Opening hours: 0800 to 1200, 1300 to 1700, Monday to Friday.

Above: Mauritius is particularly well known for its incredibly detailed model ships, which are replicas of old sea vessels.

Tastes of Mauritius

Mauritian cuisine, like so many aspects of the island, is cosmopolitan. All the dishes are derived from an Indian, a Creole, a French, or a Chinese source, but over time Mauritians, have started to create a cuisine all their own by culinary hybriding. For example, a local chef may take a typically French dish and add spices traditionally used in Indian cooking, resulting in a new, Mauritian recipe.

The other aspect that makes Mauritian cuisine different is its local ingredients. They include *cochon marron*, a type of wild boar, and *camarons*, freshwater prawns.

All this adds up to a fascinating gourmet trip for visitors willing to try a little bit of everything. Let's take an average day as an example. It is possible to wake up in the morning and have tropical fresh fruits followed by a continental breakfast of freshly baked croissants and coffee. An Indian-orientated lunch could start with an array of snacks, such as *samoosas*, *dholl poori*, and *gateaux piments* or, for a mix of two cuisines, curried chicken in a crusty French *baguette*, from the street vendors of Port Louis. This could be followed by a more substantial helping of fish *vindaye*, served with *bredes*. Dinner at a Chinese restaurant could embrace spring rolls, noodles, and Peking duck. And that's just one day . . .

Perhaps not surprisingly, given that the Indian community is by far the largest on the island, the most dominant influence in Mauritian cooking comes from the Indian sub-continent. Across the board, whether the family is of French, Indian, Chinese, or African descent, Mauritians are likely to sit down *en famille* on Sundays and eat curry. In fact, curry could almost be considered the country's national dish, so widely and so frequently is it eaten. The great thing about a curry is that it can be a cheap dish composed of potatoes, or an expensive one of lobster.

The Indian influence is most obvious in the heavy use of spices, which are the essential elements in dishes such as *vindaye*

and *briani*. Both curries can be made with any main ingredient — beef, chicken, or fish — but for an unusual and distinctly local twist, try one of venison or octopus. An interesting note about *vindaye*, which no doubt makes it popular with busy house-keepers, is that being made with oil, vinegar, onion, and garlic, it keeps for up to three weeks because of the high oil content — definitely something worth having on standby in the fridge!

One Mauritian chef admits keeping 40 spices on hand to help season dishes, but the only really essential ingredient for a true Mauritian curry is the crushed fresh leaf of the *carri poule*, which grows abundantly on the island. They say in Mauritius that 'if you don't have the leaf of the *carri poule*, you can't make a good curry'.

Dishes displaying a Creole influence include *rougaille*, which is made with ginger, onion, garlic, numerous herbs, tomato, and *daube*. A *daube*, which makes some claim to being of French influence because some Mediterranean stews are known as *daube*, is, nonetheless, similar to a *rougaille*. The ingredients are virtually the same; the only real difference lies in the consistency of the *daube*, which is much smoother than the lumpy *rougaille*. As with a curry, any number of basic ingredients — beef, fish, or chicken — can be cooked in a *rougaille* or *daube* sauce.

Curries, *rougailles*, and *daubes* are all served with rice, which may be slightly flavoured by adding a filament of saffron to the water in which the rice is boiled. Other side dishes include several chutneys, which are made from a range of vegetables and fruit, including, most commonly, coconut, tomato, and eggplant. And, of course, all are served with a variety of vegetables, many of which are probably found nowhere else in the world but are abundant in local markets. Traditional vegetables include manioc, patisson, *bredes* — which include green, leafy vegetables such as spinach — Chinese cabbage, and *chou chou* (a small, pear-shaped marrow).

Above: As one would expect with an island nation, Mauritius restaurants offer a spectacular variety of delights from the sea.

Having whetted your appetite with all these tempting dishes, perhaps now is the time to suggest where you might sample some Mauritian Indian and Creole cooking. Mauritians themselves do not like to eat in restaurants what they can eat at home.

It is thus difficult to find a restaurant serving Mauritian cuisine. However, Carri Poule and Bonne Marmite, both in Port Louis, serve Indian food with perhaps a hint of Mauritian influence, while Indra, in Domaine les Pailles, is more of a classic Indian restaurant. A restaurant serving just Creole dishes is even harder to find, but Le Pescatore in Trou aux Biches has a few typical dishes on the menu, and Cannelle Rouge in Domaine les Pailles also serves Creole food.

French cuisine probably has the least influence on Mauritian cooking, which is somewhat surprising given the heavy cultural French dominance in other aspects of the island's life. However, traditional French dishes easily adopt a Mauritian mood with the addition of a few pertinent Indian or Creole spices. Chinese cooking does not tend to interact with the other influences at work in Mauritian cuisine — this has a lot to do with the way Chinese food is cooked, essentially fast and furiously — so the Chinese food found in Mauritius is still very traditional. The only outside influence on Chinese cooking has been superficial — some have acquired French names. A bowl of *bouillon*, for example, is likely to be a traditional Chinese soup with fish balls. *Mine frit* is fried noodles, cooked in *woks* by the roadside. Chinese restaurants worth visiting include Fu Xiao, the Chinese restaurant in Domaine les Pailles which serves great Peking duck; Palais de Chine in Grand Baie, where the seafood is recommended; and Happy Valley and King Dragon in Quatre Bornes.

Typical Mauritian dishes are unique because of the basic products used, which include *cochon marron*, known as *le sanglier* in France — the meat of a dark pig that is always served with sweet potato; venison, when in season, is eaten with sugar cane.

Above: Exotic and tasty, the tropical fruits of Mauritius figure prominently in the local cuisine.

Camarons are served in a variety of ways. Traditionally the way that Mauritian families serve it at Christmas and New Year is in a red (tomato) sauce on a bed of palm heart. Braised heart of palm is also eaten with a hollandaise sauce. *Snoek*, a very smelly salted fish, is also typical, as is smoked marlin, either served straight up on toast, or as a pâté.

Other truly exotic Mauritian dishes include fried wasp larvae, which was popular a couple of generations ago; curried monkey, which is still eaten but rarely; curried *chauve-souris* (fruit bat), which is also still eaten but less frequently because it is increasingly difficult to find; curried *tang* or *tenrec*, still eaten by a few; *licorne* fish, which is eaten by the poor; and *tec tec* (a type of small clam) soup, which has almost completely disappeared.

Goat dishes are also popular on Rodrigues, where the animal is found in large numbers.

What do the local people normally eat? For breakfast, because they rush off to work very early in the morning, Mauritians do not eat a lot. Usually, they will just have time for a piece of crusty French bread covered with guava jelly (made from a recipe passed down through the generations) or cheese. In the hotels, visitors are likely to find guava jelly served up alongside a host of other preserves from local fruit, such as pineapple, banana, and passion fruit.

Lunch, carried to work in *tentes* (square woven baskets), is likely to be a sandwich stuffed with any number of things, including, perhaps, the remains of last night's supper, or it might be rice and curry. If Mauritians do not take their own food to work, they will often buy snacks off the many street vendors. Once again, these snacks are heavily Indian orientated. There are *gateaux piments* (crushed lentils and chilis fried in butter), which are hot to the uninitiated, *faratas* or *dholl pooris* (lentil pancakes filled with either *rougaille*, curry, or *achard* — finely chopped vegetables cooked with saffron, mustard, and spices) and *samoosas*, which are savoury triangular pastry cases filled with either vegetables or meat. Visitors to Port Louis who would prefer to sit down while they eat should try any of the restaurants mentioned earlier or, for a more Western light meal or sandwich, should visit La Flore Mauricienne or Le Café du Vieux Conseil. La Flore, being on a main thoroughfare, is popular with those who wish to see and be seen, while Le Café is an oasis of tranquillity, set in the picturesque courtyard of some late 18th-century buildings.

Dinner is by far the most important meal of the day, as it brings together the whole family. In winter, a lot of soups incorporating produce such as lentils and watercress are served. The main dish is likely to be a curry or a fricasse (either meat or vegetables fried quickly in oil and garlic), served with *brèdes*, lentils or beans, and rice. Sometimes, it might even be a traditional English roast and potatoes.

Pudding might be a pineapple mousse, a *crème brulée*, a *crème caramel* — sometimes referred to as *flan* (the best of which is to be found in the Cotton Bay Hotel in Rodrigues, if you feel like making the journey), or *pudding di pain*, stale bread and raisins soaked overnight in milk and then baked.

Other sweet foods include *neopolitains* (shortcake biscuits topped with pastel icing) and the fresh tropical fruits of the island, such as mangoes, pawpaws (papayas), *lychées* in summer, *longanes* — which are similar to lychées but have hard, bitter pips — wild raspberries, guavas, custard apples, melons, coconuts, pineapples, and bananas.

Accompanying this feast of food are a number of traditional and some Western drinks. On a day-to-day basis, Pepsi is virtually considered the national drink, but other carbonated drinks and fruit juices are also popular. Among the Indian community, *lassi* and *alooda* (made with agar, water, milk, rose syrup, and seeds) are typical. Non-alcoholic after-dinner beverages include locally produced coffee and tea as well as citronel, an infusion of wild lemon grass.

At weekends, when the mood is more relaxed, alcoholic drinks are the order of the day. Mauritian men usually drink whisky, while the women indulge in a fruit punch made with coconut milk and rum. The locally produced rum that has really captured the imagination of the people is Green Island, although Mainstay is also recommended. Cane spirits are a rough version of the local rum.

Rhum arrangé, drunk either as an aperitif or as a nightcap, is a type of rum that may have been flavoured with either raisins, orange, sugar cane, coconut, pineapple, or coffee. Wine is also popular, and the best is imported from South Africa and France. Wine is produced locally, but according to one expert, it is 'the headache the day after and is not recommended, not at all'.

Several beers, including Guinness — brewed under licence — are produced in Mauritius. Local beers, such as Phoenix and Stella, are definitely worth sampling, for both have won European awards. Phoenix is slightly stronger than Stella.

Cheers!

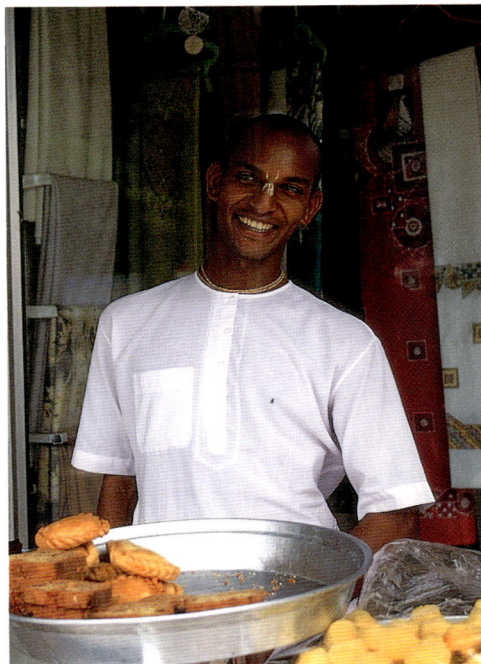

Above: Smiling street vendor offers passers-by some taste-tempting snacks.
Overleaf: Golden sundown over an Indian Ocean island paradise.

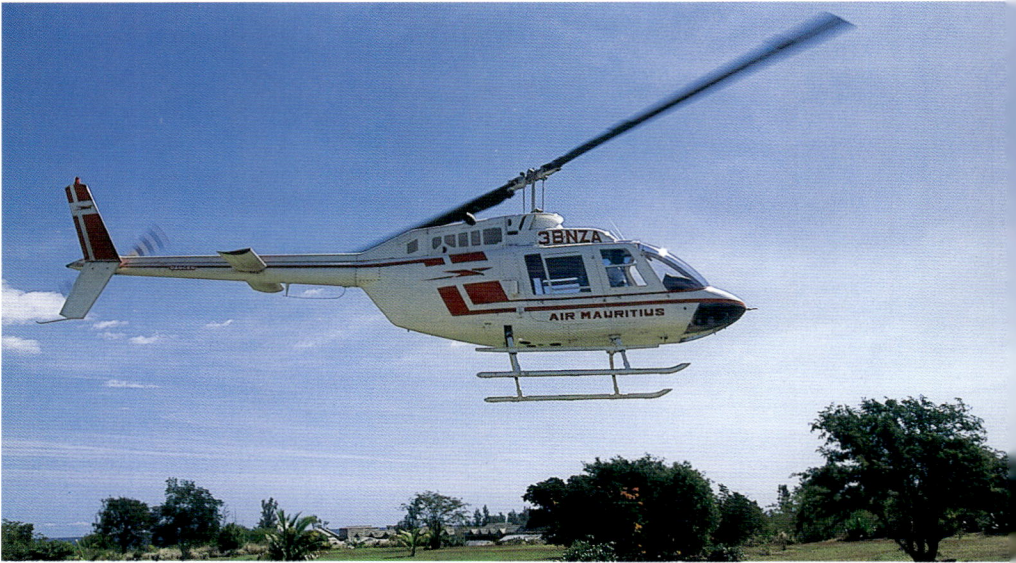

AIR MAURITIUS

The emotions aroused by a round-the-island flight in one of our helicopters is fascinating and overwhelming. One by one glorious images of this small but beautiful Indian Ocean island imprint themselves forever on your memory. Long, glistening sandy beaches with safer and colourful lagoons, the Black River Gorges, the Seven Coloured Earth of Chamarel and cascading waterfalls, the high point of Pieter Both Peak, the endless verdant green of the sugarcane plantations, unique 'Ile aux Cerfs' and the volcanic crater of Trou aux Cerfs are just some of the many, never-to-be-forgotten sights and images of Mauritius revealed from above.

Make it the highpoint of your Mauritius holiday.

We also offer transfers from the airport to all the main hotels. Sight-seeing helicopter flights depart from all hotels with a helipad.

For more information and reservations contact your travel agency or
AIR MAURITIUS HELICOPTER SERVICES
Tel: (230) 637 3552 ext 1419   Fax: (230) 637 4104

Advertisement for Berjaya Le Morne Beach Resort & Casino

You have chosen a great destination

Berjaya Le Morne Beach Resort & Casino

There is no reason why you should not choose a great hotel

Resting on an emerald gem, set in the iridescent blue of the Indian Ocean, lies the **Berjaya Le Morne Beach Resort & Casino.**

Deluxe villas with charming Malaysian style architecture and warm wood finishes. The exotic pleasures of the resort await you

Best Western
Berjaya Le Morne
Beach Resort & Casino, Mauritius

Berjaya Le Morne Beach Resort & Casino (200 Rooms) Le Morne, Case Royale, Mauritius.
Tel: (230) 6836800 Fax: (230) 6836070

PART FIVE: BUSINESS MAURITIUS

The Economy

Mauritius has been called an economic miracle. It has achieved such high rates of growth during the last 20 years that it looks set to join the ranks of such newly industrialized countries as Singapore and Taiwan.

The Mauritian economy was traditionally based on agriculture — sugar cane has been the most important crop throughout its history — but it has diversified spectacularly since setting up an Export Processing Zone (EPZ) in 1970.

In the early 1980s, Mauritius initiated a policy of fostering economic development through export processing, agricultural diversification and tourism, a policy which has produced good results. Annual Gross Domestic Product (GDP) has grown consistently in real terms, and during one year was as high as eight per cent. In a decade, the value of foreign trade quadrupled to Rs43.4 billion in 1991. In roughly the same period, Mauritius's favourable balance of payments grew tenfold to Rs5 billion in 1992. It is understood that the surplus is still effective. Foreign exchange reserves reached Rs14.6 billion at the end of 1992. Indeed, such has been the overall success of the development policy that Mauritius now has full employment, and there is even a labour shortage in some sectors.

Though sugar remains one of the island's leading exports (nearly 30 per cent of earnings), the EPZ has, in terms of contribution to export earnings, consistently outstripped sugar since 1985.

The share of sugar and its by-products in the GDP stands at about 10 per cent and the industry employs more than 40,000 people, or over 14 per cent of the working population.

The manufacturing sector, including the EPZ companies, is now the driving economic force. The EPZ has attracted investors from as far afield as Europe, South Africa, India, the Far East and Australia, as well as a great number of local entrepreneurs. In 1992 some 560 EPZ businesses employed nearly 90,000 workers, making this sector the island's largest employer and the main foreign exchange earner. Most of the large EPZ companies are producing textiles — Mauritius is the third largest producer of woollen knitwear in the world — but watches, toys, spectacle frames, electronic items, and other goods are now being manufactured. The country is also diversifying into printing and publishing, informatics, and jewellery.

Tourism, which began in 1952 when an Air France flight landed in Mauritius just after the end of World War II, has expanded rapidly. Extensive promotion campaigns were launched in the 1970s. In 1976, Mauritius welcomed 92,561 tourists and, in 1995, 422,463 visitors. Tourism and related activities, which employ some 13,855 people, are now the third largest foreign exchange earner after manufacturing and sugar, with gross receipts estimated at Rs7.4 billion in 1995.

Mauritius is hoping to add another jewel to its economic crown — as the region's financial hub. Recent deregulation measures have resulted in the establishment of a Stock Exchange with attractive tax incentives for listed firms and provision for offshore companies and banks. Consequently, the number of offshore companies has grown from 150 in 1993 to over 1,000 in 1994. A free port has been set up to complement the offshore activities, and it is hoped that this will serve as a bridge between the Far East, Europe, and continental Africa.

Investment incentive schemes

Mauritius offers incentives to investors designed to:

- encourage the investor and reward him for his entrepreneurial spirit;
- match the country's changing needs;
- channel investment in the directions most needed for economic development; and
- ensure growth with social justice.

These incentives apply to local as well as foreign entrepreneurs.

The key sectors to which fiscal incentives apply are:

- manufacturing;
- agriculture;
- services — offshore business;
- free port; and
- the Export Service Zone.

Manufacturing

Export enterprise

Activities include manufacturing goods for export and commercial fishing.

The incentives offered are:

- a corporate tax rate of 15 per cent for the company's life;
- tax free dividends for 20 years;
- no customs or excise duty, import levy or sales tax on raw materials, equipment, and export products;
- free repatriation of profits and dividends; and
- remission of 60 per cent of the duty payable on the purchase of minibuses with a seating capacity of between 50 and 25.

Strategic local enterprise
Manufacturing activities aimed at the local market that are likely to promote economic, industrial, and technological development are encouraged.

The incentives offered are:
- a corporate tax rate of 15 per cent for the life of the company; and
- tax-free dividends for 20 years.

Modernization and expansion enterprise
This category includes investment in production machinery and technology such as automation equipment and processes, computer applications for industrial design and manufacturing (CAD/CAM), and investment in anti-pollution and environment protection technology.

The incentives offered are:
- no customs duty on production equipment;
- 10 per cent income tax credit (spread over three years) on investment in new plants and machinery, provided at least Rs10 million is spent (this is in addition to the existing capital allowances amounting to 125 per cent of capital expenditure); and
- additionally, for anti-pollution and environment protection technology enterprises, an initial 80 per cent allowance for expenditure incurred on anti-pollution machinery or plants (against 50 per cent in most other cases).

Industrial building enterprise
Activities include the construction of industrial buildings of at least 1,000 square metres for letting.

The incentives offered are:
- a corporate tax rate of 15 per cent for the company's life;
- tax free dividends for 20 years;
- a 50 per cent exemption on registration dues for land purchase; and
- disapplication of the Landlord and Tenant Act, i.e., rent control.

Pioneer status enterprise
Activities involving technology and skills greater than those already existing and thus likely to enhance industrial and technological development are encouraged.

The incentives offered are:
- a corporate tax rate of 15 per cent for ten years, 35 per cent thereafter;
- tax free dividends for ten years; and
- no customs duty, import levy or sales tax on scheduled equipment or materials.

Small and medium enterprises
Any manufacturing activity, including repair, packing, and assembly of inputs into finished or semi-finished goods, provided the aggregate CIF value of production equipment does not exceed Rs5 million, is covered.

The incentives offered are:
- no customs or import duty on production equipment; and
- a corporate tax rate of 15 per cent for the company's life.

Agriculture

The incentives offered are:
- a corporate tax rate of 15 per cent for the company's life;
- tax-free dividends for the first 20 years;
- unrestricted repatriation of capital, profits and dividends;
- exemption from customs duty on machinery, equipment and spare parts; and
- exemption from 50 per cent of the normal registration fee on land and buildings purchased by the new enterprise.

Services

Offshore Business
Activities include offshore banking, offshore insurance, offshore fund management, international financial services, operational headquarters, international consultancy services, shipping and ship management, aircraft financing and leasing, international licensing and franchising, international data processing and other information technology services, offshore pension funds, international trading and assets management, and international employment services.

The incentives offered are:
- no tax on profits;
- unrestricted repatriation of profits;
- complete freedom from exhange controls;
- concessionary personal income tax for expatriate staff;
- complete exemption from duty on imported office equipment;
- complete exemption from import duties on cars and household equipment for two expatriate staff for each company;
- no withholding tax on interest payable on

deposits raised from non-residents by offshore banks; and

- no withholding tax on dividends and benefits payable by offshore entities, no estate duty or inheritance tax is payable on the inheritance of a share in an offshore entity and no capital gains tax.

Free port

Activities include transhipment and the re-export trade, for example warehousing and storage, breaking bulk, sorting, grading, cleaning, mixing, labelling, packing and repacking, minor processing and simple assembly.

The incentives offered are:

- complete exemption from payment of customs duty, import levy and sales tax on all machinery, equipment and materials imported into a free port zone for exclusive use in the free port and all goods destined for re-export;
- access to offshore banking facilities; and
- warehousing and storage fees at preferential rates.

Export Service Zone

At least 70 per cent local participation is required in an export service, such as accountancy, law, medicine, international marketing, quality testing, pre-shipment services, civil engineering, management consultancy, reinsurance, entrepôt trade, and transhipment.

The incentives offered are:

- a corporate tax of 15 per cent; and
- tax-free dividends for 20 years.

Institutional support

The Mauritian government plays an important support role in ensuring the Export Processing Zone (EPZ) success. Specialized units have been created in major departments to deal specifically with EPZ issues.

The Ministry of Industry and Industrial Technology

This ministry processes all applications in connection with manufacturing activities and normally determines project applications within four weeks of receipt. It also ensures that the clearance required by entrepreneurs for work permits, development permits, residence permits, applications for water supply, telephone and electricity, and customs facilities are processed expeditiously.

The Ministry of Industry
and Industrial Technology,
New Government Centre,
Port Louis.
Tel: (230) 201-1068
Fax: (230) 212-8201

The Mauritius Export Development and Investment Authority (MEDIA)

MEDIA is the focal point for investment and export promotion activities. It provides dedicated support to both potential investors and existing industrialists. Its services include:

- assistance in identifying investment opportunities;
- identification of joint venture partners;
- assistance in site location and factory buildings;
- help in obtaining bureaucratic clearances;
- identification of markets for Mauritian products; and
- provision of market intelligence through the Trade Information Centre.

MEDIA,
Level 2, BAI Building,
25 Pope Hennessy Street,
Port Louis.
Tel: (230) 208-7750
Fax: (230) 208-5965
MEDIA also operates several overseas offices.

The Export Processing Zone Development Authority (EPZDA)

The EPZDA provides technical assistance to companies already operating in the EPZ.
EPZDA,
5th Floor, Les Cascades,
Edith Cavell Street,
Port Louis.
Tel: (230) 212-9760
Fax: (230) 212-9767

The Mauritius Standards Bureau (MSB)

The MSB aims to promote and encourage standardization and quality control in industry and trade through the enforcement of standard codes and practices.
MSB,
c/o Ministry of Industry and Industrial Technology,
Réduit.
Tel: (230) 454-1933
Fax: (230) 464-7675

Mauritius Offshore Business Activities Authority (MOBAA)

MOBAA was set up in July 1992 to attract investment in offshore activities. The authority aims to ensure that business in the offshore sector is conducted in accordance with generally accepted international standards. It deals with all matters relating to offshore business, except banking, which is handled by the Central Bank.

MOBAA,
1st Floor, Deramann Tower,
30 Sir William Newton Street,
Port Louis.
Tel: (230) 212-9650
Fax: (230) 212-9459

Mauritius Freeport Authority (MFA)

The MFA aims to make Mauritius a hub of intercontinental maritime activity, especially trade between Asia, Europe, and Africa. The authority issues operating licences and provides bonded warehouse facilities.

MFA,
2nd Floor, Deramann Tower,
Sir William Newton Street,
Port Louis.
Tel: (230) 212-9627
Fax: (230) 212-9629

Mauritius Chamber of Commerce and Industry (MCCI)

The MCCI is the leading private-sector organization involved in the promotion of trade, industry, and tourism. It provides advice on compliance with import and export procedures, customs tariffs and practical information on certificates of origin.

MCCI,
3 Royal Street,
Port Louis.
Tel: (230) 208-3301
Fax: (230) 208-0076

Mauritius Export Processing Zone Association (MEPZA)

The objectives of MEPZA are to promote, develop, and sustain export activities in Mauritius.

MEPZA,
42 Sir William Newton Street,
Port Louis.
Tel: (230) 208-5216
Fax: (230) 212-1853

Mauritius Employers' Federation (MEF)

MEF's main aim is to promote free enterprise. However, it also provides direct advice, guidance and assistance to its members in industrial relations, economics and statistics, training and productivity, management, small scale enterprise development, and environmental management.

MEF,
Cerne House,
Chaussee,
Port Louis.
Tel: (230) 212-1599
Fax: (230) 212-6725

Financial Institutions and Services

Mauritius has a well-developed banking sector. The two largest banks are the Mauritius Commercial Bank and the State Commercial Bank. Others include Barclays Bank, Hongkong Bank, Baroda Bank, Habib Bank, South East Asian Bank, Indian Ocean International Bank, Banque Nationale de Paris Intercontinentale, and Delphis Bank. The commercial banks are of particular use to EPZ enterprises because they extend both short and long-term credit to manufacturing establishments.

Other institutions playing a crucial role in the economic growth of the country include:

- the Development Bank of Mauritius, which advances long-term loans to industries;
- the Stock Exchange, which mobilizes funds on behalf of listed companies;
- the Mauritius Leasing Company, which provides financial leases of 75 to 100 per cent of the value of production equipment for three to seven years; and
- the offshore banking sector, which is authorized to provide loans in foreign exchange to the EPZ sector at very competitive rates.

Investment

The following points were compiled in June 1994 by Imani Development (International) Limited, a management consultancy company based in Mauritius.

Bureaucracy

The overall impression of investment in Mauritius is that, while the country is generally supportive of foreign investment, and the legislation reflects this, there are certain elements of the bureaucracy which try to block it. There are extremely helpful officials and extremely obstructive ones. Foreign investment is generally more welcome where the activities are geared to offshore and export markets, rather than to the local market. There is considerable discretion in the administration of investment procedures and incentives.

Mauritius has a legion of special investment schemes, each giving various benefits and incentives. For each sector, there is a designated authority with responsibility for facilitating investment. These bodies do not, however, have full executive authority and their procedures are not transparent.

For example, the MOBAA is responsible for offshore investments; the MFA is responsible for investments in the free port; the Ministry of

Industry and Industrial Technology is, in theory, the 'one stop shop' for investment in the industrial sector, including the EPZ and pioneer status industries; and MEDIA can assist in getting permits approved, but it is only a promotional body.

In practice, each authority facilitates the process, but they have no executive powers other than basic certification of the status of the investment. They are helpful in steering applications in the right direction, but the process is still cumbersome.

Company registration is a separate process. Permission from the Prime Minister's Office is required for a foreigner to be a shareholder and for residence permits. The Ministry of Employment is responsible for work permits.

The whole process required for getting all the necessary paperwork takes a few months. Bribery is not uncommon to speed up the permit process.

Taxation

Direct tax rates are low. Investments with special certificates, for example, EPZ, Pioneer, Offshore and Freeport, all have preferential corporation tax rates, varying between zero and 15 per cent. Indirect taxes are quite high. These include an import levy of 17 per cent and sales tax of 4.5 per cent on virtually all goods. Customs duties are generally high. A family saloon car attracts 240 per cent duty, although some goods, such as computers, are duty-free. Duty exemption is granted to qualifying investments on a range of goods. There is a considerable amount of discretion in awarding incentives in this area, with no real transparency. The Ministry of Finance is responsible for determining exemptions. It can take several months for the exemption to be granted, which slows down the process. Nothing is automatic, which is a problem.

Expatriate staff

Even when work and residence permits have been granted through the above process, there are other problem areas. The Customs Department often causes problems for those importing personal effects. Not only are delays incurred, but there is no transparency in treatment. Excessive bureaucracy is rampant.

Expatriates are only allowed to maintain external bank accounts which have considerable limitations, despite the fact that Mauritius has, in theory, done away with almost all exchange control regulations.

The cost of living is high compared with the rest of the region, and is roughly on a par with Europe.

Investment sectors

Some sectors are virtually closed to foreign investors. The services sector often fits into this category, except for offshore operations and certain other approved sectors, which can include tourism.

Cost and availability of services

Electricity is relatively expensive. It is generally available, although disruptions in supply are not infrequent. The same applies to water. Land is expensive.

Local telecommunication services on the whole are of a high standard and charges are reasonable, although the local telephone network is still being upgraded. Courier and mail services are adequate.

Availability of labour and management

Labour is in short supply since the country has reached full employment. Wage rates are high in comparison with other countries in the region. Investment in non-labour intensive sectors is a higher priority now. There is a well educated population with a reasonable supply of professional and management personnel.

Investment finance

There is an embryonic stock exchange with approximately 30 listings. The banking sector is relatively advanced for the region, although there are restrictions on lending to foreign owned companies. Preferential loan rates are available for certain specified sectors and activities.

PART SIX: FACTS AT YOUR FINGERTIPS

Visa and immigration requirements

Visas are not required by the following:

- citizens of Mauritius;
- persons resident in Mauritius under the Immigration Act;
- the spouse of a Mauritius citizen;
- the child or step child or lawfully adopted child of those who come under categories a) and b) above;
- holders of diplomatic passports other than those issued by the governments of Algeria, Iraq, Iran, Libya, and Sudan;
- the crew of a vessel travelling on duty or in transit to join another vessel;
- holders of a '*Laissez Passer*' issued by the United Nations or any other internationally recognized organization;
- those who intend to remain in Mauritius only during the stay of the vessel by which they arrived and intend to depart;
- those authorized specifically by the government;
- holders of a passport issued by any of the following countries:

Antigua and Barbuda, Australia, Austria, Bahamas, Bahrain, Barbados, Belgium, Belize, Botswana, Brunei, Canada, Cyprus, Denmark, Dominica, Finland, France, The Gambia, Germany, Ghana, Greece, Grenada, Guyana, Iceland, Ireland, Israel, Italy, Jamaica, Japan, Kenya, Kiribati, Kuwait, Lesotho, Liechtenstein, Luxemburg, Malawi, Malaysia, Maldives, Malta, Monaco, Namibia, Nauru, the Netherlands, New Zealand, Nigeria, Norway, Oman, Papua New Guinea, Portugal, Qatar, (Western) Samoa, San Marino, Saudi Arabia, Seychelles, Sierra Leone, Singapore, Solomon Islands, South Africa, Spain, St Christopher (Nevis), St Lucia, St Vincent and Grenadines, Sweden, Switzerland, Tanzania, Tonga, Trinidad and Tobago, Tunisia, Turkey, Tuvalu, Uganda, the United Arab Emirates, the United Kingdom (and dependent territories), the United States of America, Vanuatu, Vatican, Zambia, Zimbabwe. Holders of a passport issued by any of the following countries may be granted a two-week visa on arrival:

Albania, Bulgaria, the Commonwealth of Independent States (including Armenia, Azerbaijan, Belarus, Kazakhstan, Kyrgystan, Moldova, Russia, Tadjikistan, Turkmenistan, Ukraine, Uzbekistan and Georgia), Comoros, the Czech Republic, Estonia, Fiji, Hungary, Latvia, Lithuania, Madagascar, Poland, Romania.

On arrival at Sir Seewoosagur Ramgoolam International Airport, completed disembarkation cards must be handed to immigration officials. It is essential to know, and write on this card, where you are going to stay, otherwise there will be problems at the immigration desk. You will also be asked to show your departure ticket from Mauritius. If you don't have one, you will be asked to buy one on the spot.

If you wish to stay longer than a maximum of one month, which you are likely to be allowed by the airport immigration officials on arrival, applications for an extension may be made to the passport and immigration officer in Line Barracks, Port Louis, provided that a valid return ticket, a valid passport or an internationally recognized travel document and adequate funds are held.

Health requirements

A yellow fever vaccination certificate is required by all travellers over one year old arriving from an infected area. Malaria prophylactics are recommended, but not absolutely necessary.

International flights

Air Mauritius, the national carrier, flies twice a week non-stop from London (Heathrow), four times a week non-stop from Paris (CDG), five times a week from Brussels, four times a week from Cape Town, twice a week from Manchester, once a week from Melbourne, twice a week from Vienna, once a week from Paris (CDG) and Frankfurt, once a week non-stop from Frankfurt, once a week non-stop from Munich, once a week from Munich and Geneva, once a week non-stop from Zurich, once a week non-stop from Rome (Fiumicino), twice a week non-stop from Johannesburg, twice a week from Johannesburg and Durban, once a week from Johannesburg and Harare, once a week non-stop from Perth, three times a week non-stop from Bombay, once a week non-stop from Singapore, once a week from Singapore and Kuala Lumpur, once a week non-stop from Hong Kong, twice a week from Nairobi and Antananarivo, twice a week from Nairobi, Moroni and Antananarivo, twice a week from Antananarivo and Réunion, and seven times a day from Réunion.

Air Austral, Air France, Air Zimbabwe, British Airways, Condor, Singapore Airlines, and South African Airways also serve Mauritius.

To reconfirm flights departing from Mauritius, please dial:

Air Austral - Tel: 208-1281
Air France - Tel: 208-1281
Air Mauritius - Tel: 208-6801
Air Zimbabwe - Tel: 212-6960
British Airways - Tel: 208-1039
Condor - Tel: 208-4802
Singapore Airlines - Tel: 208-7695
South African Airways - Tel: 208-6801

Flying times on non-stop flights from overseas destinations are as follows: London, 12 hours; Singapore, 6.5 hours; Hong Kong, 10 hours; Johannesburg, 4 hours; Nairobi, 4 hours; and Seychelles, 2.25 hours.

On arrival

The sole point of entry, by air, is Sir Seewoosagur Ramgoolam International Airport at Plaisance, three kilometres from Mahébourg, 45 kilometres from Port Louis.

A duty-free shop, foreign exchange counters, a tourist information booth, car rental company desks and in-bound tour operator desks are all to be found in the arrivals hall.

There is normally a gaggle of taxi drivers waiting for passengers outside the arrivals hall. All taxis are metered. Fares to most parts of the island hover around the Rs600 mark, but may be more if your plane has arrived in the middle of the night.

International Flight Enquiries - Tel: 208-7700 or 637-3420
Cargo Enquiries - Tel: 637-3902
Cargo Clearance and Deliveries - Tel: 637-3230

Air fares

Flights to Mauritius are, in general, expensive. The usual range of air fares is available: first, business, economy, excursion and APEX, but there are no cut price fares or charter flights because the government does not allow charters into Mauritius. Expect to pay more during the peak season, which covers the northern hemisphere winter and the Mauritian summer.

Departure tax

Exempt from paying the departure tax of Rs100 are those in transit who continue their journey by the first connecting flight within 48 hours, certain government and diplomatic officials, United Nations personnel and their families, military personnel and their families stationed in Mauritius, and children under two years.

Arrival by sea

Those arriving by ship must make contact with the Marine Authority by radio before they are allowed to access the harbour. The National Coast Guard will, once customs formalities have been completed, issue sailors with a temporary permit.

Visitors must then go to the passport and immigration officer in Line Barracks, Port Louis, to have an entry permit stamped in their passport.

Domestic flights

The only domestic service in Mauritius is the daily return flight to Rodrigues, which leaves from SSR International Airport. (During the peak tourist season, this service is increased — on most days of the week — to two flights a day.) The journey, in an ATR 42 turbo-prop plane, takes, on average, an hour and a half. A normal return flight costs Rs 5,940, and an excursion return costs Rs 2,800.

Customs

Passengers of 16 years and over may import the following into the country on a duty-free basis:

- 250 grammes of tobacco (including cigars and cigarettes)
- 1 litre of spirits
- 2 litres of wine, ale or beer
- one-quarter litre of toilet water
- a quantity of perfume not exceeding 10cl.

A plant permit must be obtained from the Ministry of Agriculture prior to the introduction of plants and plant material, including cuttings, flowers, bulbs, fresh fruits, vegetables, and seeds. All plant material must be declared to customs immediately on arrival and is subject to examination. It is prohibited to introduce sugar cane, soil micro-organisms, and invertebrate animals. Facilities for examination and certification of plant materials are available at Réduit (Tel: 454-1091), and the Sir Seewoosagur Ramgoolam International Airport offices of the Plant Pathology Division of the Ministry of Agriculture and Natural Resources (Tel: 637-3194).

All animals and animal material need an import permit from the Ministry of Agriculture and a sanitary certificate of country of origin. All animals must be declared to customs immediately on arrival; landing is allowed if certificates issued by the Veterinary Authorities of the exporting country are in conformity with the import permit.

Dogs and cats undergo a six-month quarantine; birds and other animals up to two months.

Additional information may be obtained from the Division of Veterinary Services of the Ministry of Agriculture Reduit (Tel: 454-1016).

Firearms and ammunition must be declared on arrival.

Public transport

Mauritius has a comprehensive bus service run by a combination of private operators, co-operatives and the National Transport Corporation. Together, they provide a network of services that convey passengers to virtually every part of the island.

It is a disciplined and well-run operation. Once passengers have boarded the bus, they are approached by a conductor who issues tickets. Most bus fares are less than Rs10 one way. There are 46 seats and standing room for 18 people in the coach-type buses.

Express buses take a shorter route between points, but charge the same fare as slower buses. The final destination is displayed above the front windscreen of every bus.

The buses operate from 0530 to 2000 in urban regions and from 0630 to 1830 in rural areas. A late service runs until 2300 between Port Louis and Curepipe via Rose Hill, Quatre Bornes, and Vacoas.

Taxis are numerous — recognizable by their black figures on white registration plates (private cars have black number plates with white figures). Taxi stands are usually close to bus stations in the main towns — taxis rarely roam about looking for passengers.

Taxis are normally available only at conventional times, i.e, 0600 to 2200. Outside these hours, it is advisable to order a taxi in advance. Taxi stand telephone numbers are listed in the local directory and many taxi drivers will provide you with the number of their own mobile phones.

Taxis are metered, so there should no longer be any need to haggle over fares.

'Taxi trains' are battered cars that tout for business among passengers queuing for buses and then follow a regular route picking up more passengers along the way. In effect, they charge little more for each person than the buses for a seat in a shared car.

Car hire

The main international self-drive car hire companies of Avis, Hertz and Europcar operate in Mauritius. (See Listings for addresses.)

Car company representatives are on hand at SSR International Airport and in most of the hotel lobbies should visitors decide to rent a car. All the companies offer a wide range of cars, from fun Mini Mokes to sophisticated family saloons.

Take good care on the roads as Mauritian drivers are highly undisciplined and accidents are common. Seat belts must be worn, cars must be driven on the left side of the road and speed limits (a maximum of 80kph on major roads) should be observed. Speed traps and breathalyzers are in use. In most towns, parking zones are in operation and parking tickets, available from the numerous petrol stations, must be displayed. The roads are not particularly well signposted. If you intend to spend a lot of time driving around the island and hope to get a little off the beaten track, it is worth investing in a decent map, such as the Macmillan Mauritius Traveller's Map, which can be bought from most good bookshops.

Those wishing to hire a car must be 23 years old and have held a valid driving licence for at least one year. Car rental costs vary according to the type of vehicle hired and the rental duration — check with the individual companies.

For those who do not relish the idea of driving themselves, the car hire companies will provide a driver, at an extra cost.

Ferry services

One ferry operates out of Mauritius. The Mauritius Pride has no fixed schedule but usually sails to Rodrigues and Réunion twice or three times a month. Three classes are in use on the 24-hour crossing to Rodrigues — a return ticket costs Rs1,300 in Class Loisir, Rs1,800 in Economy and Rs2,800 Class Excellence (twin-berth cabin). One way fares are half the return fares. On the 10-hour trip to Réunion, there are only two classes — return tickets in cabin class cost Rs2,700 and for a seat only, Rs1,900. These are peak season prices. Low season fares are Rs300 cheaper. The single fare is 60 per cent of the return.

Bookings should be made well ahead of departure through the Mauritius Shipping Corporation on Tel: 242-5255.

Climate

Its proximity to the Tropic of Capricorn assures Mauritius of a subtropical climate that is typically warm and humid.

There are two seasons: summer from November to April, when it is hot, and winter from May to October, when it is warm. Summer temperatures range from 24°C (75°F) at dawn to 30°C (86°F) at noon on the coast and winter ones from 18°C (64°F) at dawn to 24°C (75°F) at noon. The temperature on the central highlands is usually five degrees cooler.

Cyclones often occur in January, February, and March. April to May and September to November are generally considered the best months to visit Mauritius.

Listen to the radio or television for up-to-date weather forecasts.

Currency

The Mauritian Rupee (Rs) is divided into 100 cents (cs). Notes are issued in denominations of predominantly blue Rs1,000, brown Rs500, green Rs200, red Rs100, blue Rs50, and green Rs10. The coins are Rs5, R1, 50cs, 25cs, 20cs, 10cs and 5cs.

Currency regulations

No restriction is imposed on the importation of foreign currency in cash or drafts, letters of credit or traveller's cheques or any other banking instrument. Any excess money can be exchanged at banks or the airport bank offices.

Banks

In general, banks are open from 0915 to 1515 Monday to Friday and from 0915 to 1115 on Saturday. They are closed on Sunday and public holidays.

However, the bank counters at SSR International Airport are open for the arrival and departure of all international flights and most of the banks keep their foreign exchange counters open after normal banking hours. For example, in the touristy area of Grand Baie foreign exchange counters are open from 0800 to 1800 Monday to Saturday and on public holidays, and from 0900 to 1400 on Sunday.

Credit cards

The following credit cards are widely accepted in Mauritius: American Express, Diners, MasterCard, and Visa.

Government

Mauritius is a parliamentary democracy with universal adult franchise for all those who have reached 18 years. A general election is held every five years.

The powers of the President, although important, are limited to ceremonial functions. The real power lies with the Council of Ministers, a body of ministers (or cabinet) headed by the Prime Minister. The Prime Minister is the member of the Legislative Assembly (parliament) who appears to the President to command the support of the majority of members.

Based on the British Westminster model, the assembly has a speaker and 70 members representing 21 electoral constituencies. There are 62 directly elected seats (three each in 20 constituencies and two in Rodrigues) and eight nominated seats. The last ones go to the eight defeated party candidates who are the 'best losers' in the general election, a system conceived to ensure that every ethnic group has adequate representation in the assembly. Government by coalition is a common phenomenon in Mauritian politics.

Local government elections are held every three years on a party political basis.

The judiciary is divided into the Supreme Court, the Court of Criminal Appeal, the Intermediate Court, the Court of Civil Appeal, the Industrial Court, and 10 District Courts. The final Appeal is to the Judicial Committee of the Privy Council of the United Kingdom.

Population

At the end of 1995, the population was estimated at 1,129,428 — a mix of Indo-Mauritians, Euromauritians, Creoles (i.e., those of mixed European and African origin), and Sino-Mauritians.

Language

The official language is English, which is almost universally understood. However, Creole and French dominate in everyday life. Hindi, Tamil, and Chinese dialects are also spoken by various sectors of the population.

Religion

Given the multi-cultural nature of Mauritian society, a good many religions are practised on the island. The main ones are Christianity, Hinduism, Islam, and Buddhism. Colourful religious festivals are observed and enjoyed all year round.

Time

Mauritius is four hours ahead of Greenwich Mean Time, three hours ahead of Central European Time, and two hours ahead of South African time.

Daylight

The daylight hours are approximately 0530 to 1900 in summer (November to April) and 0645 to 1740 in winter (May to October).

Business hours

Most private businesses operate between 0830 and 1630 on Monday to Friday and between 0900 and 1200 on Saturday. Public sector offices operate between 0900 and 1600 on Monday to Saturday and between 0900 and 1200 on Saturday.

Port Louis shops open between 1000 and 1700 on Monday to Friday and between 0900 and 1200 on Saturday; those in Curepipe, Beau Bassin, Rose Hill, Quatre Bornes, Vacoas, and Phoenix open between 1000 and 1800 on Monday to Wednesday, Friday and Saturday, and between 0900 and 1200 on Thursday and Sunday.

Markets tend to open between 0600 and 1800 on Monday to Saturday and between 0600 and 1200 on Sunday.

Security

Mauritius is generally a friendly and peaceful country. Tourists should, however, be careful about their belongings at times, particularly in the towns where pickpockets often operate and on the beach where it is advisable to keep a close eye on unguarded possessions.

Women, whether single or in pairs, are advised to be on guard and, preferably, to take taxis rather than walk, when out at night as there have been a few unpleasant incidents in the north.

Communications

Mauritius Telecom (MT) operates a fairly efficient and reasonably priced telephone system, but there is a shortage of telephone lines in some areas and, for that reason, and also because businessmen worldwide now like to be in constant contact, many people make use of Emtel — the local mobile telephone service.

Public phones are few and far between, but can usually be found outside police stations and community centres. Calls can be made either using coins (the phones accept Rs5, Rs2 and R1 coins) or with MT cards, of varying denominations, which can be bought from MT and various shops.

Should you require a local telephone number, call Directory Enquiries on Tel: 90.

International direct dialling services are available out of Mauritius and calls can be made either from public phone booths (using an MT card), from the MT offices around the island or from hotel rooms, where a surcharge is usually imposed.

To make an overseas call from Mauritius dial 00 plus the country code plus the area code plus the telephone number required.

The Mauritian postal service is efficient and post offices can be found in most towns and villages. The main post office, however, is located in a majestic old building on Quay Street in Port Louis (across the M2 motorway from the main part of the capital).

The opening hours of the main Post Office are as follows: between 0815 and 1115, and 1200 and 1600, Monday to Friday and between 0800 to 1145 on Saturday.

Stamps are issued according to the size of the postcard — Rs10 for a large postcard and Rs4 for a small postcard, to European destinations.

Media

The most popular local newspapers are *Le Mauricien* and *L'Express*, published in French, although there are occasional articles, news reports and advertisements in English. A wide range of international newspapers can be bought, at inflated prices, throughout the island.

There is only one television and radio station, the Mauritius Broadcasting Corporation (MBC), and it is government-controlled. It broadcasts in a number of languages, including English, French, Creole, and Hindi. However, television viewers also receive programmes from Réunion's TV station, as well as Skynews and Canal TV. Most of the top hotels have their own in-house television programming which usually includes the Reuters news network and film channels.

Electric power

The electricity supply throughout the island is 220 volts. Power sockets take a variety of plugs including square three-pins, round three-pins, and round two-pins.

Medical services

There are several public hospitals in Mauritius where medical services are provided free, but, if in need of medical attention, it is advisable to visit a private clinic, where the standard of treatment is usually much higher.

The main hospitals, Doctor Jeetoo Hospital and Sir Seewoosagur Ramgoolam National Hospital, are in Port Louis and Pamplemousses, respectively. There is an orthopaedic hospital in Candos and an eye hospital in Moka. Private clinics are in Rose Hill, Port Louis, Réduit, Floréal, Curepipe, Quatre Bornes, and Tombeau Bay. There are two vaccination centres in Port Louis. Generally, doctors speak English and French.

Emergency services

Dial 999 and ask for the service needed police, or ambulance. For fire dial 995.

Insurance

Insurance cover can be purchased in Mauritius, but it is usually cheaper and more practical to buy it at home, prior to departure for Mauritius.

Chemists/pharmacies

Well stocked with Western medicines, pharmacies are found in all towns and most villages. In many the pharmacist is willing to prescribe certain drugs for particular ailments, thus obviating the need to visit a doctor as well.

Liquor

As would be expected on an island where vast tracts of the land are covered in sugar cane, sugar cane liquor, and rum are popular forms of alcohol.

The most popular sugar cane liquor is Goodwill, with over one million cases being sold a year. Power's No1, produced by International Distillers (ID) Mauritius, trails just behind in second place. ID also produces the very popular Green Island rum aimed at the tourist market and is the biggest seller at the airport's duty-free lounge.

Beer is also popular. Mauritius Breweries, founded in 1963, produces Phoenix (named after the area in which the brewery is located) and Stella, as well as Guinness — under licence. Both Phoenix and Stella are of a high standard, having received numerous international awards, but Phoenix is by far the more popular.

International alcohol brands are available in Mauritius, but as elsewhere in the world, prices are high in hotels, but reasonable in urban bars and nightclubs (especially compared with prices back home).

Licensing hours vary between the different types of establishment — restaurants may have to close at 2300, while nightclubs can stay open for longer.

Tipping

A 10 per cent government tax is added to all hotel and restaurant bills. Tipping is not compulsory and remains a gesture of appreciation.

Clubs

There are various social clubs in Mauritius, such as the Gymkhana Club in Vacoas, the Dodo Club in Curepipe, and the Grand Baie Yacht Club in Grand Baie. Visitors cannot gain access to these clubs unless accompanied by a member, except for the Grand Baie Yacht Club, which offers some reciprocal arrangements to visiting yachtsmen.

The Rotary Club, the Lions Club, and the Round Table all have branches in Mauritius.

There is a Chamber of Commerce. The address is as follows:
Chambre de Commerce et d'Industrie de Maurice,
3 Rue Royale,
Port Louis.
Tel: 208-3301

ENGLISH — CREOLE

Meeting and Greeting

Hello	Bonzour
Good morning	Bonzour
Good afternoon	Bonapremidi
Good evening	Bonswar
Goodbye	Orevwar
How are you?	Konman sava?
I am well	Bien mersi
Thank you (very much)	Mersi (bokou)
Please come in	Vini sivouple
Please sit down	Asize sivouple
You're welcome/ not at all	Pa dekwa
Where do you come from?	Kote ou sorte?
I come from...	Mon sorti...
What is your name?	Ki manyer ou apele?
My name is...	Mon apel...
Can you speak Creole?	Ou kabab koz Kreol?
Only a little	Zis en pe
I would like to learn more	Mon oule apran ankor
How do you find...?	Ki manyer ou vwa...?
I like Mauritius	Mon kontan avek Mauriz
The weather is hot, isn't it?	Letan is so, wi?

Useful words

Today	Ozordi
Tomorrow	Demen
Now	Konmela
Quickly	Vit
Slowly	Dousmon
Hospital	Lopital
Police	Gard
Mr	Myse
Mrs	Madam
Miss	Mamzel
I	Mon
You	Ou
He, she	Li

We	Nou
They	Zot
What?	Kwa?/Ki?
Who?	Ki?/Lekel?
When?	Kon?
How?	Ki manyer?
Why?	Akoz?
Which?	Lekel?
Yes	Wi
No	Non
Money	Larzan
Bad	Pa bon

Directions/Emergencies

Where?	Kote?
Street/road	Lari
Airport	Erport
Where is the hotel?	Lotel sivouple?
Where are you going?	Kote ou pe ale?
I am going to...	Mon pe ale...
Please stop here	Aret isi sivouple
To come	Vini
To go	Ale
To stop	Arete

Numbers

One	Enn
Two	De
Three	Twa
Four	Cat
Five	Senk
Six	Sis
Seven	Set
Eight	Weet
Nine	Nef
Ten	Dis
Eleven	Onz
Twelve	Douz
Thirteen	Trez
Fourteen	Katorz
Fifteen	Kenz
Sixteen	Sez

Seventeen	Diset	To buy	Aste
Eighteen	Disweet	To sell	Vann
Nineteen	Disnef	Shop	Laboutik
Twenty	Ven	Food	Manze
Twenty-one	Venteen	Coffee	Kafe
Twenty-two	Vende	Beer	Labyer
Twenty-three	Ventwa	Cold	Fwa
Twenty-four	Venkat	Hot	Sho
Twenty-five	Vensenk	Tea	Dite
Thirty	Trant	Meat	Lavian
Forty	Karant	Fish	Pwason
Fifty	Senkant	Bread	Dipan
Sixty	Swasant	Butter	Diber
Seventy	Swasandis	Sugar	Disik
Eighty	Katven	Salt	Disel
Ninety	Katvendis	How much?	Konbien?
One hundred	San	That's quite expensive	I ase ser
		Wait a minute	Esper mon en ti moment

Restaurants/Shops/Hotels

Hotel	Lotel	I have to get change	Mon fodre ganni larzan sanze
Room	Lasanm		
Bed	Lili	Excuse me	Ekskiz
To sleep	Dormir	Where is the toilet?	Kote kabinen sivouple?
To bathe	Banyer/Naze		
To eat	Manze	Where may I get a drink?	Kote mon kapab ganni en keksoz pou bwar?
To drink	Bwar		

In Brief

National Park/Nature Reserves

Interiors forests form the nucleus of the 14.5 square kilometres (56 sq miles) of national park and nature reserves in Mauritius. They were primarily formed to conserve and protect the island's remaining original vegetation, which is crucial for the survival of much of the endangered fauna, such as the pink pigeon, echo parakeet, and Mauritius fody. The newly-gazetted Black River Gorges National Park also offers recreation and educational facilities. No structures, firearms, animals, or rubbish dumping are allowed within the boundaries of the park or reserves. Permission from the Forestry Department (next to the Botanical Gardens in Curepipe) is required before visiting any national forest, and no person is allowed in a national forest between the hours of 1800 and 0600.

Black River Gorges National Park
Size: 65.7 sq kms (25 sq miles)
Geographical location: Savanne, Plaines Wilhelms, Black River districts.
Features: Covering 3.5 per cent of the island, this national park is the first of its kind in Mauritius

and was established in June 1994. In 1996 it was still the only national park. The park boundaries encompass the Black Rivers Gorges and environs, including the Brise Fer and Macchabée forests, Plaine Champagne, the Savanne Range, Bel Ombre forests, and much of the Black River Range. The park contains between 80 and 90 per cent of the remaining tracts of native forest in Mauritius. The higher altitudes of the park mark the most important wildlife regions, with many rare species, while the lower altitudes have been designated for picnicking, camping, walking, biking, and other recreational activities.

Bois Sec Nature Reserve
Size: 1.5 ha (3.7 acres)
Geographical location: Near Grand Bassin, Savanne District
Features: not available.

Cabinet Nature Reserve
Size: 17.73 ha (43.7 acres)
Geographical location: About 6 kilometres (3.7 miles) east of Tamarin Estate, in the Vacoas Mountains, Black River District
Features: not available.

Coin de Mire (Gunner's Quoin) Nature Reserve
Size: 75.98 ha (187.6 acres)
Geographical location: Approximately 5 kilometres (3 miles) off the northern shore of the main island of Mauritius.
Features: Plant life similar to Round Island, including a very rare endemic plant, *Lomatophyllum tormontorii*. Also home to a cave known as 'Madam's Hole', used by the British navy in the 19th century for target practice.

Combo Nature Reserve
Size: 2 sq kms (0.7 sq miles)
Geographical location: Near Mont Blanc, in the Savanne Mountains, Savanne District
Features: not available.

Corps de Garde Nature Reserve
Size: 90.33 ha (223 acres)
Geographical location: La Chaumière, near La Ferme Reservoir, Black River District.
Features: not available.

Flat Island Nature Reserve
Size: Undocumented
Geographical location: Approximately 11 kilometres (7 miles) off Cap Malheureux on the north coast of Mauritius.
Features: A lighthouse; island used often for picnic excursions. At low tide, Flat Island is joined to nearby Gabriel Island by a sand bank.

Gabriel Island Nature Reserve
Size: 42.21 ha (103 acres)
Geographical location: Approximately eleven kilometres (seven miles) off Cap Malheureux on the north coast of Mauritius.
Features: not available.

Gouly Père Nature Reserve
Size: 10.95 ha (27 acres)
Geographical location: Near Grand Bassin, Savanne District
Features: not available.

Île aux Aigrettes Nature Reserve
Size: 24.7 ha (61 acres)
Geographical location: 900 metres (980 yards) off the coast of Pointe d'Esny, Grand Port District.
Features: Many plant species found nowhere else in the world; the last remnants of coastal vegetation once prevalent on Mauritius. A Mauritian Wildlife Fund plant rehabilitation and management project was started here in 1985, and has made much progress in restoring the island's vegetation to its original condition. The island is home to a pair of rare Mauritian kestrels. Eighteen Mauritian plant species found on Île aux Aigrettes are classified as endangered or very rare, including *bois de fer*, Île aux Aigrettes ebony, Île aux Aigrettes orchid, *bois de boeuf*, and *bois de chandelle*.

Île aux Cocos Nature Reserve
Size: 14.6 ha (36 acres)
Geographical location: Approximately 3.5 kilometres (2 miles) off Pointela Fouche on the west coast of Rodrigues
Features: Surrounded by crystal-clear waters, Île aux Cocos is an important breeding ground for four tern species. It takes only one hour to walk around the sandy perimeter of the island, which offers opportunities to admire the picturesque slopes of Rodrigues from afar. It is also possible to see the remains of the coconut plantation, after which the island is named.

Île aux Sables Nature Reserve
Size: 7.8 ha (19 acres)
Geographical location: Approximately 4 kilometres (2.5 miles) off Pointela Fouche on the west coast of Rodrigues
Features: A pure beach island, tiny Île aux Sables is an important breeding ground for four tern species.

Île Marianne Nature Reserve
Size: 1.98 ha (4.8 acres)
Geographical location: Approximately 5.5 kilometres (3.4 miles) off Bois des Amourettes on the east coast of Mauritius.
Features: not available.

Les Mares Nature Reserve
Size: Undocumented
Geographical location: Near Grand Bassin, Savanne District
Features: not available.

Perrier Nature Reserve
Size: 1.5 ha (3.7 acres)
Geographical location: Between Curepipe and the Mare aux Vacoas reservoir, Plaines Wilhelms district
Features: Contains a large number of endemic species; also shows an intermediate stage between lowland and upland forest. Mauritius's smallest reserve.

Le Pouce Nature Reserve
Size: Undocumented
Geographical location: About 3 kilometres (1.8 miles) north-east of Moka, Moka and Port Louis districts.
Features: The reserve protects the area surrounding Le Pouce, the thumb-shaped mountain of 812m (2,664 feet) looming behind Port Louis.

Round Island Nature Reserve
Size: 1.6 sq kms (0.3 sq mile)
Geographical location: 22 kilometres (14 miles) off the northern shore of the main island of Mauritius.
Features: Home to some tree, lizard, and snake

species found nowhere else in the world, and harbours more endangered species per unit area than any other comparable spot on earth. Plant life includes the last remnants of palm savannah, such as the famous bottle palm, the Round Island hurrican palm, a fan palm, and a vacoas. Famous for its reptiles, the island is also an important breeding ground for several species of sea birds.

Serpent Island Nature Reserve
Size: 31.6 ha (76 acres)
Geographical location: 25 kilometres (15.5 miles) off Cap Malheureux on the north coast of Mauritius.
Features: A large barren rock with no serpents or snakes, but a sanctuary for birds.

Other Parks

Casela Bird Park
Size: 8 hectares (20 acres)
Geographical location: Near Cascavelle, just south of Bambous, Black River District.
Features: Contains more than 2,500 birds of more than 140 species, housed in 85 aviaries. There are birds from all the continents, but one of the greatest attractions is the Mauritian pink pigeon, one of the rarest birds in the world. The park also has tigers, fish ponds, tortoises, monkeys, and orchids. There is a small restaurant.

Domaine du Chasseur Game Park (privately owned)
Size: 950 ha (2,350 acres)
Geographical location: Bambou Mountains, accessed by Anse Jonchée, Grand Port and Flacq districts.
Features: Some of the last acres of private native forest, including more than 40,000 ebony trees and other tropical flora, such as bergamot, eucalyptus, traveller's palm, and wild orchids. The Domaine is also full of exotic animals (deer, monkeys, wild boar) and rare endemic birds, including the Mauritian kestrel, a couple of which are fed daily by the staff. Hunting is allowed by prior arrangement; big game fishing can also be organized. The Domaine is the only place in Mauritius to offer paragliding. There is a rustic bar and restaurant, and six guest cabins for short-term rental.

Le Val Nature Park
Size: 2 ha (5 acres)
Geographical location: On the 3,000-hectare (7,410-acre) Rose Belle Sugar Estate, Grand Port District.
Features: An example of the diversification projects now facoured by a number of sugar estates. Freshwater prawns are specially bred in chemically treated water; anthuriums, grown for export, thrive in greehouses; and huge plots of watercress is produced for home consumption. There are also deer and sheep enclosures, a duck pond, and a mini-aquarium with eels and tropical fish.

La Vanille Crocodile Park & Nature Park
Size: Undocumented
Geographical location: Sennevile, 2 kilometres (1.2 miles) south of Rivière des Anguilles, Savanne District.
Features: Nile crocodiles, farmed here for their skins, are kept in secure enclosures with noticeboards giving details of the animals within for visitors. Feeding time is usually between 1330 and 1400. The park also exhibits a wide range of Mascarene animals (monkeys, deer, giant tortoises, tenrecs, rabbits, bats, wild pigs, and a giant Telfair skink) and is now akin to a small zoo. There are freshwater streams and indigenous flora, as well as an exhibition room containing specimens of Mascarene reptiles. The park has a small snack bar and a shop.

Sir Seewoosagur Ramgoolam Botanical Gardens
Size: 93 ha (230 acres)
Geographical location: Pamplemousses, Pamplemousses District
Features: 500 plant species exist in the gardens, of which eighty are palm and 25 indigenous to the Mascarene Islands — among them palms, fruit and spice trees, ebony, mahogany, and latania. Highlights include the talipot palm, which waits 40 to 60 years to flower and then dies, and the huge 'Victoria amazonica' Amazon lilies in the water lily pond. A third of the gardens is occupied by an experimental station. There are several animal pens in the gardens, including one dedicated to giant tortoises. There is also a deer park. Entrance is free.

Wildlife and Bird Checklist

An asterisk (*) denotes an endemic species.

Mammals

INSECTIVORES
(Insectivora)
Shrew
Tenrec

BATS
(Chiroptera)
Frugivorous bats
Insectivorous bats

MONKEYS
(Primates)
Javan macaque

CARNIVORES
(Carnivora)
Small Indian mongoose
Indian Grey mongoose

EVEN-TOED UNGULATES
(Artiodactyla)
Wild Mauritian pig
Javan Rusa deer

HARES & RABBITS
(Lagomorpha)
Brown hare
European rabbit

RODENTS
(Rodentia)
Black rat
Brown rat
Mouse

SEA MAMMALS
Dugong
Sperm whale
Finback whale
Pilot whale
Beaked whale
Pygmy killer whales (possibly)
Spinner dolphin
Bottlenose dolphin

Birds

ALBATROSSES
(Diomedeidae)
Yellow-nosed albatross

PETRELS & SHEARWATERS
(Procellariidae)
Wedge-tailed shearwater
Trinidade petrel
Giant petrel
Pintado petrel (Cape pigeon)

TROPICBIRDS
(Phaethontidae)
Red-tailed tropicbird
White-tailed tropicbird

BOOBIES
(Sulidae)
Masked booby

FRIGATEBIRDS
(Fregatidae)
Lesser frigatebird

HERONS, EGRETS, & BITTERNS
(Ardeidae)
Green-backed heron
Cattle egret

FLAMINGOS
(Phoenicopteridae)
Greater flamingo

DUCKS & GEESE
(Anatidae)
Meller's duck
Mallard

FALCONS
(Falconidae)
Mauritius kestrel*

GAME BIRDS
(Phasianidae)
Indian grey francolin
Common quail
Helmeted guineafowl

CRAKES, RAILS, AND COOTS
(Rallidae)
King reed hen (purple swamp hen, Madagascar blue hen)
Madagascar moorhen

PLOVERS
(Charadriidae)
Crab plover
Grey plover
Ringed plover
Little ringed plover
Greater sand plover

SNIPE, SANDPIPERS, AND ALLIES
(Scolopacidae)
Curlew sandpiper
Sanderling
Little stint
Bar-tailed godwit
Greenshank
Redshank
Terek sandpiper
Marsh sandpiper
Common sandpiper
Wood sandpiper
Pectoral sandpiper
Whimbrel
Turnstone

COURSERS & PRATINCOLES
(Glareolidae)
Oriental pratincole
Madagascar pratincole

GULLS & TERNS
(Laridae)
Sooty tern
Lesser crested tern
Common tern
White tern
Common noddy
Brown noddy
Lesser noddy

DOVES & PIGEONS
(Columbidae)
Madagascar turtle dove
Chinese turtle dove
Striated dove
Spotted dove
Barred ground dove (zebra dove)
Rock pigeon
Pink pigeon*

PARROTS
(Psittacidae)

Mauritius echo parakeet*
Ring-necked parakeet (rose-ringed parakeet)

SWIFTS
(Apodidae)
Mascarene swiftlet*

ROLLERS
(Coraciidae)
Broad-billed roller

SWALLOWS & MARTINS
(Hirundinidae)
Mascarene swallow*

CUCKOO-SHRIKES
(Campephagidae)
Mauritius cuckoo-shrike*

BULBULS
(Pycnonotidae)
Mauritius black bulbul*
Red-whiskered bulbul (Persian nightingale)

FLYCATCHERS
(Muscicapidae)
Paradise flycatcher*

STARLINGS
(Sturnidae)
Indian mynah

WHITE-EYES
(Zosteropidae)
Mauritius grey white-eye*
Mauritius olive white-eye*

FINCHES
(Fringillidae)
Spice finch
Yellow-fronted canary

WAXBILLS
(Estrildidae)
Common waxbill

WEAVERS, SPARROWS, WHYDAHS & ALLIES
(Ploceidae)
House sparrow
Village weaver
Mauritius fody*
Madagascar red fody

CROWS & ALLIES
(Corvidae)
Indian house crow

Reptiles & Amphibians

TORTOISES & TURTLES
Geochelone inepta
Geochelene triserrata
Geochelene vosmaeri
Geochelene peltastes
Aldabran tortoise
Radiated Malagasy tortoise
Chelonia mydas
Eretmochelys imbricata
Green turtle
Hawksbill turtle
Caretta caretta
Dermochelys coriacea
Loggerhead turtle
Leatherback turtle
Soft-shelled turtle

SNAKES
Round Island burrowing boa
Round Island keel-scaled boa
Lycodon aulicus
Typhlina bramina
Pelamuis platurus
Wolf snake
Blind snake
Sea snake

LIZARDS, SKINKS & GECKOS
Agama lizard (chameleon)
Outdoor lizard
Giant skink
Telfair's skink
Bojer's skink
Bouton's (snake-eyed) skink
House (stump-eyed) gecko
Common house gecko
Rough-skinned house gecko
Tree gecko
Mourning gecko
Lesser night gecko
Night gecko
Common day gecko
Rodrigues day gecko
Forest day gecko
Ornate day gecko
Guenther's gecko
Giant gecko

CROCODILES
Nile crocodile

TOADS & FROGS
Common toad
Malagasy frog

Fish

SHARKS
Requin chasseur
Milk shark
Thresher shark
Hammerhead shark
Blue shark
Lazy shark

RAYS
Devil ray
Spotted eagle ray (duckbill ray)
Electric ray

SARDINES, HERRINGS, AND PILCHARDS
Spotted herring
Carnee sardine
Black-tailed sardine
Petite sardine (pilchard)

REEF FISH
Leiognthidae
Apogonidae
Gerridae
Pempheridae
Kyphosidae
Monodactylidae
Chaetodontidae
Pomancanthidae
Amphiprionidae
Pomacentridae
Abudefdufidae
Chromidae
Zanclidae
Platicidae
Labridae
Scaridae

OTHERS
Catfish
Barber eel
Echelidae
Congridae
Muraenidae
Milk fish
Needle fish
Flying fish
Sole
Flute mouth
Sea horse
Pipe fish
Barracuda
Lizard fish

Mullet
Lion fish
Squirrel fish
Soldier fish
Vieilles
Meron
Garoupa
Serran
Red snapper
Red emperor
Scavenger (naked head snapper)
Capitaine
Emperor
Silver bream
Red mullet
Carangue
Jack
Spanish mackerel
Yellowfin tuna
Oceanic bonito
Wahoo
Blue marlin
Black marlin
Sailfish
Scorpion fish
Stone fish
Common lionfish
Monacanthidae
Balistidae
Ostraciontidae
Puffer fish
Globe fish
Spine fish

Porcupine fish
Molidae
Salariidae

FRESHWATER FISH

Mottled fin eel
Plain long finned eel
Short finned eel
Freshwater carp
Chitte
River goby (cabot)
Gouramy
Goldfish
Tilapia

Crustaceans

FRESHWATER PRAWNS

River prawn
Colocasia prawn
Betangue
Petites chevrette
Rosenberghi

SEA WATER PRAWNS

Bambous prawn (tiger prawn)

CRABS

Thalamites
Reef crab
Carrelet crab
Grapsus crab

Ocypod crab
Ghost crab
Calling crabs

LOBSTERS

Blue lobster (*homard canal*)
Reef lobster (*langouste*)

Insects & Arachnids

ANTS & ROACHES

Black ant
Red ant
White ant (termite)
Cockroach

BEES & WASPS

Black carpenter bee
Yellow wasp

BUTTERFLIES

Papilio demodocus
Papilio manlius
Junonia rhadama
Amauris phaedon
Cathopsilla thaurana

ARACHNIDS

Grey spider
Centipedes
Scorpions

Wildlife Profile

(Creole name, if any, is indicated in parentheses after the species' Latin name.)

Shrew, *Suncus marinus*: Though to have been introduced accidentally from India in the 1700s, the insectivorous shrew is often preyed upon by the **Mauritius kestrel**.

Tenrec, *Tenrec ecaudatus* (tendrac): a yellowish-brown insectivorous mammal, the tenrec — native to Madagascar — was introduced to Mauritius at the end of the 18th century. Although in hibernation from June until September, at other times of the year the tenrec can often be seen foraging in the late afternoon or at night.

Frugivorous bat, *Pteropus rodriguensis*: Estimated at 200 in number, this small-size bat is legally protected on Rodrigues. The larger *Pteropus niger* lives in secluded spots in the forest of south-west

Mauritius. Gathering in colonies during the day, it flies at dusk to feed on eucalyptus and sisal flowers.

Insectivorous bat: Two species of small insectivorous bats inhabit Mauritius, and are believed to be rather recent arrivals to the Mascarene islands. The **white-bellied tomb bat,** *Taphozous mauritianus*, takes shelter during the day in the dark corners of roofs and caves. At night it can be seen flying about in the light of outdoor lamps catching insects. A few of these bats can sometimes be seen behind the statue of Saint Benedict on the verandah of Tamarin Church. The smaller and darker *Tadarida acetabulosus* lives in caves. The bat's excreta is attractive to cockroaches, which, when seen crawling at spots on boulders on the floor of a cave, point to the bunches of bats clinging to the roof directly above.

Javan macaque, *Macaca fascicularis*: A Javanese macaque thought to have been introduced to the country by Dutch settlers, it is responsible for the rarity of some important timber trees by destruction of their seeds. The related *Lemur catta* and *Lemur variegatus* were once often bred in captivity in Mauritius and can now be seen at Casela Bird Park.

Small Indian mongoose, *Herpestes javanicus auropunctatus*, and the **Indian grey mongoose,** *Herpestes edwardsi*: These were introduced to the island in the middle of the 19th century, but the population was not long afterwards destroyed by planters when they observed the animal's greediness for chickens and game. The mongoose was reintroduced in 1899, when what were thought to be a few males were brought in to control the rat population. There were three undetected females in the group, however, and the mongoose population multiplied quickly, resulting in the disappearance of most game birds from Mauritius. Prefers open, dry bush and savannah districts with plentiful cover. Avoids thick forest, likes to be near villages. Active by day; nights spent in abandoned holes or in self-excavated burrows or other hiding places.

Wild Mauritian pig, *Sus scrofa*: Introduced to the island in the early 1600s, pigs flourished to the extent that, as early as 1709, hunting parties had to be organized to cull the catastrophic herds. They still persist in the Mauritian forests to this day.

Javan Rusa deer, *Cervus timoriensis russa*: Brought to the country in 1639 from Java, deer rapidly flourished in the island's forests. Prefers savannahs, grassy plains, and park lands; also lives in swamps, rain forest, bushy rocky mountains, conifer forests, eucalyptus woods, and plantations. Lives on grass, herbage, leaves, sugar cane shoots, etc. In addition to the wild population that still roams, they are also reared in feed-lots and the flesh used for local consumption and export. The animal in the wild is hunted during the season, which runs from the beginning of June to the end of September.

Brown hare, *Lepus capensis*: First reported in Mauritius in 1753, the hare was once found on all the northern islets except Round Island. Today it is only found on Gunner's Quoin, where it is hunted for its meat. Prefers open country of all types. Active at dusk and at night.

European rabbit, *Oryctolagus cuniculus*: After its introduction in 1639, the rabbit was — and still is — reared as a domestic animal on Mauritius, while on Gabriel and Round islands, where there were no predators, it grew to such prolific

numbers that, in 1986, it became necessary to eradicate the species on Round Island. Prefers dry region with abundant cover and light easily excavated soil. If necessary, lives entirely above ground with refuges in dense ground cover.

Black rat, *Rattus rattus*: A climbing rat that lives in the country's forests, destroying bird eggs and nestlings. Rarely seen in towns.

Brown rat, *Rattus norvegicus*: Lives in burrows throughout the Mascarene islands.

Mouse, *Mus musculus*: First reported in the early 1700s, mice are frequently encountered in forests and towns in Mauritius.

Dogs, cats, horses, and asses were all introduced to the island between the 17th and 19th centuries and were wild for a period of time, but all are now domesticated — with the exception of some wild cats that are still present in the forests. Cattle and goats are also raised domestically.

Birdlife Profile

Albatrosses: The **yellow-nosed albatross,** *Diomedea chlororhynchos*, is an occasional visitor to Mauritius. Inhabits the open ocean; attracted to trawling grounds for fish offal.

Petrels and Shearwaters: About two to three thousand pairs of **wedge-tailed shear-waters,** *Puffinus pacificus*, return to the southern part of Round Island in September each year to nest in burrows. Of the three petrels seen around Mauritius, only the **Trinidade petrel,** *Pterodroma arminjoniana* (pétrel de la Trinité), is indigenous. It has a very restricted distribution: apart from Round Island, it nests only in one other place in the world — Trinidad, off Brazil. The **giant petrel,** *Macronectes giganteus*, and the **Pintado petrel** (or Cape pigeon), *Daption capense*, are occasional visitors.

Tropicbirds: Round Island is home to two tropicbirds: the **red-tailed,** *Phaeton rubricauda*, which nests on protected rock ledges, and the **white-tailed,** *Phaeton lepturus*, which prefers nesting in a vegetation-sheltered nook. The red-tailed species is also seen on Gunners Quoin, while the white-tailed also occurs on the main island of Mauritius, nesting in some river gorges.

Boobies: About 50 pairs of the **masked booby,** *Sula dactylatra*, maintain their numbers on Serpent Island and Pigeon Rock off Flat Island.

Frigatebirds: The **lesser frigatebird,** *Fregata ariel*, is a frequent visitor to Mauritius. The male's courting habit is particularly striking: it inflates a red pouch below its throat in a striking display to attract a female.

Herons, egrets, and bitterns: The **green-backed heron,** *Butorides striatus,* is often seen around the ponds at Curepipe Botanical Gardens. It fishes in rivers and lagoons as well, using an interesting technique of throwing small objects into the water to lure fish. The **cattle egret,** *Bubulcus ibis,* sometimes visits from Madagascar in small numbers.

Flamingos: Although not indigenous to Mauritius, about a dozen **greater flamingos,** *Phoenicopterus ruber,* are on display at Casela Bird Park.

Ducks and geese: Meller's duck, *Anas melleri,* is thought to have been a part of the local avifauna even in Dutch times. They have been privately reared very successfully for many years. The **mallard,** *Anas platyrhyncos,* the most common duck in Europe, has now become a permanent Mauritian resident after 37 chicks were imported from France in the late 1970s and later liberated. At Tamarind Falls, they have displaced Meller's ducks.

Falcons: Although reduced to only 12 individuals in 1987, the endemic **Mauritius kestrel,** *Falco punctatus* (crécerelle de Maurice), has now staged a tentative come-back because of concerted conservation measures. Related to the European and African kestrel, it has adapted itself to lizard-hunting under forest cover and has developed rounder wings, tail feathers more suited to braking, and longer legs for snatching prey off tree branches.

Game birds: The Indian grey francolin, *Francolinus pondicerianus,* was introduced to Mauritius in the 18th century and flourished until the mongoose (introduced in the early 1900s) decimated its numbers. It is still extant, however, and its call can often be heard at dawn, particularly around Port Mathurin on Rodrigues. The small **common quail,** *Coturnix coturnix africana,* is raised on Mauritius, and the **helmeted guineafowl,** *Numidia meleagris mitrata,* can still be found in small flocks in savannahs on Yemen Estate.

Crakes, rails, and coots: Most likely to be seen is the **Madagascar moorhen,** *Gallinula chloropus,* which prefers freshwater bodies like slow-flowing rivers or ponds where there is good cover for habitat. Extremely rare is the **king reed hen,** *Porphyrio madagascariensis,* also known as the purple swamp hen or Madagascar blue hen.

Plovers: Common migrants include the **greater sand plover,** *Charadrius leschenaulti,* the **grey plover,** *Pluvialis squatarola,* the **ringed plover,** *Charadius hirticula,* and the little **ringed plover,** *Charadius dubius.* Rarer is the **crab plover,** *Dromas ardeola.* All can be seen singly along the shoreline.

Snipe, sandpipers, and allies: Thirteen members of this family are migratory visitors to Mauritius; some more common than others. The most numerous is undoubtedly the **curlew sandpiper,** *Caladris ferruginea,* seen in flocks near the seaside and sometimes inland near water. Some individuals stay on the island throughout the year, but do not breed. Also resident throughout the year but not breeding are the **turnstone,** *Arenaria interpres,* and the **whimbrel,** *Numenius phaeopus.*

Coursers and pratincoles: Two species of pratincole are rare visitors to Mauritius: the **oriental pratincole,** *Glareola maldivarum,* and the **Madagascar pratincole,** *Glareola ocularis.*

Gulls and terns: Seven members of this family occur on Mauritius. Serpent Island is the home of ten to twenty thousand pairs of the **sooty tern,** *Sterna fuscata,* and four to five thousand pairs of the **brown noddy,** *Anous stolidus,* and the **lesser noddy,** *Anous tenuirostris.* The immaculate **white tern,** *Gygis alba,* is a frequent visitor.

Doves and pigeons: Of the seven members of this family present on Mauritius, only one is endemic: the **pink pigeon,** *Columba mayeri.* Dependent on the endemic forest for its diet, the bird can only be found at Macabé, Brise Fer, and Bassin Blanc in the wild; breeding at the latter place. Cage breeding saved this nearly extinct species; about 100 in various places around the world constitute a genetic reserve, while the bird is some 40-strong in nature. They can be seen at Casela Bird Park.

Parrots: The endemic **Mauritius echo parakeet,** *Psittacula eques,* was once common to the island in the mid-1800s, but as the native forest contracted, its numbers dwindled. A concerted conservation effort has offered some hope, although it is far from being taken off the danger list. Despite its smaller size, the similar **ring-necked parakeet,** *Psittacula krameri,* is often confused with the echo parakeet by the uninformed. Originating in Sri Lanka, the ring-necked (also known as the rose-ringed) parakeet was introduced to the island in 1886. It is a pest of maize in the coastal regions and is often offered for sale at the Port Louis market.

Swifts: When rain clouds threaten, the endemic **Mascarene swiftlet,** *Collocalia francica,* can often be seen flying low, insect-hunting over cane fields. The brown bird, tinged with iridescent green, nests in dark caves in lava tunnels.

Rollers: An occasional visitor to Mauritius is the **broad-billed roller,** *Eurystomus glaucurus*, of Madagascar.

Swallows and martins: A coastal bird (particularly favouring the island's west and southern coasts), the endemic **Mascarene swallow,** *Phedina borbonica*, can sometimes be seen perched on the electric wires at Grand Bassin. At Baie du Cap it is often seen near the causeway, where it can be seen flying with its bill open to take in any insects it encounters. Nests are placed in cracks and crevices of boulders or other similar shelter, and it is known to nest close to man-made structures. It is not found on Rodrigues.

Cuckoo-shrikes: It is estimated that fewer that 200 pairs of the endemic **Mauritius cuckoo-shrike,** *Coracina typica*, exist on the island today, favouring the remnants of native forest around Black River Gorges and Bel Ombre. It is not found on Rodrigues. The bird has a habit of numbing its prey — generally large insects and geckos — by knocking it against a tree branch prior to ingestion.

Bulbuls: Once a popular game bird off Asian origin, about 200 pairs of the endemic **Mauritius black bulbul,** *Hypsipetes olivacea*, still exist in the island's native forests. The most widespread bird on the island, however, is the **red-whiskered bulbul,** *Pycnonotus jocosus*. Accidently released from a cage during the cyclone of 1892, this melodious bird builds its small, cup-like nest in hedges.

Flycatchers: Suffering a steady decline throughout most of the human history of Mauritius, the beautiful **Mauritius paradise flycatcher,** *Terpsiphone bourbonnensis*, is still clinging to survival in the patchy remnants of such indigenous forests as Bassin Blanc.

Starlings: Introduced for pest control in 1763, the **mynah**, *Acridotheres tristis*, is commonly seen all over the island. They can sometimes be seen on deer and cattle, from which the birds pick off ticks. Like the magpie, it has an eye for shiny or colourful items, which it uses to adorn its nest.

White-eyes: Two endemic white-eyes exist on Mauritius: the **Mauritius grey white-eye,** *Zosterops borbonicus*, and the **Mauritius olive white-eye,** *Zosterops chloronothos*. The former is common all over the island, particularly in hotel grounds and gardens, while the latter — although closely related to the grey white-eye — has suffered a huge fall in numbers, with less that 150

pairs surviving in the undergrowth of the south-western forests of the island.

Finches: Brought from Java as a cage bird in the early 1700s, the prolific **spice finch,** *Lonchura punctulata*, has adapted well to the shady mango orchards on the island, where it hides its large round nest. Generally seen in open country, where it feeds on seeds and grains from grasses. Also a former cage bird, the **yellow-fronted canary,** *Serinus mozambicus*, has as its preferred habitat wooded areas such as the casuarina plantations near the seaside.

Waxbills: Introduced as a cage bird in the 18th century, the **common waxbill,** *Estrilda astrild*, is present on both Mauritius and Rodrigues. Locally common in open country, it gathers in flocks with **spice finches** and **Madagascar red fodys** to feed on grasses during the non-reproductive season.

Weavers, sparrows, whydahs, and **allies:** Now reduced to a small area of native forest, it is estimated that only some 90 pairs of the endemic **Mauritius fody,** *Foudia rubra*, occur today. It is primarily insectivorous. The **Madagascar red fody,** *Foudia madagascariensis*, however, is mainly a seed eater and is occasionally seen all over the island. Common throughout Mauritius is the **house sparrow,** *Passer domesticus*, which feeds on fruits, insects, seeds, and household scraps. The **yellow village weaver,** *Ploceus cucullatus*, is fairly common in various parts of the country, constructing its intricately woven nests at the extremity of palm leaves or of thin branches.

Crows and allies: Generally considered a nuisance and a menace, as they destroy the nestlings of other birds, the **Indian house crow,** *Corvus splendens*, was once centred around the Plaine Verte area of Port Louis but is spreading. An omnivore, it feeds on carrion and household refuge, among other things.

Demographic Profile

Although no official census has been taken since 1990, the population of Mauritius in 1996 was estimated at more than a million. The annual birth rate is approximately 2.1 per cent.

Population density averages 531 people to the square kilometre, with uneven distribution. The highlands in the Plaines Wilhems District is by far the most populated region, while the southern Savanne District is the least populated. The island of Rodrigues, part of the Republic of Mauritius, had an estimated 34,678 residents in 1994. Thirty-nine per cent of the population live in urban areas.

Language

Today, there are 22 languages, with 33 dialects, spoken in Mauritius. English, though little spoken, is the 'official' language and Creole is the lingua franca.

The Dutch settlers in the country, although they left behind a legacy of Dutch place names, did not have any lasting effect on local linguistics. The French language, on the other hand, still holds pride of place in Mauritian life as the dominant language in the press, as well as of everyday conversation.

The profusion of Indian immigrants from the end of the 18th century brought a number of new languages and dialects to the country. Tamil was the first Indian language spoken in Mauritius, although throughout the 19th century, Bhojpuri was — and still is — the most widely spoken Indian language. Hindi, once widely spoken at the beginning of the 20th century, is now used only in religious ceremonies and literary circles, and not as a household language. Telegu, Marathi, Gujarati, Bengali, and Punjabi are also spoken in households.

Muslim traders arriving in the 19th century brought Urdu to Mauritius. In the same century, Chinese immigrants introduced Hakka, Mandarin, and Cantonese.

In 1948, literacy in any local language became an electoral requirement. Since then, there has been a drive towards teaching all languages. In 1955, Asian-language classes were introduced in primary schools and, in 1974, in secondary schools.

Religion

There are some 87 different religious denominations represented in Mauritius, many being new sects or groupings emerging from the main religions of Hinduism, Christianity, and Islam. Visitors will see steeples of gothic-style churches, domes of gilded temples, minarets of mosques, and ornate pagodas wherever they go in Mauritius — from remote sugar cane fields to the busy streets of the nation's capital, all testifying to the complete freedom of religion in the country.

Population

1996 estimate: 1,129,428, or 554 persons a square kilometre.

(All figures below are from the last census taken in the Republic of Mauritius in 1995, and include the island of Rodrigues.)

1995 population: 1,094,426, or 587 persons per square kilometre.

Population by age and sex (1995)

	0-14	15-34	35-54	55+	Total
Males	159,335	208,603	131,477	57,564	561,505
Females	152,598	200,241	135,366	72,408	560,613

District populations (1995)

Port Louis	136,470
Pamplemousses	110,442
Rivière du Rempart	92,898
Flacq	119,151
Grand Port	102,465
Savanne	63,980
Plaines Wilhems	342,397
Moka	70,319
Black River	49,221
Island of Rodrigues	34,775
Republic of Mauritius	1,112,118

Religious affiliation

Roman Catholic	27%
Other Christian	5%
Hindu	51%
Muslim	16%
Other	1%

Gazetteer

(Second paragraph indicates kilometre distance to major towns. Populations given are current estimates. n/a: Information not available.)

BEAU BASSIN-ROSE HILL

Plaines Wilhems District.
Centre de Flacq 31.5, Chemin Grenier 47.5, Curepipe 11, Goodlands 36, Grand Baie 31.5, Mahébourg 33, Port Louis 10, Quatre Bornes 3, Rivière du Rempart 37, Triolet 25, Vacoas-Phoenix 7.
Alt: 200 m (656 ft). Pop: 95,000. Post Office. Clinique du Bon Pasteur Tel: 464 7238. Police Tel: 999. Petrol: Day hours. Hotels.

CENTRE DE FLACQ

Flacq District.
Beau Bassin-Rose Hill 31.5, Chemin Grenier 64, Curepipe 28, Goodlands 26, Grand Baie 36, Mahébourg 39, Port Louis 38.5, Quatre Bornes 31.5, Rivière du Rempart 15.5, Triolet 27, Vacoas-Phoenix 35.5.
Alt: n/a. Pop: 15,000. Hospital: none. Police Tel: 999. Petrol: Day hours. Hotel: none.

CHEMIN GRENIER

Savanne District.
Beau Bassin-Rose Hill 47.5, Centre de Flacq 64, Curepipe 34, Goodlands 81, Grand Baie 73.5, Mahébourg 40.5, Port Louis 56, Quatre Bornes 43, Rivière du Rempart 79.5, Triolet 67, Vacoas-Phoenix 39.

Alt: n/a. Pop: n/a. Post Office. Hospital: none. Police Tel: 999. Petrol: Day hours. Hotel: Pointe aux Roches.

CUREPIPE
Plaines Wilhems District.
Beau Bassin-Rose Hill 11, Centre de Flacq 28, Chemin Grenier 34, Goodlands 47, Grand Baie 42.5, Mahébourg 27, Port Louis 22, Quatre Bornes 9, Rivière du Rempart 43.5, Triolet 36, Vacoas-Phoenix 5.
Alt: 550 m (1,804 ft). Pop: 60,000+. Post Office. Clinique Ferrière Tel 676 3332; Clinique de Lorette Tel: 675 2911. Police Tel: 999. Petrol: Day hours. Hotels.

GOODLANDS
Rivière du Rempart District.
Beau Bassin-Rose Hill 36, Centre de Flacq 26, Chemin Grenier 81, Curepipe 47, Grand Baie 9.5, Mahébourg 62, Port Louis 25, Quatre Bornes 38, Rivière du Rempart 11, Triolet 14.5, Vacoas-Phoenix 42.
Alt: n/a. Pop: n/a. Post Office. Hospital: none. Police Tel: 999. Petrol: Day hours. Hotel: none.

GRAND BAIE
Rivière du Rempart District.
Beau Bassin-Rose Hill 31.5, Centre de Flacq 36, Chemin Grenier 73.5, Curepipe 42.5, Goodlands 9.5, Mahébourg 45, Port Louis 17, Quatre Bornes 30, Rivière du Rempart 20.5, Triolet 5, Vacoas-Phoenix 34.
Alt: n/a. Pop: n/a. Post Office. Hospital: none. Police Tel: 999. Petrol: Day hours. Hotels.

MAHÉBOURG
Grand Port District.
Beau Bassin-Rose Hill 33, Centre de Flacq 39, Chemin Grenier 40.5, Curepipe 27, Goodlands 62, Grand Baie 45, Port Louis 47, Quatre Bornes 36, Rivière du Rempart 54.5, Triolet 41, Vacoas-Phoenix 32.
Alt: n/a. Pop: 20,000. Airport in nearby Plaisance/Plaine Magnien. Post Office. Hospital. Police Tel: 999. Petrol: Day hours. Hotels.

PORT LOUIS
Port Louis District.
Beau Bassin-Rose Hill 10, Centre de Flacq 38.5, Chemin Grenier 56, Curepipe 22, Goodlands 25, Grand Baie 17, Mahébourg 47, Quatre Bornes 12, Rivière du Rempart 26, Triolet 13, Vacoas-Phoenix 16.
Alt: sea level. Pop: 130,000. Post Office. Dr Jeetoo Hospital Tel: 212 3201. Police Tel: 999. Petrol: Day hours. Hotels.

QUATRE BORNES
Plaines Wilhems District.
Beau Bassin-Rose Hill 3, Centre de Flacq 31.5, Chemin Grenier 43, Curepipe 9, Goodlands 38, Grand Baie 30, Mahébourg 36, Port Louis 12, Rivière du Rempart 37, Triolet 25, Vacoas-Phoenix 4.
Alt: n/a. Pop: 70,000. Clinique de Quatre Bornes Tel: 425 0423. Police Tel: 999. Petrol: Day hours. Hotels.

RIVIÈRE DU REMPART
Rivière du Rempart District.
Beau Bassin-Rose Hill 37, Centre de Flacq 15.5, Chemin Grenier 79.5, Curepipe 43.5, Goodlands 11, Grand Baie 20.5, Mahébourg 54.5, Port Louis 26, Quatre Bornes 37, Triolet 19, Vacoas-Phoenix 51.
Alt: n/a. Pop: n/a. Post Office. Hospital: none. Police Tel: 999. Petrol: Day hours. Hotel: none.

TRIOLET
Pamplemousses District.
Beau Bassin-Rose Hill 25, Centre de Flacq 27, Chemin Grenier 67, Curepipe 36, Goodlands 14.5, Grand Baie 5, Mahébourg 41, Port Louis 13, Quatre Bornes 25, Rivière du Rempart 19, Vacoas-Phoenix 29.
Alt: n/a. Pop: n/a. Post Office. Hospital: none. Police Tel: 999. Petrol: Day hours. Hotel: none.

VACOAS-PHOENIX
Plaines Wilhems District.
Beau Bassin-Rose Hill 7, Centre de Flacq 35.5, Chemin Grenier 39, Curepipe 5, Goodlands 42, Grand Baie 34, Mahébourg 32, Port Louis 16, Quatre Bornes 4, Rivière du Rempart 51, Triolet 29.
Alt: n/a. Pop: 60,000. Post Office. Hospital: none. Police Tel: 999. Petrol: Day hours. Hotel: none.

Museums

Natural History Museum (Mauritius Institute), Port Louis
District: Port Louis
Features: The remnants of the extinct dodo, plus a host of other interesting information relating to Mauritian fauna and flora. The Public Library on the first floor is a useful reference source.

Naval & Historical Museum, Mahébourg
District: Grand Port
Features: Ancient maps, historical documents, and parts of old wrecked ships are housed in a beautiful old 18th-century colonial house.

Musée de la Photographie, Port Louis
District: Port Louis
Features: A delightful collection of old newspapers, photographs, photographic equipment, and postcards, as well as a slide projector carrying old transparencies of Mauritius.

Special Mobile Force (SMF) Regimental Museum, Vacoas
District: Plaines Wilhems
Features: The museum houses a wide and intriguing array of exhibits, including military memorabilia, an aborted foetus, and a large 'Save the Whale' papier mâché display.

Eureka (La Maison Creole), Moka
District: Moka
Features: An old, wooden colonial home built in the mid-19th century which has been restored to its former glory and filled with antiques from a number of different eras.

Robert Edward Hart Museum, Souillac
District: Savanne
Features: The former home of the Mauritian poet Robert Edward Hart, now a memorial/museum dedicated to his life and work.

Public holidays

There are 13 Public holidays in Mauritius, but only six are fixed; the others are dependent on religious calendars.

January 1	New Year's Day
January 2	New Year
Jan/Feb	Chinese Spring Festival
Jan/Feb	Thaipoosam Cavadee
Feb/March	Maha Shivaratree
March 12	Republic Day
March/April	Ougadi (Telegu New Year)
May 1	Labour Day
Lunar	Id El Fitr
Aug/Sept	Ganesh Chaturthi
Oct/Nov	Diwali
November 1	All Saint's Day
December 25	Christmas Day

Due to the varied religious lives of the Mauritian people, numerous festivals take place throughout the island at different times of the year, but they are not Public holidays. Check with the MTPA or in newspapers while in Mauritius for further information.

Listings

Airlines

Air Austral
Port Louis
Tel: 208 1281

Air France
Port Louis
Tel: 208 1281

Air Madagascar
Port Louis
Tel: 208 6801

Air Mauritius
Port Louis
Tel: 208 6878
Fax: 208 8792

Air Zimbabwe
G S A Sunset
Aviation
5th Floor
Fon Sing Bldg
12 Edith Cavell St
Port Louis
Tel: 212 6960/1/2
Fax: (230) 208 8077

British Airways
Ave Duke of
Edinburgh
Port Louis
Tel: 208 1039

Cathay Pacific
Airways
Port Louis
Tel: 208 1039

Condor Airlines
Port Louis
Tel: 208 4802

Singapore Airlines
5, Ave Duke of
Edinburgh
Port Louis
Tel: 208 7695

South African
Airways
Port Louis
Tel: 208 6801
Fax: 208 8792

Airport

Air Mauritius
Helicopter Service
S S R International

Airport
Tel: 637 3420/3552
Fax: 637 4104

Art Galleries

Galerie Danielle
Poisson
21 Jemmapes St
Port Louis
Tel: 212 9771

Galerie Hélène de
Senneville
12 Belmont House
Intendance St
Port Louis
Tel: 212 8339

Galerie Stéphanie
Braud
Royal Road
St Jean Road,
Quatre Bornes
Tel: 454 1242

Henry Coombes
Art Gallery
Royal Road
Grand Baie

Max Boullé Art
Gallerie
Municipality of
Rose Hill

Port Louis Art
Gallery
Mallefille St
Port Louis

Air Mauritius Offices

Australia
MLC Center
19-29 Martin Place
Sydney NSW 2001
Tel: 221 7300
Fax: 231 1469

Austria
Hilton Center Top
1624
1030 Vienna
Tel: 71˙30 444
Fax: 71 34 036

Belgium
Boulevard Emile
Jacqmain
1000 Brussels
Tel: 218 5705
Fax: 219 1766

France
8 Rue Halevy
75441 Paris
Cedex 09
Tel: 4451 1564
Fax: 49240425

Frankfurt
Frankfurt Airport
Center
Hugo-Eckener-
Ring
60549 Frankfurt
Tel: 690 72700
Fax: 690 59206

Germany
80539 Munich
Tel: 290 03930
Fax: 290 03944

India
Air India Bldg
Ground Floor
Tel: 202 8474
Fax: 202 5340

Italy
Via Barberini 68
3rd Floor
00 187 Rome
Tel: 4742051/5
Fax: 482 5252

Kenya
1st Floor
Union Towers Bldg
Tel: 22 9166
Fax: 21 006

Mauritius
Rogers House
5, President John
Kennedy St
PO Box 441
Port Louis
Tel: 208 7700
Fax: 208 8331

Norway
Munkedamsun 38
5th Floor
0118 Oslo
Tel: 835703
Fax: 835710

Réunion
Angle des Rues
Charles
Gounod et Alexis
de Villeneuve
97400 St Denis
Tel: 202500
Fax: 200877

Rodrigues
ADS Bldg
Port Mathurin
Tel: 831 1558
Fax: 831 1954

Singapore
135 Cecil St
04-02 LKN Bldg
Singapore 0106
Tel: 222 3033
Fax: 225 9726

South Africa
701 Carlton Towers
Commissioner St
Johannesburg 2001
Tel: 331 1918
Fax: 331 1954

Spain
Plaza de Espana 18
Torre de madrid
Planta 8 -
Oficina 20
28008 Madrid
Tel: 559 3581
Fax: 547 0199

Sweden
Norriandsgatan 15
111433 Stockholm
Tel: 7230695
Fax: 7230712

Switzerland
1-3 Rue de
Chantepoulet
4th Floor
1201 Geneva
Tel: 732 0560
Fax: 731 1690

Zimbabwe
13th Floor Old
Mutual Center
3rd St
Jason Moyo Ave
Harare
Tel: 735738
Fax: 735740

Banks

Bank of Mauritius
Sir William
Newton St
PO Box 29
Port Louis
Tel: 208 6801
Fax: 208 8792

Banque
International Des
Marscareignes
4th Floor
Sir William
Newton St
Port Louis
Tel: 212 4982/78
Fax: 212 4983

Banque National de
Paris Continental
(BNPI)
5th Floor
BAI House
25 Pope Hennessy St
PO Box 494
Port Louis
Tel: 208 4147/8137
Fax: 208 8143

Banque Privée
Edmond de
Rothschild
Chancery House
Lislet Goeffroy St
Port Louis
Tel: 212 2784
Fax: 208 4561

Barclays Bank PLC
5th Floor
Moorgate House
Sir William
Newton St
Port Louis
Tel: 208 1811/1816
Fax: 208 2720

Baroda Bank
4th Floor
Baroda Bank Bldg
Sir William
Newton St
Port Louis
Tel: 208 1505/3891

Habib Bank Ltd
Sir William
Newton St
Port Louis
Tel: 208 5524

Hong Kong and
Shanghai Bank
Placed'Armes
PO Box 50
Port Louis
Tel: 208 1801/0183
Fax: 208 0183

Indian Ocean
International Bank
Ltd (IOIB)
Sir William
Newton St
Port Louis
Tel: 208 0121

Mtius Commercial
Bank Ltd (MCB)
Sir William
Newton St
Port Louis
Tel: 208 2801

State Commercial
Bank Ltd
Treasury Bldg
Intedance St
Port Louis
Tel: 208 5301

State Bank
International Ltd
10th Floor
Sincom Bldg
SC Antelme St
Port Louis
Tel: 212 2054

South East Asian
Bank Ltd
26 Bourbon St
Port Louis
Tel: 208 8826

Business Associations

Ahrim(Association
des Hoteliers et
Restaurateurs de
l'Ile Maurice)
Royal Road
Grand Baie
Tel: 263 8971
Fax: 263 7907

Chamber of
Commerce and
Industry
3, Royal Road
Port Louis
Tel: 208 3301
Fax: 208 0076

Chamber of
Agriculture
Plantation House
Duke of Edinburgh
Avenue
Port Louis
Tel: 208 9852

Chinese Chamber
of Commerce and
Industry
Joseph Rivière St
Port Louis
Tel: 212 0156

Custom and Excise
Department
IKS Bldg
Farquhar St
Port Louis
Tel: 240 9702

Mauritius Export
Development and
Investment
Association
(MEDIA)
Jamalac Bldg
Vieux Consiel St
Port Louis
Tel: 208 7750
Fax: 208 5965

Mauritius Export
Processing Zone
Association
(MEPZA)
42, Sir William
Newton St
Port Louis
Tel: 212 1853

Mauritius
Employers
Federation (MEF)
Cérne House
Cheusse
Port Louis
Tel: 212 1599

Passport and
Immigration Office
Police Hq
Line Barracks
Port Louis
Tel: 208 1212

Service Bureau
(Quick Secretarial
Services)
Place Foch
Port Louis
Tel: 212 5450/0505

Car Hire

ABC Car Rental
ABC Centre C/R
Abattoir and
Military Roads
Port Louis
Tel: 212 0291

Avis Rent A Car
Al-Madina St
Port Louis
Tel: 208 1624
Fax: 208 1014

Budget Rent A Car
Mer Rouge — Line
Road
Port Louis
Tel: 242 0341

Citer — Location
De Voitures
Grewals Lane —
Les Pailles
Tel: 211 3191

Dodo Touring and
Company Limited
Saint-Jean Road
Quatre-Bornes
Tel: 425 6810
Fax: 424 4309

Econotour
Route Saint-Jean
Quatre-Bornes
Tel: 424 4142

Europcar
Autoroute M2
Les Pailles
Tel: 208 9258
Fax: 208 4705

Endeavour Car
Rental
Tel: 212 3131

Grand Bay Top
Tours Ltd
Royal Road
Grand Baie
Tel: 263 8770

Hertz
Gustave Colin St
Forest Side
Tel: 674 3695/6
Fax: 674 3720

Jet Car Ltd
6 Sir William
Newton St
Port Louis
Tel: 212 0009

Kevtrav Ltd
3rd Floor
Discovery House
St Jean Rd
Quatre Bornes
Tel: 465 4458
Fax: 464 3777

Mauritours-
Beachcar
Rose-Hill
Tel: 454 1682
Port Louis
Tel: 208 5241

Nice Tours Ltd
Atrium Bldg
Vandermesh St
Rose-Hill
Tel: 465 4484

Societé J H A
Arnulphy Cie
Labourdonnais St
Mahebourg
Tel: 631 9806
Fax: 631 9991

Waterlily Travel
and Tours
Sir-W-Churchill St
Curepipe
Tel: 676 1496
Fax: 676 1494

Casinos

Casino de Maurice
Teste de Buch St
Curepipe
Tel: 675 5012

Casino La Progoue
Sun-Hôtel
Tel: 453 8441

Casino Trou-aux
Biches Village
Hotel
Tel: 265 6619

Casino Saint-Geran
Hôtel
Belle-Mare, Flacq
Tel: 413 2825/6

Casino Chinois
Amicale de Port
Louis

55, Route Royale
Port Louis
Tel: 242 3335

Casino Hôtel
Paradise
Le Morne
Tel: 450 5050

Casino Berjaya
Le Morne
Tel: 622 6450

Casino Belle Mare
Plage Hôtel
Tel: 415 1515

Le Grand Casino
du Domaine
Domaine Les Pailles
Tel: 211 0400

Cinemas

ABC
Royal Road
Belle Rose

Deep Sea Fishing

Beachcomber
Fishing Club
Hotel Paradis
(Challenger)
Le Morne
Tel: 450 5050
Fax: 450 5140

Black River Sport
Fishing
Organisation
La Balise
Tel: 683 6843

Centre de Peché de
l'île Maurice
Hotel Club
Rivière Noire
Tel: 683 6552/503
Fax: 683 6318

Domaine du
Pêcheur
Anse Jonchêe
Vieux Grand-Port
Tel: 631 9261

Island Sport Club
Black River
Tel: 6836 768

Killer Sportfishing
Trou aux Biches
Tel: 265 6595
Fax: 263 7888

329

La Pirogue Big
game Fishing
Flic-en-Flac
Tel: 453 8441
Fax: 453 8449

Organization de
Pechê du Nord
(Corsaire Club)
Royal Road
Trou aux Biches
Tel: 265 6267
Fax: 265 6611

Sofitel Imperial Big
Game Fishing
Wolmar
Tel: 453 8700
Fax: 453 8320

Sport Fisher
Royal Road
Grand Baie
Tel: 263 8358

Diving
Centres

Blue Water
(Diving Base)
Le Corsaire
Trou aux Biches
Hotel
Trou aux Biches
Tel: 265 7186

Canonnier Diving
Centre
Hotel Le Canonnier
Pointe aux
Cannoniers
Tel: 263 7995
Fax: 263 7864

Coral Dive (La
Croix du Sud)
Blue Bay
Tel: 631 9601

Diveplan
Beacomber Paradis
Le Morne
Tel: 683 6775

Explorer
Hotel Ambre
Palmar Belle-Mare
Tel: 415 1544

Islandive
Verandah Hotel
Grand Baie
Tel: 263 8016
Fax: 263 7369

La Pirogue
(Diving Centre)
La Pirogue Sun
Hotel
Flic en Flac
Tel: 453 8441
Fax: 453 8449

Maritim Diving
Centre
Maritim Hotel
Balaclava
Tel: 261 5600
Fax: 261 5670

Mauricia Diving
Gand baie
Tel: 263 7800

Merville Diving
Centre
Merville Beach
Hotel
Grand Baie
Tel: 263 8621
Fax: 263 8146

Paradise Diving
Royal Road
Grand Baie
Tel: 263 7220

Pierre Sport Diving
Touessrok Sun
Hotel
Trou d'Eau Douce
Tel: 419 2451
Fax: 419 2025

Saint Geran Diving
St Geran Hotel
Tel: 415 1825

Shandarani Diving
Centre
Shandarani Hotel
Blue Bay
Tel: 637 3511
Fax: 631 9313

Sindbad
Kuxville
Cap Malheureux
Tel: 262 8836

Sofitel Diving
Centre
Sofitel Imperial
Hotel
Flic en Flac
Tel: 453 8700
Fax: 453 8320

The Cap Divers
Paradise Cove
Hotel
Tel: 263 7983
Fax: 262 7736

Trou aux Biches
Diving Centre
Trou aux Biches
Hotel
Trou aux Biches
Tel: 265 6562
Fax: 265 6611

Villas Caroline
Diving Centre
Villas Caroline
Flic en Flac
Tel: 453 8450
Fax: 453 8144

Foreign
Diplomatic
Missions

Australia
High Commission
2nd Floor
Rogers House
5, John Kennedy Av
PO Box 541
Port Louis
Tel: 208 1700
Fax: 208 8878

Austria
Consulate
Rogers House
President John
Kennedy
Port Louis
Tel: 211 6801

Belgium
Consulate
New Quay St
Port Louis
Tel: 212 4811
Fax: 208 1014

Brazil
Consulate
Harel Mallac Bldg
Edith Cavell St
Port Louis
Tel: 208 5434
Fax: 208 1674

Britain
High Commission
Les Cascades Bldg
Edith Cavell St
Port Louis
Tel: 211 1361

Canada
Consulate
Pope Hennessy St
Port Louis
Tel: 208 0821

China (People's Rep)
Embassy
Royal Road
Belle Rose
Rose-Hill
Tel: 454 9111
Fax: 454 0362

Denmark
Consulate
Rogers Riche Terre
Tel: 248 9401
Fax: 248 1637

Egypt
(Arab Rep)
Embassy
8, King George V Av
Floréal
Tel: 696 5012
Fax: 686 5775

Finland
Consulate
Rogers House
5, John Kennedy St
Port Louis
Tel: 208 6801

France
Embassy
14, St George St
Port Louis
Tel: 208 2282
Fax: 208 8145

Germany
Consulate
32 B Saint
George St
Port Louis
Tel: 212 4100
Fax: 208 5330

Italy
Consulate
Air Mauritius
Rogers House
Port Louis
Tel: 208 7700

Japan
Consulate
Edith Cavell St
Port Louis
Tel: 211 1749
Fax: 211 1789

Korea (Rep)
Consulate
5th Floor
Rainbow House
Edith Cavell St
Port Louis
Tel: 212 0231

Madagascar
(Democratic Rep)
Embassy
Queen Mary Ave
Floréal
Tel: 686 5015
Fax: 686 7040

Netherlands
Consulate
New Quay St
Port Louis
Tel: 208 1241

New Zealand
Consulate
Royal Road Pailles
Port Louis
Tel: 212 4920
Fax: 208 4654

Norway
Consulate
Rogers House
5, President john
Kennedy St
Port Louis
Tel: 208 6801

Pakistan
Embassy
Anglo Mauritius
House
Intendance St
Port Louis
Tel: 212 0359

Portugal
Consulate
Harel Mallac Bldg
18, Edith Cavell St
Port Louis
Tel: 208 0861

South Africa
High Commission
British American
Insurance Bldg
Port Louis
Tel: 212 6925/6/8
Fax: 212 6936

Sweden
Consulate
Rogers House
J Kennedy St
Port Louis
Tel: 208 6801

Switzerland
Consulate
2, J Koenig St
Port Louis
Tel: 208 8763

USA
Embassy
Roger House
President John
Kennedy St
Port Louis
Tel: 208 2347
Fax: 208 9534

Russia
Embassy
Queen Mary Ave
Floréal
Tel: 696 1545
Fax: 696 5027

Hospitals and Clinics

Brown Seqauard
Hospital
Beau Bassin
Tel: 454 2071/464
0626/0731/0624

Central Flacq
Hospital
Tel: 413 532/90

City Clinic
Sir Edgar Laurent
Street
Port Louis
Tel: 220486

Clinique du Bon
Pasteur
Thomy Pitot St
Rose Hill
Tel: 464 7238

Clinique Ferriré
Curepipe
Impasse College
Lane
Tel: 676 1973

Clinique de Lorette
Higginson St
Curepipe
Tel: 675 2911

Clinique du Nord
81 Royal Road
Baie du Tombeau
Tel: 2472 532

Clinique du Dr
Darné
Curepipe Road
Curepipe
Tel: 686 1477

Clinique de
Quartre Bornes
Stevenson St
Quatre Bornes
Tel: 425 0429

Dr R A G Jeetooo
Hospital
V Pougnet St
Tel: 212 3201

Ent Hospital
Vacoas
Tel: 686 2061

Jawaharlal Nehru
Hospital
Rose Belle
Tel: 627 4951

Long Mountain
Hospital
Tel: 245 2571

Mahébourg
Hospital
Tel: 631 9556/692

Medpoint Hospital
Phoenix
Tel: 426 7777

Poudre d'Or
Hospital
Tel: 283 7568

Sir Ramgoolam
National Hospital
Pamplemousses
Tel: 243 3661/3764

Souillac Hospital
Tel: 625 5532/92

Victoria Hospital
Candos
Tel: 425 3031

Hotels

Budget Hotels
Beau Bassin
Vacances Hotel
Martindale St
Tel: 454 5249
Fax: 464 6997

Bourbon Tourist
Hotel
Jummah Mosque
Tel: 240 4407/242

City Hotel
Sir Seewoosagur
Ramgoolam St
Tel: 212 0466
Fax: 208 5340

Hotel Le Grand
Carnot
17 Dr Edouard
Laurent St
Tel: 240 3054

Le Rossignol Hotel
Jules Koenig St
Tel: 212 1983

Mountview Hotel
Trianon No 2 Ave
Tel: 464 9895/454
7058
Fax: 424 6558/454
7058

Palais d'Or Hotel
Jummah Mosque
Tel: 242 5231

Pension Arc En
Ciel
Tel: 247 2592
Fax: 247 2966

Sunray Hotel
Coromandel
Tel: 233 4777

Tandoori Hotel
Victoria Square
Tel: 212 2131/0031

Welcome Hotel
Royal Road
Curepipe
Tel: 676 1469

White House
Stanley Ave
Quatre Bornes
Tel: 464 5835
Fax: 464 5216

East Region
Ambre Hotel
Belle Mare Plage
Tel: 415 1544/45
Fax: 415 1594

Belle Mare Plage
(Golf Hotel and
Resort)
Belle Mare Plage
Tel: 415 1083
Fax: 415 1082

Blue Lagoon Beach
Hotel
Blue Bay
Mahebourg
Tel: 631 9529
Fax: 631 9045

Coco Beach
Poste de Flacq
Belle-Mare
Tel: 415 1089/10
Fax: 415 1888

Domaine du
Chasseur
Anse la Jonchée
Vieux Grand Port
Tel: 631 9261
Fax: (ditto)

Emeraude Beach
Hotel
Royal Road
Belle Mare Plage
Tel: 415 1107/8
Fax: 415 1109

La Croix du Sud
Pointe Jérôme
Mahebourg
Tel: 631 9505/9601
Fax: 631 9603

Le Flamboyant
Hotel
Blue Horizon
Hotel Ltd
Belle Mare
Tel: 1037
Fax: 415 1035

Le Palmar Hotel
Coastal Road Hotel
Mare
Tel: 415 1041/2
Fax: 415 1043

Le Surcouf Village
Hotel
Palmar Coast Road
Palmar
Tel: 419 1800/01
Fax: 212 1361

Le St Geran Sun
Hotel
Golf Club and
Casino
Tel: 415 1825/6
Fax: 415 1983

Le Tropical
Trou d'Eau Douce
Tel: 419 2300/1
Fax: 419 2302

Le Tousserok
Trou d'Eau Douce
Tel: 419 2451/6
Fax: 419 2025

Moonlight Bay
Hotel
Grand River South
East
Tel: 419 3892/4

Sandy Bay Hotel
Pointe de Flacq
Belle Mare
Tel: 413 2055
Fax: 413 2054

Silver Beach
Trou d'Eau Douce
Tel: 419 2601
Fax: 419 2604

Shandarani
Blue Bay
Tel: 637 4301/6/7
Fax: 637 4313

North Region
Bay View Hotel
Ex Arc En Ciel
Hotel
Baie du Tombeau
Tel: 247 2626/8617
Fax: 247 2772

Baie des Cocotiers
Royal Road Baie
du Tombleu
Tel: 247 2462
Fax: 247 2463

Casa Florida
Residence de
Vacances
Péreybère
Tel: 263 7371
Fax: 263 6209

Casuarina Village
Hotel
Tel: 261 5653/6552
Fax: 261 6111

Club MED
Pointe aux
Canonniers Grand
Baie
Tel: 263 7508
Fax: 263 7511

Colonial Coconut
Hotel
Pointe Malartic
Grand Baie
Tel: 263 8720/8171
Fax: 263 7116

Corotel Hotel
Le Goulet Baie du
Tombeau
Tel: 247 2355/1523
Fax: 247 2472

Coin De Mire
Village Hotel
Beau Manguier
Cap Malheureux
Tel: 262 7302/4
Fax: 262 7305

Etoile de Mer
Hotel
Coastal Road Trou
aux Biches
Tel: 261 6561
Fax: 261 6178

Fred's Apartment
and Studio
Péreybère Beach
Lane
Péreybère
Tel: 263 8830
Fax: 263 7531

Hibiscus Village
Vacances
Péreybère
Grand Baie
Tel: 263 8554/6891
Fax: 263 8553

Island View Club
Hotel
Royal Road
Grand Gaube
Tel: 283 9544/9237
Fax: 283 9233

Kuxville
Royal Road
Tel: 262 8836
Fax: 262 7407

La Maison
Route Royale
Cap Malheureux
Tel: 263 8974
Fax: 263 7009

Le Calamar Hotel
Pointe aux Piments
Tel: 261 5187-89
Fax: 261 5247

Le Canonnier
Hotel
Pointe aux
Canonniers
Tel: 263 7999
Fax: 263 7864

Le Capri
Royal Road-Baie
du Tombeau
Tel: 247 2533
Fax: 247 1071

Le Grand Gaube
Hotel
Grand Gaube
Tel: 283 9350
Fax: 283 9420
Telex: 4280 IW

Le Grand Bleu
Royal Road Trou
aux Biches
Tel: 261 5812/3
Fax: 261 5842

Le Mauricia
Beachcomber
Group
Grand Baie
Tel: 263 7800/10
Fax: 263 7888
Telex: 5326 IW

Les Mascareignes
Hotel
Coast Road Cap
Malheureux
Tel: 263 7373/4
Fax: 263 7372

Les Orchidées
Hotel
Tel: 263 8780/9
Fax: 263 8553

Le Victoria
Pointe aux Piments
Tel: 261 8124
Fax: 261 8284

Maritim Hotel
Balaclava
Turtle Bay
Terre Rouge
Tel: 261 5600/9
Fax: 261 5670

Marina Village
Hotel
Anse La Raie
Cap Malheureux
Tel: 263 7651/2
Fax: 263 7650

Merville Beach
Hotel
Royal Road Grand
Baie
Tel: 263 8621
Fax: 263 8146

Paradise Cove
Hotel
Anse la Raie
Cap Malheureux
Tel: 262 7983/4/5
262 6511/2/4/6

PLM Azur Mont
Choisy
Trou aux Biches
Tel: 265 6070/336
Fax: 265 6749

Royal Palm Hotel
Grand Baie
Tel: 263 8353
Fax: 263 8455

Troux aux Biches
(Village Hotel)
Trou aux Biches
Tel: 265 6561/2

Ventura Hotel
Royal Road
Grand Baie
Tel: 263 6030-33
Fax: 263 7479

Veranda Bungalow
Village
Grand Baie
Tel: 263 8015/2041
Fax: 263 7369

Villas Mon Plaisir
Pointe aux Piments
Tel: 261 7471/7980
Fax: 261 6600

Villas Pointe aux
Biches Hotel
Pointe aux Piments
Tel: 261 5901/2/3
Fax: 261 5904

Villa le Filao
Collendavello Lane
Péreybère
Tel: 263 6149
Fax: 637 3691

**Port Louis and
Town Hotels**
Gold Crest Hotel
Route Saint-Jean
Quatre Bornes
Tel: 454 5945/48
Fax: 454 9599

Le Saint-Georges
19 Rue St Georges
Port Louis
Tel: 211 2581/82
Fax: 211 0885

Mandarin Hotel
George-Gilbert Av
Floréal
Tel: 696 5031/2/
2288
Fax: 686 6858

Rodrigues
Auberge Anse aux
Anglais
Tel: 831 2179
Fax: 831 1973

Beau Soleil Hotel
Tel: 831 1673
Fax: 831 1916

Cotton Bay Hotel
Pointe Coton
Tel: 831 3000-02
Fax: 831 3003

Ciel d'Ete
(Pension)
Tel: 831 1587

Escale Vacances
Tel: 831 1544
Fax: 831 2075

Mourouk Ebony
Tel: 831 3350
Fax: 831 3355

Sunshine
(Pension)
Tel: 831 1674

South Region
Villas Pointe aux
Roches
Chemin Grenier
Tel: 625 5112/13
Fax: 626 2507

West Region
Berjaya Le Morne
Resort Casino
Beach Hotel
Le Morne
Tel: 450 5688/683
6800
Fax: 450 5640

Crystal Beach
Royal Road
Flic en Flac
Tel: 453 8678
Fax: 453 8688

Flic en Flac
Sea Breeze Lane
Flic en Flac
Tel: 453 8537/8834
Fax: 453 8833

Hôtel Club Centre
de Pêche
Black River
Tel: 683 6503/22
Fax: 683 6318

Island Sports Club
Hotel
Black River
Tel: 683 6769/8
Fax: 683 6547

Klondike Village
Vacances
Flic en Flac
Tel: 453 8333/6
Fax: 453 8337

Les Bougainvilliers
La Preneuse
Tel: 683 6525
Fax: 683 6332

Le Meridien
Paradise Cove
Anse la Baie
Tel: 262 7983
Fax: 262 7736

Le Pearl Beach
Hotel
Flic en Flac
Tel: 453 8406
Fax: 453 8405

Le Pirogue Sun
Hotel and Casino
Wolmar Flic en
Flac
Tel: 453 8441/2
Fax: 453 8449

Manisa Hotel
Flic en Flac
Tel: 453 8558
Fax: 453 8562

Tamarin Hôtel
Tamarin Bay
Tel: 683 6581/35
Fax: 683 6927

Villas Caroline
Flic en Flac
Tel: 453 8411/8580
Fax: 453 8144

Villas Sand N Dory
Wolmar Flic
en Flac
Tel: 453 8420/8526
Fax: 453 8640

Mauritius Missions Abroad

Australia
2 Beale Crescent
Deakin Act 2600
Canberra
Tel: (61 6) 282 4436
Fax: (61 6) 282 3235
Telex: 62863

Belgium
68 Rue des
Bollandiste
Etterbeek
1040 Bruxelles
Tel: (32 2) 733 9988
Fax: (32 2) 734
4021

Egypt
No 5-26th July St
Lebanon Square
Monadessine
Cairo
Tel: (20-2) 34 70929
Fax: (20-2) 34 52425
Telex: 93631

France
127 Rue de
Tocqueville
75017 Paris
Tel: (331) 4227 3019
Fax: (331) 4053

India
5 Kautilya Marg
Chanakyapuri
New Delhi 110021
Tel: (9111) 301
1112/3
Fax: (9111) 301
9925
Telex: 3166045
Bombay
Tel: (39 6) 354
97586
Fax: (39 6) 354
97586

Italy
Via Alfredo
Serranti 14
00136 Rome

Madagascar
Route Circulaire
Anjanahary
Boite Postale 6040

Antananarivo 101
Tel: (2612) 32157
Fax: (2612) 21939

Malaysia
14th Floor
Suite ABC
Bangunam
Angkasa Raya
Jalan Ampang
PO Box 122
50450 Kuala Lampur
Tel: (603) 241
1870/1126
Fax: (603) 241 5115

Pakistan
House No 27
St No 26
Sector F-6/2
Islamabad
Tel: (92 51) 210
145/213
Fax: (92 51) 210 076
Telex: 54 362 MAU
PK

South Africa
1163 Pretorius St
Hatfield 0083
Pretoria
Tel: (27 12) 342
1283
Fax: (27 12) 342
1286

Switzerland
Kircheweg 5
8032 Zurich
Tel: 3838788
Fax: 383 5124

United Kingdom
32/33 Elvaston
Place
London SW75 NW
Tel: (44 171) 581
0294
Fax: (44 171) 823
8437

**United States of
America**
Suite 441
4301 Connecticut
Ave NW Van
Ness Centre
Washington DC
20008 USA
Tel: (1 202) 244
1491
Fax: (1 202) 966
0983

Mauritius Tourism Promotion Authority

SSR International
Airport
Tel: 637 3635

SSR St
Port Louis
Tel: 208 6387
Fax: 212 5142

Mauritius Tourist Offices Abroad

France
120 Ave Charles-
de-Gaule
92200 Neuilly
Tel: (331) 464 03747
Fax: (331) 464
01123

Germany
Postfach 101846
600 18 Frankfurt/
Main
Tel: (6171) 980354
Fax: (6171) 980 652

Hong Kong
Suite A2, 1st Floor
Eton Bldg
288 des Voeux
Road Central
Tel: (852) 2851 1036
Fax: (852) 2805

India
Block 2-D, 3rd Floor
Phoenix Estate
462 Tulsi Pipe Rd
Bombay 400013
Tel: (9122) 493 9336
Fax: (9122) 493
9355

Italy
BMK SAS
Pibbliche Relazioni
Foro Buonapare 46
20121 Milan
Tel: (39 2) 865 984
Fax: (39 2) 864
60592

Japan
Ginza Stork
Bldg 5F
1-22-10 Ginza
Chuo-Ku
Tel: (813) 5250 0175
Fax: (813) 5250
0176

South Africa
2nd Floor
Southern Life Gdns
6 Protea Place
Sandton
Tel: (2712)784 0632
Fax: (2712) 7840635

Switzerland
Public Relations
Werbe AG
Kirchenweg 5
CH-8032 Zurich
Tel: (411) 383 8788
Fax: (411) 383 5124

United Kingdom
32/33 Elvaston
Place
Tel: (171) 584 3666
Fax: (171) 225 1135

Museums

**Natural History
Museum**
Chausée
Port Louis
Tel: 20639

Naval Museum
Mahébourg

La NeMuseum
Souillac

**S Bissoondoyal
Museums**
Tyack
Rivière des
Anguilles

SSR Museum
SSR St
Port Louis

Nightclubs

Club Climax
Grand Baie
Tel: 263 8737

Dream On
Grand Baie
Tel: 263 8434

Le Saxophone
Beau Bassin

Le Swing
Baie du Tombeau
Tel: 247 2533

Melody's Disco Club
Place Margeot
Centre
Commerciale
Rose Hill
Tel: 464 4097

Number One
Grand Baie
Tel: 263 8434

**Palladium Disco
Club**
Quatre Bornes
Tel: 454 6168

Sam's Disco
Vacoas La
Plantation
Tel: 686 5370

Public Transport

**Mauritius Bus
Transport**
Royal Road
Montagne Longue
Tel: 245 2539

**National Transport
Corporation**
Bonne Terre Road
Vacoas
Tel: 426 2938

**Rose Hill
Transport**
14 Hugnin St
Rose Hill
Tel: 464 1221

Taxi Service
17 Seeneevassen St
Cite Borstal
Tel: 233 5419

Triolet Bus Service
Triolet
Tel: 261 6516

United Bus Service
Les Cassis
Tel: 212 2028

Restaurants

Curepipe

Chez Roland
Grand Baie
Tel: 263 8326

Chinese Wok
Curepipe Road
Tel: 676 1548

Golden Lion
Restaurant
Impasse St Joseph
Tel: 676 1965

La Belle Epoque
Phoenix
Tel: 679 1386

La Nouvelle
Potinière
Hillcrest Bldg
Sir William
Churchill St
Tel: 676 2648

Maharajah
Casa Maria Bldg
College Lane
Tel: 676 2532

Nando's
Chickenland
Tel: 674 0239

Nobby's Steak
House
Royal Road
Tel: 676 2204

Tropicana
Royal Road
Tel: 676 3286

East Region

Au Val
Le Val
Tel: 633 5051

Chez Manuel
Saint Julien
Tel: 418 3599

Le Tropical
Restaurant
Trou d'Eau Douce
Tel: 419 2300

Symon's Restaurant
Belle Mare
Pointe de Flacq
Tel: 415 1135

North Region

Béatrice Restaurant
Onys Bldg
Rouge Royal
Grand Baie
Tel: 263 6944

Caféteria Péreybère
Péreybère
Tel: 263 8700

Fu Xiao
Pailles
Tel: 212 4225

Indra
Pailles
Tel: 4225

Jade Garden
Grand-Bois
Tel: 263 7214

L'Assiete du
Pêcheur
Royal Road
Grand Baie
Tel: 263 8559

La Barachois
PLM Azur
Mont Choisy
Tel: 261 6336

La Bateau Ivre
Pointe aux
Cannoniers
Tel: 263 8766

La Belle Creole
Anse La Raie
Tel: 262 7983

La Bougainville
Hôtel le Maurica
Grand Baie
Tel: 263 7800

La Case Créole
Grand Baie
Tel: 263 8432

La Cannelle Rouge
Pailles
Tel: 212 4225

La Charrette
Grand Baie
Tel: 263 8976

La Cocoteraie
Anse la Raie
Tel: 262 7983

La Dolce Vita
Pailles
Tel: 212 4225

La Jonque
Grand Baie
Tel: 263 8729

La Mediterranée
La Sapinière
Péreybère
Tel: 263 8034

Le Bigorneau
Péreybère
Tel: 263 8553/4

Le Bistrot
Tel: 263 3507

Le Café de Paris
Royal Road
Grand Baie
Tel: 263 8022

Le Capitaine
Tel: 263 8108

Le Carnivore
Restaurant
Royal Road
Pointe aux
Canoniers
Tel: 263 7020

Le Château d'Orose
Grand Baie
Tel: 263 8468

Le Clos St Louis
Pailles
Tel: 212 4225

Le Grillon
Grand Baie
Tel: 263 8540

Le Palais de Chine
Route Royale
Grand Baie
Tel: 263 7120

Le Pescatore
Route Côtière
Trou aux Biches
Tel: 265 6337

L'Epicure
Tel: 262 6711

Le Tanjore
Tel: 263 6030

Le Wahoo
(PLM Azur)
Pointe aux
Canonniers
Tel: 265 6336

Paradise
Restaurant
Pointe aux

Canonniers
Tel: 263 6355

Phil's Pub
Grand Baie
Tel: 263 8589

Restaurant Café
Péreybère
Péreybère
Tel: 263 8700

Sakura Restaurant
Route Royale
Grand Baie
Tel: 263 8092

Verandah
Grand Baie
Tel: 263 8032

Port Louis

Cannelle Rouge
Domaine Les
Pailles
Tel: 212 4225/6003

Carri Poullé
Duc-d'Edinbourg
Avenue
Tel: 212 1295

Dragon Palace
Léoville
L'Homme St
Tel: 208 0346

Foong-Teng
Rue la
Bourdonnais
Tel: 212 6468

Fu Xiao
Domaine Les
Pailles
Tel: 212 4225/6003

Kwang Chow
Cnr Queen E and
Anquetil St
Tel: 240 9735

La Bonne Marmite
Sir W Churchill
Tel: 212 2403

Lai Min
56/58 Royal Road
Tel: 242 0042

La Flore
Mauricienne
10 Intendance St
Tel: 212 2200

La Flore Orientale
53 SSR St
Tel: 240 3017

La Palmeraie
Port Louis
Tel: 212 2597

Le Boulevard
Port Louis
Tel: 208 8325

Le Café du Vieux
Conseil
Rue du Vieux
Tel: 211 0323

Palais d'Or
Jummah Mosque St
Tel: 242 5231

Paloma Léoville
L'Homme
Tel: 208 5861

Pizza Hut
Tel: 211 0708

Prestige Restaurant
Tel: 211 0566

Shamrock
Restaurant
Cnr Royal and
Corderie St
Tel: 212 5271

Snow White
Restaurant
Cnr Sir W Newton
St and Royal Road
Tel: 208 3528

Stax Steak Ranch
Tel: 211 1977

Sun Tours City
Restaurant
Remy-Ollier St
Tel: 208 1490

Tandoori
Place Victoria
Tel: 212 0031

Tung Tong
Restaurant
Royal Road
Tel: 208 6279

Underground
Bourbon St
Tel: 212 0064

Quatre-Bornes/ Vacoas

Chopsticks
St Jean Road
Quatre-Bornes
Tel: 424 7459

Golden Spur
Tel: 424 9440

Green Dragon
Trianon
Tel: 424 4564

Happy Valley
St Jean Road
Tel: 454 9208

King Dragon
La Louise
Tel: 424 7888

La Belle Epoque
Phoenix
Tel: 697 1386

La Cles des
Champs
Floreal
Tel: 686 3458

Le Perroquet
Vacoas
Tel: 696 4905

Moghal Mahal
Tel: 424 1786

Restaurant
Mandarin
Royal Road
Tel: 696 4551

Rolly's Steak and
Seafood House
Tel: 464 8267

Stephanis
Trianon
Tel: 454 7963

Rose Hill
Le Pékinois
Cnr Royal and
Ambrose St
Tel: 454 7229

Melody's
Tel: 464 4097

West Region
Crystal Beach
Hotel
Royal Road
Flic en Flac
Tel: 453 8678

Domaine du
Chasseur
Anse Jonchée
Tel: 634 5097

Golden Horse
Flic en Flac
Tel: 453 8552

La Bonne Chute
Bon Restaurant
La Preneuse
Rivière
Tel: 683 6552

Le Barachois
Vieux Grand Port
Tel: 212 8443

Le Bougainville
Blue Bay
Tel: 631 8299

Le Chamarel
Restaurant
Tel: 683 6421

Le Domino
Le Morne
Tel: 683 6675

Le Phare
Mahébourg
Tel: 631 9728

Le Sirius
Mahébourg
Tel: 631 8906

Melody's
Rose Hill
Tel: 464 4097

Mer de Chine
Flic en Flac
Tel: 453 8549

Océan
Flic en Flac
Tel: 453 8627

Pavillion de Jade
Route Royal
Rivière Noire
Tel: 683 6630

Sea Breeze
Flic en Flac
Tel: 453 8413

Varangue sur
Morne
Plaine
Champagne
Tel: 683 6610

Rodrigues Island
John's Resto
Mangue
Tel: 831 1306

Lagon Bleu
Morrisson St
Tel: 831 1635

Le Capitaine
Johnston St
Tel: 831 1581

Le Solitaire
Jenner St
Tel: 811 1540
Fax: 831 2030

Paille en Queue
Duncan St

Phoenix d'Or
Mont Lubin
Tel: 831 1417

Travel and Tour Agents

Air International
Travel and Tours
Cnr Eugéne
Laurent
SS Ramgoolam St
Port Louis
Tel: 208 0101
Fax: 212 4189

Aladdin Tours
ABC Centre
Cnr Abattoir and
Military Roads
Port Louis
Tel: 242 1168

Al-Labbaik Travel
Agency
20 Sir Virgile
Naz St
Port Louis
Tel: 212 2205
Fax: 212 6465

Atlas Travel
Services
Angle des Rues
SS Ramgoolam et
Laurent
Port Louis
Tel: 1497/0208
Fax: 208 7717

Atom Travel
Agency
22 Rue Royale
Port Louis
Tel: 212 1136/5583
Fax: 212 0555

Bonny Air Travel
Fon Sing Bldg

Budget Travel and
Tours (MTIUS)
Labama House
35 Sir William
Newton St
Port Louis
Tel: 212 4700/5753
Fax: 212 5162

Cathay Tours
Moorgate House
4/5 S W-Newton
Port Louis
Tel: 212 8584/5/6
Fax: 212 8587

Century Travel Co
Lord Kitchner St
Port Louis
Tel: 208 6707/8
Fax: 208 6707

Chinese Travel
Agency
Moorgate House
Port Louis
Tel: 212 8584
Fax: 212 8587

Clavis Travel
Bureau
1 Corderie St
Port Louis
Tel: 240 4602
Fax: 212 3435

Concorde Travel
and Tours
Chaussée St
Port Louis
Tel: 208 5041
Fax: 212 6001

Concorde Travel
Arcades
Curepipe
Tel: 675 4462
Fax: 212 2585

Edith Cavell St
Port Louis
Tel: 8540/5688
Fax: 5727

Grand-Bay Travel
and Tours Ltd
Tel: 263 8771/8273
Fax: 263 8274

Harel Mallac
Travel Ltd
18 Edith-Cavell St
Port Louis
Tel: 208 8580/4802
Fax: 208 1674

Holiday Planners
53-55 Sir S-
Ramgoolam St
Port Louis
Tel: 242 0888/3017
Fax: 242 0889

IKS Travel Agency
Cnr Farquhar and
La Paix St
Port Louis
Tel: 242 4032/5359
Fax: 240 5305

Inter Travel and
Tours
15 Bourbon St
Port Louis
Tel: 212 4369/5428
Fax: 212 1720

Matta
Cnr Sir-S-
Ramgoolam and
Sir W Newton St
Port Louis
Tel: 242 5026
Fax: 208 2417

Mauritius Travel
and Tourist
Bureau
Rue Royale
Port Louis
Tel: 208 2041/4841
Fax: 208 8607

Mauritours
10 Sir William
Newton St
Port Louis
Tel: 208 5241
Fax: 212 4465

Nice Tours Ltd
Atrium Bldg
Cnr Virgil Naz
and Vandermesh
Rose-Hill
Tel: 464 4484

Oceania Travel
44 Jummah
Mosque St
Port Louis
Tel: 242 4247
Fax: 208 8868

R Link Travel and
Tours
3 and 6 Fon Sing
Bldg
12 Edith Cavell St
Port Louis
Tel: 212 0055
Fax: 212 2413

Rogers Travel
Rogers House
John Kennedy St
Port Louis
Tel: 208 6801/0306
Fax: 212 0189

Silver Wings
Travel Ltd
19 Louis
Pasteur St
Port Louis
Tel: 242 6405/5020
Fax: 208 8133

Skyline Ltd
3 Rue Eugene-
Laurent
Port Louis
Tel: 208 5038/0549
Fax: 240 5174

Stella Travel
Agency
17 Bourbon St
Port Louis
Tel: 208 0064/0259
Fax: 212 9672

Sun Travel and
Tours Ltd
2 St George St
Port Louis
Tel: 212 1639/2771
Fax: 212 2392

Transworld Travel
Place Foch
Port Louis
Tel: 208 4110
Fax: 212 4101

Virginie Voyages
and Tours Ltd
7 Rue Saint-
Georges
Poonoosamy Bldg
Port Louis
Tel: 212 6203/6426
Fax: 212 6310

White Sand Travel
Chaussée
Port Louis
Tel: 212 6092
Fax: 208 8524

**Association of
Inbound
Operators**
Avis
Al-Madina St
Port Louis
Tel: 208 1624
Fax: 211 1420

Brisand Ltée
18 Ave Victoria
Quatre Bornes
Tel: 464 9058

Budget Holidays
M1 Motorway WS
Port Louis
Tel: 212 3493
Fax: 212 8644

Concorde Travel
and Tours
Chaussée
Port Louis
Tel: 208 5041
Fax: 212 2585

Europcar
Pailles
Tel: 208 9258
Fax: 208 4750

Hertz/Mautourco
Gustave Colin St
Forest Side
Tel: 674 3695
Fax: 674 3720

Mauritius Travel
and Tourism
Bureau
Royal Road
Floreal
Tel: 696 3001
Fax: 696 3012

Mauritours
5 Venkatasananda

Street
Rose Hill
Tel: 454 1666
Fax: 454 1682

Vacances Evasions
5 Venkatasananda
Street
Rose Hill
Tel: 454 1666
Fax: 454 1682

White Sand Tours
M1 Motorway WS
Port Louis
Tel: 212 3712
Fax: 208 8524

Theatre

Municipal Theatre
Port Louis

Yachting

Aquacat Co Ltd
(Catamaran)
Bain Boeuf
Cap Malheureux
Tel: 263 8974
Fax: 263 7009

Croisière Australes
Gustave Colin St
Forest Side
Tel: 674 3695/6
Fax: 674 3720

Croisière
Emerraude Ltée
(Catamaran)
Cap Malheureux
Tel: 263 8974
263 7009

Croisières Ltd
(Catamaran)
Riche en Eau SE
Tel: 633 5835

Le Tropical
Trou-d'Eau-Douce
Tel: 419 2300

Ocean Pearl
Charters
Royal Road
Grand Baie
Tel: 263 8899

Yacht Charters
(Schooner)
Royal Road
Grand Baie
Tel: 263 8395
Fax: 263 7814

All pictures taken by **Mohamed Amin, Duncan Willetts** and **David Lyons** except the following:

Alain Proust: pages 16 (bottom left), 24, 28, 34 (right), 66, 68, 94, 150, 152, 154, 171, 184, 187, 212, 213, 228, 249.

Sue Heady: pages 62, 63, 153, 190, 192, 193, 194, 197, 199.

Christine Pemberton: pages 125, 186, 209, 232, 258, 291, 293.

Nick Garbutt: pages 96, 138, 224, 237, 241, 251, 252, 253, 254 (bottom).

Bibliography

A la Decouverte de Rodrigues (1991), Chantal Moreau, published by Éditions de l'Océan Indien, Mauritius.

The Best of Mauritian Cooking (1986), Barry Andrews, Paul Jones and Gerald Gay, published by Les Éditions du Pacifique, Singapore.

Birds of Mauritius (1992), Claude Michel, published by Éditions de l'Océan Indien, Mauritius.

Companion to Philip's Atlas for Mauritius (1991), Dr Devi Venkatasamy, published by Éditions de l'Océan Indien, Mauritius and George Philip, England.

Exotic Cuisine of Mauritius (1988), Philippe Lenoir and R. de Ravel (translated by Maryse de Broglio-Sands), published by Éditions de l'Océan Indien, Mauritius.

Fauna of Mauritius and Associated Flora (1993), France Staub, sponsored by Mauritius Commercial Bank and British American Tobacco (Mauritius), printed by Precigraph, Mauritius.

Festivals of Mauritius (1990), Ramesh Ramdoyal, published by Éditions de l'Océan Indien, Mauritius.

Les Fleurs du Mal - et autres poèmes (1964), Charles Baudelaire, published by Garnier-Flammarion, France.

Genuine Cuisine of Mauritius (1988), Guy Felix, published by Éditions de l'Océan Indien, Mauritius.

Golden Bats and Pink Pigeons (1977), Gerald Durrell, published by Collins, England.

History of Mauritius (1977), Auguste Toussaint, published by Macmillan Education, England.

An Invitation to the Charms of Mauritian Localities (1993), Bhurdwaz Mungur and Breejan Burrun, published by Éditions le Printemps, Mauritius.

The Island of Rodrigues (1971), Alfred North-Coombes, published by the author with the assistance of the Mauritius Advertising Bureau, Mauritius.

Le Jardin Botanique de Curepipe (1990), Guy Rouillard and Joseph Gueho, published by the Société de l'Histoire de l'Ile Maurice, Mauritius.

Maisons Traditionnelles de l'Île Maurice (1978), Jean-Louis Pages, published by Éditions de l'Océan Indien, Mauritius.

Marine Molluscs of Mauritius (1988), C Michel, S Takoor and M Coowar, published by Éditions de l'Océan Indien, Mauritius.

The Mauritian Kaleidoscope - Languages and Religions (1986), Monique Dinan, printed by Best Graphics, Mauritius.

Mauritius (1974), Carol Wright, published by David and Charles, England.

The Mauritius Command (1977), Patrick O'Brian, published by Collins, England.

Mauritius from the Air (1986), photographs by Rosine Mazin and Gerard Coulon, text written by Marcelle Lagesse, published by Les Éditions du Pacifique, Singapore.

Mauritius Light and Space (1993), photographs by Christian Bossu-Picat, text written by Regis Fanchette, published by Éditions de l'Océan Indien, Mauritius.

Mauritius Traveller's Map, published by Macmillan, England.

The Mauritius Underwater Group 1963-1977 (1977), R Latimer, published and printed by Imprimerie Michel Robert & Cie, Mauritius.

Mountains of Mauritius - A Climber's Guide, Robert V R Marsh.

National Monuments of Mauritius, Vol I Port Louis District (1988), Mauritius Institute, published by Éditions de l'Océan Indien, Mauritius.

Panorama de la Peinture Mauricienne I (1986), Georges André Décotter, published by Éditions de l'Océan Indien, Mauritius.

Panorama de la Peinture Mauricienne II (1989), Georges André Décotter, published by Éditions de l'Océan Indien, Mauritius.

Parlez Creole - Guide pratique pour touristes (1988), James Burty David, Lilette David and Clarel Seenyen, published by Éditions de l'Océan Indien, Mauritius.

Paul et Virginie (1981), Bernadin de St Pierre (translated by Raymond Hein), published by Éditions de l'Océan Indien, Mauritius.

Philip's Atlas for Mauritius (1991), Dr Devi Venkatasamy, published by Éditions de l'Océan Indien, Mauritius and George Philip, England.

Port Louis - A Tropical City (1973), Auguste Toussaint (translated by W E F Ward), published by George Allen and Unwin, England.

Rodrigues Panorama (1993), Michel Pitot and Andrew Smith, published by Éditions de la Table Ovale, Mauritius.

Sea Fishes of Mauritius (1984), Michael Atchia, initiated under the auspices of the Mauritius Association for Science Education and its publication supported in part by the International Union for the Conservation of Nature and the World Wildlife Fund.

Underwater Mauritius (1989), Al J Venter, published by Ashanti Publishing, Gibraltar.

La Vegetation de l'Île Maurice (1988), Joseph Gueho, published by Éditions de l'Océan Indien, Mauritius.

The Vindication of Francois Leguat (1990), Alfred North-Coombes, published by Éditions de l'Océan Indien, Mauritius.

Wall Map of Rodrigues (1993), Dr Devi Venkatasamy and Chantal Moreau, published by George Philip, England.

338

340